# DESIGN DRAWING

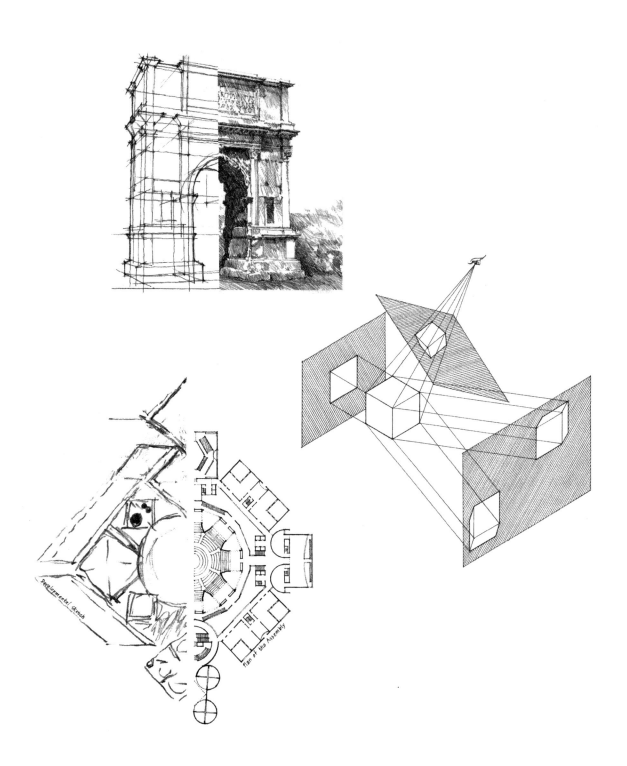

Plan of the Assembly

Developmental Sketch

# DESIGN DRAWING

Francis D.K. Ching

with Steven P. Juroszek

A VNR Book

JOHN WILEY & SONS, INC.

New York   Chichester   Weinheim   Brisbane   Singapore   Toronto

Published by John Wiley & Sons, Inc.

Published simultaneously in Canada.

**Library of Congress Cataloging-in-Publication Data:**

Ching, Frank, 1943-
    Design drawing / Frank Ching.
        p.    cm.
    Includes index
    ISBN 0-471-28654-0
    1. Architectural drawing—Technique.    I. Title.
NA2708.C49    1997
720'.22'2—dc21                                                                    97-15928

Printed in the United States of America

10   9   8   7   6

# ACKNOWLEDGMENTS

This manual began as a reader for a sequence of design drawing courses offered by the Department of Architecture at the University of Washington. Its subsequent development is largely the result of the many discussions, suggestions, and contributions of a skilled and dedicated group of teachers—Catherine Barrett, Cynthia Esselman, Kevin Kane, Anita Lehmann, Alan Maskin, Ben Sharpe, Judith Swain, Carol Thomas, Mark Wolfe, and Gail Wong.

This text is also a testimony to the efforts, accomplishments, and critical feedback of the many students who enthusiastically tested the pedagogical soundness of the material.

Finally, I would like to acknowledge those instructors who have gathered regularly at the conferences of the Design Communication Association to passionately and unselfishly share their thoughts about teaching and drawing. Their insights nurtured the progress and enhanced the dimensions of this work.

This book was prepared in part through a grant from the Graham Foundation for Advanced Studies in the Fine Arts.

# Introduction

Drawing is the process or technique of representing something—
an object, a scene, or an idea—by making lines on a surface. This
definition infers that delineation is different from painting and the
coloring of surfaces. While drawing is generally linear in nature, it
may include other pictorial elements, such as dots and brush
strokes, which can also be interpreted as lines. Whatever form a
drawing takes, it is the principle means by which we organize and
express our visual thoughts and perceptions. We therefore regard
drawing not only as artistic expression but also as a practical tool
for formulating and working through design problems.

The term design drawing brings to mind the presentation drawings used to persuade the viewer of the merits of a design proposal. Also familiar are the construction or working drawings which provide graphic instructions for the production or building of a project. But designers use both the process and products of drawing in other ways as well. In design, the role of drawing expands to include recording what exists, working out ideas, and speculating and planning for the future. Throughout the design process, we use drawing to guide the development of an idea from concept to proposal to constructed reality.

In order to learn how to draw and to use drawing effectively as an instrument in design, it is necessary to acquire certain fundamental skills, such as inscribing lines and laying down tonal values. Over time and with enough practice, anyone can learn these techniques. Skillful technique is of little value, however, unless accompanied by an understanding of the perceptual principles on which these techniques are based. Even as electronic media evolve and augment traditional drawing methods, enabling us to transfer ideas onto the computer screen and develop them into three-dimensional models, drawing remains a cognitive process that involves perceptive seeing and visual thinking.

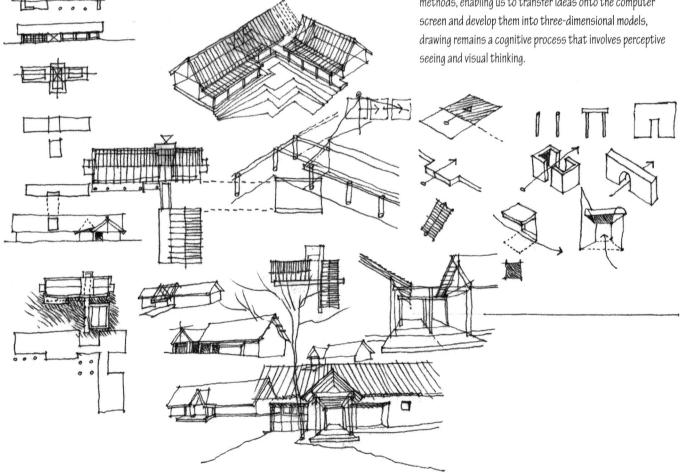

At the heart of all drawing is an interactive process of seeing, imagining, and representing images. Seeing creates the images of external reality we perceive with our eyes open, which give rise to our discovery of the world. With our eyes closed, the mind's eye presents images of an inner reality—visual memories of past events or projections of an imagined future. And then there are the images we create on paper, drawings which we use to express and communicate our thoughts and perceptions.

### Seeing

Vision is the primary sensory channel through which we make contact with our world. It is our best-developed sense, the farthest reaching, and the one we rely on the most for our day-to-day activities. Seeing empowers our ability to draw, while drawing invigorates seeing.

### Imagining

The visual data received by the eye is processed, manipulated, and filtered by the mind in its active search for structure and meaning. The mind's eye creates the images we see, and these are the images we attempt to represent in drawing. Drawing is therefore more than a manual skill; it involves visual thought which stimulates the imagination, while imagining provides impetus for drawing.

### Representing

In drawing, we make marks on a surface to graphically represent what we see before us or imagine in the mind's eye. Drawing is a natural means of expression, creating a separate but parallel world of images which speak to the eye.

The activity of drawing cannot be detached from seeing and thinking about the subject being represented. We cannot draw an object or a scene unless we see it before us as a model, or are sufficiently familiar with it to recreate it from memory or imagination. Drawing proficiency must therefore be accompanied by knowledge and understanding of what we endeavor to represent in graphic form.

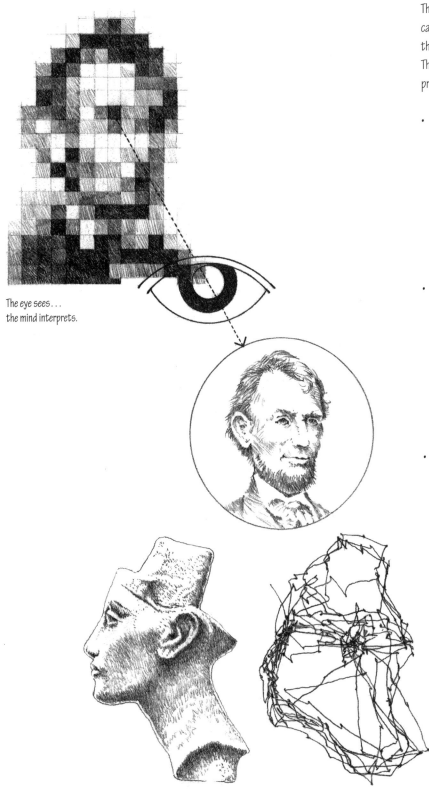

The eye sees . . .
the mind interprets.

**Bust of Queen Nefertiti**
The pattern of eye movement of a person viewing a figure, from research by Alfred L. Yarbus of the Institute for Problems of Information Transmission in Moscow.

The act of seeing is a dynamic and creative process. It is capable of delivering a stable, three-dimensional perception of the moving, changing images which make up our visual world. There are three phases in the swift and sophisticated processing which results in the images we see:

- Reception: our eyes receive energy input in the form of light—either its source or its reflection from illuminated surfaces. The optics of the eye form an upside-down image of incoming light rays on the retina, a collection of nerve cells which are an extension of the brain. These photosensitive cells convert electromagnetic energy into electrochemical signals and provide a point-by-point assessment of the intensity of light received.

- Extraction: the mind extracts basic visual features from this input. The input—basically a pattern of lights and darks—is further processed by other nerve cells in the retina and moves down the optic nerve. After an intermediate stop it arrives at the visual cortex of the brain, which has cells that extract specific features of visual input: the location and orientation of edges, movement, size, and color.

- Inference: on the basis of these extracted features, we make inferences about our world. Only a very small area of the retina is capable of distinguishing fine detail. Our eyes must therefore continually scan an object and its environment to see it in its entirety. When we look at something, what we see is actually constructed from a rapid succession of interconnected retinal images. We are able to perceive a stable image even while our eyes are scanning. Our visual system thus does more than passively and mechanically record the physical features of a visual stimulus. It actively transforms sensory impressions of light into meaningful forms.

Seeing is a vigorous, pattern-seeking process. The mind's eye uses the input extracted from the retinal image as the basis for making educated guesses about what we encounter. Inference is easy for the mind. The mind's eye actively seeks those features that fit our image of the world. It looks for closure—for meaning and understanding in the patterns that it receives. We are able to form images from the barest scaffolding of visual data, filling out the images if necessary with information that is not really there. For example, we may not understand this incomplete pattern of lights and darks, but once recognized, it cannot not be seen.

Visual perception thus is a creation of the mind's eye. The eye is blind to what the mind does not see. The picture in our head is not only based on input extracted from the retinal image but also shaped by our interests and the knowledge and experiences each of us brings to the act of seeing. Our cultural environment also modifies our perceptions and teaches us how to interpret the visual phenomena we experience.

In this illusion designed by psychologist E.G. Boring in 1930, one can see either the profile of a younger woman or the head of an older woman.

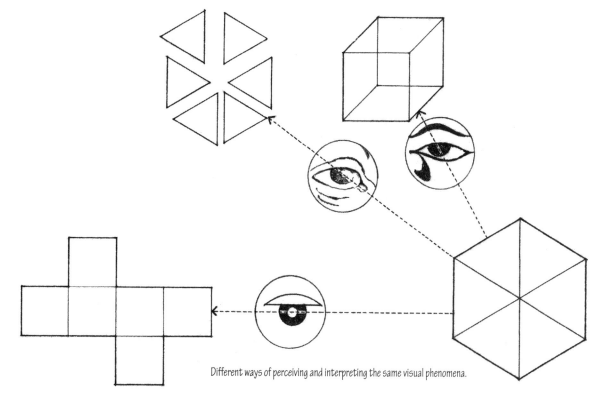

Different ways of perceiving and interpreting the same visual phenomena.

### Seeing facilitates drawing

The drawing of things we see before us, including the careful copying of a master's work, has traditionally been fundamental training for artists and designers. Drawing from observation is the classic method for developing eye-mind-hand coordination. Experiencing and examining the visible world in a direct manner through drawing makes us more conscious of the dynamics of sight. This understanding, in turn, helps us to draw.

### Drawing invigorates seeing

We normally do not see all that we are capable of seeing. Preconceived notions of what we expect or believe to be out there usually direct our seeing. Through familiarity, we tend to pass over things we confront and use every day without really seeing them. These perceptual prejudices make our life simpler and safer. We do not have to pay full attention to each and every visual stimulus as if seeing it for the first time each day. Instead we can select out only those which provide information pertinent to our momentary needs. This expeditious kind of seeing leads to our common use of stereotypical images and visual clichés.

The labeling of visual stereotypes, while necessary to avoid perceptual chaos, can also prevent us from looking anew at what we see as familiar. The visual environment is usually fuller and richer than what we normally perceive at a glance. In order to make full use of our visual faculty—to see more than symbols—we must learn to see things as if we were going to draw them.

Drawing encourages us to pay attention and to experience the full range of visual phenomena and appreciate the uniqueness of the most ordinary things. In fostering a heightened and critical awareness of the visual environment, drawing also nurtures understanding and improves our visual memory. In drawing from the imagination, we recall past perceptions and draw on these memories.

Our perception is not limited to what we can see in the here and now. Images often appear spontaneously in response to a sensory perception—something seen, touched, or smelled. Even without any sort of sensory stimulation, we have the mental faculty of recall or recreating images. Easily, almost effortlessly, you can imagine something as soon as it is suggested to you. As you read these words, you can easily visualize:

- Places, such as a childhood bedroom, the street where you live, or a scene described in a novel.
- Things, such as a triangle or square, a balloon floating in the air, or a grandfather's clock.
- People, such as a close friend, relative, or a TV newscaster.
- Activities, such as opening a door, riding a bicycle, or throwing a baseball.
- Operations, such as a cube rotating in space, a ball rolling down an incline, or a bird taking off in flight.

In responding to all of these verbal prompts, we are picturing with the mind's eye. We are thinking visually.

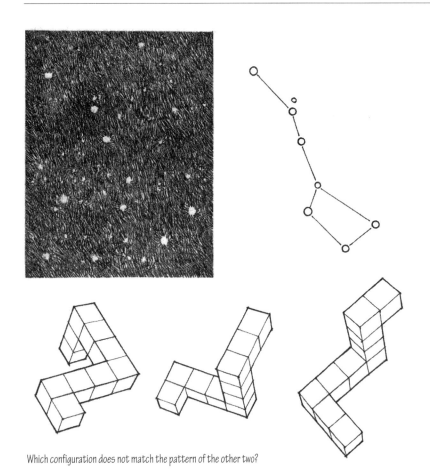

Visual thinking—thinking in images—pervades all human activity. It is an essential part of everyday life. We think in visual terms when we drive down a street looking for an address, set the table for a dinner party, or contemplate a move in a game of chess. Our thought has visual form when we search for constellations in the night sky, build a cabinet from a set of drawings, or design a building. In each of these activities, we actively seek to match the images we see with the images we hold in the mind's eye.

The images in our head are not limited to what we see in the present. The mind is capable of forming, exploring, and recombining images beyond the normal bounds of time and space. With hindsight we visualize memories of things, places, and events from the past. With foresight, we are also able to look forward in time—to use our imagination to envision a possible future. Imagination therefore enables us to have both a sense of history as well as a plan for the future. It establishes connections—visual bridges—between the past, present, and future.

Which configuration does not match the pattern of the other two?

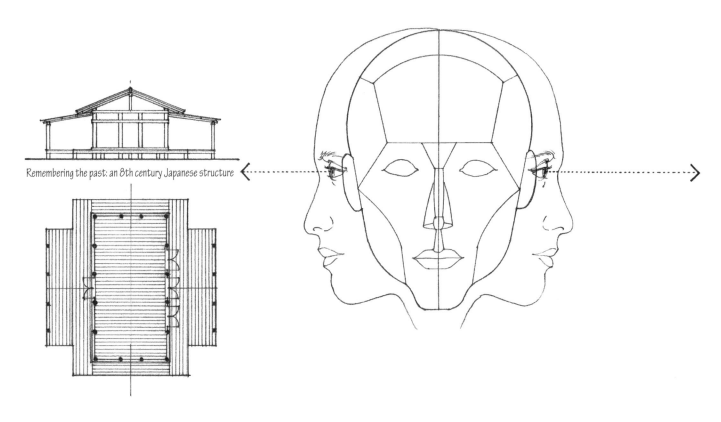

Remembering the past: an 8th century Japanese structure

## Imagination inspires drawing

The images we conjure up in the mind's eye are often hazy, brief, and all too elusive. Even if vivid and clear, they can come to mind and just as suddenly disappear. Unless captured in a drawing, they can easily be lost in awareness and replaced by others in the stream of consciousness. Drawing thus is a natural and necessary extension of visual thought. As the mental picture guides the movement of our eyes and hand on paper, the emerging drawing simultaneously tempers the image in our head. Further thoughts come to mind and are integrated into the process of imagining and drawing.

## Drawing stimulates the imagination

Drawing is a medium which influences thought just as thought directs drawing. Sketching an idea on paper enables us to explore and clarify it in much the same way as we can form and order a thought by putting it into words. Making thoughts concrete and visible enables us to act on them. We can analyze them, see them in a new light, combine them in new ways, and transform them into new ideas. Used in this way, design drawings further stimulate the imagination from which they spring.

This type of drawing is essential to the initial and developmental phases of the design process. An artist contemplating various compositions for a painting, a choreographer orchestrating a dance sequence for the stage, and an architect organizing the spatial complexities of a building—all use drawings in this exploratory way to imagine possibilities and speculate on the future.

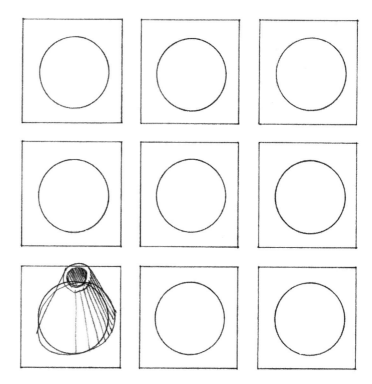

Imagine how you could transform these circles into other things by simply drawing a few lines.

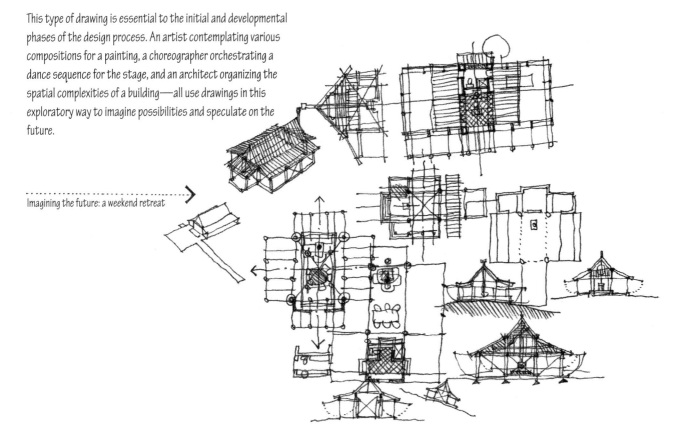

Imagining the future: a weekend retreat

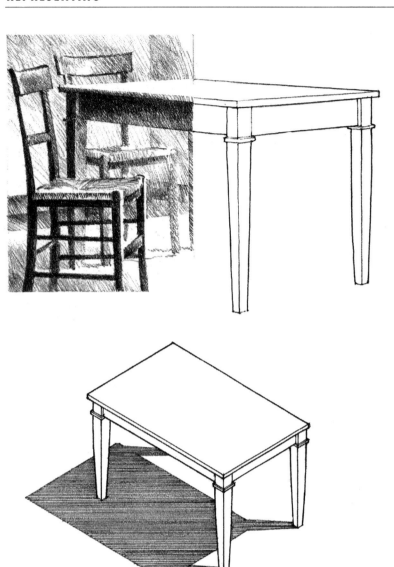

A drawing can never reproduce reality; it can only make visible our perceptions of that outer reality and the inner visions of the mind's eye. In the process of drawing, we create a separate reality which parallels our experiences.

Our perceptions are holistic, incorporating all the information we possess about the phenomena we experience. A single drawing, however, can only express a limited portion of our experience. In drawing from observation, we direct our attention to particular aspects of our vision and we choose either consciously or unconsciously to ignore others. The choice of medium and technique we elect to use also affects what we are able to convey in a drawing.

We can also draw what we know about a subject, which can be expressed in ways other than how it appears to the eye. In drawing from the imagination, for example, we are not limited to the perceptual views of optical reality. We can draw instead a conceptual view of what the mind sees. Both perceptual and conceptual views are legitimate means of representation. They represent complementary ways of seeing and drawing. The choice of one over the other depends on the purpose of the drawing and what we want to communicate of the subject.

Different ways of representing the same objective reality.

## Visual communication

All drawings communicate to the extent that they stimulate an awareness on the part of those who view them. Drawings must catch the eye before they can communicate or instruct. Once they engage the viewer, they should assist their imagination and invite a response.

Drawings are by nature information-rich. It would be difficult to adequately describe with words what a drawing is able to reveal at a glance. But just as we each see in a different way, we can each view the same drawing and interpret it differently. Even the most realistic drawing is subject to interpretation. Any drawing we use to communicate visual information should therefore represent things in a way that is comprehensible to others. The more abstract a drawing, the more it must rely on conventions and text to communicate a message or convey information.

A common form of visual communication is the diagram, a simplified drawing which can illustrate a process, clarify a set of relationships, or describe a pattern of change or growth. Another example is the set of presentation drawings which offer a design proposal to others for their review and evaluation. More utilitarian forms of graphic communication include design patterns, working drawings, and technical illustrations. These visual instructions guide others in the construction of a design or the transformation of an idea into reality.

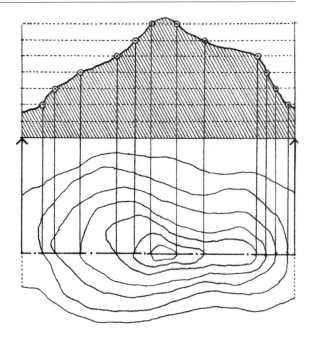

Examples of drawings which communicate relations, processes, and patterns.

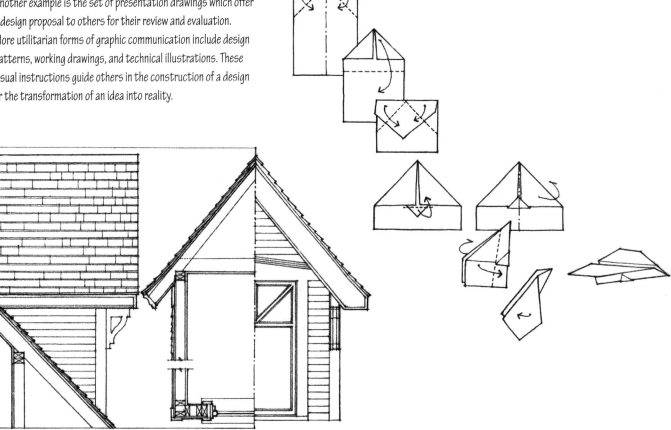

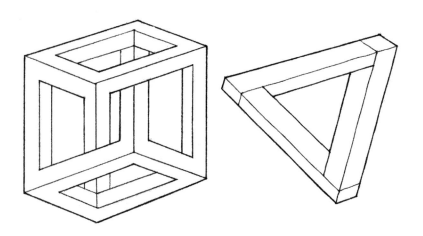

What appears to work on paper may not be possible in objective reality.

## Reading drawings

While we are able to read drawings we cannot make, the converse is not true. We cannot construct a drawing unless we are able to decipher the graphic marks we make and understand the way others might see and interpret them. An essential part of learning how to draw is learning to read the drawings we encounter as well as the ones we make.

Being able to read a drawing means that we understand the relationship between a subject and how it is represented in a drawing. For example, any drawing, whether generated on a computer screen or created by hand, can be improperly constructed and misconstrue the three-dimensional idea that it represents. We should be able to recognize when a drawing conveys something that is not possible in reality, even though the graphic image may give the opposite impression.

To better critique and improve our own drawings, we should cultivate the habit of reading them the way others might see them. It is easy to convince our eyes that a drawing we have done actually stands for what we believe it represents. It is just as easy to see mistakes in another's drawing because we see it with fresh eyes. Looking at a drawing upside down, from a distance, or through a mirror, causes us to see it in a new way. The sudden changes of view enable us to see problems we were predisposed by our mind to ignore. Even small errors that appear to be trivial are of some consequence if they muddy the message or meaning of a drawing.

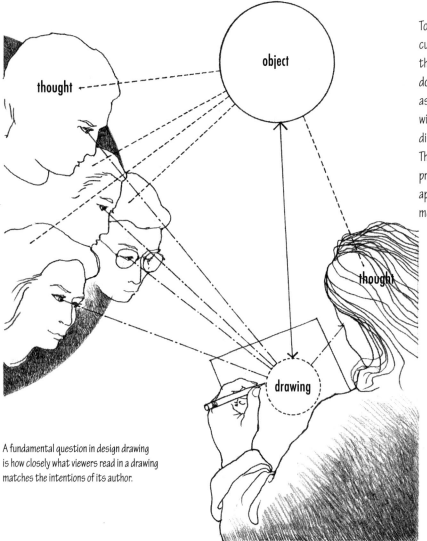

A fundamental question in design drawing is how closely what viewers read in a drawing matches the intentions of its author.

# Drawing from Observation

"Learning to draw is really a matter of learning to see—to see correctly—and that means a good deal more than merely looking with the eye. The sort of 'seeing' I mean is an observation that utilizes as many of the five senses as can reach through the eye at one time."

Kimon Nicolaïdes
*The Natural Way to Draw*

Despite the subjective nature of perception, sight is still the most important sense for gathering information about our world. In the seeing process, we are able to reach out through space and trace the edges of objects, scan surfaces, feel textures, and explore space. The tactile, kinesthetic nature of drawing in direct response to sensory phenomena sharpens our awareness in the present, expands our visual memories of the past, and stimulates the imagination in designing the future.

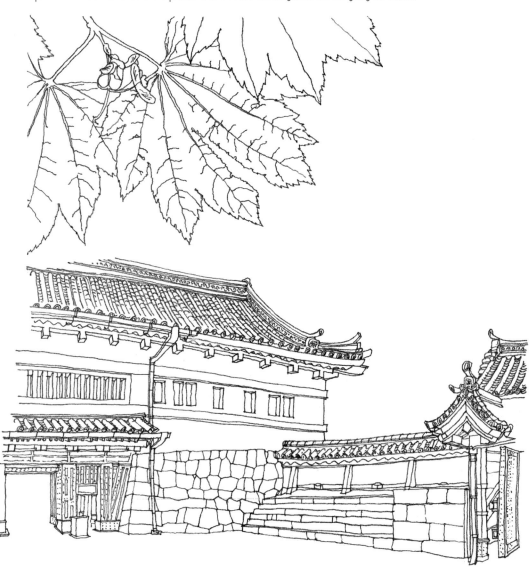

# 1
# Line and Shape

A point has no dimension or scale. When made visible as a dot, the point establishes a position in space. As the dot moves across a surface, it traces the path of a line—the quintessential element of drawing. We rely principally on the line to portray the edges and contours of objects we see in visual space. In delineating these boundaries, the line naturally begins to define shape—the pictorial element which establishes the figures in our visual field and organizes the composition of a drawing.

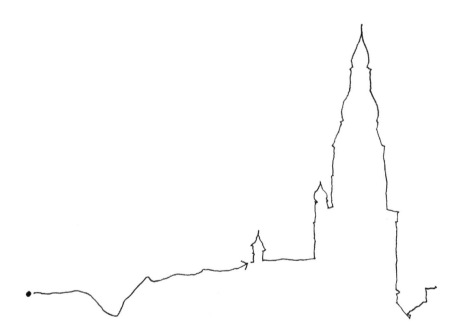

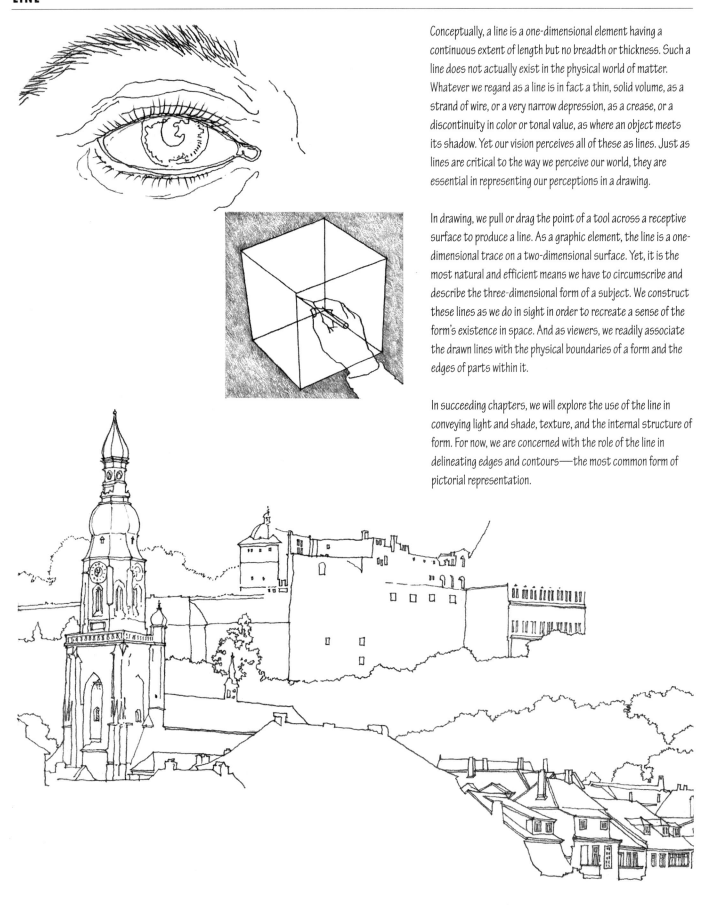

Conceptually, a line is a one-dimensional element having a continuous extent of length but no breadth or thickness. Such a line does not actually exist in the physical world of matter. Whatever we regard as a line is in fact a thin, solid volume, as a strand of wire, or a very narrow depression, as a crease, or a discontinuity in color or tonal value, as where an object meets its shadow. Yet our vision perceives all of these as lines. Just as lines are critical to the way we perceive our world, they are essential in representing our perceptions in a drawing.

In drawing, we pull or drag the point of a tool across a receptive surface to produce a line. As a graphic element, the line is a one-dimensional trace on a two-dimensional surface. Yet, it is the most natural and efficient means we have to circumscribe and describe the three-dimensional form of a subject. We construct these lines as we do in sight in order to recreate a sense of the form's existence in space. And as viewers, we readily associate the drawn lines with the physical boundaries of a form and the edges of parts within it.

In succeeding chapters, we will explore the use of the line in conveying light and shade, texture, and the internal structure of form. For now, we are concerned with the role of the line in delineating edges and contours—the most common form of pictorial representation.

Contours dominate our perception of the visual world. The mind infers the existence of contours from the patterns of light and dark the eyes receive. Our visual system seeks out and creates a cognitive line along the points where two fields of contrasting light or color meet. Some of these edges are clear; others are lost in the background as they change color or tonal value. Still, in its need to identify objects, the mind is able to fabricate a continuous line along each edge. In the seeing process, the mind enhances these edges and sees them as contours.

The most noticeable contours are those which separate one thing from another. These contours give rise to the images of objects we see in visual space. They circumscribe an object and define the outer boundary between the figure and its background. In limiting and defining the edges of things, contours also describe their shape.

But contours do more than describe the outline of a flat, two-dimensional silhouette.
- Some contours travel inward at folds or breaks in a plane.
- Others are formed by overlapping or projecting parts.
- Still other contours describe the shapes of spaces and shadows within the form.

In both seeing and drawing, we are able to follow these contours as they eloquently describe the three-dimensional nature of forms in space.

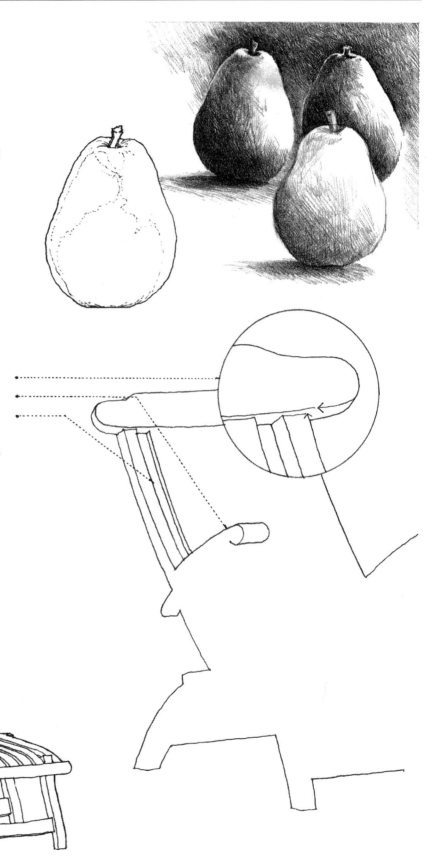

# CONTOUR DRAWING

Contour drawing is one approach to drawing from observation. Its primary purpose is to develop visual acuity and sensitivity to qualities of surface and form. The process of contour drawing suppresses the symbolic abstraction we normally use to represent things. Instead, it compels us to pay close attention, look carefully, and experience a subject with both our visual and tactile senses.

Our goal in contour drawing is to arrive at an accurate correspondence between the eye as it follows the edges of a form and the hand as it draws the lines which represent those edges. As the eye slowly traces the contours of a subject, the hand moves the drawing instrument at the same slow and deliberate pace and responds to every indentation and undulation of form. This is a meticulous and methodical process which involves working from detail to detail, part to part, and form to form.

The process is as much tactile as visual. Imagine the pencil or pen is in actual contact with the subject as you draw. Do not retrace over lines or erase them. Most importantly, draw slowly and deliberately. Avoid the temptation to move the hand faster than the eye can see; move in pace with the eye and examine the shape of each contour you see in the subject without considering or worrying about its identity.

Contour drawing is best done with a either with a soft, well-sharpened pencil or a fine-tipped pen that is capable of producing a single incisive line. This fosters a feeling of precision that corresponds to the acuity of vision which contour drawing promotes.

Blind contour drawing involves the drawing of contours while looking only at the subject, not the surface upon which we are drawing or the evolving image. Turn your body away from the paper and concentrate all of your attention on the subject. Your eyes should remain on the subject as the hand attempts to record on paper what you see.

Focus the eye on a clearly defined point along a contour of the subject. Place the tip of the pen or pencil on the paper and imagine it is actually touching the subject at that point. Slowly and painstakingly follow the contour with your eyes, observing every minute shift or bend in the contour. As your eyes move, also move your pen or pencil on the paper at the same deliberate pace, recording each variation in contour that you see.

Continue to draw each edge you see, bit by bit, at a slow, even pace. You may have to stop periodically as you continue to scan the subject, but avoid making these stopping points too conspicuous. Strive to record each contour at the very instant you see each point along the contour. Allow the eye, mind, and hand to respond simultaneously to each and every critically perceived event.

In this mode of drawing, distorted and exaggerated proportions often result. The final drawing is not intended to look like the object but rather to document and express your careful perception of its lines, shapes, and volumes.

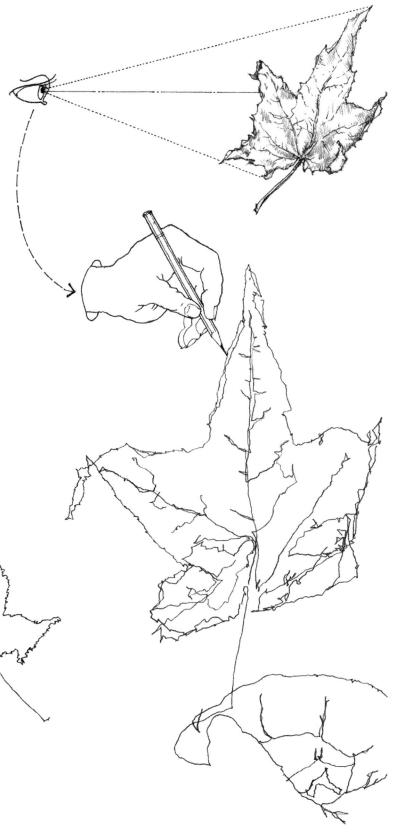

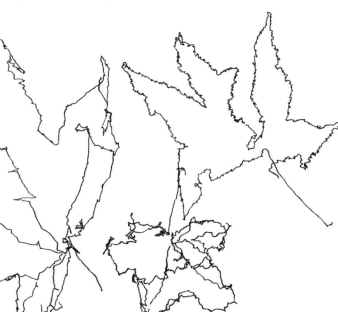

In modified contour drawing, we begin as in blind contour drawing. But in order to check relationships of size, length, and angle, we allow ourselves to glance at the emerging drawing at certain intervals.

Begin as in blind contour drawing. Select any convenient point along a contour of the subject. Place the tip of the pen or pencil on the sheet of paper and imagine it is in contact with the same point on the subject. Check the relationship of the contour to an imaginary vertical or horizontal line. As your eyes follow the contour in space, carefully draw the contour line at the same slow and deliberate pace.

Work from contour to contour, along, across, or around the edges and surfaces of a form. Respond to each and every surface modulation with equivalent hand movements. At certain points—breaks in planes or folds across contours—a contour line may disappear around a bend or be interrupted by another contour. At these junctures, look at the drawing and realign your pen or pencil with the previously stated edge to maintain a reasonable degree of accuracy and proportion. With only a glance for realignment, continue to draw, keeping your eyes on the subject.

The more we focus on what we see, the more we will become aware of the details of a form—the thickness of a material, how it turns or bends around a corner, and the manner in which it meets other materials. When confronted with a myriad of details, we must judge the relative significance of each detail, and draw only those contours which are absolutely essential to the comprehension and representation of the form. Strive for economy of line.

Do not worry about the proportions of the whole. With experience and practice, we eventually develop the ability to scan each contour of a subject, hold an image of that line in the mind's eye, visualize it on paper, and draw over the projected trace on paper.

While a true contour drawing uses a single line weight, varying the width of a line while drawing enables one to be more expressive. Thickening a line can provide emphasis, create a sense of depth, or imply a shadow. The characteristics of the line used to define a contour can communicate the nature of the form—its materiality, surface texture, and visual weight.

## Exercise 1.1

Pick a subject that has interesting contours, as your own hand, a pair of sneakers, or a fallen leaf. Focus all of your attention on the contours of the subject and draw a series of blind contour drawings. Blind contour drawing develops visual acuity, sensitivity to contours, and hand-eye-mind coordination.

## Exercise 1.2

Pair up with a friend. Draw a contour drawing of your friend's left eye using your right hand. Then draw a contour drawing of your friend's right eye using your left hand. Compare the drawing done with your normal drawing hand with that executed with the opposite hand. Drawing with your 'unfamiliar hand' forces you to draw more slowly and be more sensitive to the contours you see. This exercise may also be done by looking in a mirror and drawing your own pair of eyes.

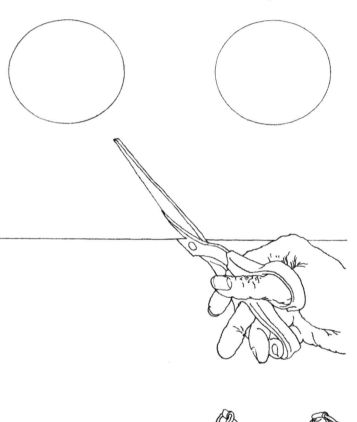

## Exercise 1.3

Compose a still life of objects having different forms—flowers and a hand tool, several fruit and bottles, leaves and a handbag. Draw a series of modified contour drawings of the composition. Try not to name or identify the things you are drawing, which can lead to the drawing of symbols. Rather, pay close attention to, sense, and record the differing nature of the edges and contours as you see them.

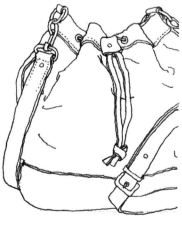

# CROSS-CONTOUR DRAWING

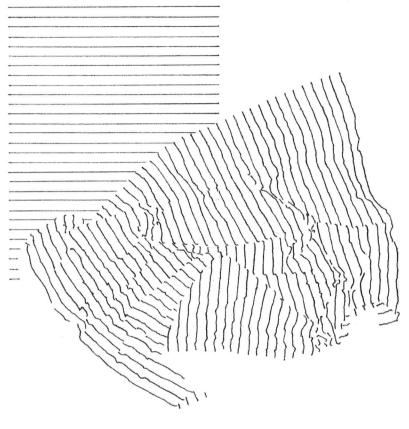

In cross-contour drawing, we draw lines not as we perceive them but as they would appear if inscribed across the surfaces of the object we see. So rather than depict the spatial edges of a form, cross-contours emphasize the way its surfaces turn and shift in space.

We use cross-contours to explore and represent the volumetric nature of an object, especially when its form is not comprised of flat planes or is organic in character. Cross-contours flow along the ridges and hollows of a surface. Where the surface is indented, the cross-contour line indents; where the surface rises, then the cross-contour line rises as well.

To better visualize the spatial turns and shifts that occur along the surfaces of an object, imagine cutting a series of equally spaced, parallel planes through the form. Then draw the series of profiles which result from the cuts. Through the series of closely spaced cross-contour lines, the form of the object will emerge.

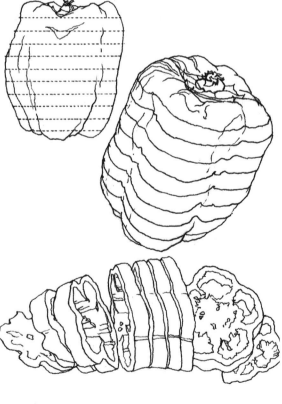

The lines we see in visual space correspond to discernible changes in color or tonal value. In contour drawing, we use visible lines to represent these lines of contrast that occur along the edges of objects and spaces. The contour lines delineate where one area or volume begins and another apparently ends. Our perception and drawing of the boundary lines that separate one thing from another leads to our recognition and description of shape.

Shape is the characteristic outline or surface configuration of a figure or form. As a visual concept in drawing and design, shape refers specifically to a two-dimensional area enclosed by its own boundaries and cut off from a larger field. Everything we see—every area in our field of vision enclosed by a contour line or bounded by an edge between contrasting colors or tonal values—has the quality of shape. And it is by shape that we organize and identify what we see.

A shape can never exist alone. It can only be seen in relation to other shapes or the space surrounding it. Any line that defines a shape on one side of its contour simultaneously carves out space on the other side of its path. As we draw a line, therefore, we must be conscious not only of where it begins and ends, but also how it moves and the shapes it carves and molds along the way.

At the threshold of perception, we begin to see parts of a visual field as solid, well-defined objects standing out against a less distinct background. Gestalt psychologists use the term figure-ground to describe this property of perception. Figure-ground is an essential concept in the ordering of our visual world, for without this differentiation of figure from ground, we would see as if through a fog. A figure emerges from a background when it has certain characteristics.

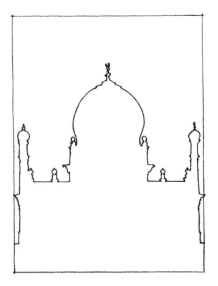

The contour line which borders a figure appears to belong to it rather than to the surrounding background.

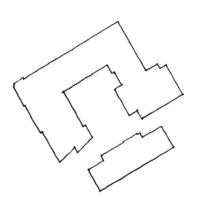

The figure appears to be a self-contained object, while its background does not.

The figure appears to advance in front of a continuous, receding background.

The figure has a color or tonal value which is more solid or substantial than that of the background.

The figure appears to be closer and the background more distant.

The figure appears to dominate its field and be more memorable as a visual image.

The visual environment is in reality a continuous array of figure-ground relationships. No part of a visual field is truly inert. A thing becomes a figure when we pay attention to it. When we fix our gaze on a book on a crowded desk, it becomes a figure while the rest of the desktop dissolves into the background. As we shift our awareness to another book, a stack of papers, or a lamp, each can become a figure seen against the ground of the desktop. Broadening our view, the desk can be seen as a figure against the ground of a wall, and the wall can become a figure seen against the enclosing surfaces of the room.

# POSITIVE AND NEGATIVE SHAPES

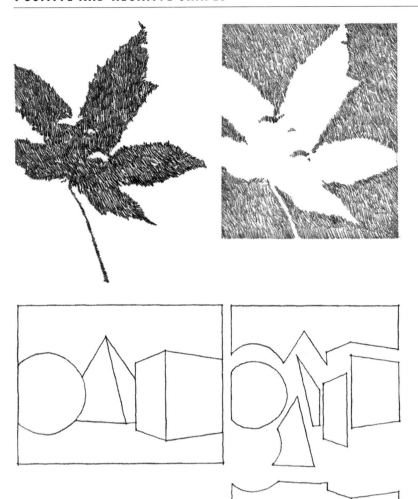

A figure that we can see relatively clearly against a background is said to have a positive shape. By comparison, the figure's rather shapeless background is said to have a negative shape. The positive shapes of figures tend to advance and be relatively complete and substantial, while their background appears to recede and be comparatively incomplete and amorphous.

We are conditioned to see the shapes of things rather than the shapes of the spaces between them. While we normally perceive spatial voids as having no substance, they share the same edges as the objects they separate or envelop. The positive shapes of figures and the shapeless spaces of backgrounds share the same boundaries and combine to form an inseparable whole—a unity of opposites.

In drawing, also, negative shapes share the contour lines that define the edges of positive shapes. The format and composition of a drawing consists of positive and negative shapes that fit together like the interlocking pieces of a jigsaw puzzle. In both seeing and drawing, we should raise the shapes of negative spaces to the same level of importance as the positive shapes of figures and see them as equal partners in the relationship. Since negative shapes do not always have the easily recognizable qualities of positive shapes, they can be seen only if we make the effort.

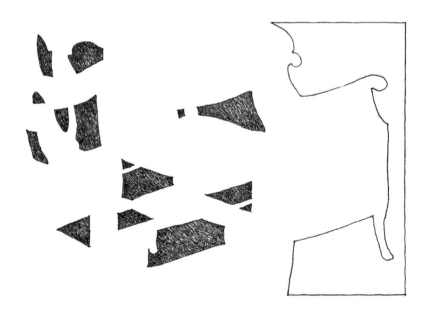

### Exercise 1.4

Copy these letter shapes line by line using the guidelines provided. Drawing something upside-down compels us to be less concerned with its identity and more focused on the shapes of the contours and spaces we see.

### Exercise 1.5

Place several paper clips on a sheet of paper, overlapping them to create a number of interesting spaces. Using a soft pencil or black pen, focus on and draw the shapes of the paper surface you see within and in-between the paper clips. Do similar drawings of negative shapes by substituting compositions of small objects which have notched, indented, or complex profiles, such as leaves, keys, or silverware.

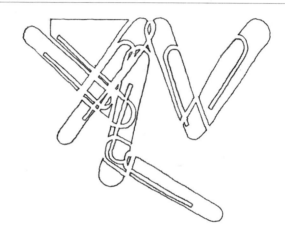

### Exercise 1.6

Compose several chairs containing openings within their form. Overlap them to create interesting spaces. Using a soft pencil or black pen, focus on and draw the shapes of the negative spaces created by the overlapping chairs.

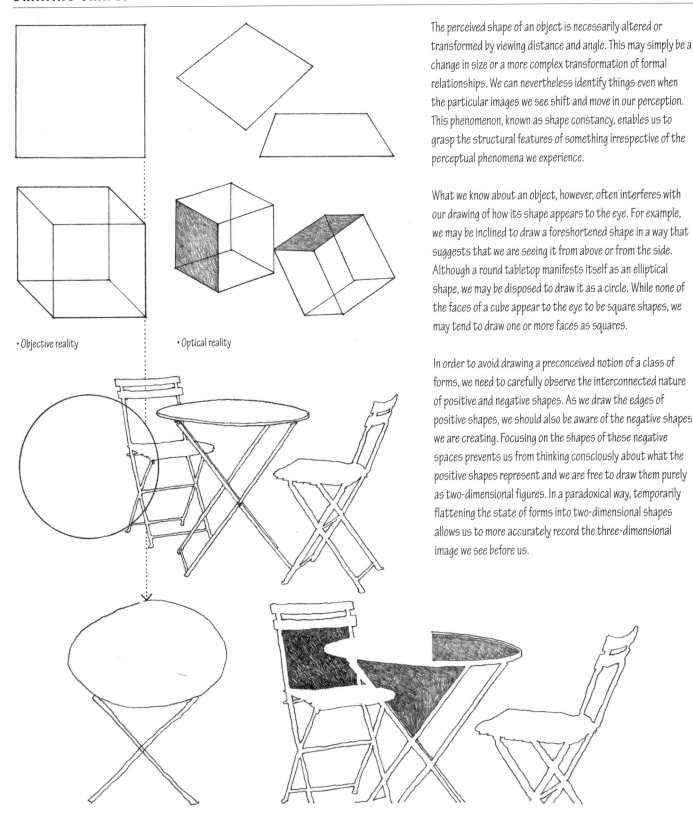

• Objective reality

• Optical reality

The perceived shape of an object is necessarily altered or transformed by viewing distance and angle. This may simply be a change in size or a more complex transformation of formal relationships. We can nevertheless identify things even when the particular images we see shift and move in our perception. This phenomenon, known as shape constancy, enables us to grasp the structural features of something irrespective of the perceptual phenomena we experience.

What we know about an object, however, often interferes with our drawing of how its shape appears to the eye. For example, we may be inclined to draw a foreshortened shape in a way that suggests that we are seeing it from above or from the side. Although a round tabletop manifests itself as an elliptical shape, we may be disposed to draw it as a circle. While none of the faces of a cube appear to the eye to be square shapes, we may tend to draw one or more faces as squares.

In order to avoid drawing a preconceived notion of a class of forms, we need to carefully observe the interconnected nature of positive and negative shapes. As we draw the edges of positive shapes, we should also be aware of the negative shapes we are creating. Focusing on the shapes of these negative spaces prevents us from thinking consciously about what the positive shapes represent and we are free to draw them purely as two-dimensional figures. In a paradoxical way, temporarily flattening the state of forms into two-dimensional shapes allows us to more accurately record the three-dimensional image we see before us.

What we draw is often a compromise between what we know of an object and the optical image we see.

Sighting is a means of measuring by eye with the aid of any of several devices. A well-known historical example is Albrecht Dürer's device of a transparent grid through which he viewed his subject. The grid allowed Dürer to transfer specific points or line segments in the subject to the picture plane of the drawing.

A similar but more portable device is a viewfinder constructed by neatly cutting a 3" x 4" rectangle in the middle of an 8-1/2" x 11" sheet of dark gray or black cardboard. Bisect the opening in each direction with two black threads secured with tape. The viewfinder helps us compose a view and gauge the position and direction of contours. More importantly, looking through the rectangular opening with a single eye effectively flattens the optical image and makes us more conscious of the unity of both the positive shapes of matter and the negative shapes of spaces.

We can also use the shaft of a pencil or pen as a sighting device. With the pencil or pen held out at arm's length, in a plane parallel with our eyes and perpendicular to our line of sight, we can use it to gauge the relative lengths and angles of lines.

90°

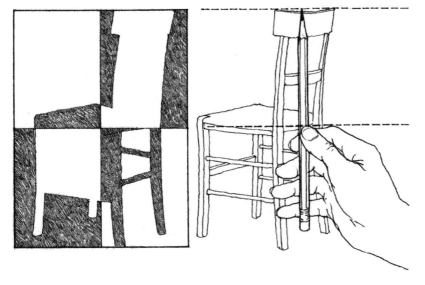

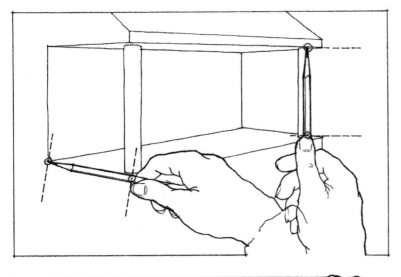

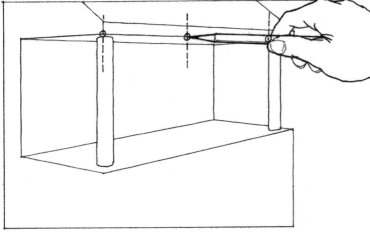

We can use either the viewfinder or the shaft of a pen or pencil to measure and compare the relationships of points, lengths, angles, and alignments in what we see and draw.

Finding the midpoint of the image is a simple matter of using the crosshairs of the viewfinder. Dividing the image into halves helps to place the image on the sheet of paper and sharpens our perception of shapes. To find the midpoint of a shape or group of shapes, we use the shaft of the pen or pencil to first estimate where the center is. Then we check to see if one half equals the other.

To make a linear measurement, we align the pencil's tip with one end of a line we see and use our thumb to mark the other end. We then shift the pencil to another line and, using the measurement as a unit of length, measure the second line's relative length. We normally use a short line segment to establish the unit of measurement so that other, longer line segments are multiples of that unit.

To gauge the apparent slopes or angles of lines, we use vertical and horizontal lines. These reference lines may be the edges or crosshairs of the viewfinder, or the shaft of the pen or pencil held horizontally or vertically at arm's length. We align one end of an angled line with the vertical or horizontal reference line and visually gauge the angle between the two. We then transfer this angular measurement to the drawing using as guides the edges of the drawing surface which correspond to the horizontal and vertical reference lines.

We can also use the same reference lines to see which points in the image align vertically or horizontally with other points. Checking alignments in this way effectively controls the proportions and relations of both positive and negative shapes.

With training and experience, we can utilize sighting techniques without an external device such as a pencil or ruler. Instead, we can develop the ability to measure the dimensions of a form and gauge relationships with our eyes alone. To do this, we must be able to hold in our mind's eye a visual measuring stick, based on one aspect of a form. We can then project this image over other parts or aspects of what we are drawing. When making visual judgments, it is important that any preliminary assumptions be checked against what we actually see. When drawing from imagination or memory, we must be able to evaluate what we have drawn in light of what we want to convey.

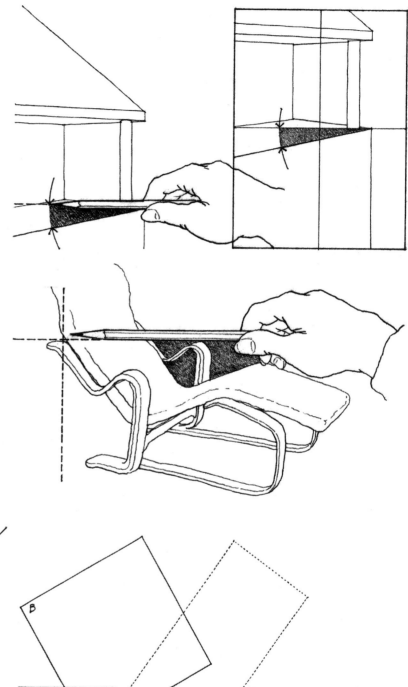

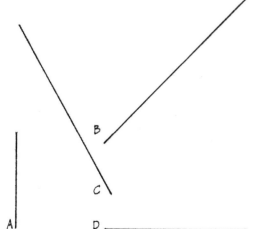

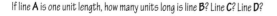

If line **A** is one unit length, how many units long is line **B**? Line **C**? Line **D**?

If **A** is a square, what proportion is rectangle **B**? Rectangle **C**? The rectangle that encloses the quadrilateral **D**?

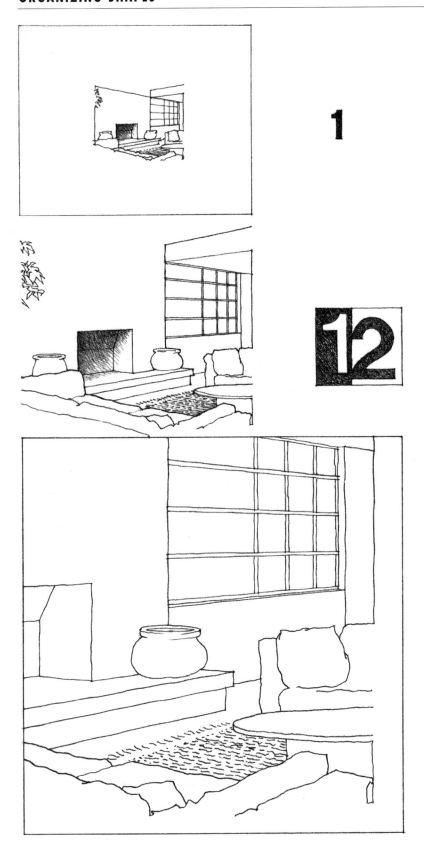

Organizing the composition of a drawing or design is basically the arrangement of shapes. When we begin to draw on a piece of paper, we face decisions as to how large the image will be, where it will be, and what orientation it will have, relative to the size, shape, and edges of the sheet. We also have to determine what is to be included and what is to be omitted from what we see or envision. These decisions affect the way we perceive the resulting figure-ground relationships between positive and negative shapes.

When a figure floats, isolated in a sea of empty space, its presence is emphasized. This type of figure-ground relationship is easy to see. The figure stands out clearly as a positive shape against an empty, diffuse, and shapeless background.

When a figure crowds its background field or overlaps other figures in its field, it begins to organize the surrounding spaces into recognizable shapes. A more interactive and integrated figure-ground relationship develops. Visual movement occurs between positive and negative shapes and the resulting visual tension creates interest.

When figures and background both have positive shape qualities or when we render overlapping shapes transparently, then the figure-ground relationship becomes ambiguous. Initially, we may see certain shapes as figures. Then, with a shift in view or understanding, we might see what were formerly background shapes as the positive figures. This ambiguous relationship between positive and negative shapes can be desirable in certain situations and distracting in others, depending on the purpose of a drawing. Any ambiguity in a figure-ground relationship should be intentional, not accidental.

## Exercise 1.7

Arrange a still life of objects and use your viewfinder to study alternative compositions. Vary your viewing distance to create an isolated figure against a shapeless background, an interactive figure-ground pattern of shapes, and finally, a composition of ambiguous figure-ground relationships.

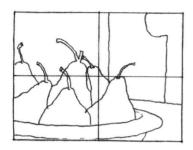

## Exercise 1.8

Do similar studies of how you might frame an outdoor scene to create a vignette, an interactive figure-ground pattern of shapes, and finally, a composition of ambiguous figure-ground relationships.

## A search for pattern

What we see and draw often consists of a complex composition of lines and shapes. There may exist not one but a whole array of interrelated sets of figure-ground patterns. How do we make sense of such a complex visual field? We see not individual shapes, but rather a pattern of relationships. According to the Gestalt theory of perception, we tend to simplify what we see, organizing complex stimuli into simpler, more holistic patterns. This grouping can occur according to certain principles.

• Similarity
   The perceptual principle that we tend to group things which have some visual characteristic in common, such as a similarity of shape, size, color, detail, alignment, or orientation.

• Proximity
   The perceptual principle that we tend to group those elements which are close together, to the exclusion of those which are further away.

• Continuity
   The perceptual principle that we tend to group elements which continue along the same line or in the same direction.

These perceptual tendencies lead us to see the relationships between the graphic elements of a composition. If these relationships form a relatively regular pattern of shapes, then they can organize a complex composition into a perceptually simpler and more comprehensible whole. The principle of grouping thus helps promote the coexistence of unity, variety, and visual richness in a drawing.

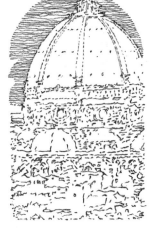

## A search for stability

Closure refers to the tendency for an open or discontinuous figure to be seen as if it were a closed or complete and stable shape. Given a pattern of dots, virtual lines connect the points in such a way that a regular, stable shape results. These lines are similar to the ones that complete a regular shape even when part of that shape is hidden. Incomplete figures tend to complete themselves according to simplicity and regularity of form.

There are situations where even if a line does not in fact exist, the mind's eye creates the line in an attempt to regularize a shape and make it visible. These seen but nonexistent lines are illusory and have no physical basis. We see them in visual areas which are completely homogeneous. They can be either straight or curved. While they appear to define opaque shapes, the figures can also be transparent. In any case, what we tend to perceive are the simplest, most regular structure of lines which can complete the shape we see.

The principle of closure prompts the viewers of a drawing to mentally complete interrupted lines and fill in discontinuous shapes. We can therefore use this property of perception to suggest shapes without actually drawing them. This can lead to a more economical use of line and greater efficiency in drawing.

What do you see in this pattern of light and dark shapes?

## A search for meaning

The grouping principles of similarity, proximity, and continuity operate without regard for representational meaning. They aid us in organizing even the most abstract patterns. Since the mind's eye constantly searches for meaning in what we see, we also tend to group shapes into familiar images.

Merely looking at an apparently amorphous shape can sometimes bring to a prepared, interested, and searching mind a more specific image. In its search for meaning, the mind's eye imagines and projects familiar images onto seemingly shapeless patterns until if finds a match that makes sense. It attempts to complete an incomplete pattern, or find a meaningful pattern embedded in a larger one, in accordance with what it already knows or expects to see. Once seen and understood, it is difficult to not see the image.

The manner in which the mind assigns meaning to what it encounters is often unpredictable. We must therefore be continually aware that others may see something other than what we intend or expect them to see in our drawings.

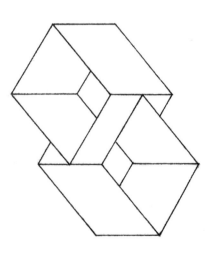

Drawings do not speak for themselves. What possible meanings could this drawing have for the viewer?

## Exercise 1.9

Exercise your mind's tendency to project meaning onto unfamiliar or ambiguous images. How many different things can you see in this inkblot?

## Exercise 1.10

A tangram is a Chinese puzzle consisting of a square cut into five triangles, a square, and a rhomboid, which can be reassembled into a great variety of figures. Make a copy of the tangram and cut apart on the heavy lines. Can you arrange the pieces to form the examples? How many other identifiable patterns can you form?

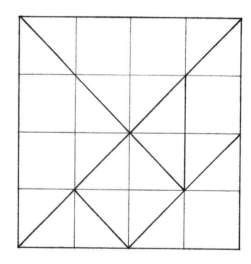

"...when you look at a wall spotted with stains, you may discover a resemblance to various landscapes, beautified with mountains, rivers, rocks, trees...Or again you may see battles and figures in action, or strange faces and costumes and an endless variety of objects which you could reduce to complete and well-known forms. And these appear on such walls confusedly, like the sound of bells in whose jangle you may find any name or word you choose to imagine."
—Leonardo da Vinci

# 2
# Tone and Texture

While lines are essential to the task of delineating contour and shape, certain visual qualities of surface and volume cannot be fully described by line alone. Even when we vary the weight of a line to imply a shift in the direction of a surface or an overlapping of forms, the effect is subtle. In order to accentuate shape and model the surfaces of forms, we rely on the rendering of tonal values. Through the interplay of tonal values we are able to convey a vivid sense of light, mass, and space. And through a combination of lines and tonal values, we create the tactile sensation and appearance we call texture.

Vision results from the stimulation of nerve cells in the retina of the eye, signaling patterns of light intensity and color. Our visual system processes these patterns of light and dark and extracts specific features of our environment—edges, contours, size, movement, and color. This assessment gives rise to our perception of separate objects in space.

The light and dark patterns we see emanate from the interaction of light with the objects and surfaces around us. The reflection of radiant energy from illuminated surfaces creates areas of light, while comparatively darker areas occur where there is an absence of light, either because surfaces are turned away from a light source or an opaque body intercepts the rays from the light source.

Just as seeing patterns of light and dark is essential to our perception of objects, the representation of tonal values in a drawing is necessary to depict the lightness or darkness of objects, describe the effect of light on their forms, and clarify their arrangement in space. Before proceeding on to creating and using tonal values to model form and convey the presence of light, it is necessary to understand the relationship between color and value.

Color is a phenomenon of light and visual perception that may be described in terms of an individual's perception of hue, saturation, and lightness for objects, and hue, intensity, and brightness for light sources. We refer to the relative lightness or brightness of a color as value. Of the properties of color, value is the most critical in seeing and drawing.

• Some hues reflect more light than others, which is why we perceive them as being lighter or paler than others.
• Shades of the same hue vary in tonal value. For example, sky blue and indigo blue are the same hue, but the former is inherently lighter in value than the latter.
• The way light illuminates a color and makes it visible affects its apparent value. A highlight on a colored surface will appear much lighter than the same hue seen in shade or within a shadow.
• Surrounding hues or values alter our perception of a color or value.

Every color has a tonal value, but it is often difficult to discern. If we squint at an object or scene, however, our perception of hues diminishes and patterns of light and dark values begin to emerge. Seeing color values in this way and being able to translate them into equivalent tonal values are essential tasks in drawing with the traditional media of pencil and pen.

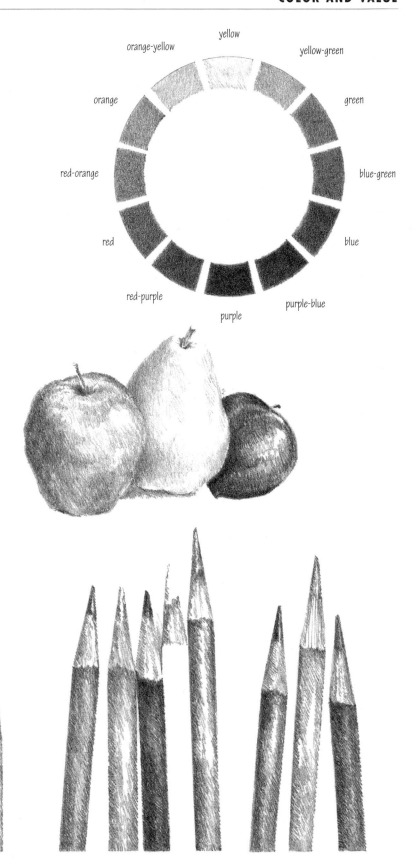

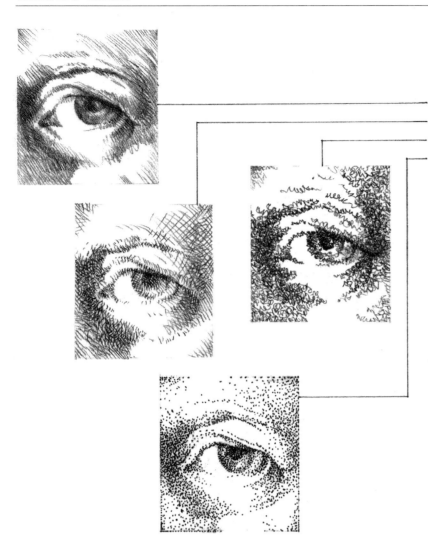

Using the traditional media of pencil and pen-and-ink to make dark marks on a light surface, there are several basic techniques for creating tonal values.

- Hatching
- Crosshatching
- Scribbling
- Stippling

These shading techniques all require a gradual building up or layering of strokes or dots. The visual effect of each technique varies according to the nature of the stroke, the medium, and the texture of the drawing surface. Regardless of the shading technique we use, we must be fully aware of the tonal value being achieved.

Since tonal value is expressed primarily through the relative proportion of light to dark areas on the drawing surface, the most important characteristic of these techniques is the spacing and density of the strokes or dots. Secondary characteristics include the visual texture, grain, and direction of the strokes. When rendering the darkest values, we should be careful not to lose the white of the paper. Covering the paper surface entirely can cause a drawing to lose depth and vitality.

Spacing

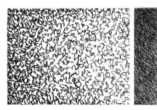

Texture

Density

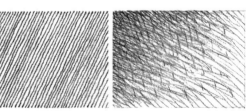

Direction

## Hatching

Hatching consists of a series of more or less parallel lines. The strokes may be long or short, mechanically ruled or drawn freehand, and executed with either a pen or a pencil on smooth or rough paper. When spaced closely, the lines lose their individuality and merge to form a tonal value. Therefore, we rely primarily on the spacing and density of lines to control the lightness or darkness of a value. While thickening the linear strokes can deepen the darkest values, using too thick of a line can result in an unintentional coarseness and heaviness of texture.

To produce a range of values with a pencil, we can vary the grade of lead as well as the pressure with which we draw. Be careful not to use too dense a grade of lead or press so hard that the pencil point embosses the drawing surface.

Unlike a pencil line, the tonal value of an ink line remains constant. We can only control the spacing and density of the hatching. When using a pen with a flexible nib, however, we can alter the pressure to subtly alter the thickness of the stroke.

The most flexible freehand technique for hatching utilizes relatively short, rapid, diagonal strokes. To define a precise edge, fix the beginning of each stroke with slight pressure. Feather the ends of the strokes to depict curved surfaces, a texture gradient, or subtleties of light and shade. When extending a tonal value over a large area, avoid the effect of banding by softening the edges and overlapping each set of strokes in a random manner.

By applying additional layers of diagonal strokes at only slightly different angles to the preceding sets, we can build up the density and therefore the tonal value of an area. Maintaining the diagonal direction of the strokes in this manner avoids confusion with the underlying drawing and unifies the various tonal areas of a drawing composition.

The direction of hatching can also follow the contours of a form and emphasize the orientation of its surfaces. Remember that direction alone, however, has no impact on tonal value. With texture and contour, the series of lines can also convey material characteristics, as the grain of wood, the marbling of stone, or the weave of fabric.

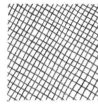

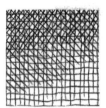

## Crosshatching

Crosshatching utilizes two or more series of parallel lines to create tonal values. As with hatching, the strokes may be long or short, mechanically ruled or drawn freehand, and executed with either a pen or a pencil on smooth or rough paper.

The simplest crosshatching consists of two perpendicular sets of parallel lines. While the resulting weave may be appropriate for describing certain textures and materials, the pattern can also produce a stiff, sterile, and mechanical feeling, especially when the lines are ruled and widely spaced.

Using three or more sets or layers of hatching provides more flexibility in generating a greater range of tonal values and surface textures. The multidirectional nature of the hatching also makes it easier describe the orientation and curvature of surfaces.

In practice, we often combine hatching and crosshatching into a single technique. While simple hatching creates the lighter range of values in a drawing, crosshatching renders the darker range.

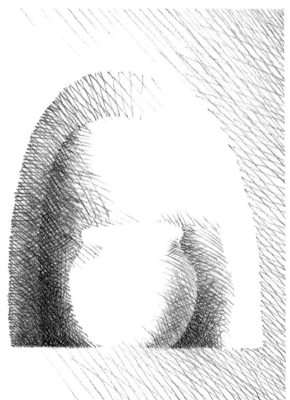

## Scribbling

Scribbling is a shading technique that involves drawing a network of random, multidirectional lines. The freehand nature of scribbling gives us great flexibility in describing tonal values and textures. We can vary the shape, density, and direction of the strokes to achieve a wide range of tonal values, textures, and visual expression.

The strokes may be broken or continuous, relatively straight or curvilinear, jagged or softly undulating. By interweaving the strokes, we create a more cohesive structure of tonal value. By maintaining a dominant direction, we produce a grain that unifies the various areas and shades of value.

As with hatching, we must pay attention to both the scale and density of the strokes, and be aware of the qualities of surface texture, pattern, and material they convey.

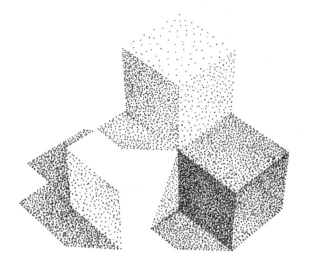

### Stippling

Stippling is a technique for shading by means of very fine dots. The best results occur when using a fine-tipped ink pen on a smooth drawing surface.

Applying stippling is a slow and time-consuming procedure that requires the utmost patience and care in controlling the size and spacing of the dots. Rely on density to control tonal value. Resist the temptation to deepen a value by enlarging the dots. If the scale of the dots is too large for the toned area, too coarse a texture will result.

We use stippling to establish tonal values in pure-tone drawings—drawings that rely on value alone to define edges and contours. We apply stippling over faintly drawn shapes of the areas to be toned. We first cover all shaded areas with an even spacing of dots to create the lightest value. Then we establish the next value step with additional stippling. We continue to add stippling in a methodical manner until the darkest tonal values are established.

Since there are no objective lines to describe contour and shape in a pure-tone drawing, we must rely on a series of dots to profile spatial edges and define the contours of forms. We use tightly spaced dots to define sharp, distinct edges, and a looser spacing of dots to imply softer, more rounded contours.

White represents the lightest possible value and black the darkest. In between exists an intermediate range of grays. A familiar form of this range is represented by a value or gray scale having ten equal gradations from white to black.

As we begin to see value relationships, we must develop the ability to create corresponding tones using a variety of media and techniques. To this end, producing both a stepped series and a graduated scale of tonal values is beneficial and rewarding. Explore all of the shading techniques described on the preceding pages. Also investigate the possibility of executing a gray scale on a tinted or colored surface, using a black pencil to define values darker than the tone of the surface and a white pencil to establish the lighter values.

After each attempt, carefully evaluate the tonal order from a distance. Check to see if there are any breaks in value and if an even progression of values exists from white to black. With disciplined practice, we should be able to develop the control necessary to replicate any desired tone and maintain the required value contrasts in a drawing.

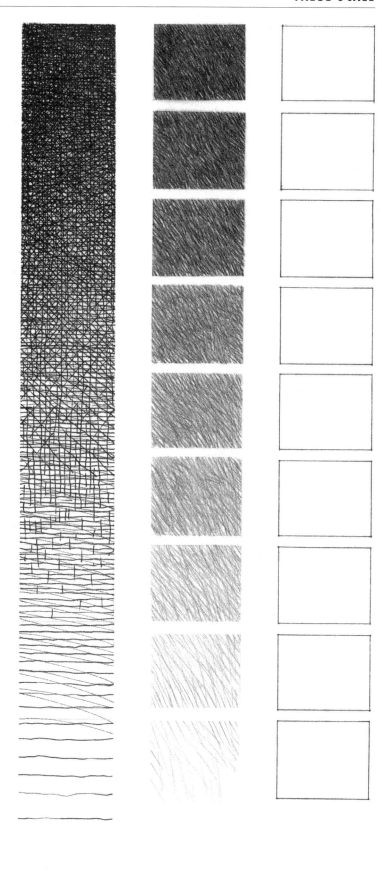

Modeling refers to the technique of rendering the illusion of volume, solidity, and depth on a two-dimensional surface by means of shading. Shading with tonal values extends a simple drawing of contours into the three-dimensional realm of forms arranged in space.

The modeling of values from light to dark can describe the nature of a surface—whether it is flat or curved, smooth or rough. Areas of light can emerge from a dark background like mounds rising from the earth, while dark areas can appear to recede into the depth of the drawing surface. Gradual transitions from light to dark occur along the surfaces of cylinders, cones, and organic forms, whereas abrupt changes in value pronounce the angular meeting of planes in cubes, pyramids, and other prismatic forms.

Since defining edges helps us recognize shape, we look to edges to discover the configuration of the surfaces of a three-dimensional form. We must be careful how we define the nature of the edge or boundary where two shapes of contrasting values meet. The skillful manipulation of tonal edges is critical to defining the nature and solidity of a surface or object.

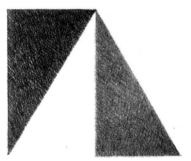

Hard edges delineate sharp breaks in form or describe contours that are separated from the background by some intervening space. We define hard edges with an abrupt and incisive shift in tonal value. Soft edges describe indistinct or vague background shapes, gently curving surfaces and rounded forms, and areas of low contrast. We create soft edges with a gradual change in tonal value or diffuse tonal contrast.

Hard edges

Soft edges

Hard and soft edges

### Exercise 2.1

Use a soft pencil to create a range of tonal values which convert the two-dimensional circle, triangle, and polygon into a three-dimensional sphere, cone, and cube. Experiment with hatching, crosshatching, and scribbling techniques to create the desired range of tonal values.

### Exercise 2.2

Repeat the above exercise but this time use a fine-tipped black pen and experiment with hatching, crosshatching, and stippling techniques to create the desired range of tonal values.

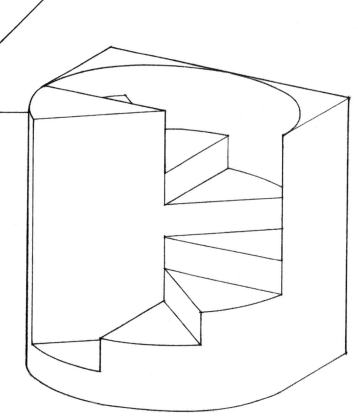

### Exercise 2.3

Use a soft pencil to create a range of tonal values which clarify the three-dimensional form of this object. Experiment with hatching, crosshatching, and scribbling techniques to create the desired range of tonal values. Repeat this exercise using a fine-tipped black pen and experiment with hatching, crosshatching, and stippling techniques to create the tonal values.

While tonal values can imply depth on a flat drawing surface, we turn to light to more vividly describe the three-dimensional qualities of forms and spaces in our environment. Light is the radiant energy that illuminates our world and enables us to see three-dimensional forms in space. We do not actually see light but rather the effects of light. The way light falls on and is reflected from a surface creates areas of light, shade, and shadow, giving us perceptual clues about its three-dimensional qualities. Tonal value is the graphic equivalent of shade and shadow and can only indicate light by describing its absence. In rendering the resulting patterns of light and dark shapes, we invest a form with mass and volume and create a sense of spatial depth.

Almost everything we see comprises a combination of one or more relatively simple geometric forms—the cube, the pyramid, the sphere, the cone, and the cylinder. If we understand that light illuminates each of these fundamental solids in a logical and consistent way, we can better render the effects of light on more complicated subjects. When light strikes an object, it creates a light side, a shaded side, and a cast shadow. Within this light-dark pattern, we can recognize the following elements:

- Light values occur on any surface turned toward the light source.

- Tonal values shift as a surface turns away from the light source, with intermediate values occurring on surfaces which are tangent to the direction of the light rays.

- Highlights appear as luminous spots on smooth surfaces that directly face or mirror the light source.

- Shade refers to the comparatively dark values of surfaces turned away from the light source.

- Areas of reflected light—light cast back from a nearby surface—lighten the tonal value of a portion of a shaded surface or a shadow.

- Shadows are the dark values cast by an object or part of an object upon a surface that would otherwise be illuminated by the light source.

In modeling, we tend to consider first the local value of a surface. Local value describes how light or dark the material of a surface is. It is a constant property of the surface and has nothing to do with light. The quality of light that illuminates a surface, however, modifies its local value. For example, naturally light colors can appear darker in shade than those that are normally deeper in value but illuminated by light. In rendering tonal values, we should attempt to communicate this interplay of local value, light, and shade.

It is important to remember that we perceive tonal values relative to their context. The law of simultaneous contrast states that the stimulation of one color or tonal value leads to the sensation of its complement, which is projected instantaneously on a juxtaposed color or value. For example, when two colors of contrasting value are juxtaposed, the lighter color will deepen the darker color while the darker color will lighten the lighter one. In a similar manner, a tonal value superimposed upon a darker tone will appear lighter than the same value set against a lighter tone.

Local values      +      Light-shade pattern

= Value pattern

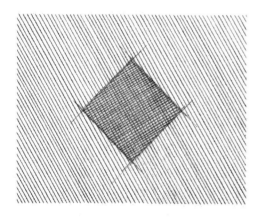

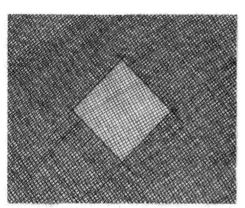

# LIGHT, SHADE, AND SHADOW

Brilliant light

Diffused light

In order to render the effects of light, we must be able to comprehend the nature of the light source, its spatial relationship to the objects it illuminates, as well as the three-dimensional nature of the forms themselves.

The clarity and tonal value of shaded surfaces and cast shadows provide clues to the quality of the light source.

- Brilliant light produces strong light-dark contrasts with sharply defined shadows.
- Diffused light creates less value contrast between lit surfaces and shadows.

Cast shadows disclose the relative position of objects in space.

- Cast shadows anchor an object to the surface on which it sits.
- Cast shadows reveal the distance between forms and the surfaces upon which they are cast.
- Cast shadows clarify the form of the surfaces upon which they are cast.

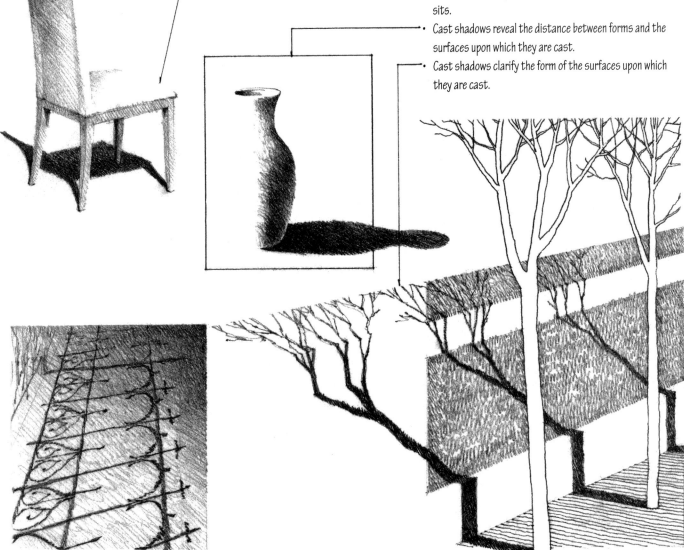

Even when forms are hidden from view, the shadows they cast can reveal their shape.

The shape and path of a shadow conveys both the location of a light source and the direction of its rays.

- Cast shadows retreat in the direction opposite of that of the light source.
- Frontlighting creates deep shadows behind the subject which recede from the viewer.
- Toplighting creates shadows that are shallow or directly beneath the subject.
- Sidelighting throws one side of the subject into shade and casts shadows in the direction opposite of the light source.
- Three-quarter lighting, from above and over the shoulder of the viewer, creates a strong sense of volume and reveals the surface texture of the subject.
- Backlighting creates deep shadows toward the viewer and emphasizes the silhouette of the subject.

Frontlighting

Toplighting

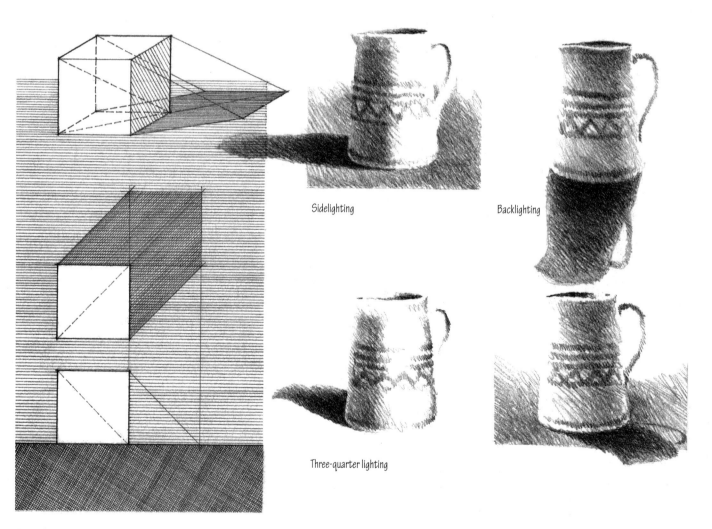

Sidelighting

Backlighting

Three-quarter lighting

For the formal construction of shade and shadows in architectural drawings, refer to Multiview Drawings.

Shaded surfaces and cast shadows are usually neither opaque nor uniform in value. We should avoid employing large areas of solid dark tones that obliterate detail and disrupt our reading of the form of a surface. Instead, apply shades and shadows as transparent washes that belong to the form and through which we can read the texture and local color of the surface.

Shade becomes shadow along spatial edges or shifts in planes. In order to retain a sense of three-dimensional forms occupying space, we should distinguish between the values of surfaces in shade and those of cast shadows. Shaded surfaces are often lighter in value than shadows, but this value relationship should be confirmed by careful observation.

Cast shadows are generally darkest where they meet a surface in shade, becoming lighter toward its outer edges. The boundaries of cast shadows are distinct in brilliant light, but softer in diffuse light. In either case, we should define the outer edges of shadows with a contrast in value, never with a drawn line.

Areas of shade or shadow are almost never uniform in value. Light reflecting back from nearby surfaces illuminates surfaces in shade or on which shadows are cast. To depict the modifying effects of reflected light, we vary the tonal value of surfaces in shade and those on which shadows are cast. The effects of reflected light, however, should be suggested in a subtle way so as not to disrupt the nature of the surface in shade or shadow.

## Exercise 2.4

Arrange a still-life composition on a horizontal surface near a window or under a desk lamp so that clear and distinct shadows are cast by the objects. Squint and focus on the shapes and tonal values of the shaded areas and cast shadows. Use a soft pencil and your choice of modeling technique to render the tonal values you observe.

## Exercise 2.5

Repeat the above exercise, using a fine-tipped black pen to render the shaded areas and cast shadows.

## Exercise 2.6

Arrange another still-life composition by a window or under a desk lamp. This time, instead of rendering the darker tones with a graphite pencil or ink pen, draw the lighter values on black construction paper with a white pencil.

## MAPPING VALUES

The mapping of light-dark patterns is the easiest way to begin modeling. Mapping involves breaking down all areas of light, shade, and shadow that we see on a subject or in a scene into definite shapes. Decisiveness is necessary. When a shade or shadow seems indistinct, we must impose boundaries anyway. In doing this, we create an organized map of interlocking shapes that serves as a starting point for later refinements.

Mapping requires reducing the many tonal variations that we see into just a few. We begin by sorting the range of tonal values into two groups—light and dark; or three—light, medium, and dark. Within each group, the tonal value can vary to articulate the nature of the surfaces, but the overall mapping of the values should remain clear. Squinting through half-closed eyes makes this task easier. Another method is to view a scene through tinted glass or acetate, which reduces the number of colors and simplifies the values we see.

The pattern of values establishes the underlying structure that holds a modeled drawing together and gives it unity and strength. If the value pattern is fragmented, then the composition will be incoherent, no matter how carefully rendered or technically competent the individual drawing elements may be. Thumbnail sketches are effective devices for studying alternative value patterns and developing a strategy for the range, placement, and proportion of tonal values in a drawing.

Once the overall value pattern is established, we work from light to dark. We can always darken a tonal value, but once a tone has been darkened, it is difficult to reestablish a lighter value. Here are a few additional points to remember in modeled drawing:

- Layer areas of value. Avoid drawing values sequentially from part to part of a drawing. Doing so can fragment a drawing and obscure our reading of a form. Establish broad groupings of tonal value before layering the smaller, more specific tones that constitute them. Establish each increase in value with an additional layer of tone. Continue to add layers of tone until the darkest tonal values are established.
- Establish grain. Maintaining a consistent direction to the strokes unifies the various areas of tonal value and infuses a drawing with a cohesive quality.
- Maintain the distinction between the sharp tonal contrasts of hard edges and the diffuse contrasts of soft edges.
- Retain highlights. It is extremely important not to lose areas in light. While these areas can be reclaimed in a pencil drawing by erasure, no such opportunity exists when drawing in ink.

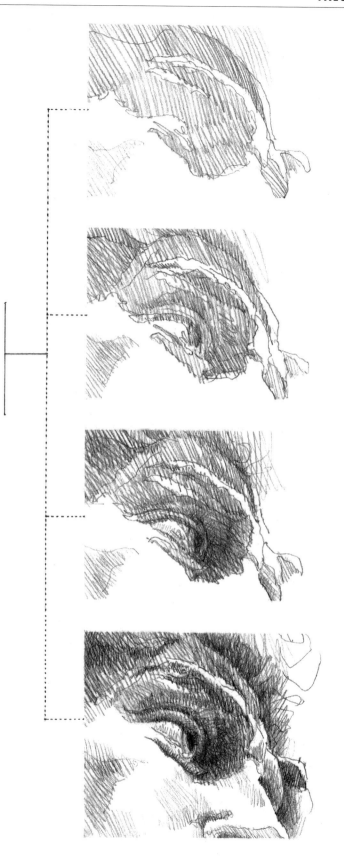

Tight range

Broad range

High contrast

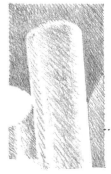

The range of tonal values we use in a drawing influences the weight, harmony, and atmosphere of the composition. Sharp contrasts in value vividly define and draw attention to the tonal shapes. A broad range of tonal values, with intermediate values providing a transition from the lightest to the darkest tones, can be rich and visually active. Too broad a range of values, however, can fragment the unity and harmony of a drawing's composition. Closely related values tend to produce more restful, subtle, and restrained effects.

The relative proportion of light and dark values defines the dominant tonal value or key of a drawing.

- A predominantly light range of values or high key conveys delicacy, elegance, and a sense of illuminating light.

- A medium range of tonal values or middle key imparts a feeling of harmony and balance. Without some positive contrasts, however, a middle-key drawing can become bland and lifeless.

- On the other hand, the somber quality of a moderately dark tonal range or low key can have a calming effect and establish a feeling of strength and stability.

When an intermediate tone is the dominant value of a drawing, it is convenient to draw on a gray or colored surface, which automatically establishes the tonal value. This tint of the surface serves as an effective foil for darker values established with a black pencil and lighter values rendered with a white pencil.

## Exercise 2.7

Arrange a still life on a window sill or under a desk lamp so that a clear pattern of light, shade, and shadow emerges. Using only the white of the paper plus two values—a light and a middle gray, develop a mapping study of the composition.

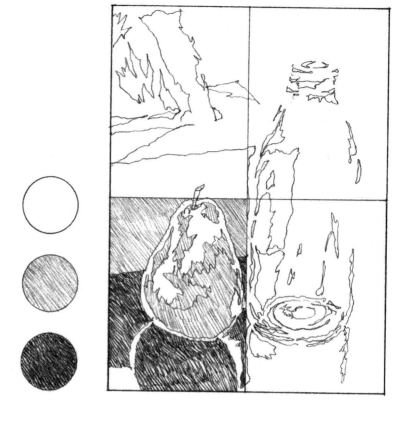

## Exercise 2.8

Find an exterior landscape containing both near and distant elements. Using a viewfinder to establish the limits of your visual field, develop a value pattern which describes the shapes and tonal values you see in the landscape.

## Exercise 2.9

Repeat the above exercises, but this time develop each drawing further by layering additional, intermediate tonal values within each value area.

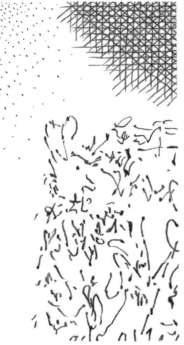

Physical texture

Visual texture

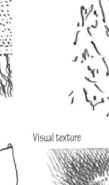

Whenever we use hatching or stippling to create a tonal value, we simultaneously create texture. Likewise, as soon as we begin to describe the nature of a material with lines, we simultaneously create a tonal value. We should always be aware of this relationship between tonal value and texture, whether smooth or rough, hard or soft, polished or dull. In most cases, tonal value is more critical than texture to the representation of light, shade, and the way it models forms in space.

We use the term texture most often to describe the relative smoothness or roughness of a surface. It can also describe the characteristic surface qualities of familiar materials, as the hewn appearance of stone, the grain of wood, and the weave of a fabric. This is tactile texture that can be felt by touch.

Visual texture is the representation of the structure of a surface as distinct from color or form. It can be either felt or perceived in a drawing. All tactile textures provide visual texture as well. Visual texture, on the other hand, may be illusory or real.

Our senses of sight and touch are closely intertwined. As our eyes read the visual texture of a surface, we often respond to its apparent tactile quality without actually touching it. The visual texture prompts memories of past experiences. We remember what certain materials felt like as we ran our hands across their surfaces. We base these physical reactions on the textural qualities of similar materials we have experienced in the past.

The scale of the strokes or dots we use to create a tonal value, relative to the size of the toned area and the drawing composition, inherently conveys the visual texture of a surface.

Visual texture can also result from the interaction between medium and drawing surface. Drawing on a rough surface breaks up the deposits of ink or graphite. Lightly drawn strokes deposit the medium only on the raised portions of the surface, while increased pressure forces the medium also into the low-lying areas. In effect, the physical texture of the drawing surface bestows a visual grain and texture on the drawing itself.

Another way to impose a textural quality on an area of tonal value is through frottage. Frottage refers to the technique of obtaining textural effects by rubbing graphite or charcoal over paper laid on a granular, pitted, or other roughly textured surface. This method of producing a textured tonal value is especially useful to prevent overworking a dark tonal value, which can cause a drawing to lose its freshness and spontaneity.

Small-scale strokes and dots

Large-scale strokes and dots

Smooth strokes

Irregular strokes

Frottage

Smooth drawing surface

Coarse drawing surface

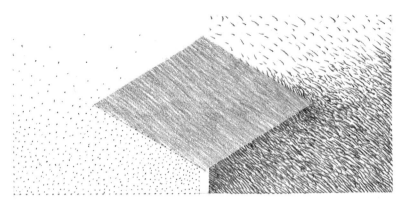

Contrast

Scale and distance

Light

## Modifying Factors

Contrast, scale, distance, and light are important modifying factors in our perception of texture and the surfaces they articulate. Whenever representing texture in a drawing, consider the following factors.

Contrast influences how strong or subtle a texture will appear to be. A texture seen against a uniformly smooth background will appear more obvious than when placed in juxtaposition with a similar texture. When seen against a coarser background, the texture will appear to be finer and reduced in scale.

The relative scale of a drawing determines whether we read a texture as blades of grass, a field of grain, or a patchwork quilt of fields. The relative scale of a texture also affects the apparent shape and position of a plane in space. Textures with directional grain can accentuate the length or width of a plane. Coarse textures can make a plane appear closer, reduce its scale, and increase its visual weight. In general, textures tend to visually fill the space they occupy.

All materials have some degree of texture, but the finer the scale of a texture, the smoother it will appear to be. Even coarse textures, when seen from a distance, can appear to be relatively smooth. Only upon closer viewing would the coarseness of a texture become evident.

Light influences our perception of texture and, in turn, is affected by the texture it illuminates. Smooth, shiny surfaces reflect light brilliantly, appear sharply in focus, and attract our attention. Surfaces having a matte texture absorb and diffuse light unevenly and therefore appear less bright than a similarly colored but smoother surface. Coarse surfaces, when illuminated with direct lighting, cast distinct shadow patterns of light and dark upon itself and discloses its textural quality. Diffused lighting de-emphasizes physical texture and can even obscure its three-dimensional structure.

### Exercise 2.10

Select two or more objects having decidedly different textures. Possibilities include a paper bag and a glass bottle, an egg and a spoon or fork on a piece of fabric, or various fruit in a ceramic bowl. Arrange the objects on a window sill or under a desk lamp so that the lighting emphasizes the various textures. Describe the contrasting textures using any of the modeling techniques.

### Exercise 2.11

Repeat the above exercise, but this time move in very close to one of the overlapping edges. Focus on this edge and describe the enlarged surface textures where they meet.

### Exercise 2.12

Repeat the above exercises several times, experimenting with both pencil and pen-and-ink media, and working on both smooth as well as rough drawing surfaces.

# 3
# Form and Structure

"All pictorial form begins with the point that sets itself in motion...
The point moves...and the line comes into being—the first dimension.
If the line shifts to form a plane, we obtain a two-dimensional element.
In the movement from plane to spaces, the clash of planes gives rise to a
(three-dimensional) body...A summary of the kinetic energies which move
the point into a line, the line into a plane, and the plane into a spatial
dimension."

—Paul Klee
*The Thinking Eye*

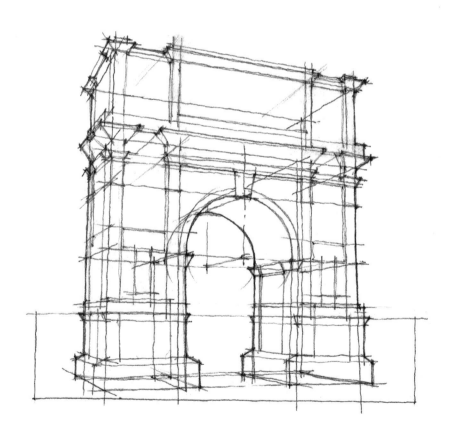

# FORM

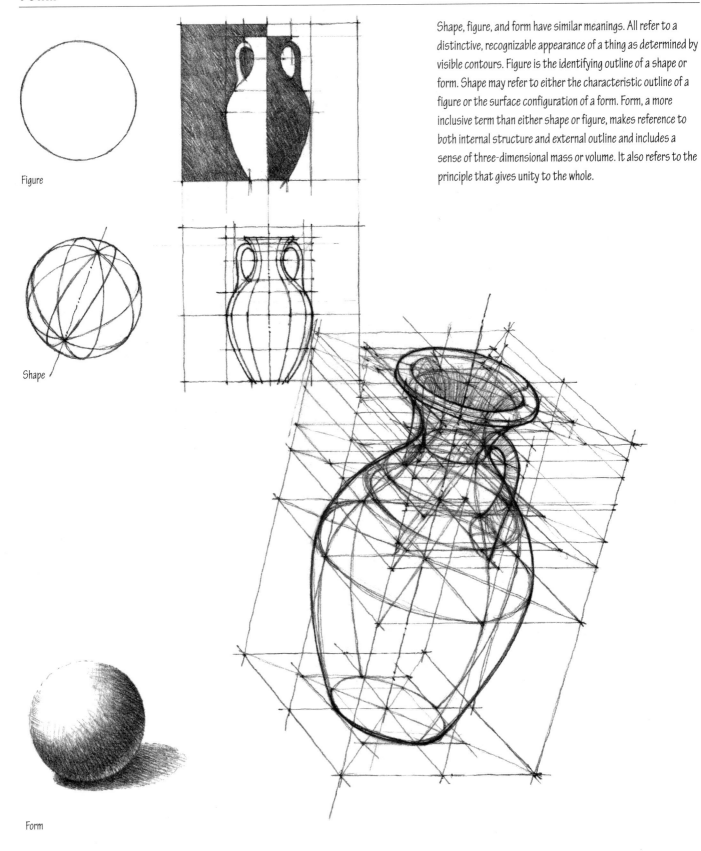

Figure

Shape

Form

Shape, figure, and form have similar meanings. All refer to a distinctive, recognizable appearance of a thing as determined by visible contours. Figure is the identifying outline of a shape or form. Shape may refer to either the characteristic outline of a figure or the surface configuration of a form. Form, a more inclusive term than either shape or figure, makes reference to both internal structure and external outline and includes a sense of three-dimensional mass or volume. It also refers to the principle that gives unity to the whole.

Volume refers to the three-dimensional extent of an object or region of space. Conceptually, a volume is bound by planes and has three dimensions of width, height, and depth. In drawing, we endeavor to convey the illusion of three-dimensional volumes of mass and space on a two-dimensional surface.

All objects fill a volume of space. Even thin, linear objects occupy space. We can pick up a small object and turn it around in our hands. Each turning of the object displays a different shape because the relationship between the object and our eyes changes. In seeing the object from different angles and distances, our vision assembles the shapes into a three-dimensional form.

A drawing presenting a view from a fixed angle and distance can only illustrate a single moment of our perception. If this is a frontal view that shows only width and height, the image would appear flat. But turning the view to expose three adjacent sides of the object reveals the third dimension of depth and clarifies its form. Paying attention to the planar shapes helps us see how they combine to convey the three-dimensional form of the volume.

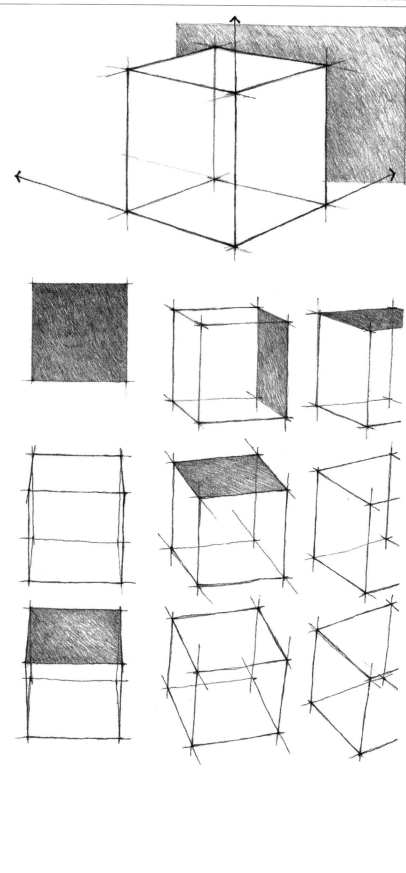

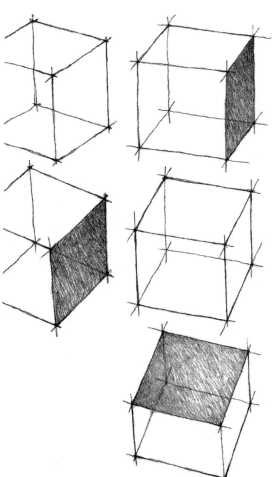

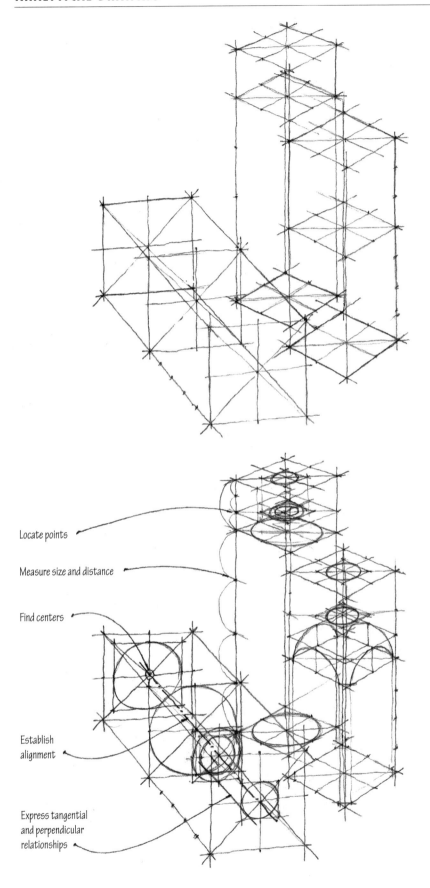

Locate points

Measure size and distance

Find centers

Establish alignment

Express tangential and perpendicular relationships

A drawing can describe the outer configuration of surfaces of an object or explain its inner structural nature and the way its parts are arranged and joined in space. In drawing analytically, we seek to merge these two approaches.

Unlike contour drawing, in which we proceed from part to part, analytical drawing proceeds from the whole to the subordinate parts and finally the details. Subordinating parts and details to the structure of the overall form prevents a piecemeal approach that can result in faulty proportional relationships and a lack of unity.

We begin an analytical drawing with light, freely drawn lines using a soft, well-sharpened pencil. We draw these lines in a tentative and exploratory manner to block out and establish a transparent volumetric framework for a form. Imagine a transparent box whose sides touch the front, back, top, bottom, and both sides of an object. This imaginary container describes the extent and relations of the object's three dimensions. Visualizing this enveloping volume of an object helps us to draw its three-dimensional form.

These lines are diagrammatic in nature, serving to establish and explain not only the appearance of exterior surfaces but also the underlying geometry and structure of the subject. We call these initial lines regulating lines since they order relationships and control the placement, size, and proportion of the fundamental parts of a form. In the process of blocking out the enveloping shapes and volume of an object, we use regulating lines to locate points, measure size and distance, find centers, express perpendicular and tangential relationships, and establish alignments and offsets.

Drawing approximate lines first helps the eye seek the correct ones. They represent visual judgments to be confirmed or adjusted. We do not erase any previously drawn lines. If necessary, we restate a line, correcting basic shapes and checking the relative proportions between the parts, always striving for incremental improvement over the last line drawn.

Because of their constructive nature, regulating lines are not limited by the physical boundaries of objects. They can cut through forms and extend through space as they link, organize, and give measure to the various parts of an object or composition. In ordering formal and spatial relationships, they establish a planar or spatial framework on which we can build up a drawing in stages, similar to the armature upon which a sculptor molds clay.

Drawing both unseen and visible parts of the subject makes it easier to gauge angles, control proportions, and see the optical appearance of shapes. The resulting transparency also conveys a convincing sense of volume occupied by the form. Working in this way prevents the appearance of flatness that can result from concentrating too much on surface rather than volume.

Through a continual process of elimination and intensification, we gradually build up the density and weight of the final contour or object lines, especially at critical points of intersection, connection, and transition. Having all lines remain visible in the final drawing intensifies the depth of the image and reveals the constructive process by which it was generated and developed.

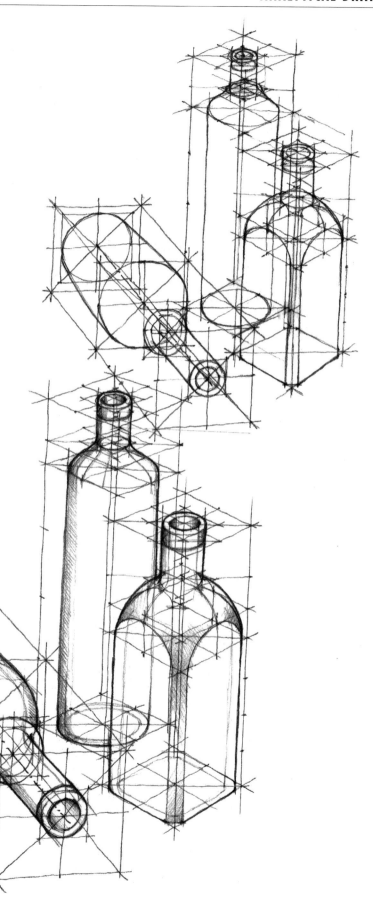

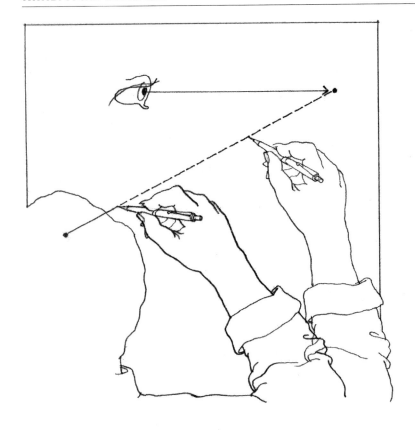

When blocking out light construction lines, hold the pen or pencil lightly as you draw. Squeezing the pen or pencil too tightly creates tension that interrupts the fluid nature of a freehand line. Instead, try to feel the drawing surface through the point of the instrument.

Before actually drawing a line, practice the eye-mind-hand movement by marking the beginning and end of the intended line with dots. Draw lines by pulling the pencil, never pushing it. For righthanders, this means drawing lines from left to right and from top to bottom; lefthanders should draw lines from right to left and from top to bottom. Keep a disciplined eye on where the line is headed, not where it's been. Avoid scratching in lines with short, feeble strokes. Instead, draw lines continuously.

For short strokes or when applying considerable pressure, swing the hand at the wrist, or let the fingers perform the necessary motions. For longer strokes, swing the entire forearm and hand freely from the elbow, with a minimum of wrist and finger movement. Only as you approach the end of the stroke should you bring the wrist and fingers into motion to control where the line ends.

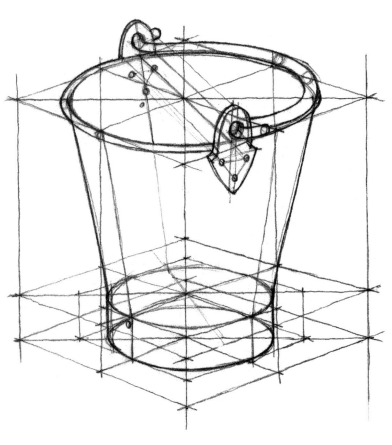

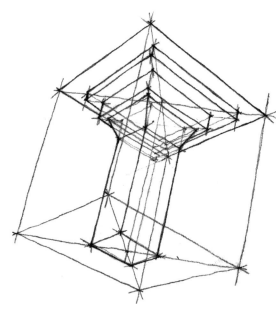

## Exercise 3.1

Using the analytical process of drawing, practice drawing cubes from a variety of viewpoints.

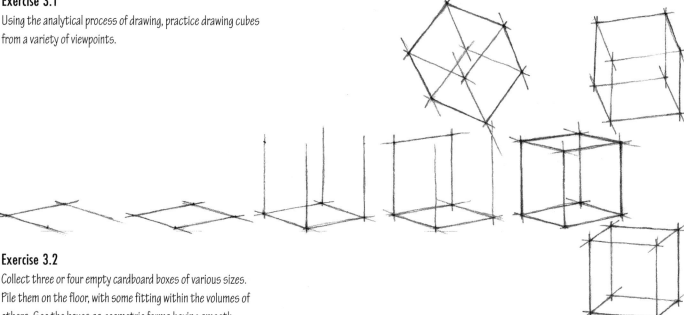

## Exercise 3.2

Collect three or four empty cardboard boxes of various sizes. Pile them on the floor, with some fitting within the volumes of others. See the boxes as geometric forms having smooth rectangular planes intersecting along straight lines. Using the analytical process of drawing, describe the geometric forms of the boxes.

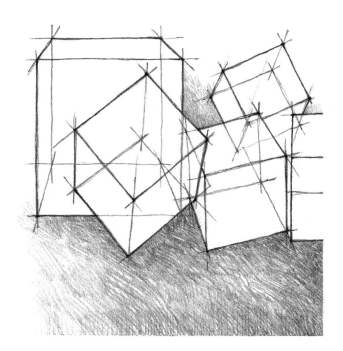

## Exercise 3.3

Collect two glass bottles, one having a tall, cylindrical body and another having a square or rectilinear cross section. Arrange the bottles with one standing on its end and the other laying on its side. Using the analytical process of drawing, describe the geometric forms of the bottles. Pay careful attention to important axial and proportional relationships.

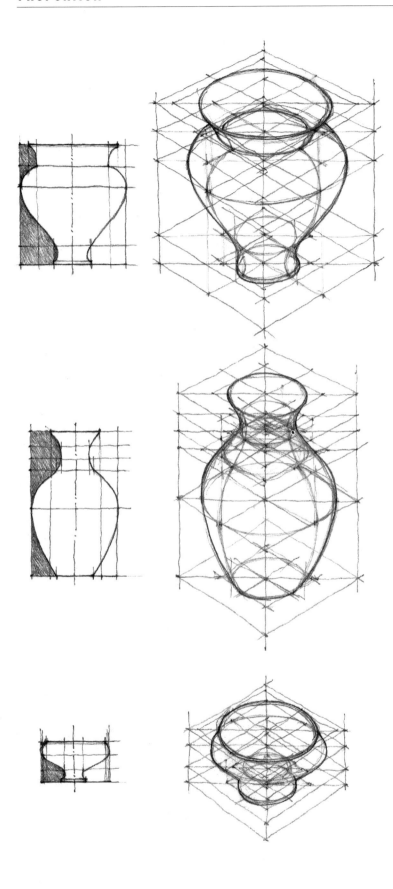

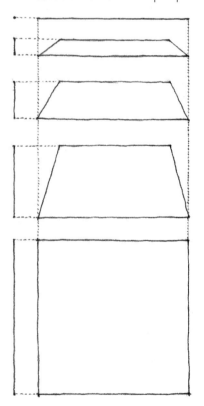

As we become more sensitive to the unique visual characteristics of what we see and draw, we should not lose sight of the total image. No single element in a drawing stands alone in the composition. All of the parts depend on one another for their visual impact, function, and meaning. To ensure things remain in their proper place and relationship to one another—to see both the trees and the forest and to avoid making mountains out of molehills—we must pay attention to proportion.

Proportion is the comparative, proper, or harmonious relation of one part to another or to the whole with respect to magnitude, quantity, or degree. Proportional relations are a matter of ratios, and ratio is the relationship between any two parts of a whole, or between any part and the whole. In seeing, we should pay attention to the proportional relationships that regulate our perception of size and shape.

Although often defined in mathematical terms, proportion refers to any consistent set of visual relationships among the parts of a composition. It can be a useful design tool in promoting unity and harmony. Our perception of the physical dimensions of things is, however, often imprecise. The foreshortening of perspective, viewing distance, and even cultural bias can distort our perception.

Proportion is primarily a matter of critical visual judgment. In this respect, significant differences in the relative dimensions of things are important. Ultimately, a proportion will appear to be correct for a given situation when we sense that neither too little nor too much of an element or characteristic is present.

These are some important points to remember in gauging or using proportion in a drawing:

- The apparent size of an object is influenced by the relative size of other objects in its environment.
- When dealing with the form of volumes, we must be concerned with proportion in three dimensions.
- Verbalize the proportions as you draw to remind yourself of the proper ratios.
- Be careful not to rectify the shape to correspond to the shape of the format or the sheet of paper on which you are drawing.
- When drawing complex shapes, look for shapes you understand, such as squares.
- Even subtle changes in proportion can have a powerful effect on the visual identity and aesthetic quality of an image. Cartoonists use this deliberate distortion to advantage in creating caricatures.
- If the diagonals of two rectangles are either parallel or perpendicular to one another, they indicate the two shapes have similar proportions.

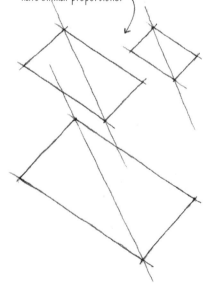

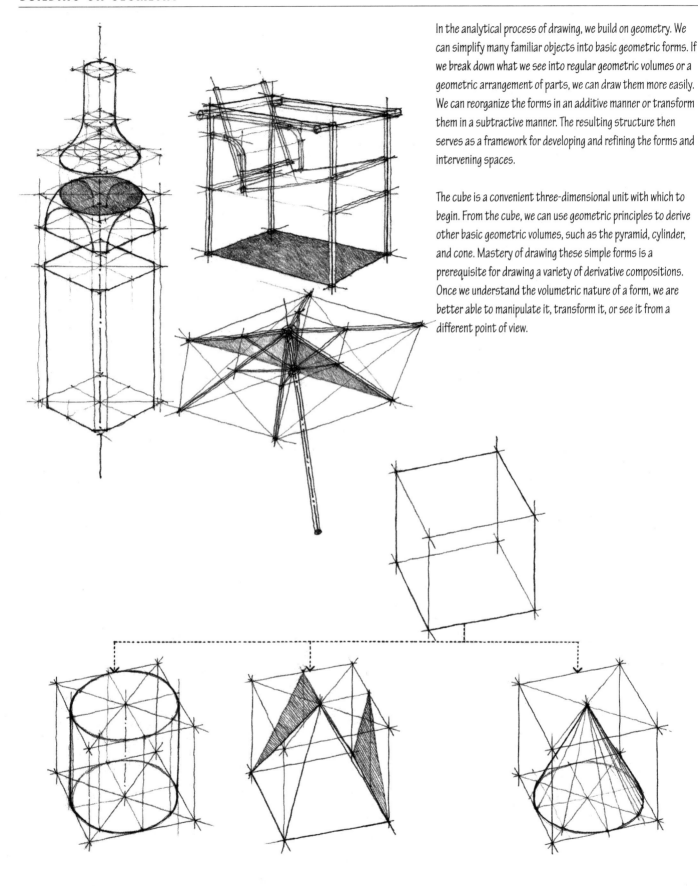

In the analytical process of drawing, we build on geometry. We can simplify many familiar objects into basic geometric forms. If we break down what we see into regular geometric volumes or a geometric arrangement of parts, we can draw them more easily. We can reorganize the forms in an additive manner or transform them in a subtractive manner. The resulting structure then serves as a framework for developing and refining the forms and intervening spaces.

The cube is a convenient three-dimensional unit with which to begin. From the cube, we can use geometric principles to derive other basic geometric volumes, such as the pyramid, cylinder, and cone. Mastery of drawing these simple forms is a prerequisite for drawing a variety of derivative compositions. Once we understand the volumetric nature of a form, we are better able to manipulate it, transform it, or see it from a different point of view.

### Exercise 3.4

Using the analytical process of drawing, transform each of the cubes into a pyramid or other prismatic form.

### Exercise 3.5

Using the analytical process of drawing, copy each of the cubes and transform each into a cone, cylinder, or similar form based on the circle.

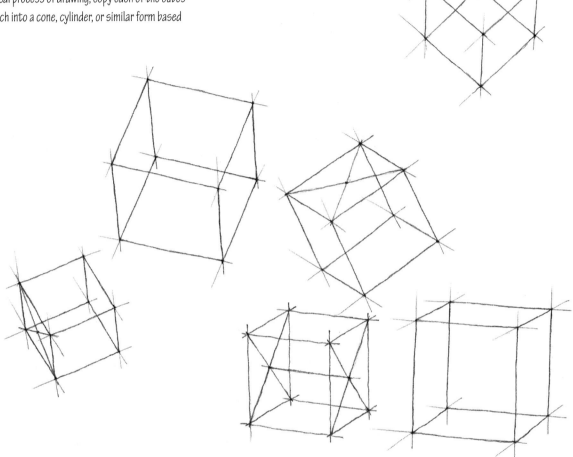

### Exercise 3.6

Building on the geometry of the forms you developed in the preceding two exercises, transform each into a familiar object.

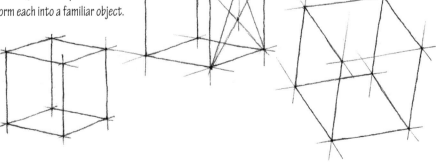

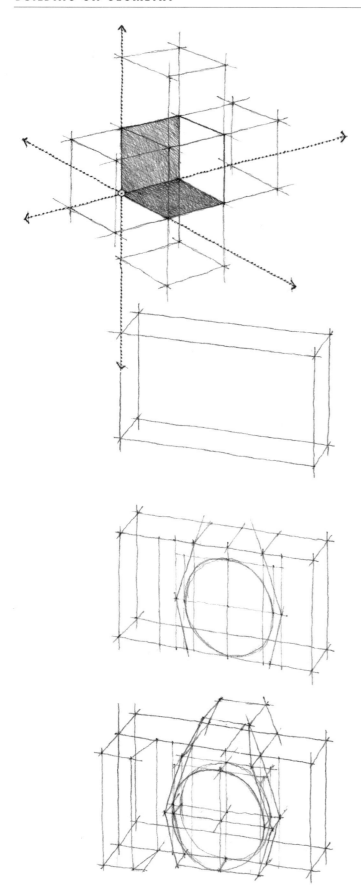

## Additive Forms

We can extend a cube horizontally, vertically, as well as into the depth of a drawing. A number of cubic volumes or derivative forms can link, extend, or grow along axes and tangents into centralized, linear, symmetrical, or clustered compositions.

We can also extend the base of a cube into a two-dimensional grid upon which we can explore relationships of shape and size. A grid may consist of dots, lines, or shapes. Dots are subtle reminders of position. Lines represent the vertical and the horizontal, and regulate the spacing of elements. Shapes define areas and emphasize space rather than position.

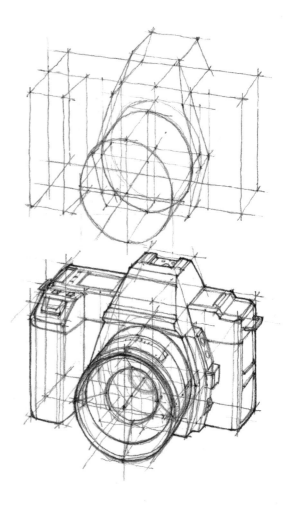

## Subtractive Forms

Working from a simple, regular form, we can selectively remove or carve out portions to generate a new form. In this subtractive process, we use the solid-void relationship between form and space to guide us as we draw the proportion and development of the parts. The procedure is similar to a sculptor who projects a mental image onto a block of stone and systematically carves away material until the image is realized.

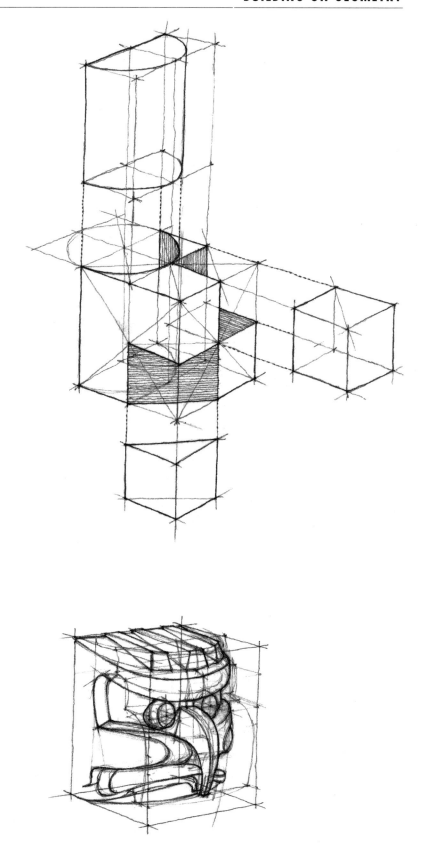

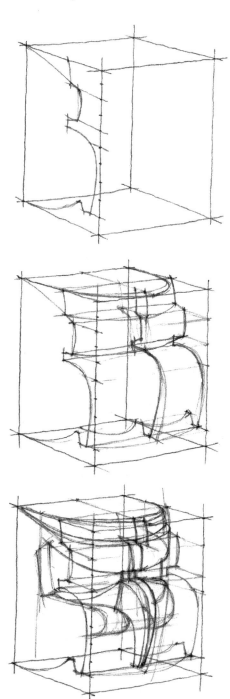

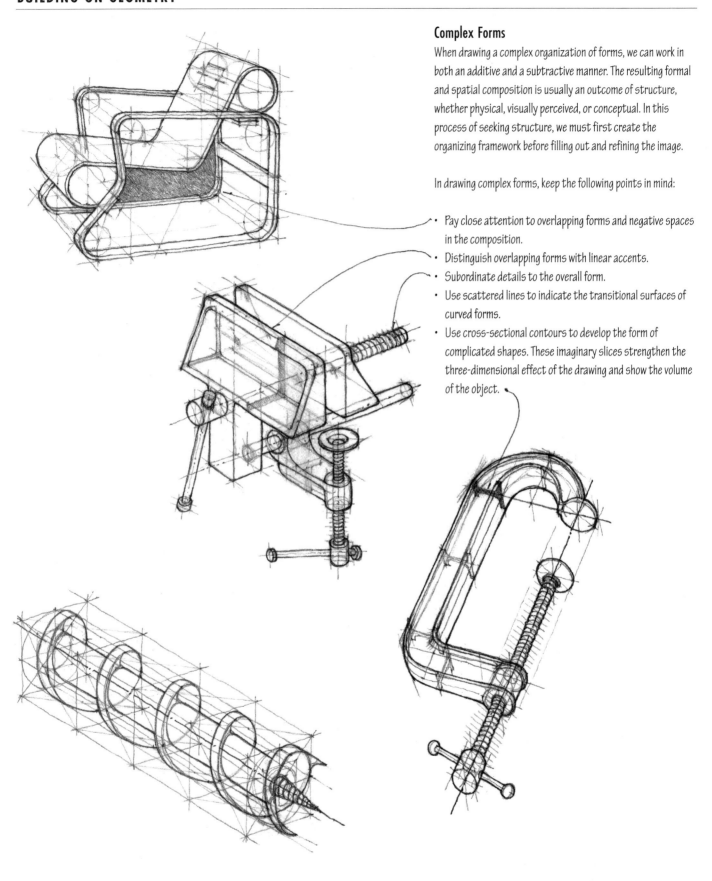

## Complex Forms

When drawing a complex organization of forms, we can work in both an additive and a subtractive manner. The resulting formal and spatial composition is usually an outcome of structure, whether physical, visually perceived, or conceptual. In this process of seeking structure, we must first create the organizing framework before filling out and refining the image.

In drawing complex forms, keep the following points in mind:

- Pay close attention to overlapping forms and negative spaces in the composition.
- Distinguish overlapping forms with linear accents.
- Subordinate details to the overall form.
- Use scattered lines to indicate the transitional surfaces of curved forms.
- Use cross-sectional contours to develop the form of complicated shapes. These imaginary slices strengthen the three-dimensional effect of the drawing and show the volume of the object.

## Exercise 3.7

Extend each cube horizontally, vertically, or into the depth of the drawing. Transform one or two of the cubes into a chair.

## Exercise 3.8

Transform one or two of the cubes by slicing off pieces and reattaching them to the original cube in new positions.

## Exercise 3.9

Select a small hand tool or kitchen utensil having a clear geometric order. Carefully study the geometric and proportional relationships among the constituent parts. Use the analytical process to draw the object from two different points of view.

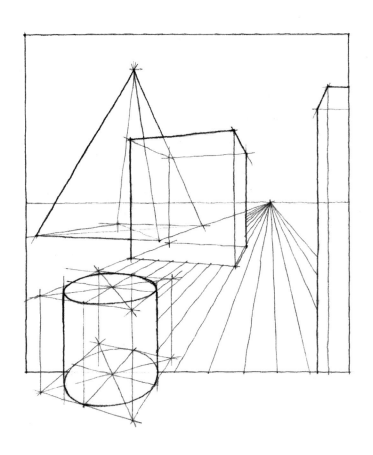

# 4
# Space and Depth

We live in a three-dimensional world of objects and space. Solid objects occupy, define the limits of, and give form to space. Space, on the other hand, surrounds and colors our vision of objects. A fundamental challenge in drawing is how to convey the existence of three-dimensional objects in space by describing lines, shapes, and tonal values on a flat, two-dimensional surface.

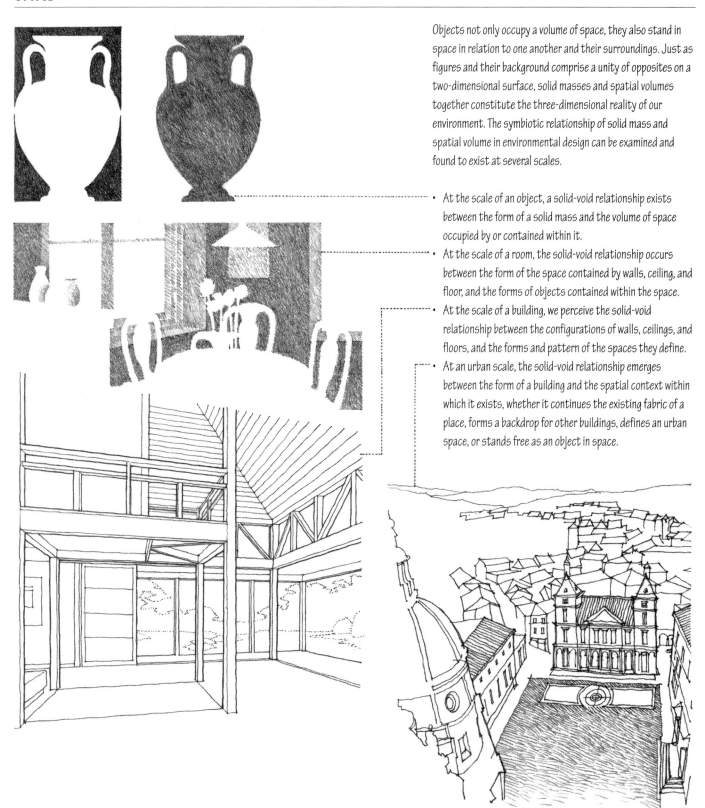

Objects not only occupy a volume of space, they also stand in space in relation to one another and their surroundings. Just as figures and their background comprise a unity of opposites on a two-dimensional surface, solid masses and spatial volumes together constitute the three-dimensional reality of our environment. The symbiotic relationship of solid mass and spatial volume in environmental design can be examined and found to exist at several scales.

- At the scale of an object, a solid-void relationship exists between the form of a solid mass and the volume of space occupied by or contained within it.
- At the scale of a room, the solid-void relationship occurs between the form of the space contained by walls, ceiling, and floor, and the forms of objects contained within the space.
- At the scale of a building, we perceive the solid-void relationship between the configurations of walls, ceilings, and floors, and the forms and pattern of the spaces they define.
- At an urban scale, the solid-void relationship emerges between the form of a building and the spatial context within which it exists, whether it continues the existing fabric of a place, forms a backdrop for other buildings, defines an urban space, or stands free as an object in space.

Pictorial space is the illusion of space or depth depicted on a two-dimensional surface by various graphic means. This pictorial space may be flat, deep, or ambiguous, but in all cases, it is illusory. Certain arrangements of lines, shapes, values, and textures on a drawing surface, however, can trigger the perception of a three-dimensional world by our visual system. If we understand how we infer three-dimensional form and space in what we see, we can use this information to make the drawn image of an object appear flat or volumetric. We can project the image forward toward the viewer or recede deeply into the depth of a drawing. We can, on a two-dimensional surface, establish and illuminate the three-dimensional relationships between objects.

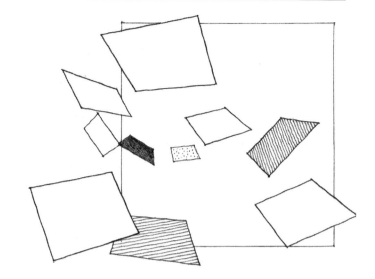

In The Perception of the Visual World, the psychologist James J. Gibson identifies 13 varieties of perspective. Gibson uses the term perspective to describe various "sensory shifts"—visual impressions that accompany our perception of depth over a continuous surface. Of these 13, eight are particularly effective in provoking the illusion of space and depth in a drawing:

- Continuity of outline
- Size perspective
- Vertical location in the visual field
- Linear perspective
- Atmospheric perspective
- Perspective of blur
- Texture perspective
- Shift of texture or linear spacing
- Transitions between light and shade

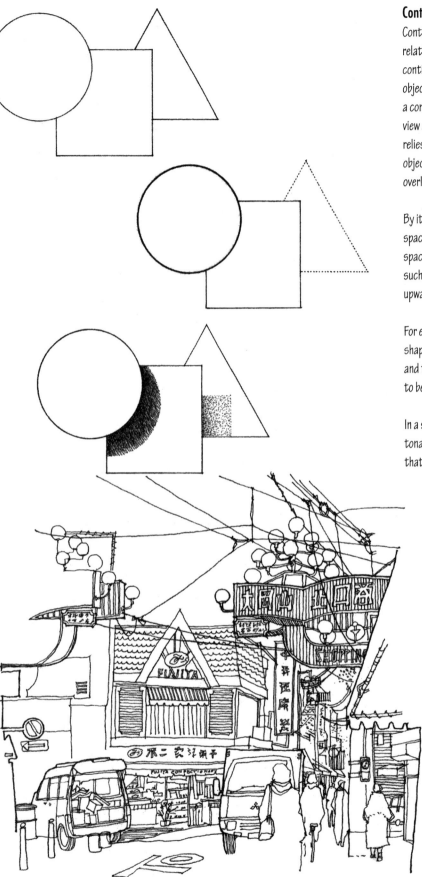

## Continuity of Outline

Continuity of the outline of an object helps us identify its depth relative to other objects in our visual field. A shape having a continuous outline visibly disrupts or obscures the profile of an object behind it. Therefore, we tend to perceive any shape having a complete outline as being in front of and concealing from our view a part of the shape behind it. Since this visual phenomenon relies on nearer objects overlaying or projecting in front of objects farther away, we often refer to the depth cue simply as overlap.

By itself, overlap tends to create relatively shallow intervals of space. However, we can achieve a greater sense of intervening space and depth if we combine overlap with other depth cues, such as atmospheric perspective or a shift in texture, and upward location in the visual field.

For example, we can enhance the spatial effect of overlapping shapes by varying the line weights of a pureline drawing. Darker and thicker profile or contour lines tend to advance and appear to be in front of lighter and thinner outlines.

In a similar manner, any shift in texture or sharp contrast in tonal value along an overlapping edge amplifies the perception that space intervenes between two overlapping shapes.

## Size Perspective

Size perspective refers to the apparent reduction in size of an object as it moves farther away from us. Our perception of size differences is based on the phenomenon known as size or object constancy, which leads us to imagine categories of objects as being uniform in size with constant color and texture. If we understand or know two objects to be the same size, but they appear to be different in size, then the larger will seem to be nearer than its smaller counterpart.

In reading size differences to assess scale and depth in a drawing, we must base our visual judgment on objects of known size, as human figures, or on objects of similar size in the visual field, as a series of windows, tables, or lamp posts.

Consider this example. When we observe two people, we naturally assume they are approximately the same height and possess similar proportions. If in a photograph or drawing we perceive one to be discernibly larger than the other, we conclude the smaller image represents a person that is more distant than the other. Otherwise, one would be a midget or the other a giant.

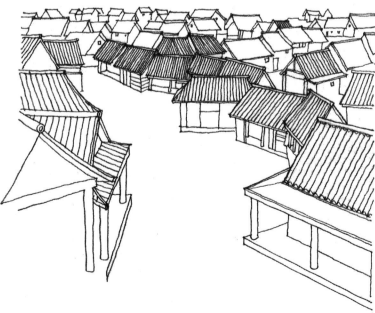

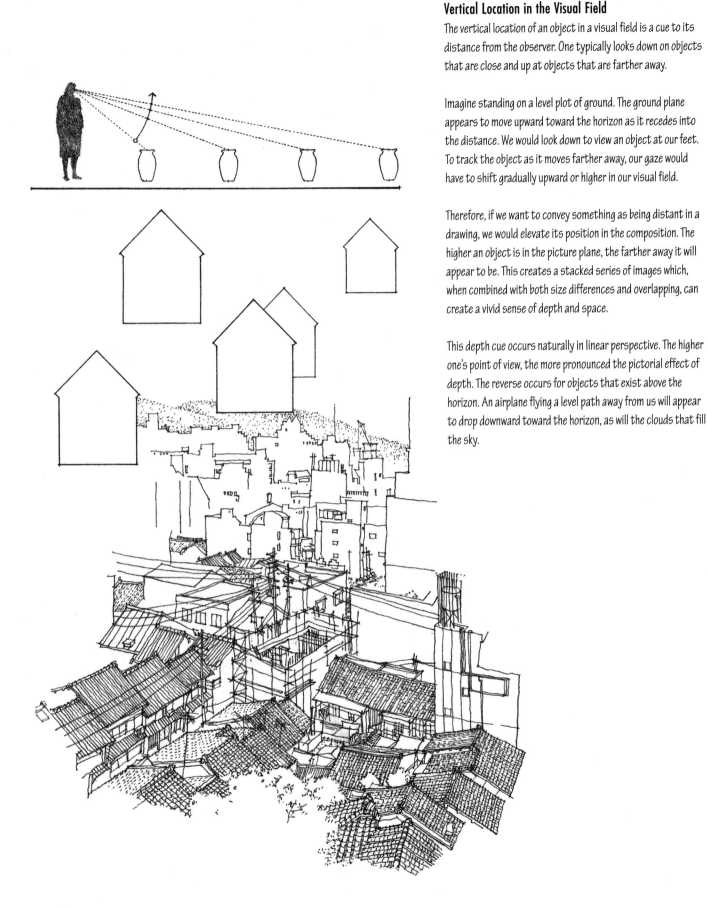

### Vertical Location in the Visual Field

The vertical location of an object in a visual field is a cue to its distance from the observer. One typically looks down on objects that are close and up at objects that are farther away.

Imagine standing on a level plot of ground. The ground plane appears to move upward toward the horizon as it recedes into the distance. We would look down to view an object at our feet. To track the object as it moves farther away, our gaze would have to shift gradually upward or higher in our visual field.

Therefore, if we want to convey something as being distant in a drawing, we would elevate its position in the composition. The higher an object is in the picture plane, the farther away it will appear to be. This creates a stacked series of images which, when combined with both size differences and overlapping, can create a vivid sense of depth and space.

This depth cue occurs naturally in linear perspective. The higher one's point of view, the more pronounced the pictorial effect of depth. The reverse occurs for objects that exist above the horizon. An airplane flying a level path away from us will appear to drop downward toward the horizon, as will the clouds that fill the sky.

## Exercise 4.1

Analyze the photograph below for examples of overlap, indicating which objects are closer and which objects are farther away. Lay a sheet of tracing paper over the photograph and draw the examples you discover.

## Exercise 4.2

Repeat the above exercise, but this time search for examples of size perspective indicating which objects are closer and which objects are farther away.

## Exercise 4.3

Repeat the Exercise 4.1, but this time search for examples of vertical location indicating which objects are closer and which objects are farther away.

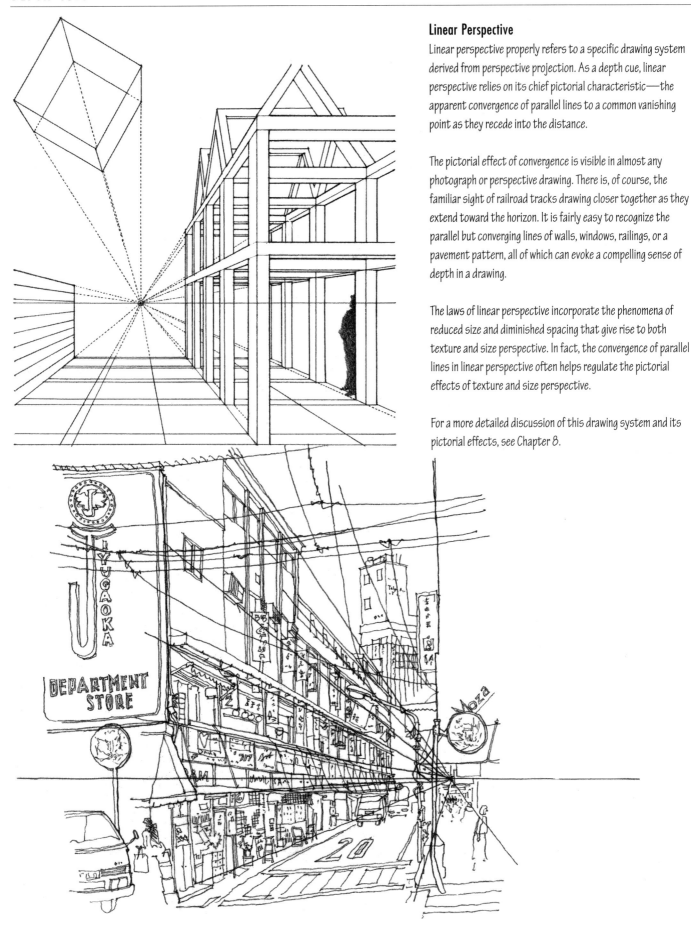

## Linear Perspective

Linear perspective properly refers to a specific drawing system derived from perspective projection. As a depth cue, linear perspective relies on its chief pictorial characteristic—the apparent convergence of parallel lines to a common vanishing point as they recede into the distance.

The pictorial effect of convergence is visible in almost any photograph or perspective drawing. There is, of course, the familiar sight of railroad tracks drawing closer together as they extend toward the horizon. It is fairly easy to recognize the parallel but converging lines of walls, windows, railings, or a pavement pattern, all of which can evoke a compelling sense of depth in a drawing.

The laws of linear perspective incorporate the phenomena of reduced size and diminished spacing that give rise to both texture and size perspective. In fact, the convergence of parallel lines in linear perspective often helps regulate the pictorial effects of texture and size perspective.

For a more detailed discussion of this drawing system and its pictorial effects, see Chapter 8.

## Exercise 4.4

Analyze the photograph below for examples of convergence of parallel lines. Make a photocopy of the photograph and lay a large sheet of tracing paper over it. Draw the lines which are parallel in space and which appear to converge in linear perspective. Extend them until they meet at their respective vanishing points. Note that there are two major sets of horizontal lines, one converging toward the left and the other converging toward the right. Connecting the vanishing points for each set should establish a horizontal line in the drawing which represents the horizon line of the observer.

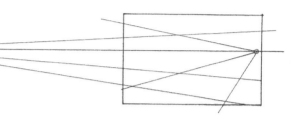

How many examples of the depth cues of overlap, size perspective, and vertical location can you find in the photograph?

## Exercise 4.5

Find a window that looks onto a scene exhibiting lines which are parallel in space. How many sets of converging parallel lines can you observe?

Tape a sheet of acetate to the glass. Focus on a point in the scene, hold your head steady, and maintain a level line of sight. With one eye closed, use a pen that will mark on the acetate to draw the sets of parallel lines you observe. Extend them to see if each set meets at a common vanishing point.

## Atmospheric Perspective

Atmospheric perspective refers to the progressive muting of hues, tonal values, and contrast that occur with increasing distance from the observer. Objects seen up close in the foreground of our visual field typically possess dark, saturated colors and sharply defined contrasts in value. As they move farther away, their colors become lighter and more subdued, and their tonal contrasts more diffuse. In the background, we see mainly shapes of grayed tones and muted hues.

These apparent changes in color and definition result from the diffusing quality of dust particles or pollution in the intervening atmosphere between viewer and object. This haze obscures the colors and distinctness of more distant forms. Since atmospheric perspective represents the combined effect of distance and the quality of the air that separates an object from the observer, it is also referred to as aerial perspective. This term should not be confused with a linear perspective drawn from an aerial point of view.

The graphic technique for rendering atmospheric perspective involves executing scaled variations of color and tone.

To move objects back:

- mute colors
- lighten values
- soften contrast

To bring objects forward:

- saturate colors
- darken values
- sharpen contrast

## Perspective of Blur

Perspective of blur refers to the indistinct form or outline of objects in any visual plane other than the one on which the eyes are focused. This depth cue reflects the fact that we normally associate clarity of vision with nearness and blurring of outlines with farness.

When we focus on an object within our visual field, there exists a range of distances through which we see sharply defined images. Within this depth of field, we see the edges, contours, and details of objects clearly. Beyond this range, the shape and form of objects appear less distinct and more diffuse. This visual phenomenon is closely related to and often incorporated into the pictorial effects of atmospheric perspective.

Critical to the reading of perspective blur in a drawing is a discernible contrast between the sharply defined edges and contours of foreground elements and the more indistinct shapes that occur in the background. The graphic equivalent of perspective blur is a diminishing or diffusion of the edges and contours of more distant objects. We can use either a lightly drawn line or a broken or dotted line to delineate these edges of shapes and contours of forms that exist beyond the focus of a drawing.

## Texture Perspective

Texture perspective refers to the gradual increase in the density of the texture of a surface as it recedes into the distance. The texture gradient that we perceive on a receding surface results from the continuous reduction in size and diminished spacing of the elements that comprise the surface texture.

Consider this example. When we view a brick wall up close, we can discern the individual bricks as well as the thickness of the mortar joints. As the wall surface recedes in perspective, the brick units diminish in size and the mortar joints appear simply as lines. As the wall continues to recede still further, the brick surface becomes denser and consolidates into a tonal value.

The graphic technique for depicting the visual phenomenon of texture perspective involves gradually diminishing the size, proportion, and spacing of the graphic elements used to portray a surface texture or pattern, whether they be dots, lines, or shapes of tonal values. Proceed from identifying units in the foreground to delineating a textured pattern in the middleground, and finally to rendering a tonal value in the background. Strive for smooth transitions and be careful that the resulting tonal values do not negate the principles of atmospheric perspective.

## Exercise 4.6

Draw the scene in the photograph below. Use the depth cue of atmospheric perspective to convey a sense of depth as one moves from the passage in the foreground to the gateway in the middleground and finally to the space beyond.

## Exercise 4.7

Redraw the scene in the photograph, but this time focus on the middleground and utilize perspective of blur to provoke a sense of depth in the scene.

## Exercise 4.8

Analyze the photograph for examples of texture perspective. Can you also find examples of size perspective and overlap in the photograph? Draw the scene a third time, employing these depth cues to convey the illusion of space and depth in your drawing.

## Shift of Texture or Linear Spacing

A discernible shift of texture or linear spacing conveys an interval of space between foreground and background. The degree of change depends on the actual distance that exists between the surface or object nearer to us and a more distant one.

Consider this example. We see the individual leaves of a tree that is close to us, but perceive the foliage of a tree further away as a textured aggregate of leaves. Trees in the distance emerge simply as masses of tonal value. The sudden changes in scale, texture, and spacing of the leaves signal significant intervals of depth.

Any shift in texture is related to texture perspective. If we take a receding plane of fabric and fold it over unto itself, what was originally a gradual increase in density of texture will now appear as a sudden shift in texture. The foreground pattern will overlap and juxtapose itself against a smaller background pattern.

Similarly, any shift in linear spacing is related to size perspective. The interval between the edges of equally spaced objects gradually diminish as they recede into the distance. Any sudden change in this interval will evoke a jump in distance between the foreground elements and those in the background.

## Transition between Light and Shade

Any abrupt shift in brightness stimulates the perception of a spatial edge or profile separated from a background surface by some intervening space. This depth cue implies the existence of overlapping shapes and the use of contrasting tonal values in a drawing.

Any line of tonal contrast is a potent depth cue that can enhance the sense of overlap and the pictorial effect of atmospheric perspective. The greater the spatial interval between overlapping shapes, the sharper the contrast between light and dark tonal values. While an abrupt change in tonal value indicates the profile of a corner or a spatial edge, a gradual transition in brightness leads to a perception of curvature and roundness.

In the three-dimensional modeling of forms, we rely on a discernible range of tonal values to depict and differentiate surfaces in light, shaded surfaces, and cast shadows. The resulting shifts in brightness can intensify the illusion of depth in multiview, paraline, and perspective drawings. For more information on the construction of architectural shade and shadows in these drawing systems, refer to the respective sections in Chapters 6, 7, and 8.

### Exercise 4.9

Observe where shifts in texture occur in the photograph below. Draw the setting, employing this depth cue to convey a sense of depth as the wall planes step back away from the observer.

### Exercise 4.10

Draw the scene in the photograph again, this time ignoring the colors and textures of the forms. Instead, record only the shapes and values of the shaded surfaces and cast shadows you see. To articulate the spatial edges of overlapping forms, emphasize the lines of contrast where shifts in brightness or tonal value occur.

Every drawing evolves over time. Knowing where to begin, how to proceed, and when to stop are crucial to the process of drawing. Whether we are drawing from observation or the imagination, we should develop a strategy for organizing the sequence in which we draw.

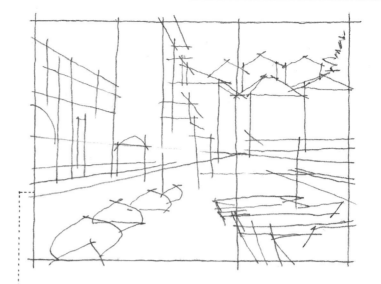

Building up a drawing in a systematic way is an important concept. We should advance by progressive stages and construct a drawing from the ground up. Each successive iteration or cycle through the drawing process should first resolve the relationships between the major parts, then resolve the relationships within each part, and finally readjust the relationships between the major parts once again.

A sequential approach of tediously finishing one part of a drawing before going on to the next can easily result in distorting the relationships between each part and the rest of the composition. Maintaining a consistent level of completeness or incompleteness across the entire surface of a drawing is important to preserving a unified, balanced, and focused image.

The following procedure prescribes a way of seeing as well as drawing. It involves building up a drawing in the following stages:

• Establish composition and structure
• Layer tonal values and textures
• Add significant details

We normally select from what we see what is of interest to us. Since our perception is discriminating, we should also be selective in what we draw. How we frame and compose a view, and what we emphasize with our drawing technique will tell others what attracted our attention and what visual qualities we focused on. In this way, our drawings will naturally communicate our perceptions with an economy of means.

Composing a view of a scene involves positioning ourselves at a particular point in space and deciding how to frame what we see. In order to convey the sense that the viewer is within a space rather than on the outside looking in, we must establish three pictorial regions: a foreground, a middleground, and a background. All three should not have equal emphasis; one should dominate to heighten the pictorial space of the drawing.

When portraying a specific aspect of an object or scene, a closer viewpoint may be necessary so that the size of the drawing can accommodate the rendering of tonal value, texture, and light.

### Exercise 4.11

Explore alternative ways of composing the view in the photograph below. The shape and orientation of the frame and the positions of elements within the frame interact to influence the pictorial space and composition of a drawing. Compare the spatial effects of a vertical or portrait format with those of a horizontal or landscape layout. How does a square format alter these effects?

### Exercise 4.12

Explore alternative ways of cropping the view in the photograph below. Compare a broad or distant view with close-in views that focus on only certain aspects or features of the scene.

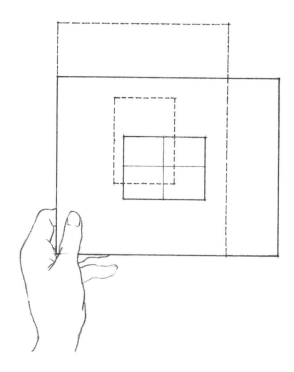

Without a cohesive structure to hold it together, the composition of a drawing collapses. Once the composition for a view is established, we use the analytical process of drawing to establish its structural framework. We begin with regulating lines that examine and verify the position, shape, and proportions of major elements. As we establish these first few lines, a tentative armature emerges that both holds and guides further observations and ideas. We draw further perceptions over this framework, which in turn, is adjusted in response to our perceptions. Let this structure remain visible, for it clarifies pictorial relationships and serves as a preparatory underdrawing for what comes later.

We see little dimensional foreshortening in relatively small objects. The eye perceives vertical lines as parallel and perpendicular to the ground plane, in contrast to optical reality. Therefore, in drawing small-scale objects, we preserve the verticality of vertical edges.

In drawing an environment—an outdoor space or an interior room—we view the scene from a fixed position in space. The structure, therefore, must be regulated by the principles of linear perspective. We are concerned here principally with the pictorial effects of linear perspective—foreshortening and the convergence of parallel lines. Our mind interprets what we see and presents an objective reality based on what we know of an object. In drawing a perspective view, we attempt to illustrate the visual aspects of an optical reality. These two are often at odds, and the mind usually wins out.

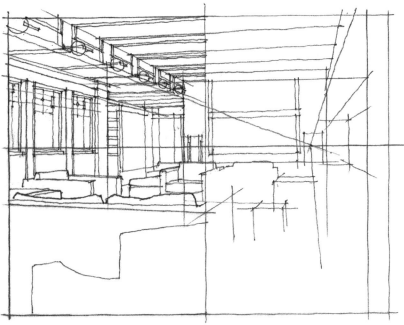

Begin by drawing the perceived shape of a vertical plane facing you. This plane may be the wall of a room, the façade of a building, or an implied plane defined by two vertical elements, such as the corners of two buildings. Use any of the sighting techniques described in Chapter 2 to ensure that the shape of the plane is properly proportioned.

Next, establish your eye level relative to that plane. Focus on a specific point, and draw a horizontal or horizon line through that point. Notice that horizontal elements situated above your eye level slope downward toward the horizon, while horizontal elements below rise upward. Draw human figures in the foreground, middleground, and background to establish a vertical scale.

Use sighting techniques to gauge the slopes of horizontal edges that pass through points in the vertical plane and recede into the distance. Visually extend these lines to determine their vanishing points. If these vanishing points lie off the sheet of the drawing, draw the front and rear vertical edges of a receding face and judge what proportion of the vertical leading edge lies above the horizon line and what lies below. Reproduce the same proportions for the rear vertical edge. Use the established points to guide the drawing of the inclined lines in perspective. These receding lines along with the horizon line then serve as visual guides for any other lines that converge at the same point.

To ensure the correct foreshortening of receding planes, you must be able to flatten their state into two-dimensional shapes and correctly judge the relative proportion between their width and depth.

Remember to draw these regulating lines in a continuous manner to construct a spatial framework for the drawing. As you proceed, compare every part in its proper relation to others in the perspective layout. Recalling the following depth cues will help regulate the shapes you see in perspective:

• Overlap
• Size perspective
• Location in visual field

For a more detailed discussion of this drawing system and the pictorial effects of convergence and foreshortening, see Chapter 8.

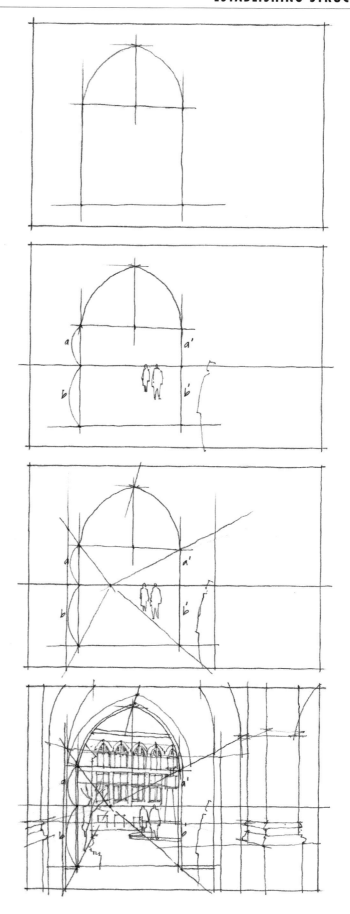

### Exercise 4.13

Use the analytical process of drawing to establish the underlying structure of the scene in the photograph below. Do not add tonal values or details. Start with a series of five-minute sketches before proceeding on to longer drawings.

### Exercise 4.14

Find an outdoor or interior space that exhibits a clear geometric structure and the convergence of parallel lines in linear perspective. Use the analytical process of drawing to establish the underlying structure of the scene. Do not add tonal values or details. Start with a series of five-minute sketches before proceeding on to longer drawings.

Scale refers to apparent size—how large or small a thing appears to be relative to some other thing. In order to measure scale, therefore, we must have something of known size to which we can refer.

## Visual Scale

Visual scale refers to the how big something appears to be when measured against other things around it. Thus, an object's scale is often a judgment we make based on the relative or known size of nearby or surrounding elements. For example, a table can appear to be in scale or out of scale with a room, depending on the relative size and proportions of the space. In drawing, we can emphasize or reduce the significance of an element by manipulating its scale relative to other elements.

Depending on the scale of what we are drawing, what we judge to be significant or trivial affects what we measure and the degree of accuracy that is required. The overall proportions of an object are important, as is its scale, relative to other things around it. But the degree of accuracy required really depends on whether or not we perceive differences. Are these differences significant and can we see them?

We are speaking of relative dimensions, not absolute meters, feet, or inches. Therefore, if something is $3\,^{29}/_{32}$ of an inch thick, this dimension is perhaps not as significant as whether we see it as being thin. And whether we see it as being thin really depends on what we are measuring it against. In other words, if it is thin, then something else must be thick. If something is short, we must be measuring it against something which is long.

How large is this wall?

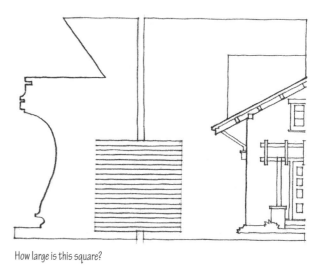

How large is this square?

## HUMAN SCALE

Human scale refers to how big or small something makes us feel. If the dimensions of an interior space or the size of elements within it make us feel small, we can say they lack human scale. If, on the other hand, the space does not dwarf us or if the elements offer a comfortable fit with our dimensional requirements of reach, clearance, or movement, we can say they are human in scale.

In what we see and draw, we often use the human figure to establish how large or small other things are. This comparison is based on our familiarity with our own body dimensions and the result can make us feel large or small, or it can make the thing we are measuring seem large or small. Other scale-giving elements are implements we use often and are sized to our dimensions, such as chairs and tables.

Human figures give a sense of size and scale, while furniture arrangements define areas of use. Therefore, in recording a scene or developing a design idea, it is important to draw at a scale that allows people and the furnishings they use to be included. For more information about drawing the human figure, see Chapter 11.

In linear perspective, the heads of people will appear to be approximately at your eye level if they are standing or walking on the same horizontal plane as the one on which you are standing.

### Exercise 4.15

Draw a series of cubes. Alter the relative scale of the cubes by drawing different-sized human figures next to each. Then transform each of the cubes into something in scale with the human figures: e.g., a chair, a room, or a building.

### Exercise 4.16

Visit two public spaces occupied by a number of people, one that is relatively small in scale and the other having a larger, more monumental scale. Draw the people in each space, paying attention to their relative heights and positions in space. Use the figures as measuring devices to establish the structure and scale of each space. In addition to size and proportion, what other attributes contribute to the perceived scale of each space?

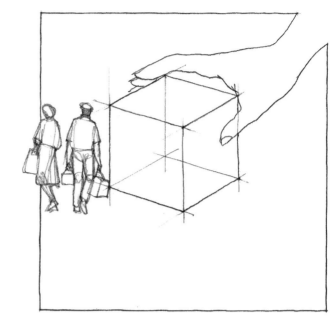

In composing and establishing the structure of a drawing, we create a framework of lines. To this scaffolding, we add tonal values to represent light and dark areas of the scene, define planes in space, model their form, describe surface color and texture, and convey spatial depth.

We should work from light to dark by mapping and layering shapes of tonal value over preceding areas of value. If an area is too light, we can always darken it. But once an area has been darkened too much and becomes muddy, it is difficult to correct. The freshness and vitality of a drawing is fragile and easily lost.

In rendering tonal values, keep in mind the depth cues of:

• Atmospheric perspective
• Texture perspective
• Perspective of blur

## Exercise 4.17

Follow the procedure outlined in Exercises 4.13 and 4.14 to establish the underlying structure of the scene in the photograph below. Over this framework, add tonal values to define planes in space, model forms, and convey spatial depth. Pay careful attention to the shapes, pattern, and range of tonal values; work from large areas of similar value, and then layer darker tones within these areas. Allow about five minutes for establishing the structure and another five minutes for the rendering of tonal values.

## Exercise 4.18

Find a public outdoor or interior space. Compose the scene with your viewfinder and repeat the above exercise. Practice a series of ten-minute structure-and-value sketches before proceeding on to longer drawings.

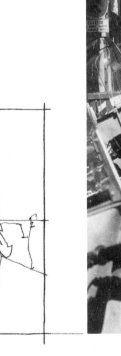

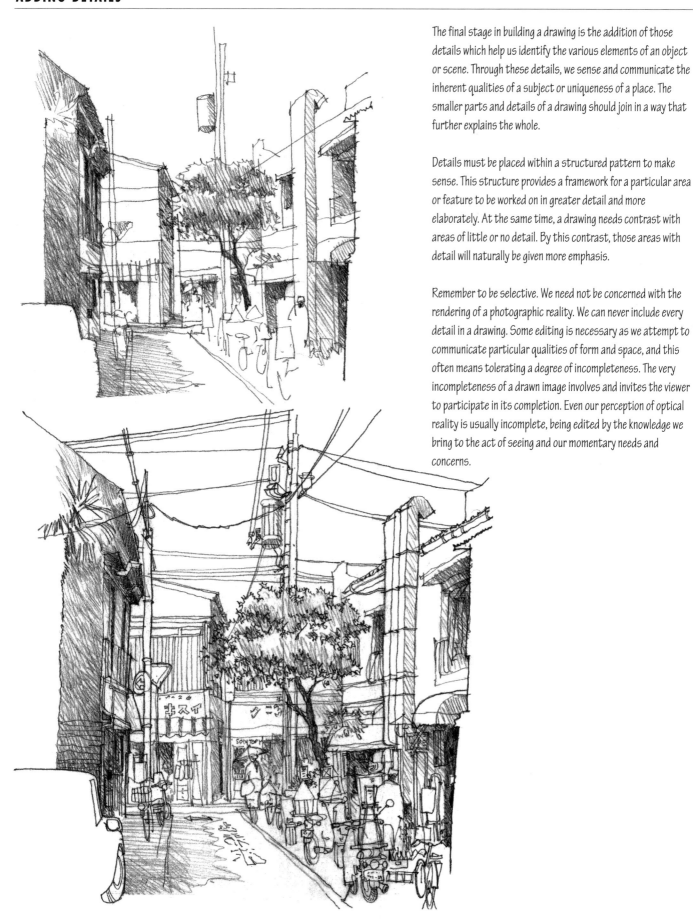

The final stage in building a drawing is the addition of those details which help us identify the various elements of an object or scene. Through these details, we sense and communicate the inherent qualities of a subject or uniqueness of a place. The smaller parts and details of a drawing should join in a way that further explains the whole.

Details must be placed within a structured pattern to make sense. This structure provides a framework for a particular area or feature to be worked on in greater detail and more elaborately. At the same time, a drawing needs contrast with areas of little or no detail. By this contrast, those areas with detail will naturally be given more emphasis.

Remember to be selective. We need not be concerned with the rendering of a photographic reality. We can never include every detail in a drawing. Some editing is necessary as we attempt to communicate particular qualities of form and space, and this often means tolerating a degree of incompleteness. The very incompleteness of a drawn image involves and invites the viewer to participate in its completion. Even our perception of optical reality is usually incomplete, being edited by the knowledge we bring to the act of seeing and our momentary needs and concerns.

## Exercise 4.19

Follow the procedures outlined in Exercises 4.13 and 4.17 to establish the underlying structure and value pattern of the scene in the photograph below. To this, add those details that help identify and clarify objects in the foreground. Deepen tonal values as necessary to emphasize spatial edges and convey spatial depth. Allow about ten minutes for establishing the structure and rendering the tonal values, and another five minutes for adding significant details.

## Exercise 4.20

Find a public outdoor or interior space. Compose the scene with your viewfinder and build a drawing by establishing the structure, layering tonal values, and adding details. Practice a series of fifteen-minute sketches before proceeding on to longer drawings.

# Drawing Systems

A central problem in drawing is how to represent aspects of three-dimensional reality on a surface which has only two dimensions. In the course of human history, various empirical methods evolved to represent the depth of space and objects within it. Manifestations of what we now call orthographic projection occur on Egyptian temple walls and in Greek vase paintings. There are numerous examples of oblique projection in Indian, Chinese, and Japanese art. We even find instances of linear perspective in Roman murals.

Today, these visual systems of representation constitute a formal language of design drawing governed by a consistent set of theories, principles, and conventions. We categorize these modes of representation into distinct types of drawing systems. We refer to these as systems in order to distinguish them from drawing techniques, which pertain to how we make marks on a sheet of paper or a computer screen.

In design, drawing systems provide alternative ways of thinking about and representing what we see before us or envision in the mind's eye. Each drawing system involves a built-in set of mental operations that directs our exploration of a design problem. In selecting one drawing system over another to convey visual information, we make conscious as well as unconscious choices as to which aspects of our perception or imagination can or should be expressed. The choice of a drawing system is as much a question of what to conceal as it is a decision about what to reveal.

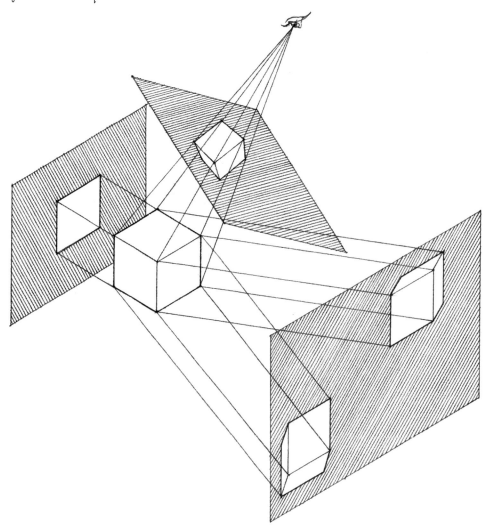

# 5
# Pictorial Systems

We classify drawing systems according to method of projection as well as by resulting pictorial effect. Projection refers to the process or technique of representing a three-dimensional object by extending all its points by straight lines, called projectors, to a picture plane, an imaginary transparent plane assumed to be coextensive with the drawing surface. We also call the picture plane the plane of projection.

There are three major types of projection systems—orthographic projection, oblique projection, and perspective projection. The relationship of the projectors to each other as well as the angle at which they strike the picture plane differentiate each projection system from the other two. We should recognize the particular nature of each projection system and understand the principles that guide the construction of each drawing type within the system. These principles define a common language that allows us to read and understand one another's drawings.

In addition to its utility as a means of communication, projection drawing both requires and facilitates learning how to think spatially in three dimensions. In working through the process of constructing a projection, we navigate through a three-dimensional field of space in order to locate points, determine the length and direction of lines, and describe the shape and extent of planes. Projection drawing thus embraces the system of Cartesian coordinates and the principles of descriptive geometry.

## PICTORIAL SYSTEMS

When we lay out the major types of projection systems, it becomes apparent that the images they present of an object vary in appearance. It is easiest to discern both the pictorial similarities and differences by studying how each projection system represents the same cubic form as having mutually perpendicular sets of lines and planes.

Based on similarities of appearance, there are three major categories of pictorial systems—multiview drawings, paraline drawings, and perspective drawings. Multiview drawings represent a three-dimensional subject through a series of distinct but related two-dimensional views. Both paraline and perspective drawings, on the other hand, depict two or more facets of a three-dimensional structure in a single image. The major pictorial difference between the two is that parallel lines remain parallel in paraline drawings while they appear to converge in perspective drawings.

Multiview, paraline, and perspective drawings represent a range of choices for the designer. We should not only know how to construct each drawing type but also understand the particular pictorial effects that each projection system produces. No one drawing system is superior to the others; each has inherent pictorial characteristics that influence how we think about what we are illustrating and what others read into it. Each defines a unique relationship between subject and viewer, and describes different aspects of a subject. For every aspect revealed by a particular drawing system, other aspects are concealed. In the end, the selection of a drawing system should be appropriate to the nature of the subject and the requirements of communication.

### Projection System

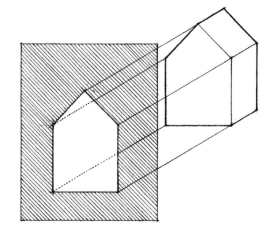

#### Orthographic Projection

Projectors are parallel to each other and perpendicular to picture plane; see Chapter 6.

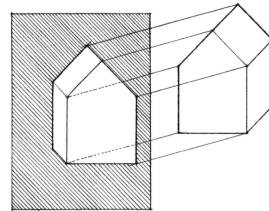

#### Oblique Projection

Projectors are parallel to each other and oblique to picture plane; see Chapter 7.

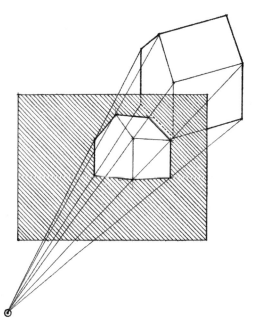

#### Perspective Projection

Projectors converge to a point that represents the eye of the observer; see Chapter 8.

## Projection System

### Orthographic Projection

**Plan, section, elevation**
Principal face of rectangular form in each view is parallel to the picture plane.

— Multiview Drawings

### Axonometric Projection
*See Chapter 7.*

**Isometric**
Three major axes make equal angles with the picture plane.

**Dimetric**
Two of the three major axes make equal angles with the picture plane.

**Trimetric**
Three major axes make different angles with the picture plane.

— Paraline Drawings

### Oblique Projection

**Elevation Oblique**
Principal vertical face of rectangular form is parallel with the picture plane.

**Plan Oblique**
Principal horizontal face of rectangular form is parallel with the picture plane.

### Perspective Projection

**1-point Perspective**
One horizontal axis is perpendicular to the picture plane; the other horizontal axis and the vertical axis are parallel with the picture plane.

**2-point Perspective**
Both horizontal axes are oblique to the picture plane; vertical axis remains parallel with the picture plane.

**3-point Perspective**
Three major axes of rectangular form are oblique to the picture plane.

— Perspective Drawings

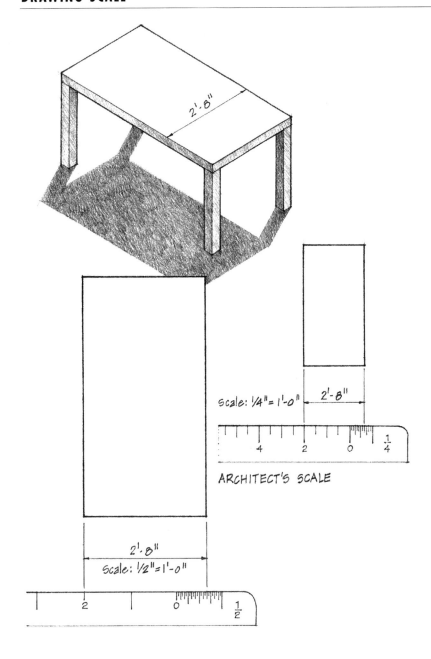

Scale: $1/4" = 1'-0"$

2'-8"

ARCHITECT'S SCALE

2'-8"

Scale: $1/2" = 1'-0"$

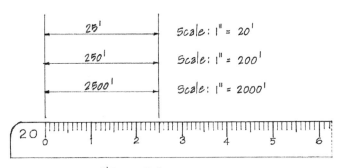

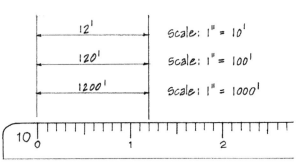

Mechanical scale is the calculation of the physical dimensions of an object according to a standard system of measurement. For example, we can say that a table, according to the U.S. Customary System, measures 5' long, 32" wide, and 29" high. If we are familiar with this system and to objects of similar size, we can visualize how big the table is. Using the International Metric System, however, the same table would measure 1524 mm long, 813 mm wide, and 737 mm high.

The drawings we use to represent this table or any other design must fall within the confines of the drawing surface. Since a design object or construction is usually much larger than the drawing surface, we must reduce the size of the drawing to fit. We refer to the proportional reduction in drawing size as the scale of the drawing.

To construct an accurate representation of a design, we use a proportional measuring system. When we say a drawing is made to scale, we mean that all of its dimensions are related to the full-size object or construction by a chosen ratio. For example, when we draw at a scale of $1/4" = 1'-0"$, each $1/4"$ in the drawing represents a foot in the full-size object or construction. In a large-scale drawing, the size reduction is relatively small, while in a small-scale drawing, the size reduction is considerable.

The term scale also refers to the device we use to accurately make measurements. Architect's scales have one or more sets of graduated and numbered spaces, each set establishing a proportion of a fractional part of an inch to one foot. Engineer's scales have one or more sets of graduated and numbered spaces, each set divided into multiples of ten parts per inch.

25'   Scale: $1" = 20'$

250'   Scale: $1" = 200'$

2500'   Scale: $1" = 2000'$

ENGINEER'S SCALE

12'   Scale: $1" = 10'$

120'   Scale: $1" = 100'$

1200'   Scale: $1" = 1000'$

In all drawing systems, object lines define the shape and form of the physical entity or construction we are designing. We draw all object lines visible to the eye as solid, continuous lines. Depending on our point of view, however, the contour that an object line represents may appear to be a spatial edge, an intersection of two visible planes, or simply a change in material or color. To represent and communicate these distinctions, we use a hierarchy of line weights.

• Spatial Edges

The most important object lines are those which depict the edges where solid matter meets spatial void. These contours define the shape and profile of objects and distinguish one object from another where they overlap in space. We typically use the heaviest line weight to delineate these edges of space.

• Planar Corners

The second most important object lines are those which describe contours appearing within the outer silhouette of a three-dimensional volume. These interior contours articulate the surface structure of a three-dimensional volume. To distinguish these inner edges from the outer profile of a form, we use an intermediate range of line weights.

• Surface Lines

The third type of object line simply indicates discernible changes in color, tonal value, or texture on the surface of a plane or volume. To indicate these lines of tonal or textural contrast, we use the lightest range of line weights. When the slimmest possible solid line is not light enough in value, a dashed or dotted line may be used to preserve the hierarchy of line weights.

• Hidden Lines

Hidden lines reveal edges which would be concealed otherwise by another part of the object in a particular view. Hidden lines consist of a series of closely spaced dashes or dots.

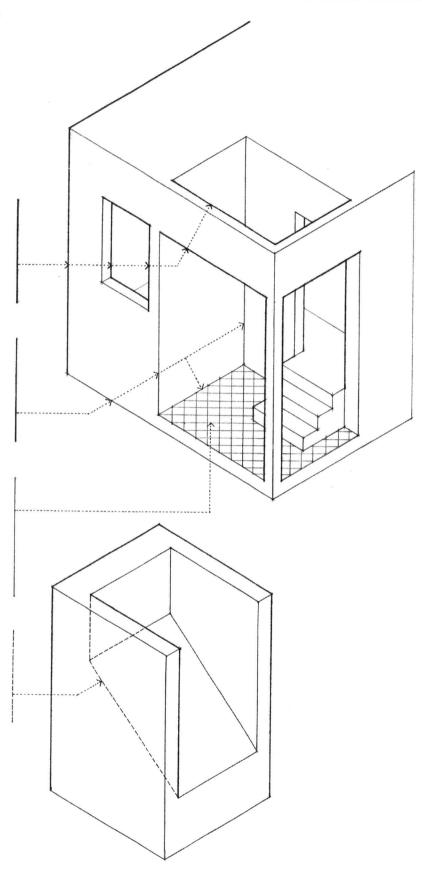

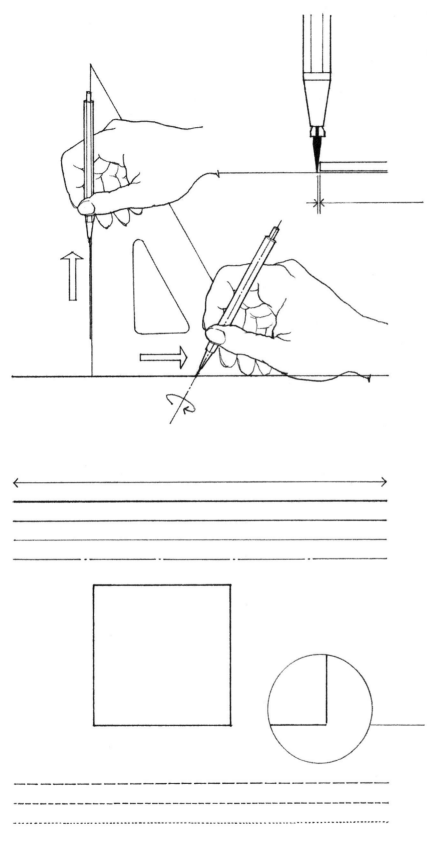

We rule lines by using the straightedge of a T-square, parallel rule, or triangle as a guide as we pull a pencil point or pen nib in the direction of the line being drawn. Ruling or drafting lines is necessary when clarity, precision, and accuracy are paramount in the communication of a design. Ruled lines should therefore be uniform in thickness and density, have definite endpoints, and meet other lines cleanly.

When ruling lines, keep the following points in mind:

• Always draw over the straightedge, leaving a very slight gap between the edge and the point of the pencil or tip of the pen.
• Hold the barrel of the pen or shaft of the pencil in a vertical plane perpendicular to the drawing surface and tilt it in the direction of movement. With pens, maintain an angle of about 80°; hold pencils at an angle from 45° to 60°.
• Always pull the pen or pencil in the direction of the line being drawn. Never push the pen tip or pencil point, as this makes it difficult to control the quality of the line, and can also damage both the pen tip and the drawing surface.
• When drafting with a pencil, it is important to have a well-sharpened point that is neither too stubby nor too rounded. To maintain the sharpness of a pencil point and maintain a uniform thickness, practice rotating the pencil between thumb and forefinger as you draw each line.

• Strive for consistently crisp, clear lines. Each object line should start and end in a precise manner. Back up slightly and exert a little extra pressure at both the beginning and the end of each stroke so that every line begins and ends in a positive manner.
• Draw at a steady pace and strive for a line that is uniform in thickness and density. A ruled line should appear as if it were stretched tightly between two points.

• Define corners with a very slight overlap.
• Avoid exaggerating the length of the overlap; the amount of overlap depends on the scale of the drawing.
• Corners appear rounded when lines do not meet in an explicit manner.

• Maintain the continuity of dashed and dotted lines by spacing the dashes or dots as closely and evenly as possible.

## Exercise 5.1

With a mechanical pencil and a T-square or parallel rule, draw three sets of alternating thick and thin dark lines six inches long. Are the ends of each line clearly defined? Is each line uniformly dense? Is there sufficient contrast in adjacent line thicknesses to discern the different line weights?

## Exercise 5.2

With a mechanical pencil, a drafting triangle, and a T-square or parallel rule, draw a composition of three squares with sides of 1", 2½", and 4¾". Is there a consistency of line density and thickness? Do the lines meet crisply at corners? Repeat this exercise, using a mechanical pen.

## Exercise 5.3

With a mechanical pencil, a drafting triangle, and a T-square or parallel rule, draw this diagram at twice its size. Use an architect's scale to determine the overall dimensions of the largest rectangle when measured at the following scales: ⅛" = 1'-0", ¼" = 1'-0", ¾" = 1'-0", 1" = 1'-0", 1½" = 1'-0".

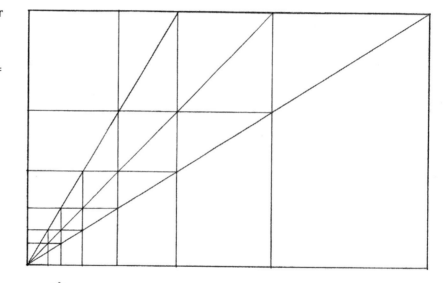

## Exercise 5.4

With a mechanical pencil, 30°-60° and 45°-45° drafting triangles, and a T-square or parallel rule, copy the drawings below at twice their size. Use a hierarchy of line weights to differentiate spatial edges, planar corners, and surface lines. Repeat this exercise, using a mechanical pen.

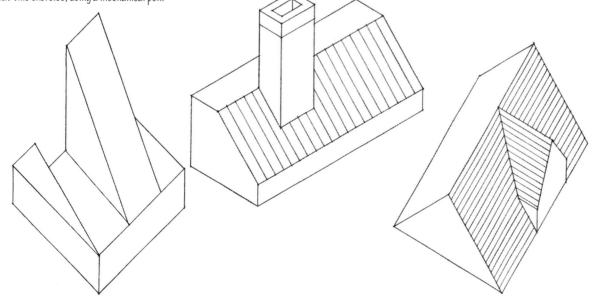

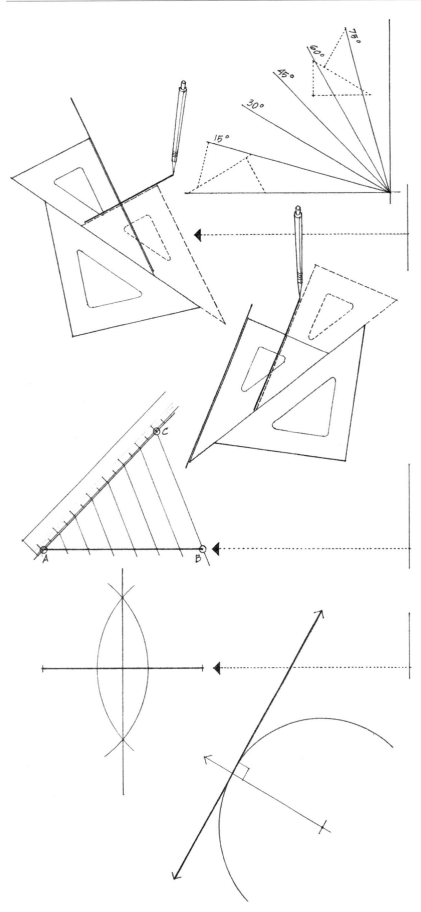

It is useful to understand how to draw common geometric shapes and perform certain geometric constructions.

### Angled Lines

We can use the standard 45°-45° and 30°-60° triangles either singly or in combination to draw angled lines in 15° increments from 15° to 90°.

### Drawing a Perpendicular

We can use a pair of triangles to draw a perpendicular to any line. First position the hypotenuse of each triangle against each other and align one side of the upper triangle with the line. Then hold the bottom triangle in position while you slide the upper triangle until the perpendicular side is in the proper position.

### Drawing a Series of Parallel Lines

We can use a pair of triangles to draw a series of lines parallel to one already drawn. First position the hypotenuse of each triangle against each other and align the longer side of the upper triangle with the drawn line. Then hold the second triangle in position and slide the first triangle to the desired positions of the parallel lines.

### Subdividing a Line

To subdivide a line AB into a number of equal parts, draw a second line at any angle between 10° and 90° from point A. Use a scale to mark off the desired number of equal divisions along the second line. Draw line BC. Then use a pair of triangles to draw a series of parallel lines which transfer the scaled divisions to line AB.

### Bisecting a Line

To bisect a line, construct circular arcs with a compass from each of the endpoints of the line. Then draw a line through the two points where the arcs intersect. This line not only bisects the first line but is also perpendicular to it.

### Drawing a Tangent to a Circular Arc

To draw a tangent to a circle or circular arc, first draw the radius from the center of the circle or circular arc to the point of tangency. Then construct a line perpendicular to the radius through the point of tangency.

## Exercise 5.5

With a compass, draw a 6"-diameter circle. Construct a pentagon as shown in the diagram to the right. Within this pentagon, draw a gradated series of pentagrams.

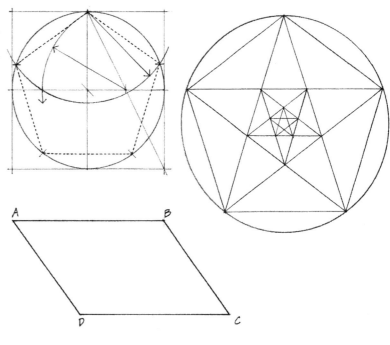

## Exercise 5.6

Divide the long side of the parallelogram ABCD into seven equal parts. Then draw lines from each of these points parallel to AD.

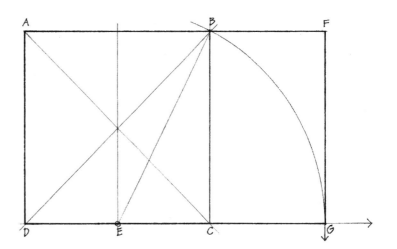

## Exercise 5.7

At a scale of ³/₄" = 1'-0", draw the profile of a stair having nine risers and eight treads from point A to point B.

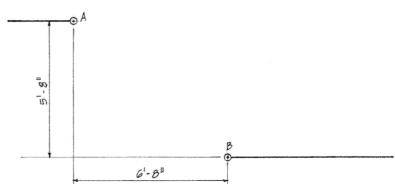

## Exercise 5.8

Construct a rectangle for which the ratio between the shorter and the longer sides is the Golden Section or Golden Mean. First draw the square ABCD with 2" sides. Find the center of the square by drawing two diagonals. Through this center draw a vertical line down to the base of the square to locate point E midway between DC. With E as the center and EB as the radius, swing an arc down to a horizontal extension of the base of the square. Then draw the rectangle AFGD. The ratio of AD to DG is the Golden Section, a ratio of approximately 0.618 to 1.000.

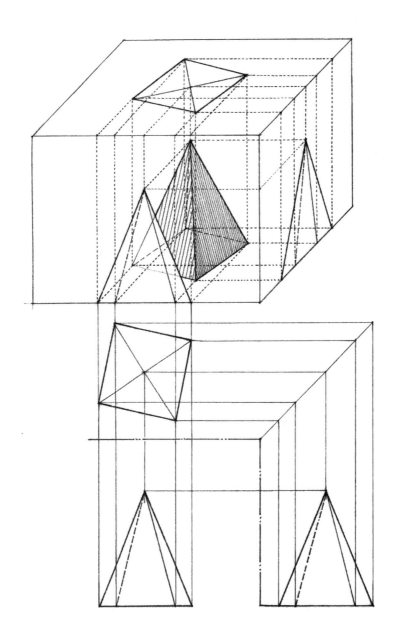

# 6
# Multiview Drawings

Multiview drawings comprise the drawing types we know as plans, elevations, and sections. Each is an orthographic projection of a particular aspect of an object or construction. These orthographic views are abstract in the sense that they do not match optical reality. They are a conceptual form of representation based on what we know about something rather than on the way it is seen from a point in space. There is no reference to an observer, or if there is, the spectator's eye is an infinite distance away.

In orthographic projection, parallel projectors meet the picture plane at right angles. Therefore, the orthographic projection of any feature or element which is parallel to the picture plane remains true in size, shape, and configuration. This gives rise to the principal advantage of multiview drawings—the ability to precisely locate points, gauge the length and slope of lines, and describe the shape and extent of planes.

During the design process, multiview drawings establish two-dimensional planar fields on which we can study formal patterns and scale relationships in a composition, as well as impose an intellectual order on a design. The ability to regulate size, placement, and configuration also makes multiview drawings useful in communicating the graphic information necessary for the description, fabrication, and construction of a design.

On the other hand, a single multiview drawing can only reveal partial information about an object or construction. There is an inherent ambiguity of depth as the third dimension is flattened onto the picture plane. Whatever depth we read in a solitary plan, section, or elevation must be implied by such graphic depth cues as hierarchical line weights and contrasting tonal values. While a sense of depth can be inferred, it can be known with certainty only by looking at additional views. We therefore require a series of distinct but related views to fully describe the three-dimensional nature of a form or composition—hence the term multiview.

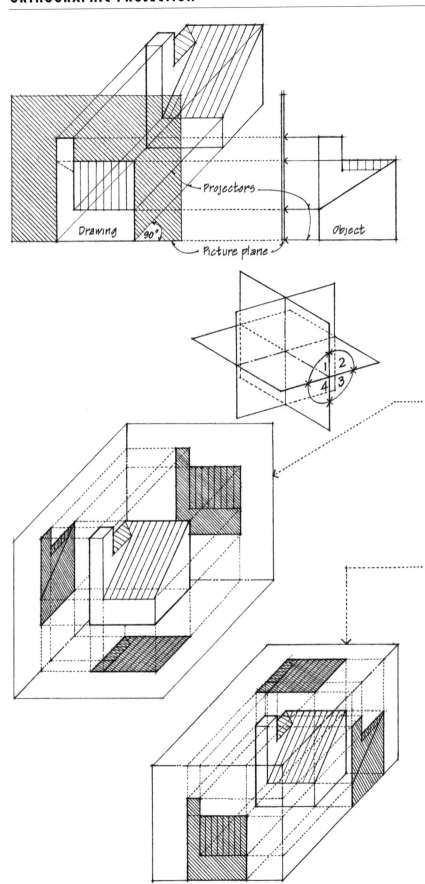

Orthographic projection is a system of projection which represents an object by projecting lines perpendicular to the picture plane. To construct an orthographic projection, we draw parallel projectors from the various points in the object to intersect the picture plane at right angles. We then connect the projected points in their proper order to obtain the view of the object on the picture plane. We refer to the resulting image on the picture plane as an orthographic view.

A single orthographic view is insufficient to fully describe a three-dimensional object. We need a set of related orthographic views. There are two conventions for regulating the relationship between orthographic views: first-angle projection and third-angle projection. To understand the distinction between the two, imagine three mutually perpendicular picture planes—one horizontal and two vertical. The frontal picture plane and the horizontal picture plane intersect to form four dihedral angles, numbered one through four in a clockwise direction starting with the upper front quadrant.

### First-angle Projection

Gaspard Monge, a French physicist and military engineer responsible for the design of fortifications, devised first-angle projection in the eighteenth century. In first-angle projection, we locate the object in the first quadrant and project the images of the object back like shadows to the inner faces of the picture planes. What is projected back through the object are those aspects of the object nearest to the viewer.

### Third-angle Projection

If we place the object in the third quadrant, the result is third-angle projection. Since the picture planes lie between the object and viewer, we project the images of the object forward to the picture planes. We therefore draw and view the images on the outer faces of the transparent picture planes.

If we enclose an object within a transparent picture-plane box, we can name the principal picture planes and the images projected orthographically onto these planes. Each orthographic view represents a different orientation and a particular vantage point from which to view the object. Each plays a specific role in the development and communication of a design.

## Principal Planes

A principal plane is any of a set of mutually perpendicular picture planes on which the image of an object is projected orthographically.

### Horizontal Plane

The principal level picture plane on which a plan or top view is projected orthographically.

### Frontal Plane

The principal vertical picture plane on which an elevation or front view is projected orthographically.

### Profile Plane

The principal vertical picture plane on which a side or end view is projected orthographically.

### Fold Line

The trace representing the intersection of two perpendicular picture planes.

### Trace

A line representing the intersection of two planes.

## Principal Views

The principal orthographic views are the plan, the elevation, and the section.

### Plan

A principal view of an object projected orthographically on a horizontal picture plane; also called top view. In architectural drawing, there are distinct types of plan views for representing various horizontal projections of a building or site.

### Elevation

A principal view of an object projected orthographically on a vertical picture plane. An elevation view may be a front, side, or rear view, depending on how we orient ourselves to the object or assess the relative significance of its faces. In architectural graphics, we label elevation views in relation to the compass directions or to a specific feature of a site.

### Section

An orthographic projection of an object as it would appear if cut through by an intersecting plane.

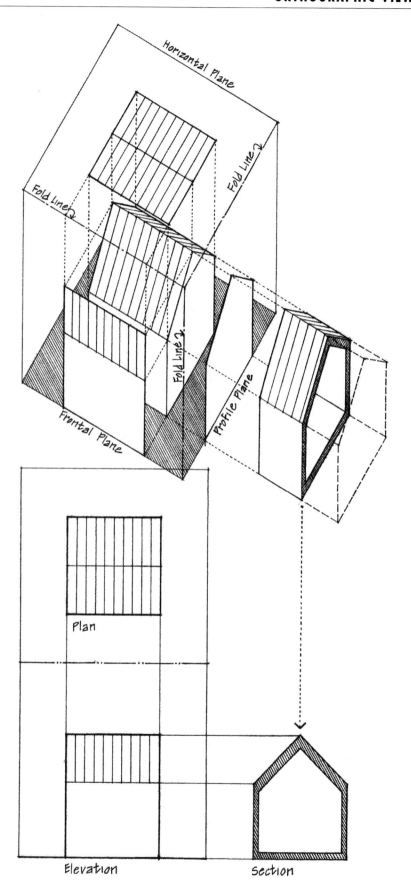

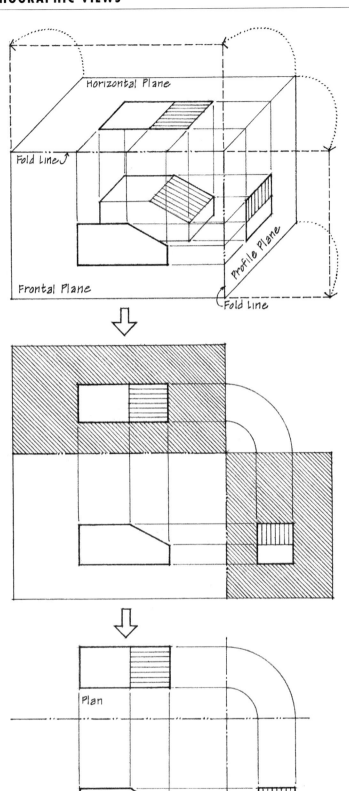

### Arranging Views

To make it easier to read and interpret how a series of orthographic views describes a three-dimensional whole, we arrange the views in an orderly and logical fashion. The most common arrangement of plan and elevations results from unfolding the transparent picture-plane box in third-angle projection.

After each view is projected, we rotate the views about the fold lines into a single plane represented by the drawing surface. The top or plan view revolves upward to a position directly above and vertically aligned with the front or elevation view, while the side or profile view revolves to align horizontally with the front view. The result is a coherent set of related orthographic views separated by fold lines.

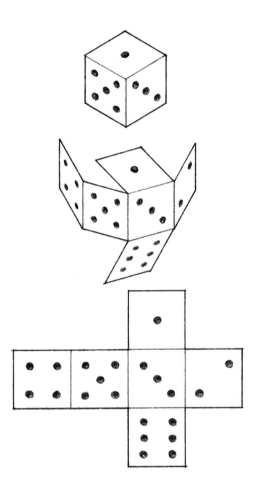

## Number of Views

The number of orthographic views necessary to completely describe the three-dimensional form of an object varies with its geometry and complexity.

Symmetrical conditions often eliminate the need for one or more views. For example, a form or composition characterized by axial or bilateral symmetry has two sides which are mirror images of each other. Therefore, one side view would be redundant and could be omitted. Similarly, multiple elevation views of a radially symmetrical form or composition would be unnecessary if a single elevation replicated the same information. The omission of a view, however, can lead to ambiguity if a symmetrical condition does not in fact exist.

Most objects require a minimum of three related views to describe their form. Complex forms and compositions may require four or more related views, especially if they have a number of oblique faces.

## Auxiliary Views

For each oblique face of an object or construction, an auxiliary view is necessary to describe its true size and shape. We establish an auxiliary view by inserting a fold line which represents the edge view of an auxiliary picture plane parallel to the inclined or oblique face.

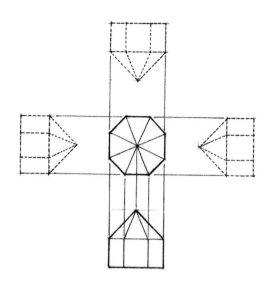

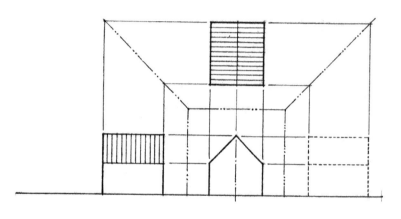

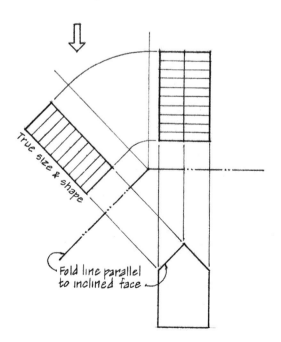

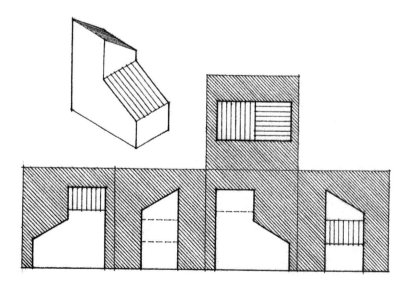

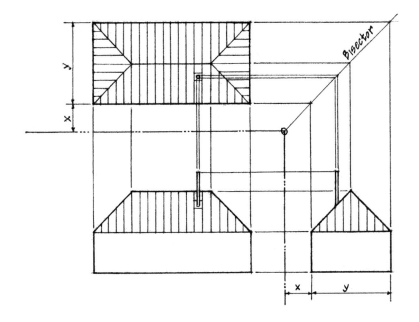

## Constructing Views

Whenever possible, align related orthographic views so that points and dimensions can be transferred easily from one view to the next. This relationship will not only facilitate the construction but also makes the drawings more understandable as a coordinated set of information. For example, once a plan is drawn, we can efficiently transfer the horizontal dimensions of length vertically on the drawing surface to the elevation below. In a similar manner, we can project the vertical dimensions of height horizontally on the drawing surface from one elevation to one or more adjacent elevations.

Always project points to an adjacent view with projectors drawn perpendicular to the common fold line. Since any point is the same distance away from the fold line in all views related to a common view, we can transfer a distance from the horizontal plane to the profile plane by constructing a diagonal bisector at the intersection of the fold lines. An alternative is to use the intersection of the fold lines as the center for a series of quarter-circular arcs.

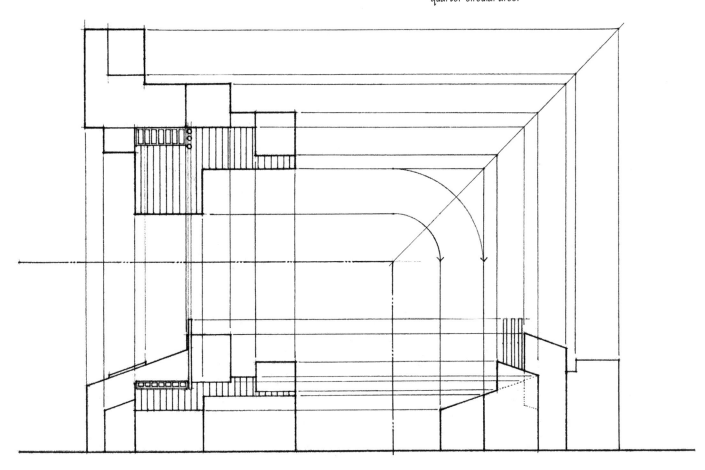

## Principles and Techniques

The orthographic projection of any line or plane parallel to the picture plane is true to whatever scale to which a drawing is being constructed.

- To determine the true length of a line, establish a fold line parallel to the line and project its end points across the fold line.
- The orthographic projection of any line perpendicular to a picture plane is a point. To show the point view of a line, one view must first reveal its true length. Then establish a fold line perpendicular to the true-length line and project across the fold line.

- The orthographic projection of any plane perpendicular to a picture plane is a straight line. If a line which lies in a plane appears as a point, the plane will appear as a line in the same view. Therefore, to show the edge view of a plane, find the point view of a true-length line in the plane and project the points defining the plane into the same view.
- To find the true size and shape of a plane, establish a fold line perpendicular to the edge view of the plane and project the points defining the plane across the fold line.

- If two or more lines are parallel in space, their orthographic projections are parallel in all views.
- The size of an element remains constant in any single view regardless of its distance from the picture plane.

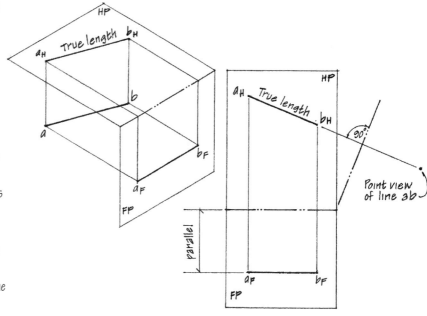

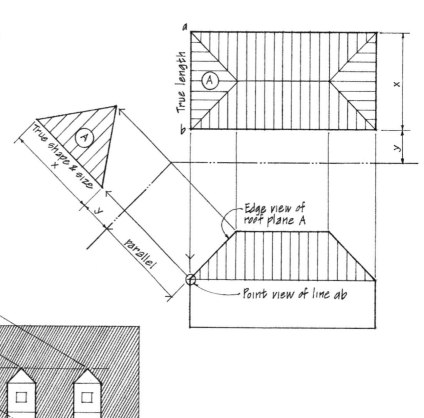

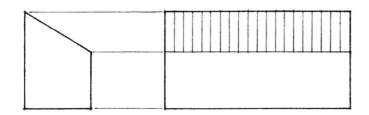

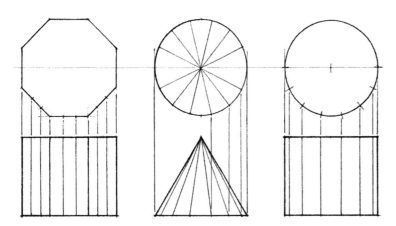

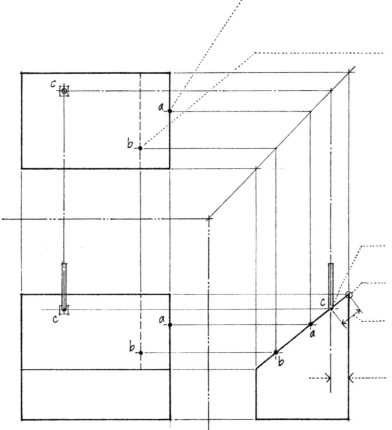

## Principles and Techniques

- The orthographic projection of any line or plane oblique to the picture plane is always foreshortened. To draw the foreshortened view of an oblique line or plane, one view must show the true length of the line or the edge view of the plane.

- To determine an orthographic projection of a curve, first draw the curve in the view that shows its true shape or contour. Then establish equidistant points along this profile and transfer them to the related view. The finer the divisions, the smoother and more accurate the representation.

- To project a point on a line in one view to the same location in an adjacent view, project the point across the fold line until it meets the line in the adjacent view.

- To project a point on a plane from one view to another, construct a line within the plane that contains the point. Project this line from one view to the next and then project the point from line to line.

- The point of intersection between a line and a plane appears in the view that shows the edge view of the plane.

- The line of intersection between two nonparallel planes appears in a view that shows one of the planes as an edge.

- The shortest distance between a point and a line appears in a view where the line appears as a point. The perpendicular distance is a straight line connecting the two points.

- The shortest distance from a point to a plane appears in a view that shows the edge view of the plane. The perpendicular extends from the point to the edge view of the plane.

### Principles and Techniques

- The true angle between two intersecting lines appears when the true length of both lines show in the same view. If two intersecting lines are perpendicular to each other, the 90° angle will remain true in any view that shows the true length of one of the lines.

$acb$ = True ∡
TL = True length

- The true angle between a line and a plane appears in the view that shows the edge view of the plane and the true length of the line.

- The true angle between two planes appears in the view that shows their line of intersection as a point.

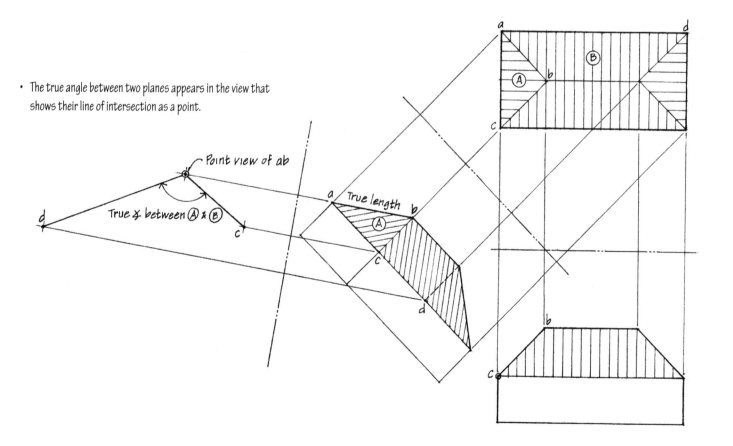

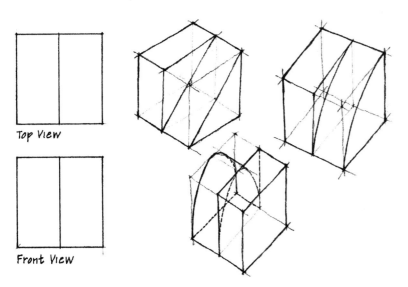

Top View

Front View

The top and front views can describe a number of different objects. Presented here in pictorial form are three possibilities. How many more can you visualize?

Multiview drawings comprise a series of related but partial views of a three-dimensional reality. Orthographic plans, sections, and elevations do not convey how we normally see our visual world. Even when embellished with visual depth cues, they remain essentially a conceptual system of representation that is more abstract than pictorial. Learning to draw plans, sections, and elevations, therefore, also requires learning how to read and interpret the graphic language of multiview drawings. Anyone using multiview drawings to think about, make, and communicate design decisions must understand how the individual views relate to each other to describe a three-dimensional object or space. From this reading, one should be able to assemble the series of partial and fragmentary views in the mind's eye to recreate an understanding of the whole. Similarly, given a three-dimensional construct, one should be able to develop a representation of the whole through a series of multiview drawings.

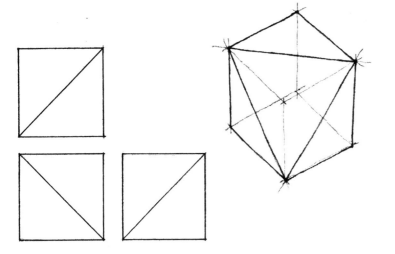

### Exercise 6.1

Visualizing the three-dimensional form of an object described in a set of multiview drawings requires mental trial and error. Drawing possible solutions out on paper helps us work through the problem. To experience this, try to sketch a pictorial view of the object described in each set of orthographic projections.

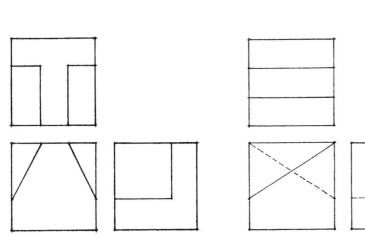

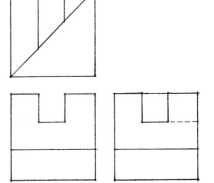

## Exercise 6.2

For each pair of orthographic projections, draw a third orthographic view as well as a three-dimensional pictorial view of the object described.

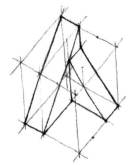

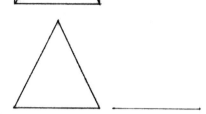

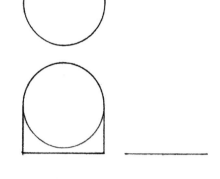

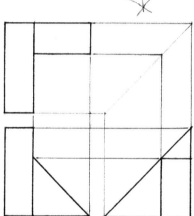

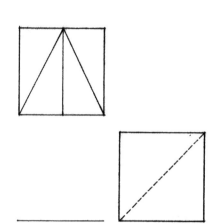

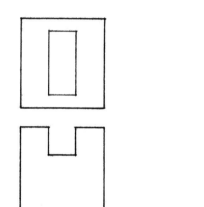

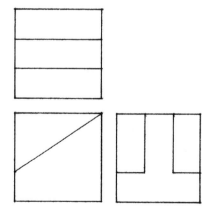

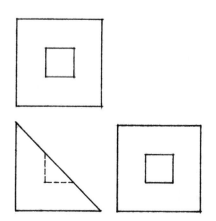

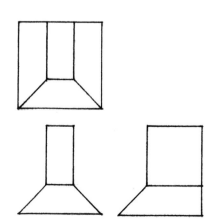

## Exercise 6.3

Study each set of orthographic projections and try to visualize the object described. Which set, if viewed in third-angle projection, contains views that are inconsistent or illogical?

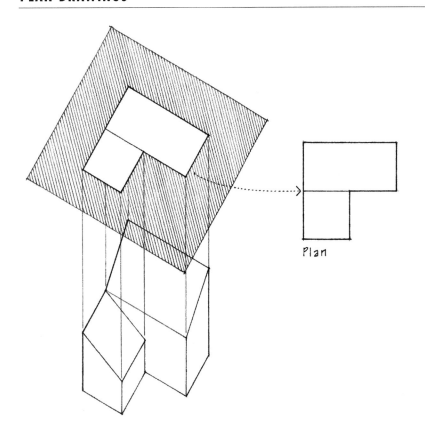

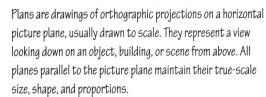

Plan

Plans are drawings of orthographic projections on a horizontal picture plane, usually drawn to scale. They represent a view looking down on an object, building, or scene from above. All planes parallel to the picture plane maintain their true-scale size, shape, and proportions.

Plans reduce the three-dimensional complexity of an object to its two-dimensional horizontal aspects. They depict width and length but not height. This emphasis on the horizontal is both the plan's limitation as well as its strength. It is ironic that while plan drawings are relatively easy to generate in comparison to the intricacies of linear perspectives, they are essentially abstract constructs which can be difficult to read and understand. They depict an aerial viewpoint that we seldom experience except in the mind's eye.

In eliminating certain aspects from consideration, however, plans emphasize the horizontal arrangements and patterns of what we see or envision. These may be relationships of function, form, interior or exterior space, or of parts within a greater whole. In this way, plans match our mental map of the world and display a field of action for our thoughts and ideas.

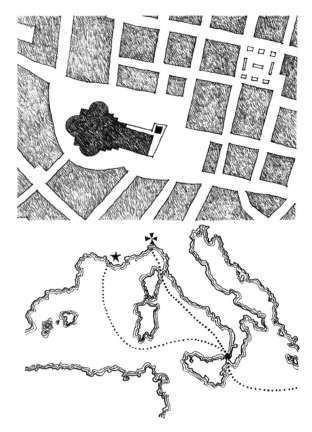

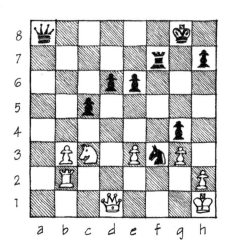

Charles Bradley's Twist: Black to move and mate in three.

A floor plan represents a horizontal section of a building as it would appear if cut through by an intersecting plane. After a horizontal plane slices through the construction, we remove the upper part. The floor plan is an orthographic projection of the portion that remains.

Floor plans open up the interior of a building to reveal a view that would otherwise not be possible. They unveil horizontal relationships and patterns not easily detected when walking through a building. On a horizontal picture plane, floor plans are able to disclose the configuration of walls and columns, the shape and dimensions of spaces, the pattern of window and door openings, and the connections between spaces as well as between the interior and exterior.

The horizontal plane of a plan slices through walls, columns, and other vertical elements of a building, as well as through all window and door openings. The plane of the cut is usually about 4 feet above the floor, but its height can vary according to the nature of the building design. Beyond the plane of the cut, we see the floor, counters, tabletops, and similar horizontal surfaces.

Critical to reading a floor plan is the ability to distinguish between solid matter and spatial void and to discern precisely where mass meets space. It is therefore important to emphasize in a graphic way what is cut in a floor plan, and to differentiate the cut material from what we can see through space below the plane of the cut. In order to convey a sense of the vertical dimension and the existence of a spatial volume, we must utilize a hierarchy of line weights or a range of tonal values. The technique we use depends on the scale of the floor plan, the drawing medium, and the required degree of contrast between solid matter and spatial void.

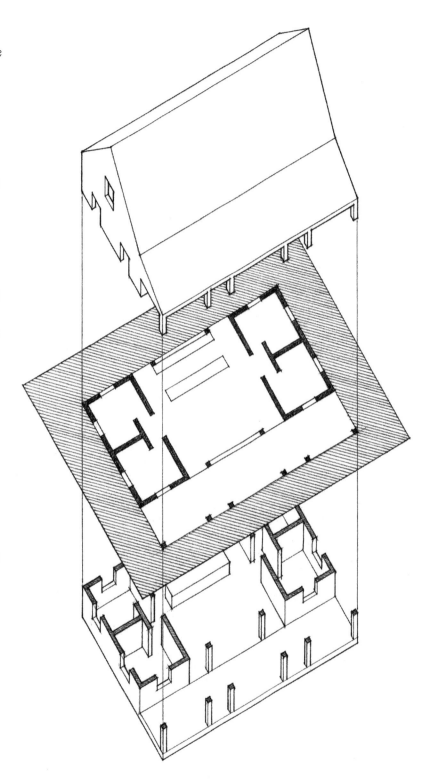

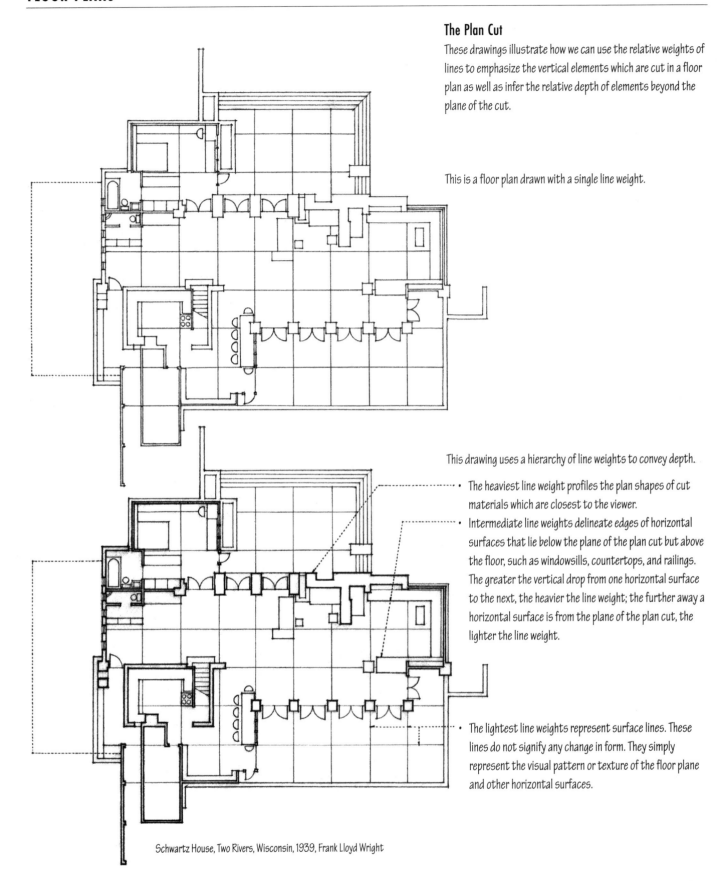

Schwartz House, Two Rivers, Wisconsin, 1939, Frank Lloyd Wright

### The Plan Cut

These drawings illustrate how we can use the relative weights of lines to emphasize the vertical elements which are cut in a floor plan as well as infer the relative depth of elements beyond the plane of the cut.

This is a floor plan drawn with a single line weight.

This drawing uses a hierarchy of line weights to convey depth.

- The heaviest line weight profiles the plan shapes of cut materials which are closest to the viewer.
- Intermediate line weights delineate edges of horizontal surfaces that lie below the plane of the plan cut but above the floor, such as windowsills, countertops, and railings. The greater the vertical drop from one horizontal surface to the next, the heavier the line weight; the further away a horizontal surface is from the plane of the plan cut, the lighter the line weight.
- The lightest line weights represent surface lines. These lines do not signify any change in form. They simply represent the visual pattern or texture of the floor plane and other horizontal surfaces.

## Exercise 6.4

The pictorial view to the right is cut at an elevation of about four feet above the floor level. Draw the floor plan at a scale of ¼" = 1'-0". Initially use a single, thin line weight. Then use a hierarchy of line weights to convey the relative depth of elements. Use the heaviest line weight to profile the plan cuts, intermediate line weights to describe the edges of horizontal surfaces below the plane of the plan cut, and the lightest line weight to indicate surface lines.

## Exercise 6.5

To the right is the first floor plan of the Vanna Venturi House in Philadelphia, designed by Robert Venturi in 1962. Draw the plan at twice the scale. Follow the same procedure outlined in the previous exercise. Initially use a single, thin line weight. Then use a hierarchy of line weights to convey the relative depth of elements in the floor plan. If there are doubts regarding what is cut, draw out the possibilities on overlays of tracing paper and try to visualize which alternatives would make the most sense if extended into the third dimension.

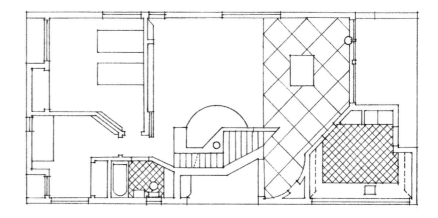

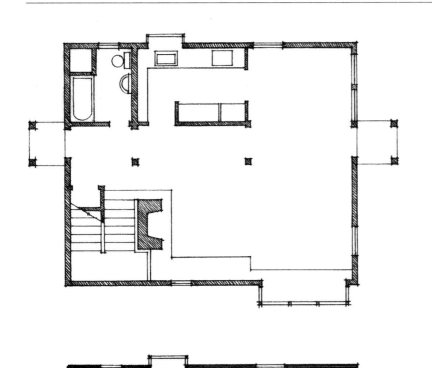

## Poché

In a line-and-tone or pure tone drawing, we emphasize the shape of cut elements with a tonal value that contrasts with the spatial field of the floor plan. We refer to this darkening of cut walls, columns, and other solid matter as poché.

It is typical to blacken the cut elements in small-scale plans in order to give them prominence. If only a moderate degree of contrast with the drawing field is desired, use a middle-gray value to illuminate the shape of the cut elements. This is especially important in large-scale plans when large areas of black can carry too much visual weight or create too stark a contrast. However, if plan elements such as flooring patterns and furniture give the field of the drawing a tonal value, a dark gray or black tone may be necessary to produce the desired degree of contrast between solid matter and spatial void.

Poché establishes a figure-ground relationship between solid and void—between container and contained. We tend to read the cut elements of a floor plan as figures and the bounded space as background. To focus on the shape of space as figure, we can reverse the normal pattern of dark marks drawn on a light surface and instead produce light marks on a dark surface.

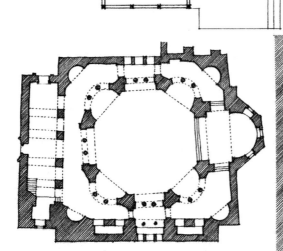

S.S. Sergius and Bacchus, Constantinople (Istanbul), 525–30 A.D.

## Exercise 6.6

To the right is illustrated the first floor plan of the Fisher House in Hatboro, Pennsylvania, designed by Louis Kahn in 1960. Draw the floor plan at a scale of ¼" = 1'-0", profiling the elements that are cut in the plan view with a heavy line weight. Redraw the floor plan a second time and render the shapes of the cut elements with poché or dark tonal value. Compare the differences between the two floor plans. In which plan are the shapes and pattern of both the cut elements and defined spaces more dominant?

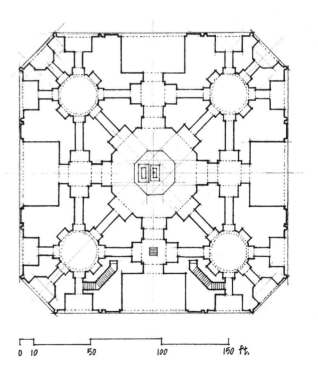

## Exercise 6.7

Make two drawings of each of the floor plans. On the first set of drawings, render the shapes of the cut elements with poché. On the second set, reverse the dark-light pattern and render the shapes of the spaces defined by the cut elements. Compare the two sets of drawings. In which set of floor plans are the shapes of the enclosed spaces more dominant or easier to read?

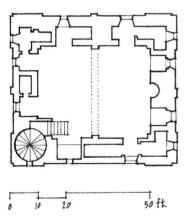

Hedingham, a Romanesque castle in Essex County, England

Ground Floor Plan of the Taj Mahal, the Tomb of Mumtaz Mahal in Agra, India, 1632–54

# FLOOR PLANS

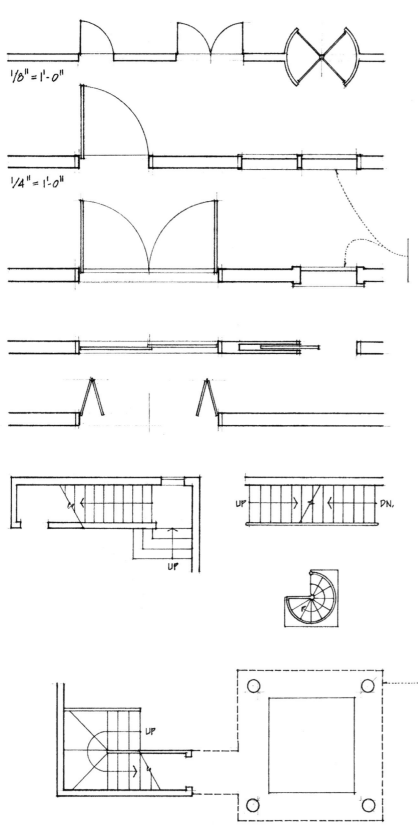

1/8" = 1'-0"

1/4" = 1'-0"

UP

UP    DN.

UP

UP

## Doors and Windows

We are not able to show the appearance of doors in a plan view. For this information, we must rely on elevations. What a floor plan does show, however, are the location and width of door openings, and to a limited degree, the door jambs and type of door operation—whether a door swings, slides, or folds open. For example, we typically draw a swinging door perpendicular to the plane of the wall and denote the door swing with a lightly drawn quarter circle.

Neither can we show the appearance of windows in a plan view. A floor plan does disclose the location and width of window openings, and to a limited degree the presence of window jambs and mullions. But the plan view should include the windowsill below the plane of the plan cut, which passes through the glass panes and frame of a window.

## Stairs

Plan views are able to show the run of a stairway—its horizontal treads and landings—but not the height of the vertical risers. The path of travel terminates where the stairway passes through the plane of the plan cut. We use a diagonal line to indicate this cut in order to more clearly distinguish it from the parallel lines of the stair treads. An arrow specifies the direction up or down from the level of the floor plan. Above the plan cut, we can use a dashed line to complete the opening through which a stairway rises.

## Elements Above or Below Plan Cut

Dashed lines indicate major architectural features that occur above the plane of the plan cut, as lofts, lowered ceilings, exposed beams, skylights, and roof overhangs. Dashed lines may also disclose the hidden lines of features concealed from view by other opaque elements. The common convention is to use longer dashes to signify elements that are removed or above the plane of the plan cut, and shorter dashes or dots for hidden elements below the plan cut.

## Drawing Scale

We normally draw floor plans at a scale of ⅛" = 1'-0" or ¼" = 1'-0". We may use a smaller scale for large buildings and complexes, or a larger scale for the floor plan of a single room. Room plans are especially useful for studying and presenting highly detailed spaces, such as kitchens, bathrooms, and stairways. The larger scale enables information about floor finishes, fittings, and trimwork to be included.

The larger the scale of a floor plan, the more detail we must include. This attention to detail is most critical when drawing the thickness of construction materials and assemblies that are cut in the plan view. Pay careful attention to wall and door thicknesses, wall terminations, corner conditions, and stair details. A general knowledge of how buildings are constructed is therefore extremely beneficial when executing large-scale floor plans.

We crop a drawing either when its size is too large to fit on a single sheet or when the entire drawing is not required to convey the desired information. To indicate where a portion of a drawing has been cut off and removed, we use a break line—a broken line consisting of relatively long segments joined by short zigzag strokes.

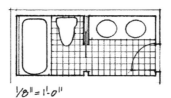

⅛" = 1'-0"

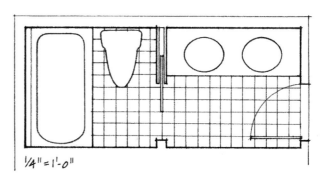

¼" = 1'-0"

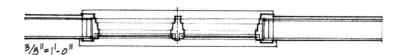

⅛" = 1'-0"

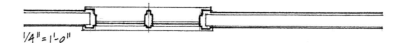

¼" = 1'-0"

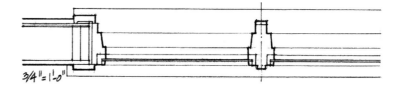

⅜" = 1'-0"

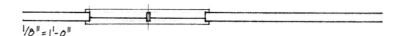

¾" = 1'-0"

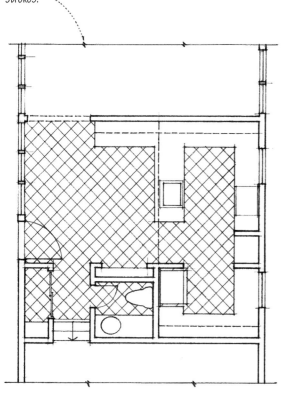

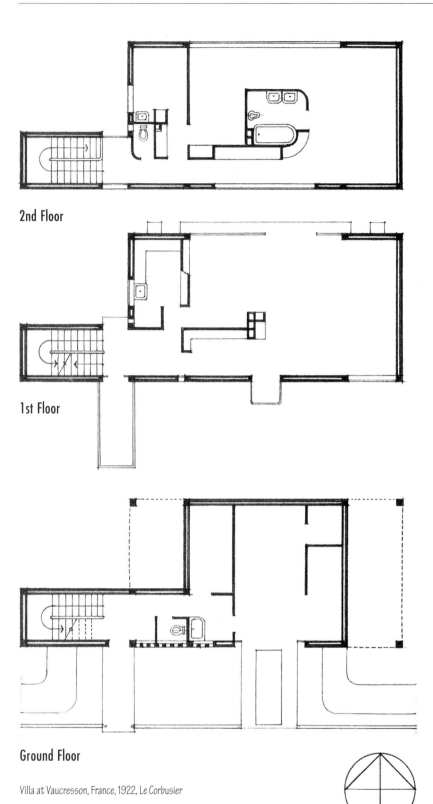

**2nd Floor**

**1st Floor**

**Ground Floor**

*Villa at Vaucresson, France, 1922, Le Corbusier*

### Orientation

To orient the viewer to the surrounding environment, we accompany a floor plan with a north arrow. The normal convention is to orient floor plans with north facing up or upward on the drawing sheet.

If a major axis of the building is less than 45° east or west of north, we can use an assumed north to avoid wordy titles for the building elevations, as 'north-northeast elevation,' or 'south-southwest elevation.'

Whenever possible, orient the floor plan of a room with its entrance at the bottom of the drawing so that we can imagine entering the room in an upward direction. When keying a room plan to a floor plan of a building, however, orienting both plans in the same manner takes precedence.

### Arrangement

In laying out the floors plans of a multistory building, align the plans either vertically, directly above one another, or horizontally side by side. Vertical arrangements should begin with the lowest level at the bottom and rise to the highest level at the top. Horizontal arrangements should generally proceed from the lowest floor to the upper levels, reading from left to right.

Aligning a series of floor plans in these two ways makes it easier to read and understand the vertical relationships between elements that occur or rise through two or more floor levels of a building. To strengthen this reading, relate the plans of linear buildings along their long side whenever possible.

The first or ground floor plan often extends out to include adjacent outdoor spaces and features, as courtyards, landscaping, and garden structures.

assumed north

A ceiling plan involves a horizontal cut through the vertical walls and columns that define the space of a room. Once a horizontal plane slices through the room, we flip the upper part so that we can project its image orthographically onto a horizontal picture plane. This results in a ceiling plan that is a mirror image of the floor plan.

We typically draw ceiling plans at the same scale as the floor plan. As with floor plans, it is important to profile all vertical elements that rise to meet the ceiling.

### Reflected Ceiling Plans

In order for a ceiling plan to have the same orientation as the floor plan, we draw what is called a reflected ceiling plan. A reflected ceiling plan represents what we would see if we placed a large mirror on the floor and looked down at the reflection of the ceiling above.

A ceiling plan is probably the least common type of plan view. It becomes necessary when we wish to show such information as the form and material of a ceiling, the location and type of lighting fixtures, exposed structural members or mechanical ductwork, as well as skylights or other openings in the ceiling.

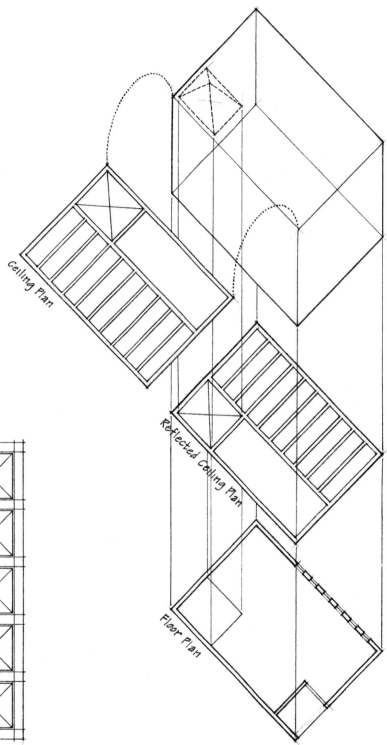

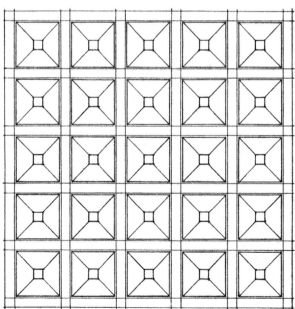

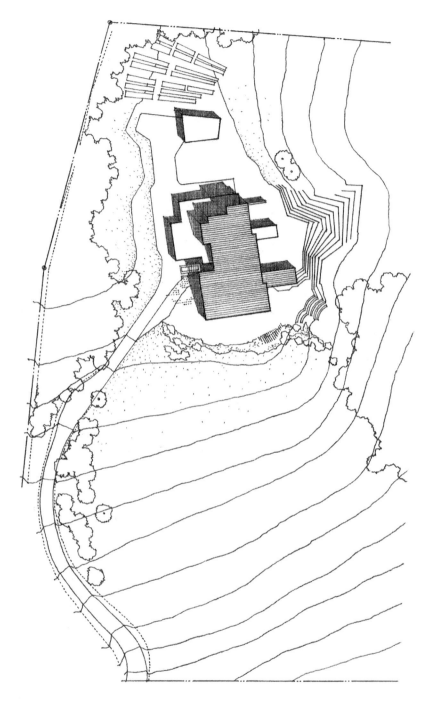

A site plan describes the location and orientation of a building or building complex on a plot of land and in relation to its context. Whether this environment is urban or rural, the site plan should describe the following:

- the legally recorded boundaries of the site, indicated by a broken line consisting of relatively long segments separated by two short dashes or dots;
- the physical topography of the terrain with contour lines;
- natural site features, as trees, landscaping, and watercourses;
- existing or proposed site constructions, as walks, courts, and roadways;
- architectural structures in the immediate setting that impact the proposed building.

In addition, a site plan may include:

- legal constraints, as zoning setbacks and right-of-ways;
- existing or proposed site utilities;
- pedestrian and vehicular entry points and paths;
- significant environmental forces and features.

### Scale

To reduce the physical size of a site plan and balance its impact in relation to the other drawings in a presentation, we usually draw site plans at a smaller scale than building plans, elevations, and sections. Depending on the size of the site and available drawing space, we can use an engineering scale of 1" = 20' or 40', or an architectural scale of $1/16$" = 1'-0" or $1/32$ = 1'-0". To illustrate more detail and if space permits, we may also use an architectural scale of $1/8$" = 1'-0" or $1/4$" = 1'-0". At larger scales, a site plan may include the first or ground floor plan of the building. This depiction is particularly appropriate for illustrating relationships between interior and outdoor spaces.

### Orientation

To make the relationship between site plans and floor plans clear, they should have the same orientation throughout a presentation.

Site Plan, Carré House, Bazoches-sur-Guyonne, France, 1952–56, Alvar Aalto

## Roof Plans

Site plans typically include the roof plan or top view of the proposed building or building complex. A roof plan is most useful when it describes the form, massing, and material of a roof or the layout of rooftop features, as skylights, decks, and mechanical housings.

Depending on the scale of the drawing, the depiction of a roofing material can infuse a roof plan with both visual texture as well as a tonal value. We must consider these graphic attributes carefully in planning the range and pattern of tonal values in a site plan drawing. The depiction can focus attention on either the plan shape of the building or the features of the outdoor spaces surrounding the building.

## Conveying Depth

There are two principal ways to achieve the desired degree of tonal contrast between a building form and the surrounding space. The first is rendering the building as a darker figure against a lighter background. This approach is especially appropriate when indicating the roofing material of the building invariably establishes a tonal value and texture against which the surrounding context must contrast.

The second approach defines the building as a lighter shape against a darker background. This technique is necessary when rendering shadows cast by the form of the building, or when landscaping elements impart a tonal value to the surrounding context.

To enhance the illusion of a three-dimensional ground surface, we can use a stepped series of tonal values which appear to ascend or descend with the elevation of the contours. The easiest way to create the tonal values is to introduce hatching perpendicular to the contour lines.

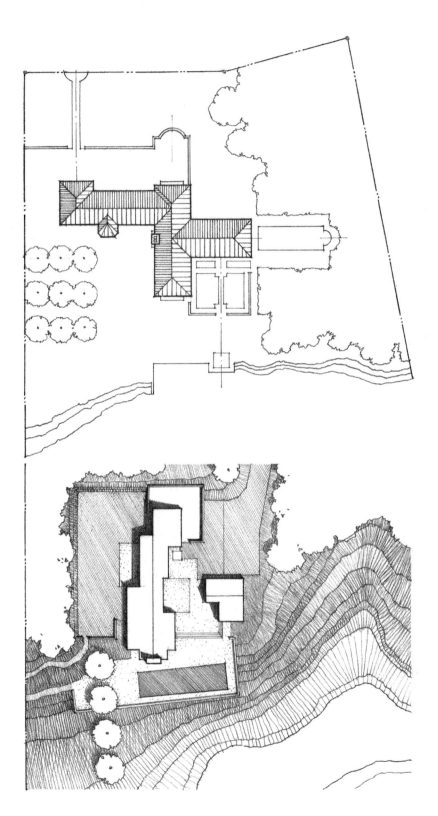

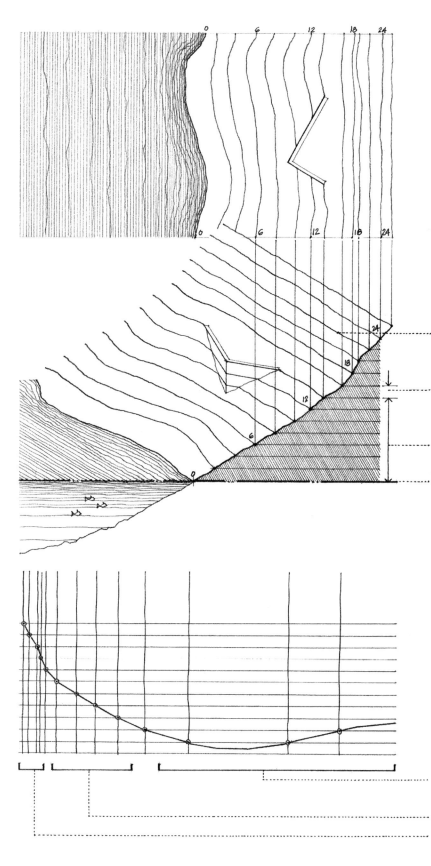

## Site Contours

The response of a building design to its context includes consideration of the physical characteristics of its site, especially the surface configuration of the terrain. A series of site sections can effectively represent this information. On a site plan, however, it is difficult to describe the vertical aspect of an undulating ground surface. Contour lines are the graphic convention we use to convey this information.

One way to visualize contour lines is to imagine that horizontal slices cut through the landform at regular intervals, the profile of each cut being represented by a contour line. The trajectory of each contour line indicates the shape of the land formation at that elevation. Contour lines are always continuous and never cross one another. They coincide in a plan view only when they cut across a vertical surface.

### Contour Line
An imaginary line joining points of equal elevation on a ground surface.

### Contour Interval
The difference in elevation represented by any two adjacent contour lines on a topographic map or site plan.

### Elevation
The vertical distance of a point above or below a datum.

### Datum
Any level surface, line, or point used as a reference from which elevations are measured.

Contour interval is determined by the scale of a drawing, the size of the site, and the nature of the topography. The larger the area and the steeper the slopes, the greater the interval between contours. For large or steeply sloping sites, 10', 25', or 50' contour intervals may be used. For small sites having relatively gradual slopes, 5', 2', or 1' contour lines may be used.

The horizontal distances between contour lines in a site plan are a function of the slope of the ground surface. We can discern the topographical nature of a site by reading this horizontal spacing.

- Contours spaced far apart indicate a relatively flat or gently sloping surface.
- Equally spaced contours indicate a constant slope.
- Closely spaced contours indicate a relatively steep rise in elevation.

## Exercise 6.8

Make two copies of the site plan of Sea Ranch Condominium and develop two value schemes which enhance the reading of the building forms as well as the enclosed and surrounding spaces. In the first scheme, render the buildings as darker figures against the lighter context of the site. In the second scheme, define the structures as light figures contrasting with the darker contextual field of the topography.

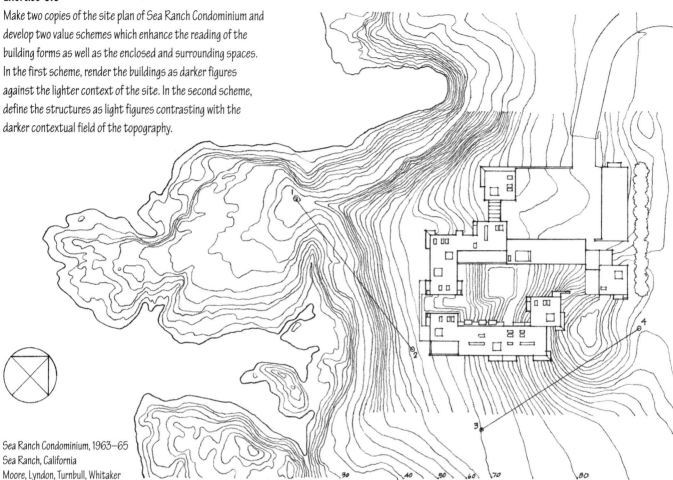

Sea Ranch Condominium, 1963–65
Sea Ranch, California
Moore, Lyndon, Turnbull, Whitaker

## Exercise 6.9

Which profile matches the line drawn from point 1 to point 2 on the site plan of Sea Ranch Condominium? (A) (B) (C) (D)

## Exercise 6.10

Which profile matches the line drawn from point 3 to point 4 on the site plan of Sea Ranch Condominium? (A) (B) (C) (D)

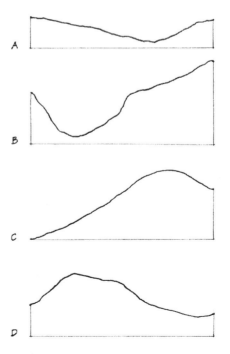

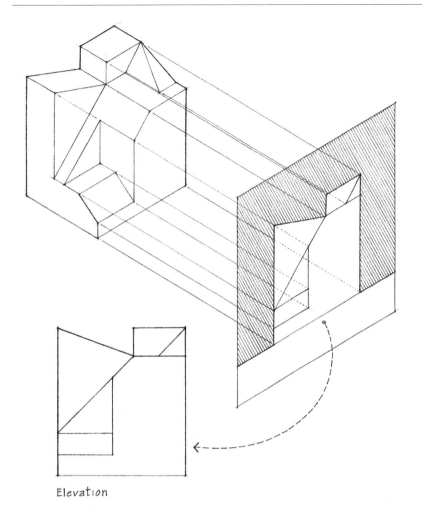

Elevation

An elevation is an orthographic projection of an object or construction on a vertical picture plane parallel to one of its sides. As with other orthographic projections, all planes parallel to the picture plane maintain their true-scale size, shape, and proportions. Conversely, any plane that is curved or oblique to the picture plane will be foreshortened in the orthographic view.

Elevations reduce the three-dimensional complexity of an object to two dimensions—height and either width or length. Unlike a plan, an elevation mimics our upright stance and offers a horizontal viewpoint. Unlike a section, it does not involve a cut through the object being depicted. Instead, the elevation offers an exterior view that closely resembles the natural appearance of the object. Even though elevation views of vertical surfaces are closer to perceptual reality than either plans or section views, they cannot represent the diminishing size of planes as they recede from the spectator. When we draw objects and surfaces in elevation, we must rely on graphic cues to convey depth, curvature, or obliqueness.

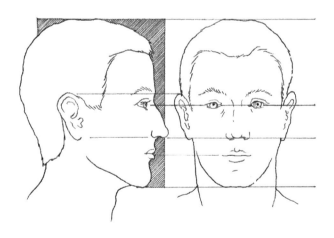

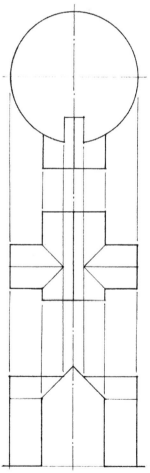

The two different plan views can generate the same elevation.

A building elevation is a horizontal view of the image of a building projected orthographically onto a vertical picture plane. We normally orient the picture plane to be parallel to one of the principal faces of the building.

Building elevations convey the external appearance of a building, compressed onto a single plane of projection. They therefore emphasize the exterior vertical surfaces of a building parallel to the picture plane and define its silhouette in space. We use building elevations to illustrate the form, massing, and scale of a building, the texture and pattern of its materials, as well as the location, type, and dimensions of window and door openings.

In order to show a building's relationship to the ground plane, building elevations should always include a section cut through the ground mass on which the structure sits. This vertical cut is typically at some distance in front of the building. This distance varies according to what information we wish to display in front of the building and to what degree this context will obscure the form and features of the building.

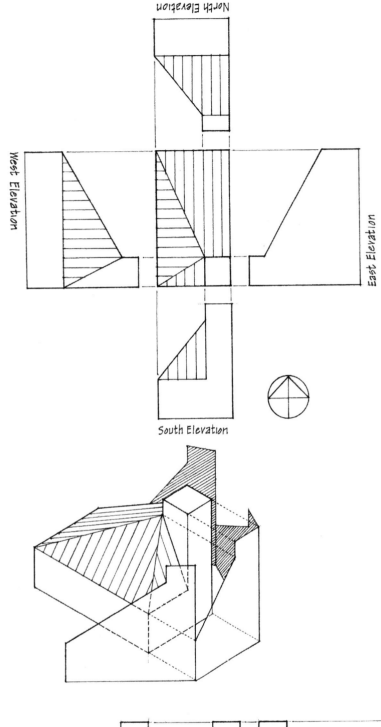

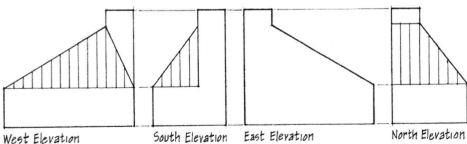

### Arrangement

As we move around a building, we see a series of related elevations that change as our position in space changes. We can logically relate these views to each other by unfolding the vertical picture planes on which they are projected. They can form a horizontal sequence of drawings, or be related in a single, composite drawing around a common plan view.

While an elevation drawing can show the context of objects and the relationships between a number of forms in space, they do not reveal any information about their interiors. We can combine elevations and sections, however, when drawing symmetrical forms and constructions.

### Orientation

To orient the viewer, we label each elevation drawing according to its relationship to an assumed front face, the compass direction it faces, or the context from which the elevation is seen. An elevation view may be a front view if projected on a frontal plane of projection, and a side view if projected on the profile plane, depending on how we orient ourselves to the object or assess the relative significance of its faces.

In architectural graphics, however, the orientation of a building to the compass points is an important consideration when studying and communicating the effect of sun and other climatic factors on the design. Therefore, we most often name a building elevation after the direction the elevation faces: e.g., a north elevation is the elevation of the façade that faces north. If the face is oriented less than 45°off the major compass points, an assumed north may be used to avoid wordy drawing titles.

When a building addresses a specific or significant feature of a site, we can name a building elevation after that feature: e.g., a street elevation is the the elevation of the façade that faces a street.

## Drawing Scale

We usually draw building elevations at the same scale as the accompanying floor plans—$\frac{1}{8}$" = 1'-0" or $\frac{1}{4}$" = 1'-0". We may use a smaller scale for large buildings and complexes, or a larger scale for the interior elevations of a single room. Interior elevations are especially useful for studying and presenting highly detailed spaces, such as kitchens, bathrooms, and stairways.

The larger the scale of an elevation, the more detail we must include. This attention to detail is most critical when drawing the appearance of wall surfaces, window and door units, and roof coverings. Pay careful attention to the texture and pattern of materials, the thicknesses of frames and joints, the exposed edges of planes, and how planar constructions turn corners. A general knowledge of how buildings are constructed is therefore extremely beneficial when executing large-scale building elevations.

As always, including human figures in elevation drawings help establish a sense of scale and remind us of the intended patterns of activity and use.

## Conveying Depth

Since planes perpendicular to the picture plane appear as lines in orthographic projection, there are no inherent depth cues in a building elevation. Regardless of their distance in space, all lines and planes parallel to the picture plane retain their true-scale size. In order to convey a sense of depth, we must utilize a hierarchy of line weights or a range of tonal values. The technique we use depends on the scale of the building elevation, the drawing medium, and the technique for depicting the texture and pattern of materials.

This series of drawings illustrates ways to convey a sense of depth in a building elevation.

- This is a building elevation drawn with a single line weight.
- This drawing uses a hierarchy of line weights to convey depth.
- The heaviest line weight defines the groundline of the section cut in front of the building. Extend this groundline into the adjoining space to describe the topographical nature of the setting.
- The next heaviest line weight profiles the planes closest to the plane of projection.
- Progressively thinner and lighter lines indicate increasing distance from the picture plane.
- The lightest line weights represent surface lines. These lines do not signify any change in form. They simply represent the visual pattern or texture of surfaces.

We use tonal values in an elevation drawing to render cast shadows as well as establish three pictorial zones: the foreground space between the section cut and the facade of the building, the middleground that the building itself occupies, and the background of sky, landscape, or structures beyond the building.

- First establish the tonal range of the building; then establish contrasting values for the foreground and background.
- Darker planes may front progressively lighter planes in the distance or vice versa.
- Using the depth cue of transition between light and shade, define sharper tonal contrasts to project elements forward, and diminish areas of contrast to push areas into the background.
- Using the depth cue of atmospheric perspective, delineate the material and texture of surfaces more distinctly in the foreground and diffuse the edges and contours of more distant surfaces in the background.
- Sharpness and clarity of detail focus attention on the parts of the building which are closest to the picture plane.

For information on architectural shade and shadows, see pages 165–171.

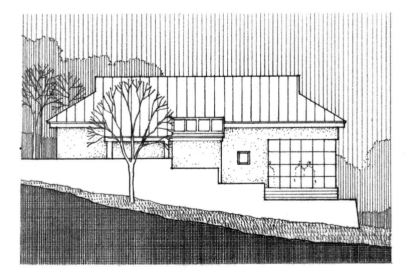

### Exercise 6.11

At a scale of ⅛" = 1'-0", draw the south and east elevations of the structure illustrated in the pictorial view. Use a hierarchy of line weights to imbue a sense of depth and convey which elements project forward of other elements.

### Exercise 6.12

On the same drawings developed in Exercise 6.11, explore how a pattern and range of contrasting tonal values can silhouette the structure and establish three pictorial zones: foreground, middleground, and background.

### Exercise 6.13

On a sheet of tracing paper, draw the elevations a second time at the same scale. Investigate how a pattern and range of contrasting tonal values can convey which elements project forward of other elements within the structure itself.

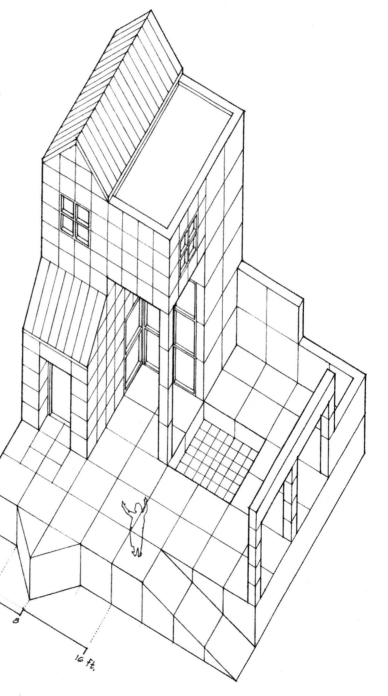

# SECTION DRAWINGS

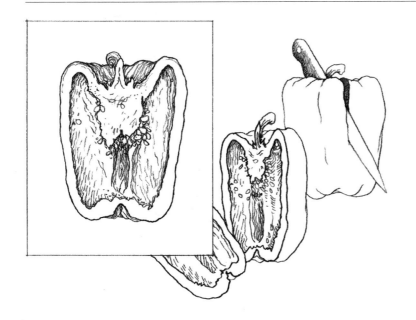

A section is an orthographic projection of an object as it would appear if cut through by an intersecting plane. It opens up the object to reveal its internal material, composition, or assembly. In theory, the plane of the section cut may have any orientation. But in order to distinguish a section drawing from a floor plan—the other type of drawing that involves a slice—we usually assume the plane of the cut for a section is vertical and the view is horizontal. As with other orthographic projections, all planes parallel to the picture plane maintain their true-scale size, shape, and proportions.

Sections reduce the three-dimensional complexity of an object to two dimensions—height and either width or length. We often use section drawings to design and communicate the details of a building's construction as well as the assembly of furniture and cabinetry. In architectural graphics, however, the building section is the premier drawing for studying and revealing the vital solid-void relationship between the floors, walls, and roof structure of a building, and the vertical dimensions and relationships of the contained spaces.

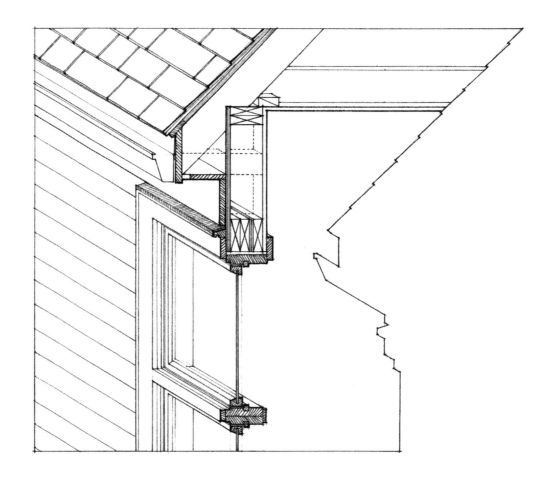

A building section represents a vertical section of a building. After a vertical plane slices through the construction, we remove one of the parts. The building section is an orthographic projection of the portion that remains, cast onto a vertical picture plane parallel to the plane of the incision.

Building sections combine the conceptual qualities of plans with the perceptual qualities of elevations. In cutting through walls, floors, and the roof structure of a building, as well as through window and door openings, we open up the interior of a building to reveal conditions of support, span, and enclosure, as well as the vertical arrangement of spaces. On a vertical picture plane, building sections are able to unveil the vertical dimension, shape, and scale of interior spaces, the impact of window and door openings on these spaces, and the vertical connections between the internal spaces, as well as between the interior and exterior. Beyond the plane of the cut, we see elevations of interior walls as well as objects and events that occur in front of them but behind the vertical plane of the section cut.

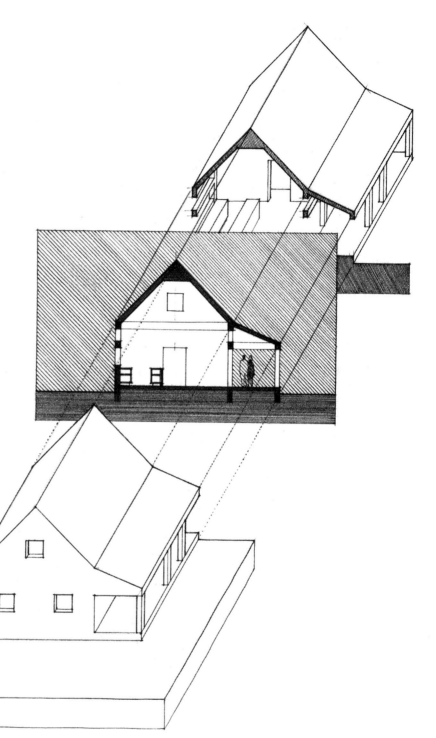

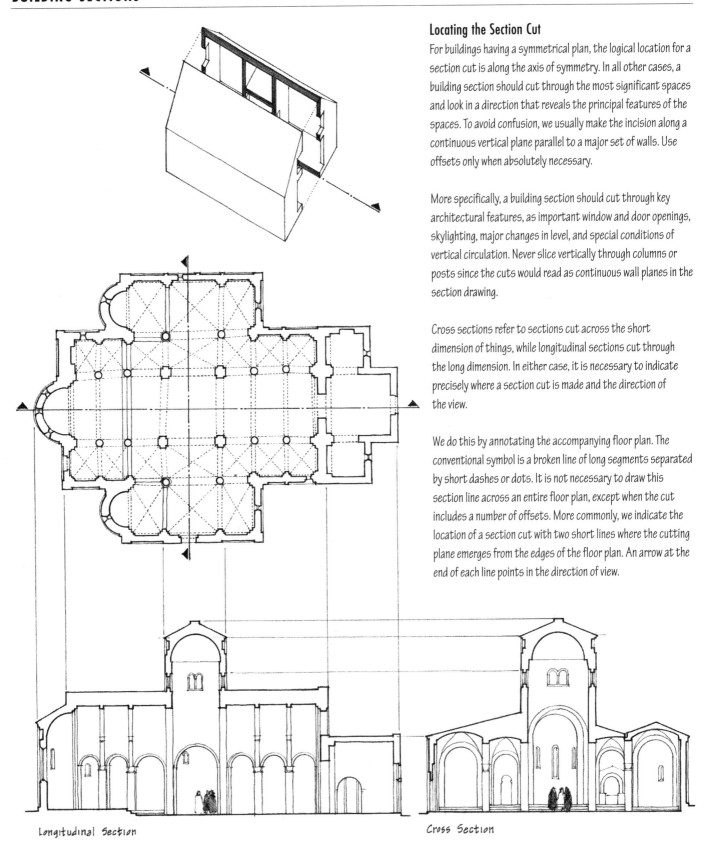

### Locating the Section Cut

For buildings having a symmetrical plan, the logical location for a section cut is along the axis of symmetry. In all other cases, a building section should cut through the most significant spaces and look in a direction that reveals the principal features of the spaces. To avoid confusion, we usually make the incision along a continuous vertical plane parallel to a major set of walls. Use offsets only when absolutely necessary.

More specifically, a building section should cut through key architectural features, as important window and door openings, skylighting, major changes in level, and special conditions of vertical circulation. Never slice vertically through columns or posts since the cuts would read as continuous wall planes in the section drawing.

Cross sections refer to sections cut across the short dimension of things, while longitudinal sections cut through the long dimension. In either case, it is necessary to indicate precisely where a section cut is made and the direction of the view.

We do this by annotating the accompanying floor plan. The conventional symbol is a broken line of long segments separated by short dashes or dots. It is not necessary to draw this section line across an entire floor plan, except when the cut includes a number of offsets. More commonly, we indicate the location of a section cut with two short lines where the cutting plane emerges from the edges of the floor plan. An arrow at the end of each line points in the direction of view.

Longitudinal Section

Cross Section

Abbey Church of S. Maria, Portonovo, Italy, 12th Century

## Interior Elevations

Interior elevations are orthographic projections of significant interior walls of a building. While normally included in the drawing of building sections, they may stand alone to illustrate the interior features of a room, such as doorways and built-in furnishings and fixtures. In this case, instead of profiling the section cut, we emphasize instead the boundary line of the interior wall surfaces.

## Scale

We normally draw interior elevations at the same scale as the accompanying floor plans—$\frac{1}{8}" = 1'-0"$ or $\frac{1}{4}" = 1'-0"$. In order to show a greater amount of detail, we may use a scale of $\frac{1}{2}" = 1'-0"$.

## Orientation

To orient the viewer, we label each interior elevation according to the compass direction toward which we look in viewing the wall. An alternative method is to key each interior elevation to a compass on the floor plan of the room.

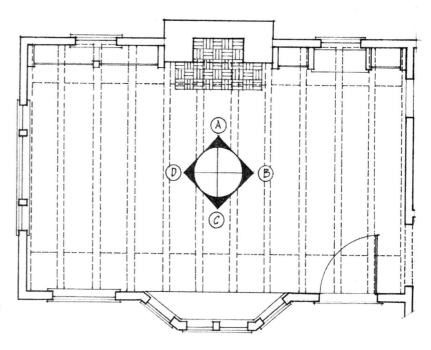

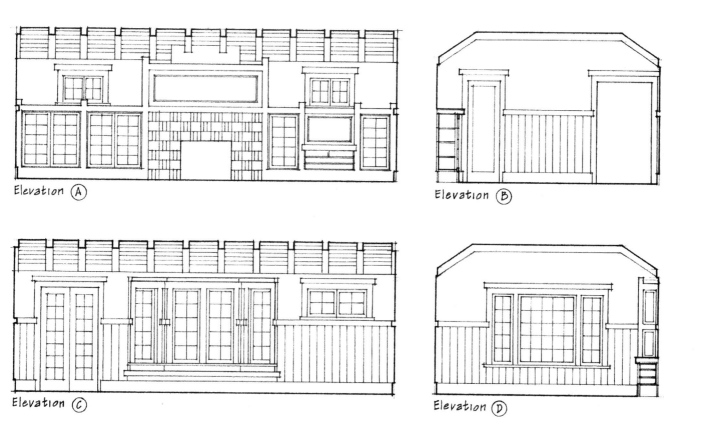

Elevation Ⓐ

Elevation Ⓑ

Elevation Ⓒ

Elevation Ⓓ

### The Section Cut

As with floor plans, it is critical to distinguish between solid matter and spatial void and to discern precisely where mass meets space in a building section. In order to convey a sense of depth and the existence of spatial volumes, we must utilize a hierarchy of line weights or a range of tonal values. The technique we use depends on the scale of the building section, the drawing medium, and the required degree of contrast between solid matter and spatial void.

This series of drawings illustrates ways to emphasize the solid material that is cut in a line drawing of a building section.

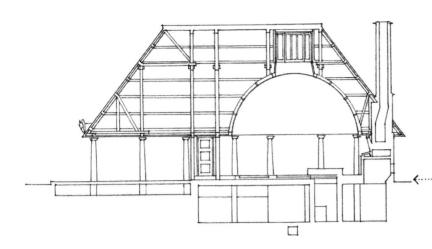

• This is a building section drawn with a single line weight.

• This drawing uses a hierarchy of line weights to convey depth.

• The heaviest line weight profiles the shape of cut materials that are closest to the viewer.

• Intermediate line weights delineate edges of vertical surfaces that lie beyond the plane of the section cut. A decreasing line weight delineates the edges of progressively more distant objects from the plane of the cut.

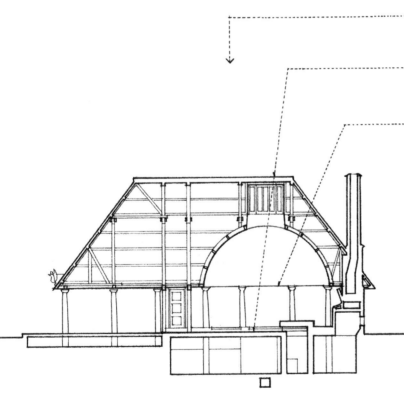

Woodland Chapel, Stockholm, Sweden, 1918–20, Erik Gunnar Asplund

The lightest line weights represent surface lines. These lines do not signify any change in form. They simply represent the visual pattern or texture of wall planes and other vertical surfaces parallel to the picture plane.

## Poché

In a line-and-tone or pure tone drawing, we emphasize the shape of cut elements with a tonal value that contrasts with the spatial field of the building section. The purpose is to establish a clear figure-ground relationship between solid matter and spatial void—between container and contained.

It is typical to blacken or poché the floor, wall, and roof elements which are cut in small-scale building sections. If only a moderate degree of contrast with the drawing field is desired, use a middle-gray value to illuminate the shape of the cut elements. This is especially important in large-scale sections when large areas of black can carry too much visual weight or create too stark a contrast. However, if vertical elements such as wall patterns and textures give the field of the drawing a tonal value, a dark gray or black tone may be necessary to produce the desired degree of contrast between solid matter and spatial void. In this value scheme, use progressively lighter values for elements as they recede into the third dimension.

A second approach is to reverse the value scheme and render the cut elements as a white figure against a spatial field of darker tonal values. Reversing the normal dark-light pattern in this way emphasizes the figure of the contained space. Be sure, however, that there is enough tonal contrast to distinguish the cut elements. If necessary, outline the profile of the cut elements with a heavy line weight and use progressively darker values for elements or planes as they recede into the third dimension.

Remember that the ground mass is also cut in building and site sections. The tonal value of the cut elements should therefore continue into the supporting ground mass. If we show a building's foundation in a section drawing, we should be careful to delineate its walls and footings below-grade as an integral part of the surrounding ground mass. We must represent the substructure in such a way that we maintain the reading that the vertical plane of the section cuts through both the foundation and the surrounding mass of the earth.

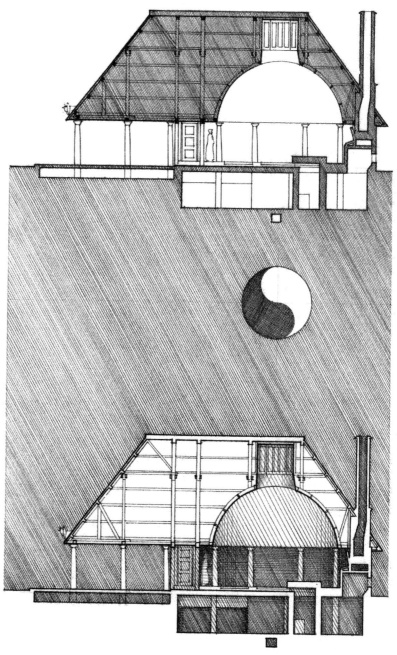

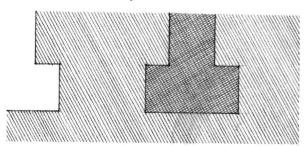

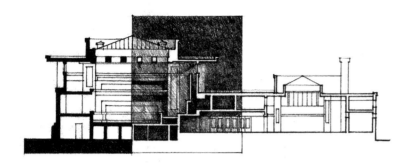

### Exercise 6.14

Make two copies of the longitudinal section of Unity Temple illustrated below. On the first drawing, render the shapes of the cut elements with poché. On the second drawing, reverse the dark-light pattern and render the shapes of the spaces defined by the elements cut by the vertical plane of the section. Compare the two section drawings. In which section are the shapes of the enclosed spaces more dominant or easier to read?

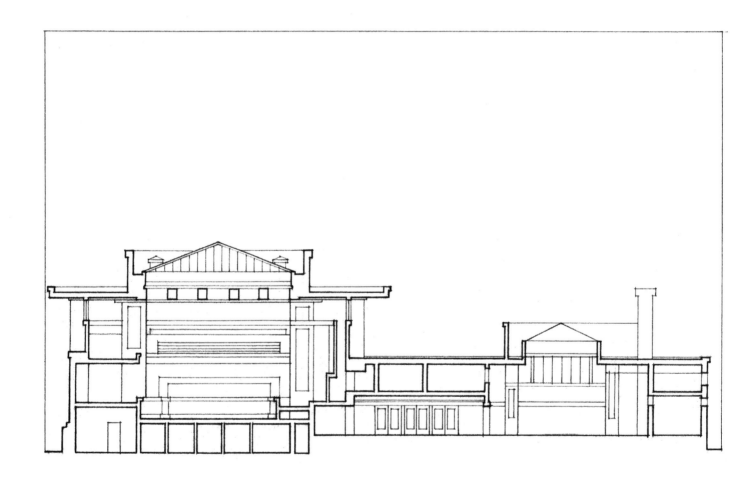

## Drawing Scale

We usually draw building sections at the same scale as the accompanying floor plans—$\frac{1}{8}$" = 1'-0" or $\frac{1}{4}$" = 1'-0". We may use a smaller scale for large buildings and complexes, or a larger scale for the section and interior elevations of a single room. Room sections are especially useful for studying and presenting highly detailed spaces, such as kitchens, bathrooms, and stairways.

The larger the scale of a section, the more detail we must include. This attention to detail is most critical when drawing the thickness of construction materials and assemblies which are cut in the section view. Pay careful attention to wall thicknesses, corner conditions, and stair details. A general knowledge of how buildings are constructed is therefore extremely beneficial when executing large-scale sections.

As always, including human figures in section drawings establishes a sense of scale and reminds us of patterns of activity and use.

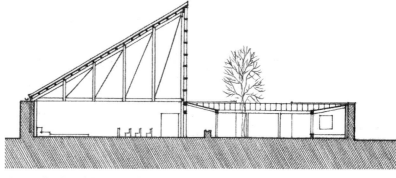

Mountain Church on Winkelmoosalm, Germany, 1975, J. Wiedemann

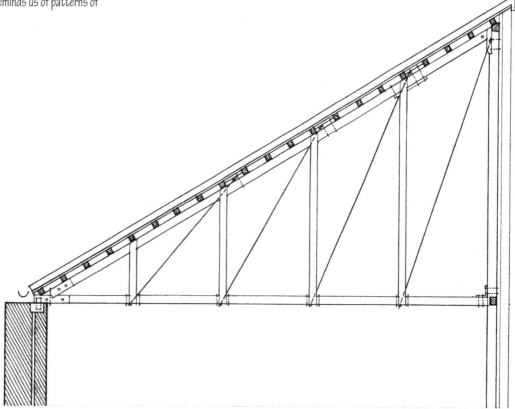

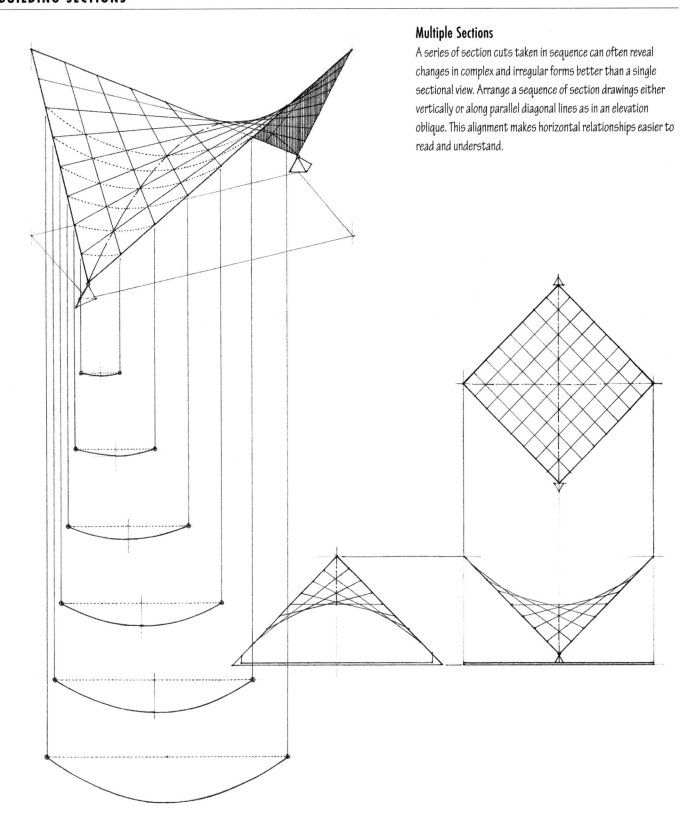

### Multiple Sections

A series of section cuts taken in sequence can often reveal changes in complex and irregular forms better than a single sectional view. Arrange a sequence of section drawings either vertically or along parallel diagonal lines as in an elevation oblique. This alignment makes horizontal relationships easier to read and understand.

Section drawings often extend outward to include the context of a building's site and environment. They are exceptionally capable of describing the relationship of a proposed structure to the surrounding ground plane and disclosing whether a proposed structure rises from, sits on, floats above, or becomes embedded within the earth of the site. In addition, section drawings can effectively illustrate the relationship between the interior spaces of a building and adjoining exterior spaces.

Whenever possible, but especially in urban settings, building sections should include adjacent structures either cut through simultaneously in the section or seen in elevation beyond the plane of the cut.

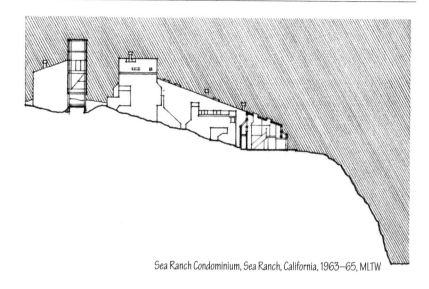

Sea Ranch Condominium, Sea Ranch, California, 1963–65, MLTW

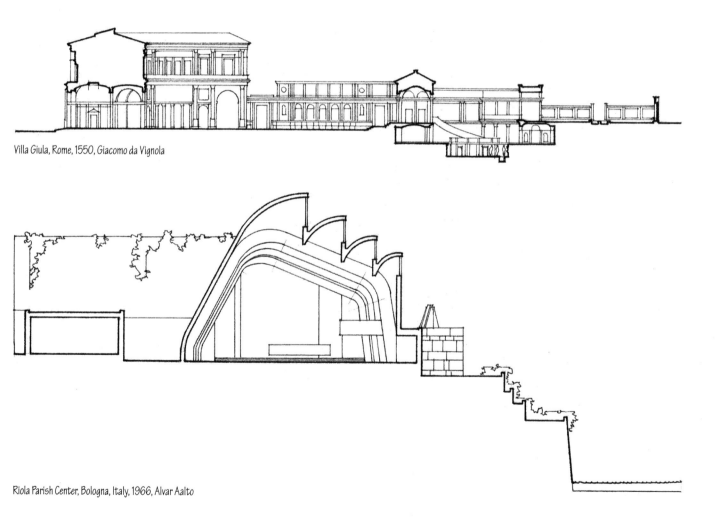

Villa Giula, Rome, 1550, Giacomo da Vignola

Riola Parish Center, Bologna, Italy, 1966, Alvar Aalto

# SHADE AND SHADOWS

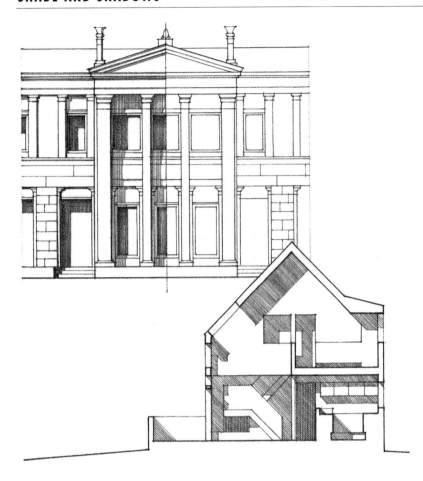

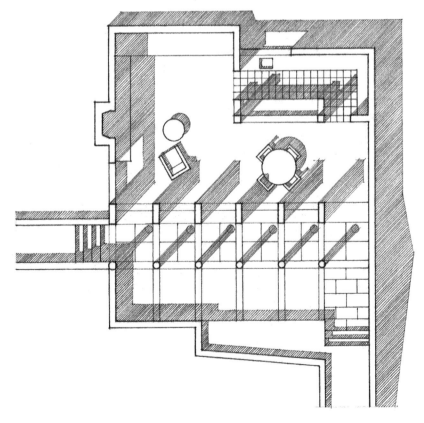

Shade and shadows refers to the technique of determining areas in shade and casting shadows on surfaces by means of projection drawing. The casting of shade and shadows is especially useful to overcome the flatness of multiview drawings and enhance the illusion of depth.

In an elevation, shade and shadows clarify the relative depth of projections, overhangs, and recesses within the massing of a building as well as model the relief and texture of surfaces receiving the shadows.

In a building section, the shadows cast by the cut elements provide a sense of how far they project in front of surfaces seen in elevation beyond the plane of the cut.

In a site plan, shade and shadows convey the relative heights of building masses and elements as well as reveal the topographical nature of the ground plane on which shadows are cast.

In a floor plan, the shadows cast by the cut vertical elements and objects within the space give us an indication of their height above the floor or ground plane.

An understanding of shade and shadows is vital not only to the presentation of a design proposal but also to the study and evaluation of the design itself. The interplay of light, shade, and shadow models the surfaces of a design, describes the disposition of its masses, and articulates the depth and character of its details. Depending on the technique used in rendering tonal values, shade and shadows can also communicate the vivid quality of light that illuminates forms and animates a space.

## Basic Elements

### Light Source

An illuminating source, as the sun or an electric lamp, that makes things visible. In architectural shade and shadows, we normally assume the sun to be the light source.

### Light Ray

Any of the lines or narrow beams in which light appears to radiate from a luminous source. The light rays emanating from the sun travel a distance of 93 million miles (150 million km) to reach the earth's surface. The sun is so large and distant a source that its light rays are considered to be parallel. On the other hand, artificial light sources, being relatively small and much closer to what they illuminate, emit radial light rays.

### Sun Angle

The direction of the sun's rays, measured in terms of bearing and altitude.

### Bearing

A horizontal direction expressed in degrees east or west of a true or magnetic north or south direction.

### Azimuth

The angle of horizontal deviation, measured clockwise, of a bearing from a standard north direction.

### Altitude

The angular elevation of a celestial body above the horizon.

### Shade

A relatively dark area on those parts of a solid that are tangent to or turned away from a theoretical light source.

### Shadow

A relatively dark figure cast upon a surface by an opaque body or part of a body intercepting the rays from a theoretical light source.

### Shade Line

A line on an object that separates an illuminated surface from one in shade. Also called casting edge.

### Shadow Plane

A plane of light rays that passes through adjacent points of a straight line.

### Shadow Line

The shadow that a shade line casts on a receiving surface.

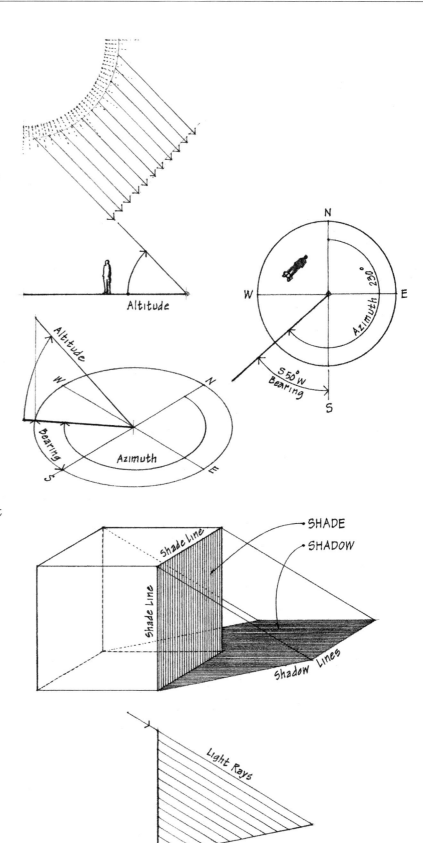

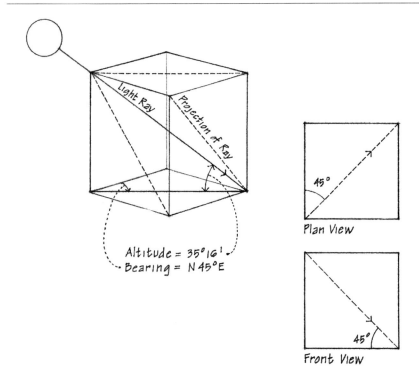

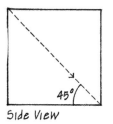

In multiview drawings, we assume the conventional direction of sunlight to be parallel to the diagonal of a cube from the upper left front corner to the lower right rear corner. While the true altitude of this diagonal is 35° 16′, in plan and elevation views, this direction is seen as the 45° diagonal of a square. This convention produces shadows of width or depth equal to the width or depth of the projections that cast the shadows.

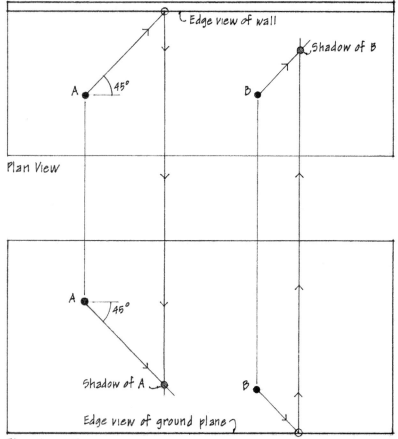

### Shadow of a Point

• The shadow of a point occurs where the light ray passing through the point meets an intercepting surface.

The casting of shade and shadows in multiview drawings generally requires two related views—either a plan and elevation or two related elevations—and the transferring of information back and forth from one view to the other.

The process begins with drawing a 45° light ray through a point along a casting edge in both views. In the view showing the edge view of the receiving surface, extend the ray until it intersects the receiving surface. Project this intersection to the related view. The intersection of this transferred line with the ray in the adjacent view marks the shadow of the point.

## Shadow of a Line

- The shadow of a straight line is the intersection of its shadow plane with the surface receiving the shadow. The hypotenuse of the triangular shadow plane establishes the direction of the light rays, and its base describes their bearing.
- The shadow of a straight line on a flat surface is the line that connects the shadows of its end points.
- The shadow of a line that intersects a surface begins where the line meets the surface.
- A vertical line casts its shadow onto a horizontal surface in the bearing direction of the light rays.
- A straight line casts onto a parallel plane a shadow that is parallel to itself. This is also true when the line is parallel to the straight lines in a curved surface receiving the shadow.

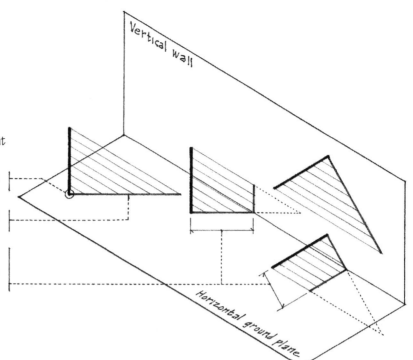

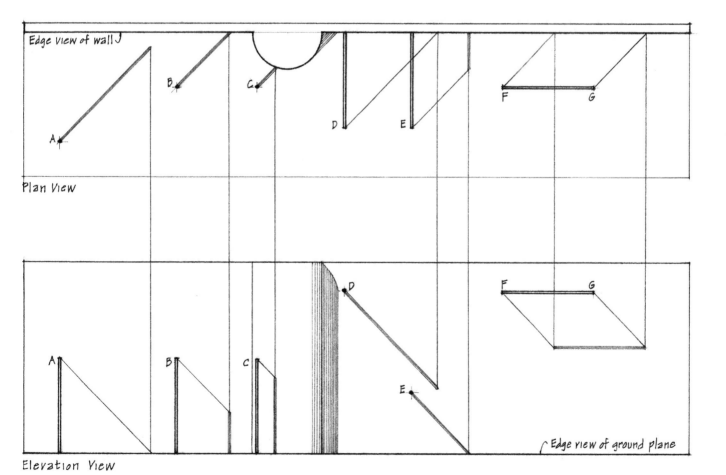

Plan View

Elevation View

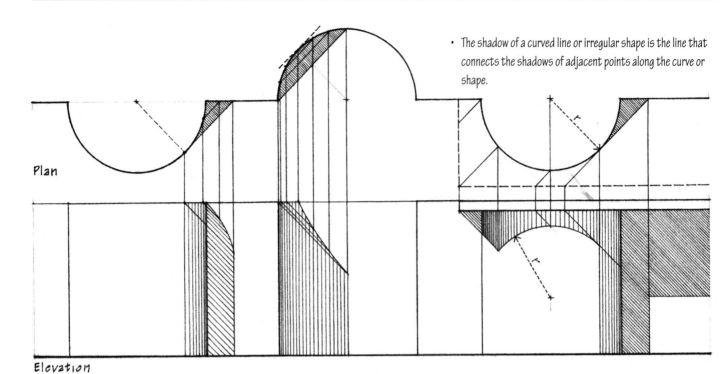

Plan

Elevation

- The shadow of a curved line or irregular shape is the line that connects the shadows of adjacent points along the curve or shape.

## Shadow of a Plane

- The shadow of a plane figure on a parallel plane is identical in size and shape to the figure.
- The shadow of a polygonal figure on a plane is circumscribed by the shadows of its shade lines.
- The shadow of a circle is the intersection of the cylinder of light rays passing through adjacent points of the circle and the surface receiving the shadow. The shape of the shadow is elliptical since the section of a cylinder cut by any plane oblique to its axis is an ellipse. The most convenient method of determining the shadow of a circle is to determine the shadow of the square or octagon circumscribing the given circle and then to inscribe within it the elliptical shadow of the circle.

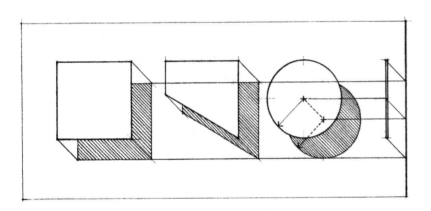

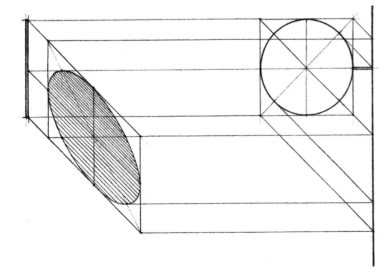

## Shadow of a Solid

- The shadow of a solid is bound by the shadows of the shade lines of the object. It is usually best to begin by determining the shadows of significant points in the form, such as the end points of straight lines and the tangent points of curves.
- The shadow cast by a complex composition of masses is a composite of the shadows of its simplest geometric components.
- A shadow line changes direction where it crosses a corner, edge, or other break in the continuity of a surface.

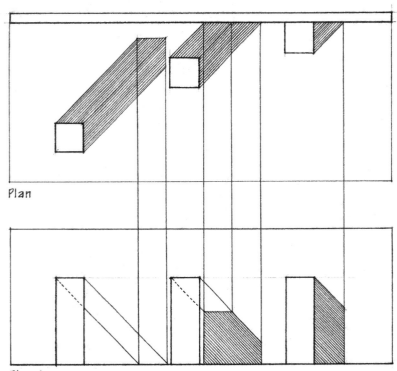

Plan

- Shadows of parallel lines are parallel when they fall on the same plane or on parallel planes.

Sometimes it is necessary to construct an additional elevation in order to find where the light rays through the corner points of a solid intersect the surface receiving the shadow.

Elevation

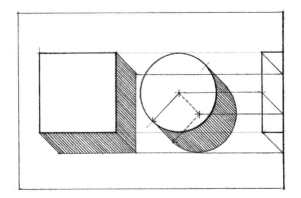

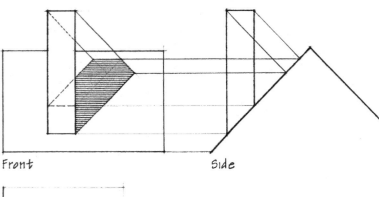

Front                    Side

In addition to the general principles outlined previously, the following tenets apply specifically to casting shade and shadows in multiview drawings:

- A vertical shade line appears as a point in a plan view and its shadow falls along the bearing direction of the light rays through that point.
- When the observer looks at the end of a straight line, the line is seen as a point, and the shadow of the line will also appear to be straight regardless of the shape of the surface receiving the shadow.

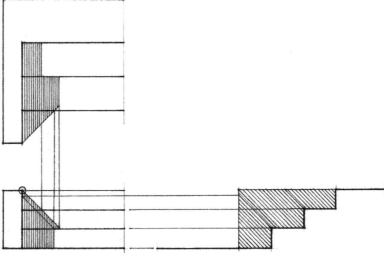

Illustrated on this page are examples of the shadows cast by typical architectural elements. Two fundamental principles to keep in mind are:

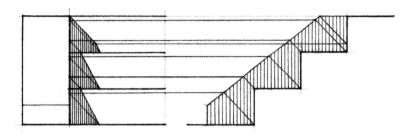

- Every part of an object in light must cast a shadow. The corollary to this is that any point not in light cannot cast a shadow because light does not strike it.
- A shadow is visible only when there is an illuminated surface to receive the shadow. A shadow can never be cast on a surface in shade, nor can it exist within another shadow.

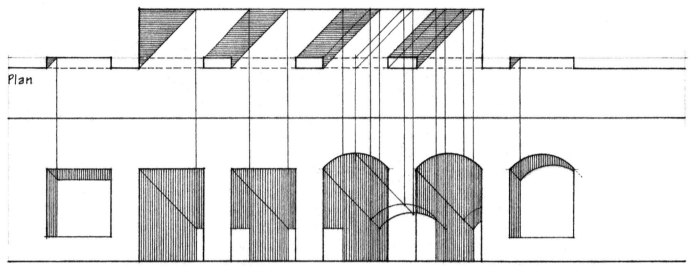

Plan

Elevation

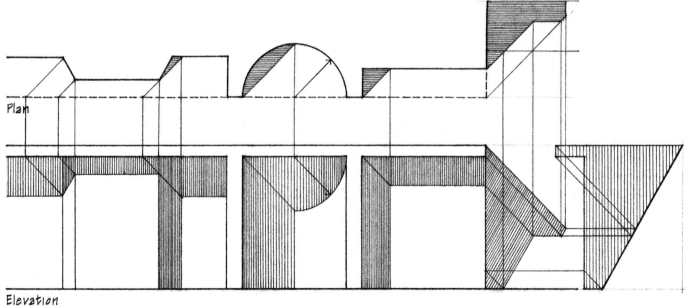

Plan

Elevation

### Exercise 6.15

Using the conventional direction of light rays for multiview drawings, determine the surfaces in shade and cast their shadows in the plans and elevations of the two building forms illustrated to the right and below.

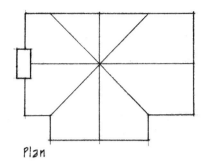

Plan

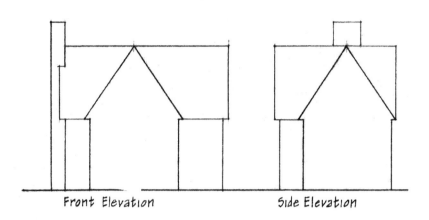

Front Elevation          Side Elevation

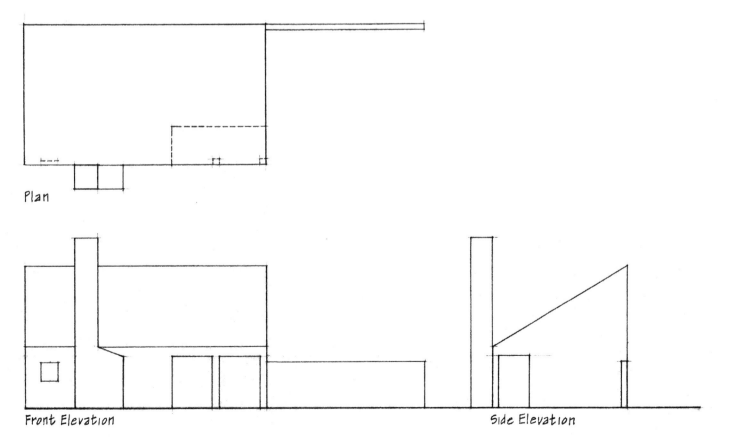

Plan

Front Elevation                                    Side Elevation

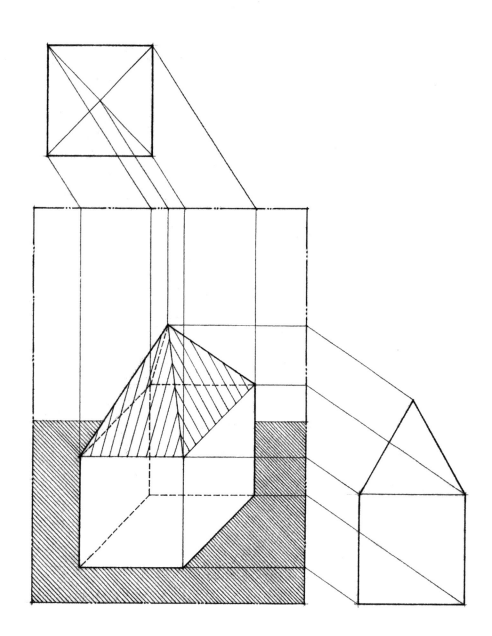

# 7
# Paraline Drawings

Paraline drawings include a subset of orthographic projections known as axonometric projections—the isometric, dimetric, and trimetric—as well as the entire class of oblique projections. Each type offers a slightly different viewpoint and emphasizes different aspects of the subject. As a family, however, they combine the measured precision and scalability of orthographic multiview drawings and the pictorial nature of linear perspective.

Paraline drawings communicate the three-dimensional nature of an object or spatial relationship in a single image. Hence, they are also called single-view drawings to distinguish them from the multiple and related views of plans, sections, and elevations. They can be distinguished from the other type of single-view drawing, linear perspective, by the following pictorial effects. Parallel lines, regardless of their orientation in the subject, remain parallel in the drawn view; they do not converge to vanishing points as in linear perspective—hence the term paraline. In addition, any linear measurement parallel to the three major axes can be made and drawn to a consistent scale.

Because of their pictorial nature and ease of construction, paraline drawings are appropriate for visualizing an emerging idea in three dimensions early in the design process. They are capable of fusing plan, elevation, and section and illustrating three-dimensional patterns and compositions of space. They can be cut or made transparent to see inside and through things, or expanded to illustrate the spatial relationships between the parts of a whole. They can even serve as a reasonable substitute for a bird's-eye perspective.

Paraline views, however, lack the eye-level view and picturesque quality of linear perspectives. They present instead either an aerial view looking down on an object or scene, or a worm's-eye view looking upward. In either case, the drawing system can be extended to include a boundless and unlocalized field of vision, unlike perspective drawings which are strictly limited in scope by the size of the visual angle. It reveals the view from an infinite set of positions rather than from a specific point in space. The viewer can move in on a portion of the drawing or move back to take in a broader vista.

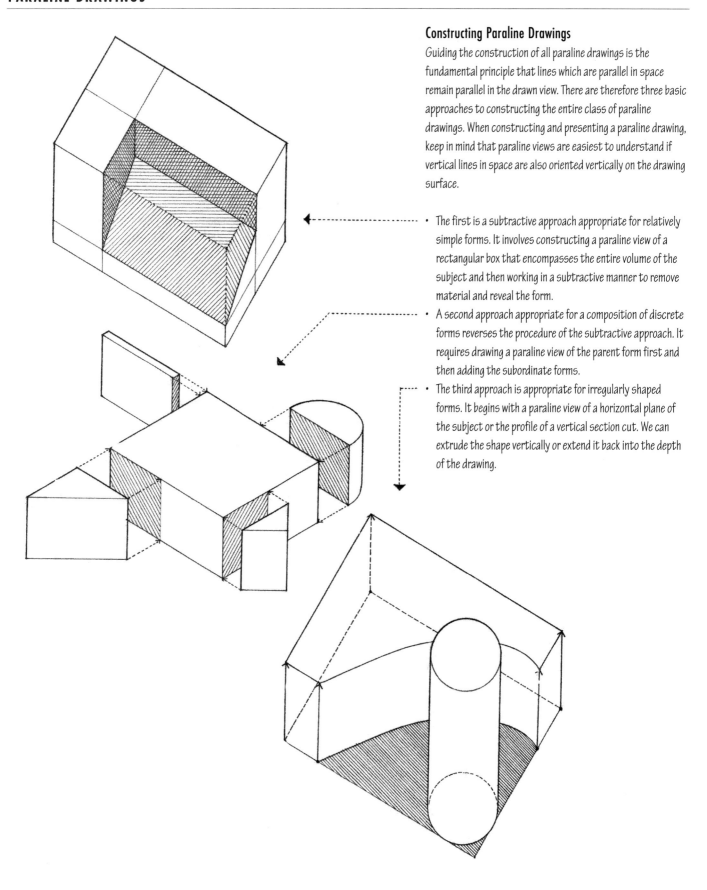

### Constructing Paraline Drawings

Guiding the construction of all paraline drawings is the fundamental principle that lines which are parallel in space remain parallel in the drawn view. There are therefore three basic approaches to constructing the entire class of paraline drawings. When constructing and presenting a paraline drawing, keep in mind that paraline views are easiest to understand if vertical lines in space are also oriented vertically on the drawing surface.

- The first is a subtractive approach appropriate for relatively simple forms. It involves constructing a paraline view of a rectangular box that encompasses the entire volume of the subject and then working in a subtractive manner to remove material and reveal the form.
- A second approach appropriate for a composition of discrete forms reverses the procedure of the subtractive approach. It requires drawing a paraline view of the parent form first and then adding the subordinate forms.
- The third approach is appropriate for irregularly shaped forms. It begins with a paraline view of a horizontal plane of the subject or the profile of a vertical section cut. We can extrude the shape vertically or extend it back into the depth of the drawing.

### Axial Lines

Axial lines refer to those lines which are parallel to any of the three principal axes. Regardless of the approach we take in constructing a paraline drawing, we can measure dimensions and draw to scale only along axial lines. Axial lines naturally form a rectangular grid of coordinates which we can use to find any point in three-dimensional space.

### Non-axial Lines

Non-axial lines refer to those lines which are not parallel to any of the three principal axes. We cannot measure dimensions along these non-axial lines, nor can we draw them to scale. To draw non-axial lines, we must first locate their end points using axial measurements, and then connect these points. Once we establish one non-axial line, however, we can draw any line parallel to that line since parallel lines in the subject remain parallel in the drawing.

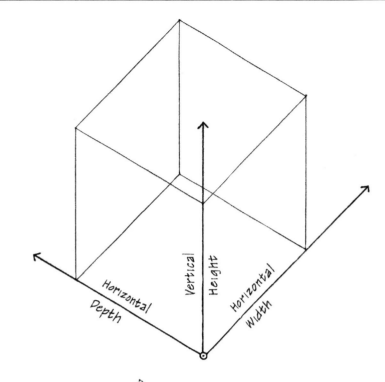

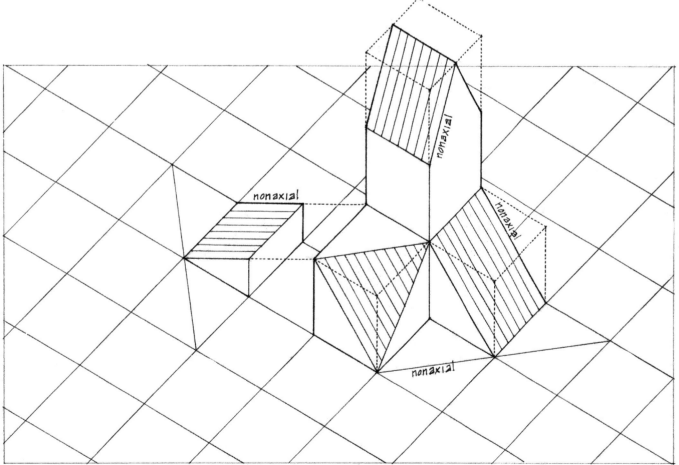

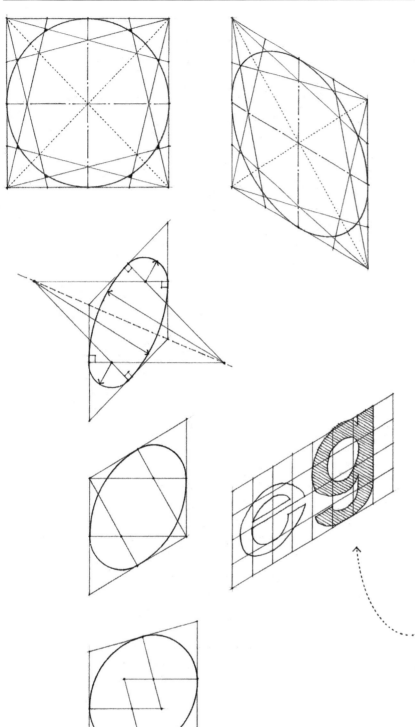

## Circles

Any circle oblique to the picture plane appears as an ellipse. In order to draw such a circle in a paraline drawing, we must first draw a square that circumscribes the circle. Then we can use either of following two approaches to drawing the circle within the square.

- If we can divide the square into quadrants and draw the diagonals we can establish eight points along the circumference of the circle.
- The four-center method uses two sets of radii and a compass or circle template. First draw the paraline view of the square that circumscribes the circle. From the midpoints of the sides of the rhombus, extend perpendiculars until they intersect. With the four points of intersection as centers and with radii $r^1$ and $r^2$, describe two sets of arcs in equal pairs between the origin points of the perpendiculars.

## Curves

We can draw a paraline view of any curved line or surface by using offset measurements to locate the positions of significant points along the line or surface.

## Freeform Shapes

In order to draw a freeform shape in a paraline drawing, first construct a grid over a plan or elevation view of the shape. This grid may either be uniform or correspond to critical points in the shape. The more complex the shape, the finer the grid divisions should be. Construct the same grid in the paraline view. Next, locate the points of intersection between the grid and the freeform shape and plot these coordinates in the paraline view. Finally, we connect the transferred points in the paraline view.

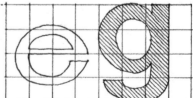

## Exercise 7.1

Use the three cubes as a guide to draw paraline views of a cylinder, a cone, and a pyramid.

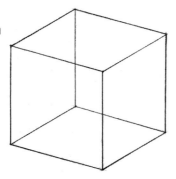
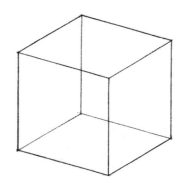
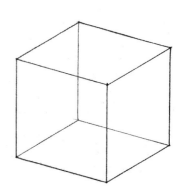

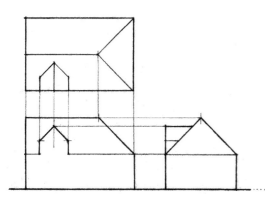

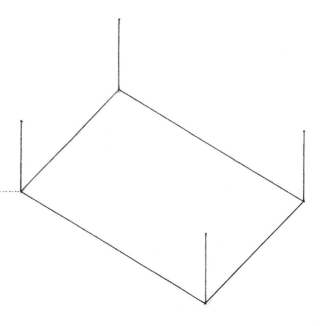

## Exercise 7.2

Construct a paraline drawing of the form described by the set of multiview drawings. Use the principal axes shown and double the scale.

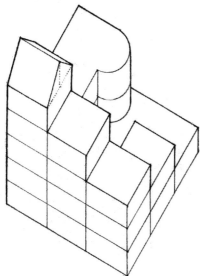

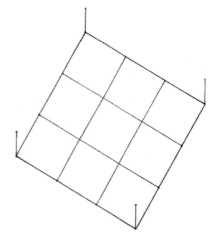

## Exercise 7.3

Using the same principal axes, construct a paraline drawing of the form as it would be seen from the opposite direction.

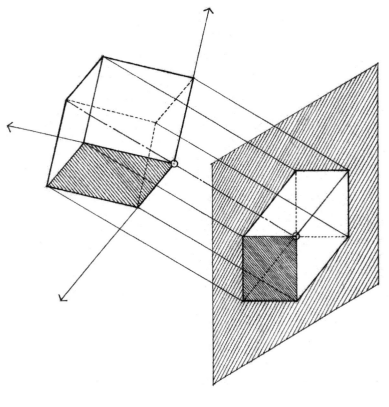

Axonometric = axono + metric or axis-measurement. The term axonometric is often used to describe paraline drawings of oblique projections or the entire class of paraline drawings. Strictly speaking, however, axonometric projection is a form of orthographic projection in which the projectors are parallel to each other and perpendicular to the picture plane. The difference between orthographic multiview drawings and an axonometric single view drawing is simply the orientation of the object to the picture plane.

## Axonometric Projection

Axonometric projection is an orthographic projection of a three-dimensional object inclined to the picture plane in such a way that its three principal axes are foreshortened. The family of axonometric projection includes isometric, dimetric, and trimetric projections. They differ according to the orientation of the three principal axes of a subject to the picture plane.

There is a significant difference between an axonometric projection and a drawing of that projection. In a true axonometric projection, the three principal axes are foreshortened to varying degrees, depending on their orientation to the picture plane. However, in an axonometric drawing, we draw the true length of one or more of these axes to exact scale. Axonometric drawings are therefore slightly larger than their corresponding axonometric projections.

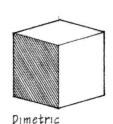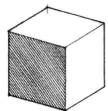

Isometric

Dimetric

Dimetric

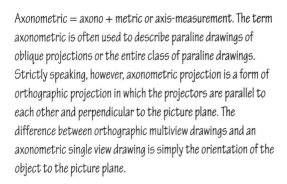

Dimetric

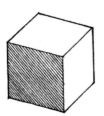

Trimetric

An isometric projection is an axonometric projection of a three-dimensional object inclined to the picture plane in such a way that the three principal axes make equal angles with the picture plane and are equally foreshortened.

To better visualize this, construct an isometric projection of a cube in the following manner.

- Establish a fold line parallel to a diagonal in a plan or elevation view of the cube.
- Project the cube into the auxiliary view.
- Construct a second fold line perpendicular to the diagonal in the auxiliary view of the cube.
- Project the cube into the second auxiliary view.

In developing an isometric projection of a cube, we find that the three principal axes appear 120° apart on the picture plane and are foreshortened to 0.816 of their true length. The diagonal of the cube, being perpendicular to the picture plane, is seen as a point and the three visible faces are equivalent in shape and proportion.

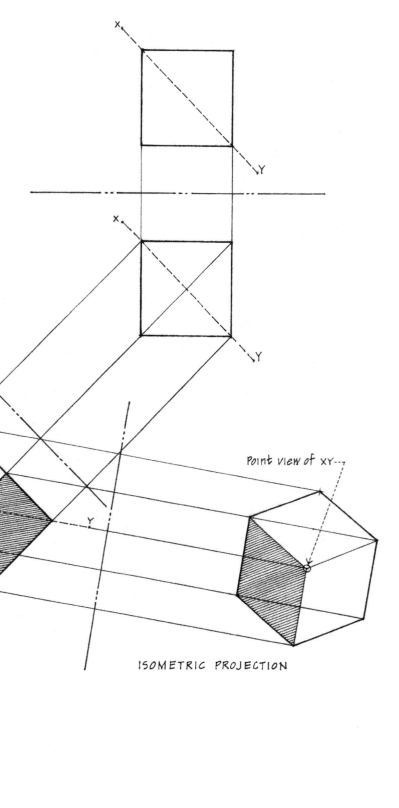

Point view of XY

ISOMETRIC PROJECTION

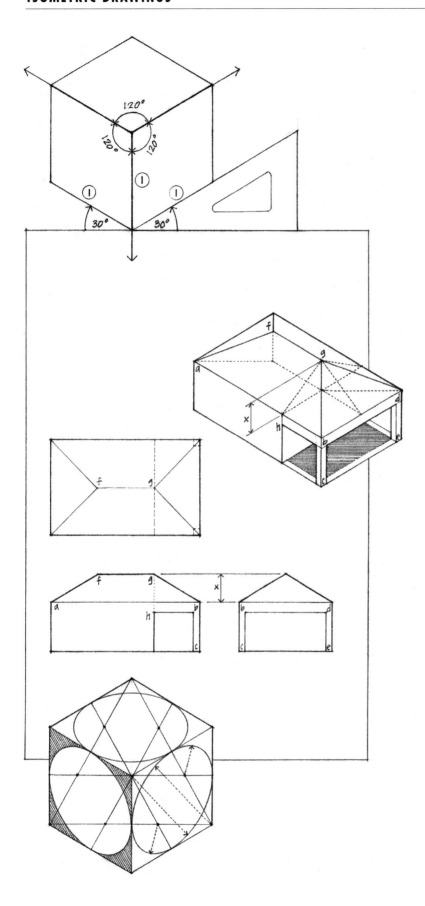

Instead of developing an isometric projection from a set of plan, elevation, and auxiliary views, it is common practice to construct an isometric drawing in a more direct manner. First, we establish the direction of the three principal axes. Since they are 120° apart on the picture plane, if we draw one axis vertically, the other two axes make a 30° angle with a horizontal on the drawing surface.

To save time, we disregard the normal foreshortening of the principal axes. Instead, we lay out the true lengths of all lines parallel to the three principal axes and draw them to the same scale. Thus, an isometric drawing is always slightly larger than an isometric projection of the same subject.

An isometric drawing establishes a lower angle of view than a plan oblique and gives equal emphasis to the three major sets of planes. It preserves the relative proportions of the subject and is not subject to the distortion inherent in oblique views. Isometric drawings of forms based on the square, however, can create an optical illusion and be subject to multiple interpretations. This ambiguity results from the alignment of lines in the foreground with those in the background. In such cases, a dimetric or oblique might be a better choice.

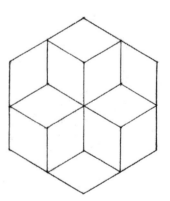

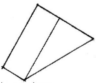

Isometric

Dimetric

**Exercise 7.4**

Construct an isometric drawing of the construction
described in the paraline view.

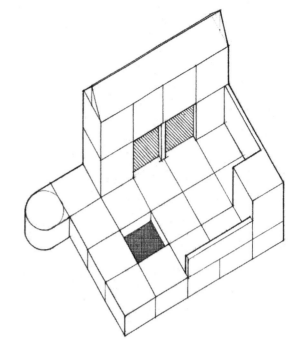

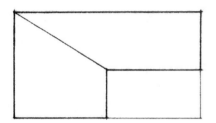

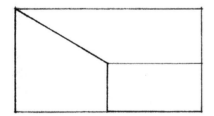 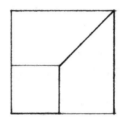

**Exercise 7.5**

Construct an isometric drawing of the structure described by
the set of multiview drawings.

**Exercise 7.6**

Construct an isometric drawing of the object as it would be
seen from the direction indicated.

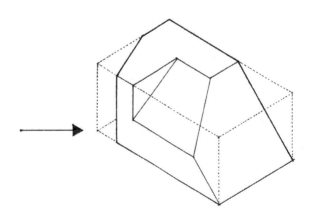

# DIMETRIC PROJECTION

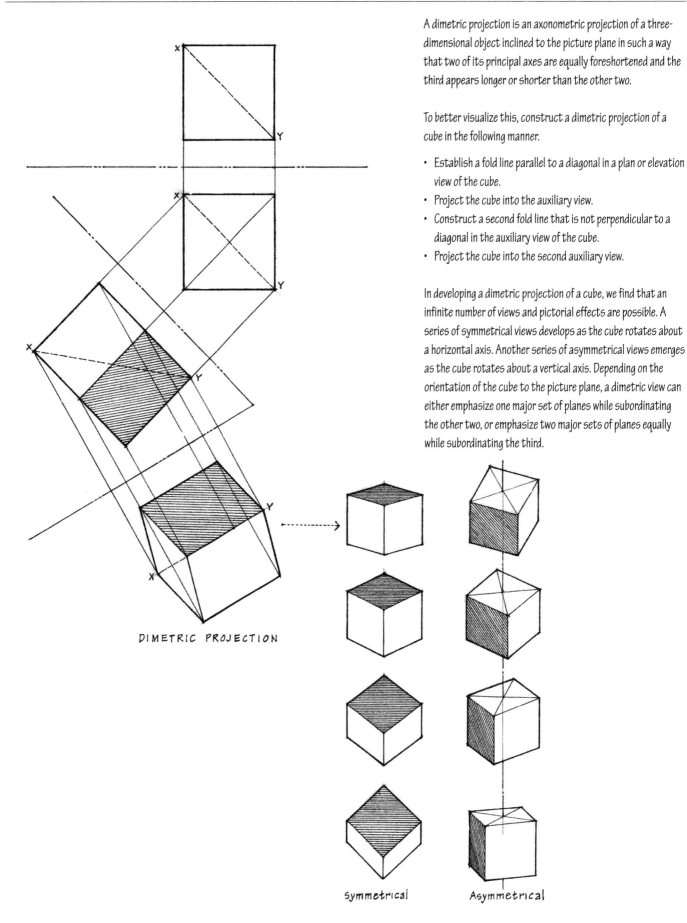

A dimetric projection is an axonometric projection of a three-dimensional object inclined to the picture plane in such a way that two of its principal axes are equally foreshortened and the third appears longer or shorter than the other two.

To better visualize this, construct a dimetric projection of a cube in the following manner.

- Establish a fold line parallel to a diagonal in a plan or elevation view of the cube.
- Project the cube into the auxiliary view.
- Construct a second fold line that is not perpendicular to a diagonal in the auxiliary view of the cube.
- Project the cube into the second auxiliary view.

In developing a dimetric projection of a cube, we find that an infinite number of views and pictorial effects are possible. A series of symmetrical views develops as the cube rotates about a horizontal axis. Another series of asymmetrical views emerges as the cube rotates about a vertical axis. Depending on the orientation of the cube to the picture plane, a dimetric view can either emphasize one major set of planes while subordinating the other two, or emphasize two major sets of planes equally while subordinating the third.

DIMETRIC PROJECTION

symmetrical          Asymmetrical

A dimetric is a paraline drawing of a dimetric projection, having all lines parallel to two of the principal axes drawn to true length at the same scale, and lines parallel to the third either elongated or foreshortened.

As with isometric drawings, we usually construct dimetric drawings in a direct manner. We first establish the direction of the three principal axes. Assuming one principal axis remains vertical, we can lay out the angles of the two horizontal axes in several ways. While these angles do not correspond exactly with the angles that result from dimetric projection, they are convenient to use when drafting with 30°/60° and 45°/45° triangles.

We can now lay out the lengths of all lines parallel to the three principal axes. Two of the three principal axes make the same angle with the picture plane. We draw lines parallel to these two axes at the same scale, and lines parallel to the third at a proportionately greater or smaller scale. The circled numbers indicate the whole and fractional scales at which we draw the three principal axes in each dimetric view.

The use of two scales and odd angles make dimetric drawings slightly more difficult to construct than isometric drawings. On the other hand, they offer a flexibility of viewpoint that can overcome some of the pictorial defects of isometric drawings. A dimetric view can emphasize one or two of the major sets of planes as well as provide a clearer depiction of 45° lines and surfaces.

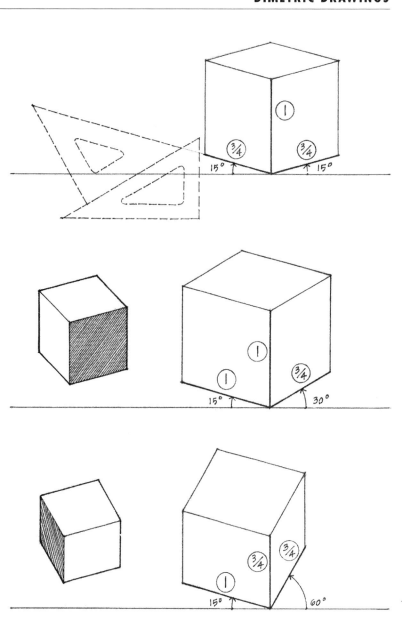

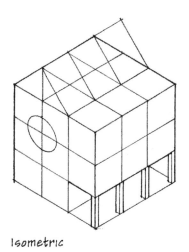

Isometric

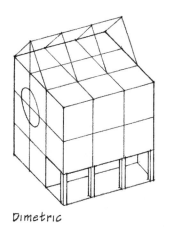

Dimetric

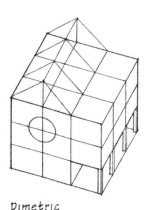

Dimetric

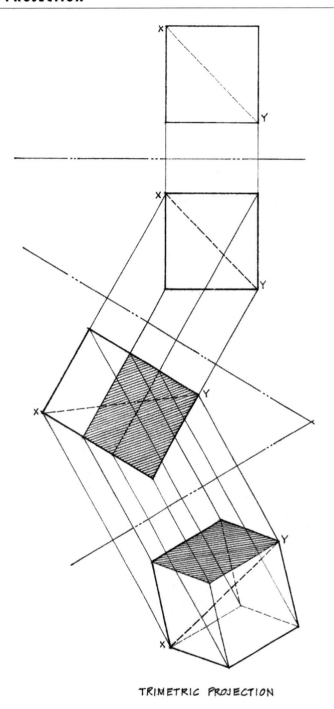

TRIMETRIC PROJECTION

A trimetric projection is an axonometric projection of a three-dimensional object inclined to the picture plane in such a way that all three principal axes are foreshortened at a different rate.

### Trimetric Drawings

A trimetric is a paraline drawing of a trimetric projection, showing all three principal axes foreshortened at a different rate and therefore drawn at different scales. Trimetrics naturally emphasize one major set of planes over the other two. We rarely use trimetrics because what they reveal does not justify their complex construction. Isometric and dimetric views are simpler to construct and just as satisfactory for most purposes.

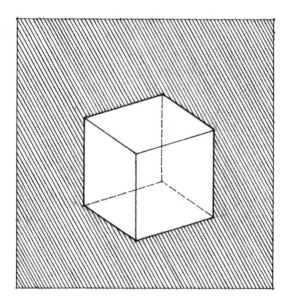

Oblique projection is one of three major types of projection drawing. The images that emerge from oblique projections belong to the pictorial family of paraline drawings but are distinct from the isometric and dimetric views that develop from orthographic projection. In oblique projection, a principal face or set of planes in the object is oriented parallel to the picture plane as in orthographic multiview drawing, but the image is transmitted by means of parallel projectors oriented at any angle other than 90° to the picture plane.

Oblique drawings show the true shape of planes parallel to the picture plane. Onto this frontal view, top and side views are attached and projected back into the depth of the drawing. This yields a three-dimensional image that represents what we know rather than how we see. It depicts an objective reality that corresponds more closely to the picture in the mind's eye than the retinal image of linear perspective. It represents a mental map of the world that combines plan and elevational views into a single expression.

The ease with which we can construct an oblique drawing has a powerful appeal. If we orient a principal face of an object parallel to the picture plane, its shape remains true and we can draw it more easily. Thus, oblique views are especially convenient for representing an object which has a curvilinear, irregular, or complicated face.

While oblique projection can suggest the solidity of a three-dimensional object and produce a powerful illusion of space, it also allows the composition of lines to remain on the surface as a flat pattern. This can lead to optical illusions and therefore ambiguity in the reading of an oblique drawing.

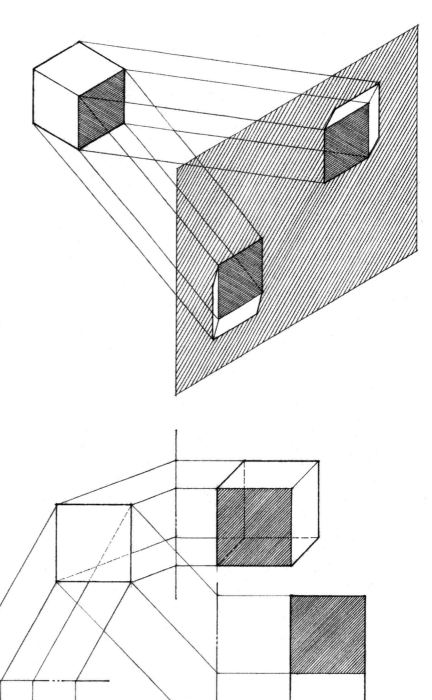

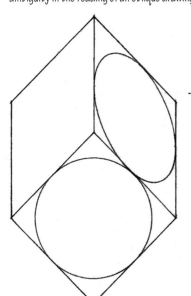

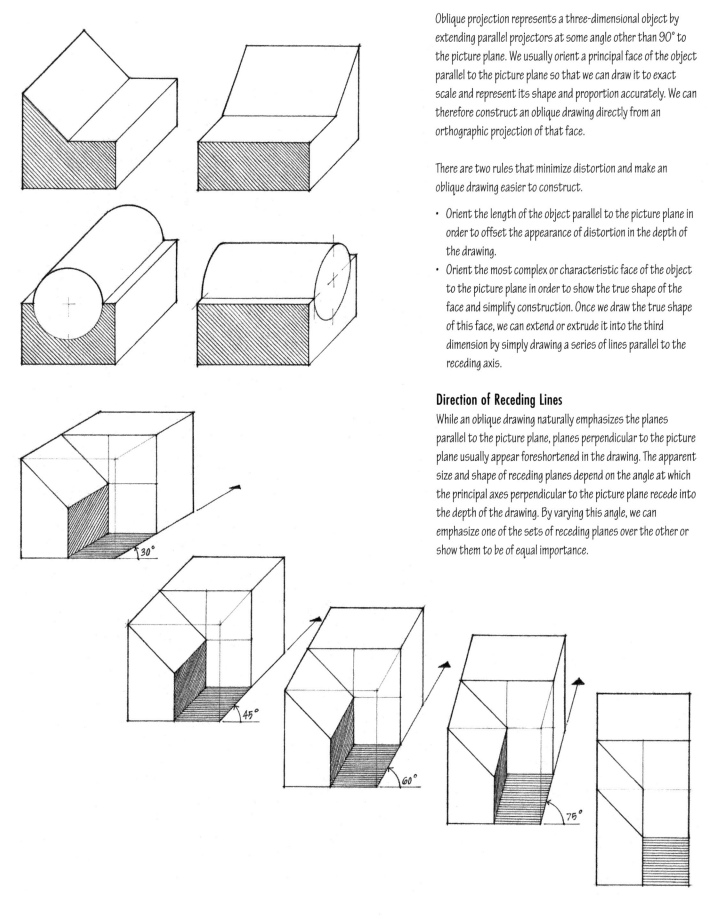

Oblique projection represents a three-dimensional object by extending parallel projectors at some angle other than 90° to the picture plane. We usually orient a principal face of the object parallel to the picture plane so that we can draw it to exact scale and represent its shape and proportion accurately. We can therefore construct an oblique drawing directly from an orthographic projection of that face.

There are two rules that minimize distortion and make an oblique drawing easier to construct.

• Orient the length of the object parallel to the picture plane in order to offset the appearance of distortion in the depth of the drawing.
• Orient the most complex or characteristic face of the object to the picture plane in order to show the true shape of the face and simplify construction. Once we draw the true shape of this face, we can extend or extrude it into the third dimension by simply drawing a series of lines parallel to the receding axis.

### Direction of Receding Lines

While an oblique drawing naturally emphasizes the planes parallel to the picture plane, planes perpendicular to the picture plane usually appear foreshortened in the drawing. The apparent size and shape of receding planes depend on the angle at which the principal axes perpendicular to the picture plane recede into the depth of the drawing. By varying this angle, we can emphasize one of the sets of receding planes over the other or show them to be of equal importance.

## Length of Receding Lines

The angle that the oblique projectors make with the picture plane determines the lengths of the receding axial lines in an oblique drawing. If the projectors are at a 45° angle to the picture plane, the receding lines will be projected in their true length. At other angles, the projectors will cause the receding lines to appear either longer or shorter than their true length. In practice, we can lay out and draw the receding lines of an oblique drawing to their true lengths or at a reduced scale to offset the appearance of distortion.

## Cavalier Projection

The term cavalier derives from the past use of this projection system in drawing fortifications. In cavalier projection, the projectors form a 45° angle with the picture plane. We can therefore draw the receding axial lines at the same scale as the lines parallel to the picture plane.

While the use of a single scale for all three principal axes greatly simplifies the construction of an oblique drawing, the lengths of receding lines can sometimes appear too long. To offset the appearance of distortion, we can foreshorten the receding lines by drawing their lengths at the same reduced scale, usually ²/₃ to ³/₄ of their true length.

## Cabinet Projection

The term cabinet comes from its use in the furniture industry. In cabinet projection, a three-dimensional object is represented by an oblique drawing having all lines parallel to the picture plane drawn to exact scale and receding lines reduced to half-scale. Cabinet drawings suffer from a major pictorial defect—the length of receding lines can sometimes appear too short.

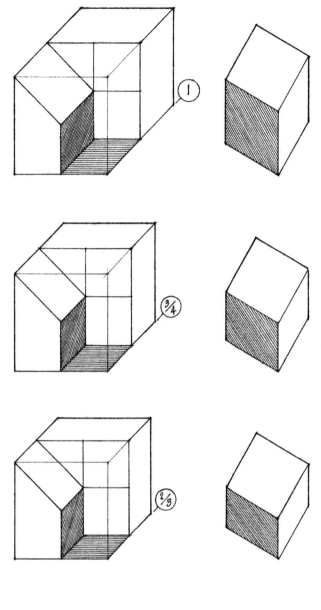

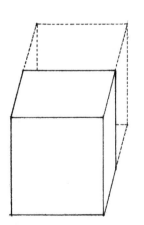
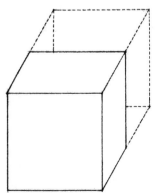
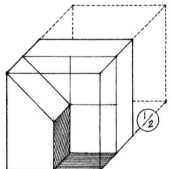
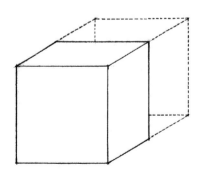

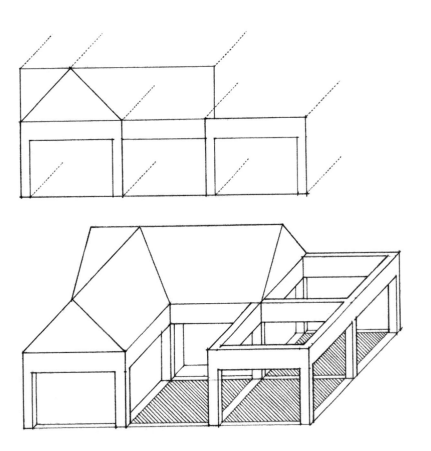

In architectural graphics, the two major types of oblique drawings are elevation obliques and plan obliques. Most of the examples on the previous two pages are elevation obliques.

An elevation oblique orients a principal vertical face parallel to the picture plane and therefore reveals its true shape and size. We can therefore construct an elevation oblique directly from an elevation view of the principal face. This face should be the longest, the most significant, or the most complex façade of the subject.

From significant points in the elevation view, we project the receding lines back at the desired angle into the depth of the drawing. In drafting with triangles, we typically use 30°, 45°, or 60° angles for the receding lines. In sketching, we need not be as precise, but once we establish an angle for the receding lines, we should apply it consistently.

Remember that the angle we use for the receding lines alters the apparent size and shape of the receding planes. By varying the angle, the horizontal and vertical sets of receding planes can receive different degrees of emphasis. In all cases, the primary emphasis remains on the vertical faces parallel to the picture plane.

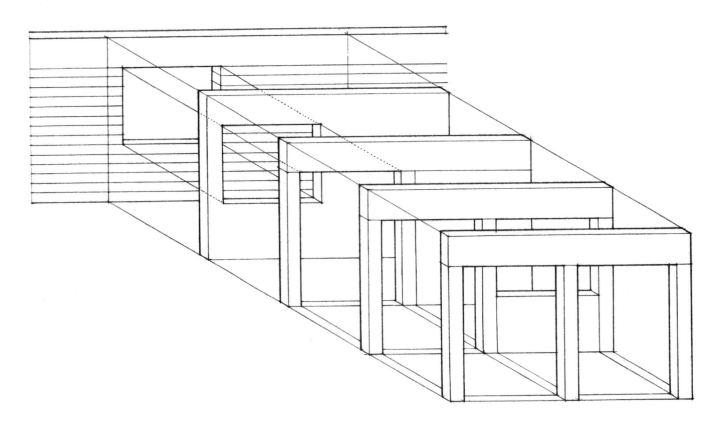

### Exercise 7.7

Construct two series of elevation obliques of the building form
described in the set of multiview drawings. In the first series,
draw the lines parallel to the receding axis at full scale but vary
their direction—draw the receding lines first at 30° to the
horizontal, then at 45° to the horizontal, and finally at 60° to
the horizontal.

In the second series, draw the receding axis at 45° to the
horizontal but vary its scale—draw the lines parallel to the
receding axis first at three-quarter scale, then at two-third
scale, and finally at one-half scale.

Compare the pictorial effects of the various elevation obliques.
Do any of the elevation obliques appear to be too deep? Do any
appear too shallow? Which sets of receding planes does each
elevation oblique emphasize?

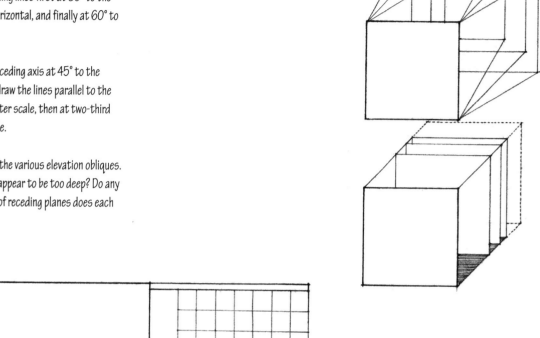

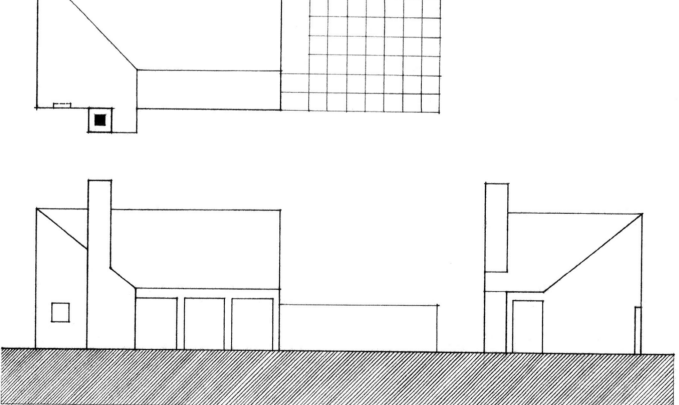

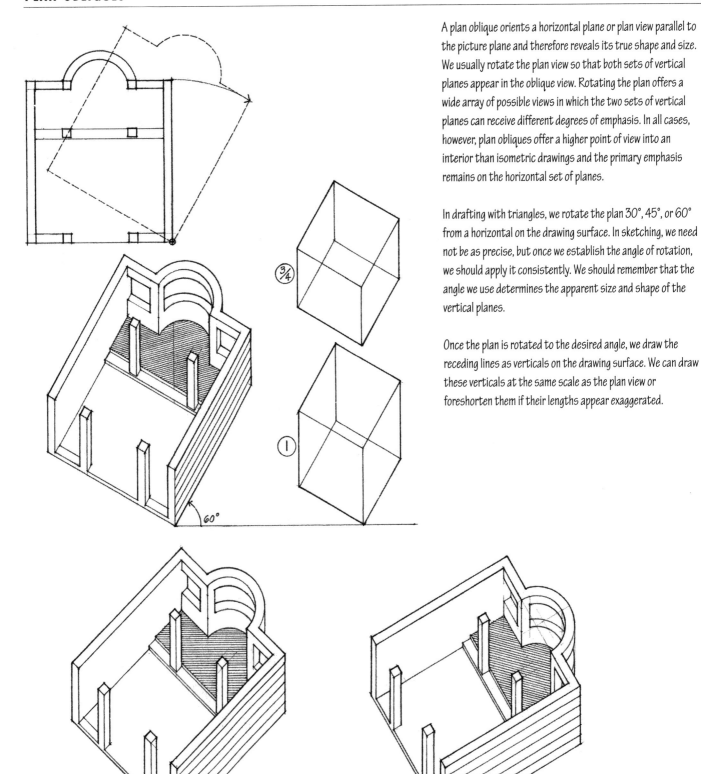

A plan oblique orients a horizontal plane or plan view parallel to the picture plane and therefore reveals its true shape and size. We usually rotate the plan view so that both sets of vertical planes appear in the oblique view. Rotating the plan offers a wide array of possible views in which the two sets of vertical planes can receive different degrees of emphasis. In all cases, however, plan obliques offer a higher point of view into an interior than isometric drawings and the primary emphasis remains on the horizontal set of planes.

In drafting with triangles, we rotate the plan 30°, 45°, or 60° from a horizontal on the drawing surface. In sketching, we need not be as precise, but once we establish the angle of rotation, we should apply it consistently. We should remember that the angle we use determines the apparent size and shape of the vertical planes.

Once the plan is rotated to the desired angle, we draw the receding lines as verticals on the drawing surface. We can draw these verticals at the same scale as the plan view or foreshorten them if their lengths appear exaggerated.

### Exercise 7.8

Construct two pairs of plan obliques of the building form described in the set of multiview drawings. In the first series, draw the lines parallel to the vertical axis at full scale but rotate the plan view 30° clockwise about point A, then 45° clockwise about point A, and finally 60° clockwise about point A.

In the second pair, rotate the plan view in the same way, but draw the lines parallel to the vertical axis at three-quarter scale.

Compare the pictorial effects of the various plan obliques. Do any of the plan obliques appear to be too tall? Do any appear too short? Which sets of vertical planes does each plan oblique emphasize?

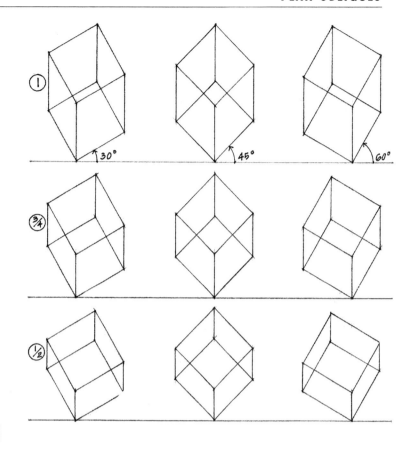

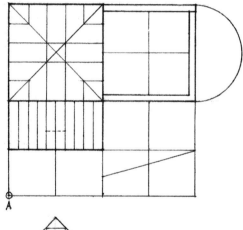

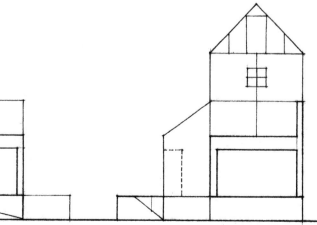

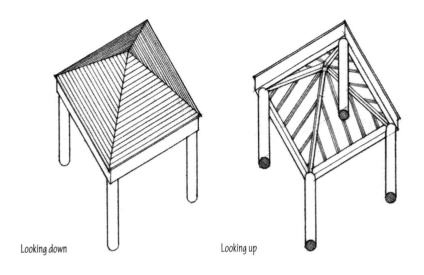

Looking down          Looking up

### Paraline Views

Even though a paraline drawing always presents either an aerial view or a worm's-eye view of a subject, we can construct a paraline view in any of several ways to reveal more than the exterior form and configuration of a design. These techniques allow us to gain visual access to the interior of a spatial composition or the hidden portions of a complex construction. We categorize these techniques into phantom views, cutaway views, and expanded views.

### Phantom Views

A phantom view is a drawing having one or more parts made transparent to permit representation of internal information otherwise hidden from our view. This strategy effectively allows us to unveil an interior space or construction without removing any of its bounding planes or encompassing elements. Thus we are able to simultaneously see the whole composition as well as its internal structure and arrangement.

We use a phantom line to represent the transparency of a part, an alternative position of a moving part, the relative position of an absent part, or a repeated detail or feature. A phantom line is a broken line consisting of relatively long segments separated by two short dashes or dots. In practice, phantom lines may also consist of dashed, dotted, or even delicately drawn lines. The graphic description should include the thickness or volume of the transparent part as well as any details that may exist within its boundaries.

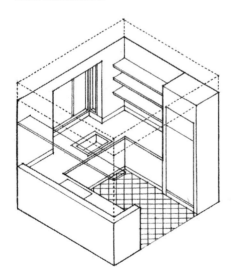

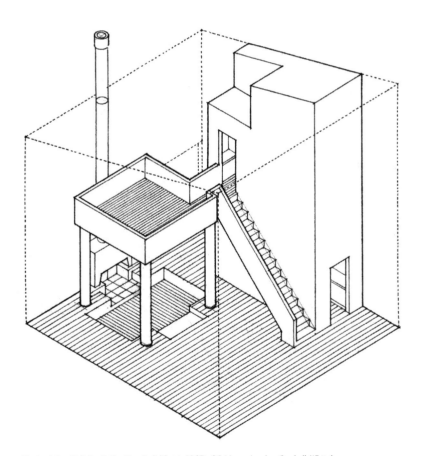

Condominium Unit No. 5, Sea Ranch, California, 1963–65, Moore, Lyndon, Turnbull, Whitaker

## Cutaway Views

A cutaway view is a drawing having an outer section or layer removed to reveal an interior space or an internal construction. This strategy can also effectively manifest the relation of an interior to the exterior environment.

The simplest method for creating a cutaway view is to remove an outer or bounding layer of a composition or construction. For example, removing a roof, ceiling, or wall allows us to look down and see into an interior space. Removing a floor permits a view up into a space.

We can remove a larger section by slicing through the heart of a composition. When a composition exhibits bilateral symmetry, we can make this cut along the axis and indicate the footprint or plan view of the part removed. In a similar fashion, we can create a cutaway view of a radially symmetrical composition by slicing through the center and removing a quadrant or similar pie-shaped portion.

In order to reveal a more complex composition, the cut may follow a three-dimensional route. In this case, the trajectory of the cut should clarify the nature of the internal organization and arrangement, and be clearly articulated by a contrast in line weights or tonal values.

Even though a portion is removed in a cutaway view, its presence can remain in the drawing if we delineate its outer boundaries with a dotted, dashed, or delicate line. Indicating the external form of what is removed helps the viewer retain a sense of the whole.

While a paraline is a single-view drawing useful in displaying three-dimensional relationships, a series of paraline views can effectively explain processes and phenomena that occur in time or across space. A progression of paraline drawings can explain a sequence of assembly or the stages of a construction, with each view successively building upon the preceding one.

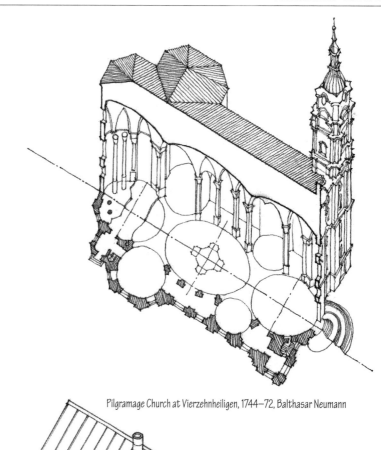

Pilgramage Church at Vierzehnheiligen, 1744–72, Balthasar Neumann

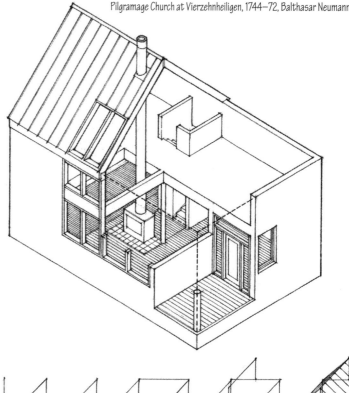

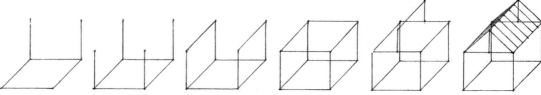

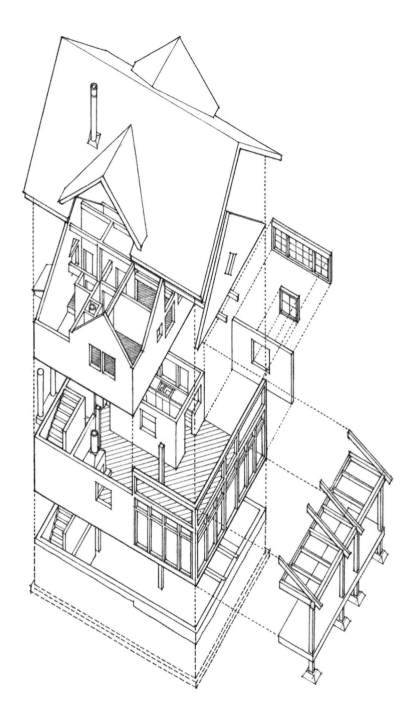

## Expanded Views

The portions removed from a drawing may not disappear but merely shift to new positions in space, developing into what we call an expanded or exploded view. An expanded view shows the individual components of a construction or assembly separately but indicates their proper relation to each other and to the whole. The finished drawing appears to be an explosion frozen at a point in time when the relationships between the parts are most clear.

The displacement of the parts should be in the order and direction in which they fit together. For axial compositions, the expansion occurs either along the axis or perpendicular to it. For rectangular compositions, the parts relocate along or parallel to the principal axes. In all cases, we indicate the relationships between the parts to each other and to the whole with dotted, dashed, or delicately drawn lines.

Expanded views are extremely useful in describing the details, layering, or sequence of a construction assembly. At a larger scale, expanded views can effectively illustrate vertical relationships in buildings as well as horizontal connections across space. In clarifying spatial relationships and organizations through displacement, expanded views can simultaneously combine the revealing aspects of phantom and cutaway views.

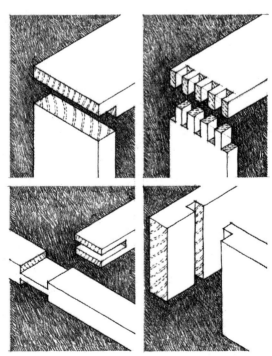

## Conveying Depth

Even a simple line drawing of a paraline view induces a powerful sensation of space. This is due not only to the depth cue of overlap, but also our perception of parallelograms as rectangles occupying space. We can enhance the perceived depth of a paraline drawing by contrasting line weights or tonal values.

We use a hierarchy of line weights to distinguish between spatial edges, planar corners, and surface lines.

1. Spatial edges are the boundaries of a form separated from their background by some intervening space.
2. Planar corners are the intersections of two or more planes which are visible to the eye.
3. Surface lines are lines that represent an abrupt contrast in color, tonal value, or material; they do not represent a change in form.

In order to separate planes in space, clarify their different orientations, and especially to distinguish between the horizontal and the vertical, we can use contrasting tonal values, textures, or patterns. The most important distinction to establish is the orthogonal relationship between horizontal and vertical planes. Applying a tonal value to the horizontal planes in a paraline view not only establishes a visual base for the drawing but also aids in defining the shape and orientation of the vertical planes.

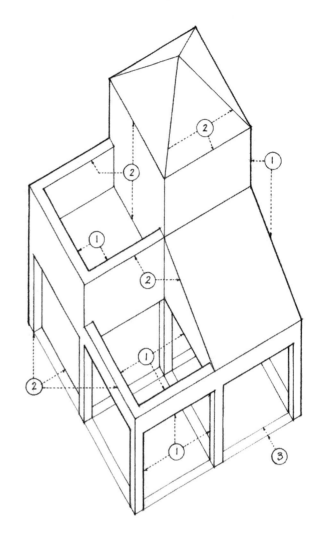

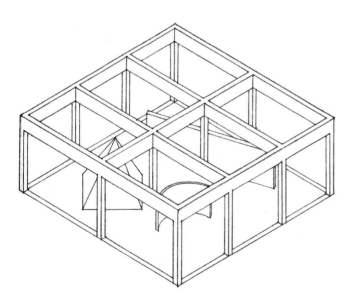

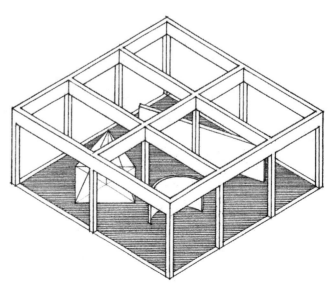

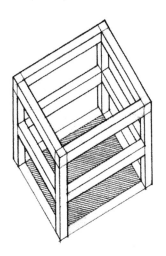

### Exercise 7.9

Illustrated is a paraline view of the Hirabayashi Residence in Yamada, Japan, designed by Tadao Ando in 1975. First draw the paraline view with a single line weight. Then use a hierarchy of line weights to differentiate spatial edges, planar corners, and surface lines.

Remember that line weight is not simply a matter of density. Rather, we rely on contrasting line thicknesses to distinguish one line weight from another.

### Exercise 7.10

For more practice in articulating spatial edges, planar corners, and surface lines, apply a hierarchy of line weights to any of the paraline views executed in Exercises 7.4 through 7.8.

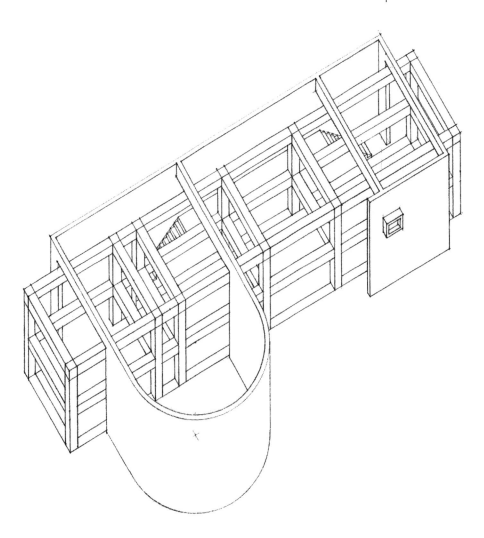

## Shade and Shadows

The casting of shade and shadows in a paraline drawing enhances our perception of the three-dimensional nature of volumes and masses and articulates their spatial relationships. In addition, the tonal values used in rendering shades and shadows can help differentiate between vertical, horizontal, and sloping planes. For the basic concepts and terminology of shade and shadows, refer back to Chapter 6.

It is convenient to visualize the three-dimensional relationships between light rays, shade lines, and cast shadows in paraline views because they are pictorial in nature and display the three major spatial axes simultaneously. In addition, parallel light rays and their bearing directions remain parallel in a paraline drawing.

In order to construct shade and shadows, it is necessary to assume a source and direction of light. Deciding on a direction of light is a problem in composition as well as communication. Remember that cast shadows should clarify rather than confuse the nature of the forms and their spatial relationships. The lower the angle of light, the deeper the shadows; the steeper the angle, the shallower the shadows. In any case, the resulting shadow patterns should not conceal more than they reveal about the forms being depicted.

Occasionally it may be desirable to determine the actual conditions of light, shade, and shadow. For example, when studying the effects of solar radiation and shadow patterns on thermal comfort and energy conservation, it is necessary to construct shades and shadows using the actual sun angles for specific times and dates of the year.

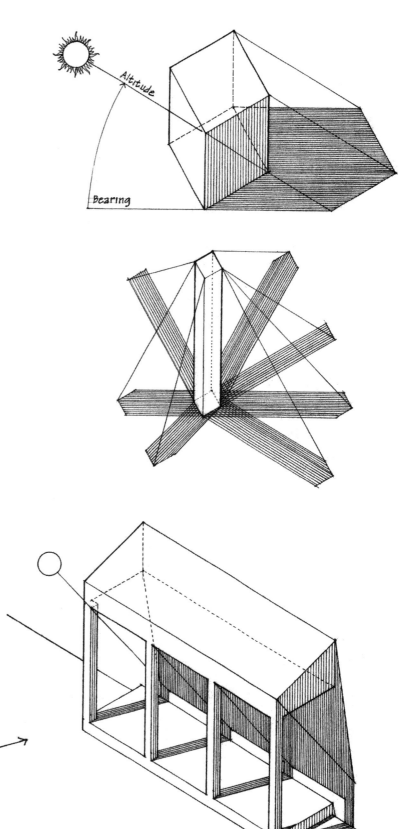

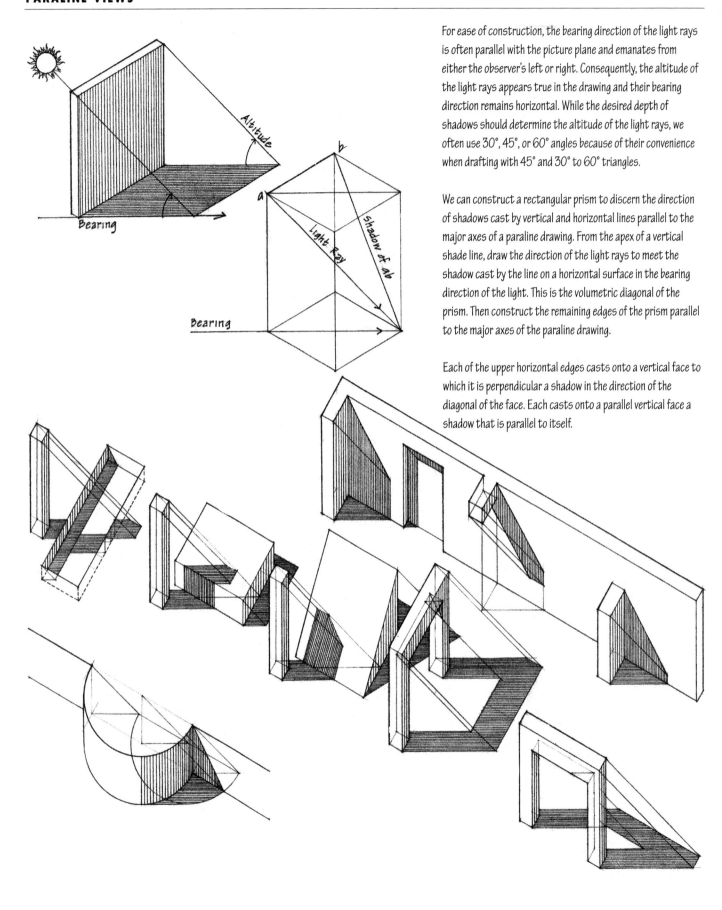

For ease of construction, the bearing direction of the light rays is often parallel with the picture plane and emanates from either the observer's left or right. Consequently, the altitude of the light rays appears true in the drawing and their bearing direction remains horizontal. While the desired depth of shadows should determine the altitude of the light rays, we often use 30°, 45°, or 60° angles because of their convenience when drafting with 45° and 30° to 60° triangles.

We can construct a rectangular prism to discern the direction of shadows cast by vertical and horizontal lines parallel to the major axes of a paraline drawing. From the apex of a vertical shade line, draw the direction of the light rays to meet the shadow cast by the line on a horizontal surface in the bearing direction of the light. This is the volumetric diagonal of the prism. Then construct the remaining edges of the prism parallel to the major axes of the paraline drawing.

Each of the upper horizontal edges casts onto a vertical face to which it is perpendicular a shadow in the direction of the diagonal of the face. Each casts onto a parallel vertical face a shadow that is parallel to itself.

## Exercise 7.11

Construct the shade and shadows for the structure described in the paraline view below. Assume the parallel light rays of the sun have an altitude of 45° and a bearing direction to the right and parallel to the picture plane.

## Exercise 7.12

For more practice, assume the same direction of light rays and construct shade and shadows for the structure described in Exercise 7.4.

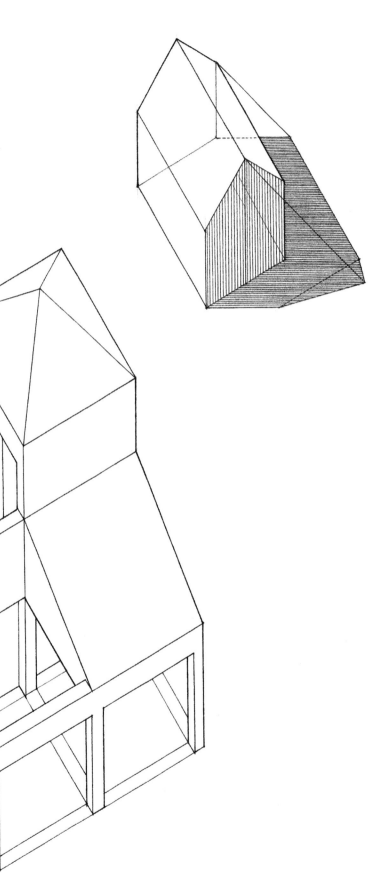

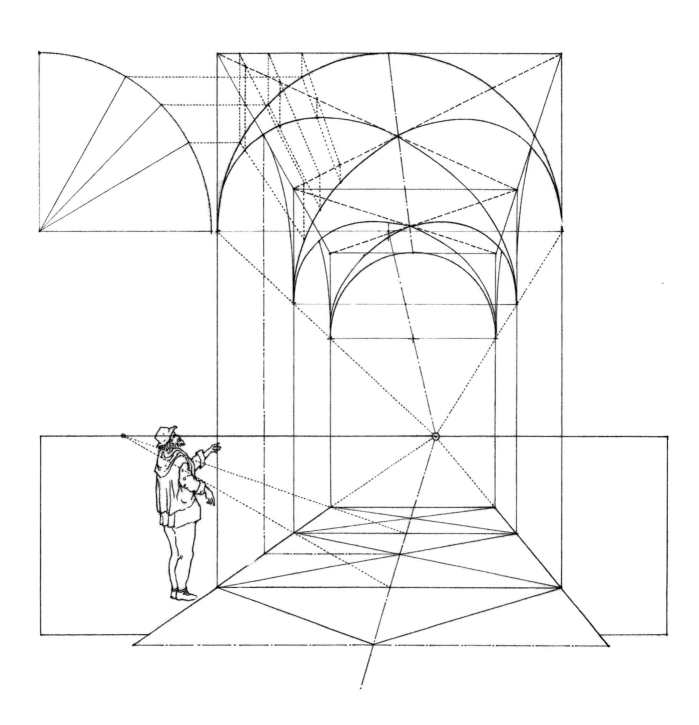

# 8
# Perspective Drawings

Perspective properly refers to any of various graphic techniques for depicting volumes and spatial relationships on a flat surface, such as size and atmospheric perspective. The term perspective, however, most often brings to mind the drawing system of linear or artificial perspective.

Linear perspective is the art and science of describing three-dimensional volumes and spatial relationships on a two-dimensional surface by means of lines which converge as they recede into the depth of a drawing. While multiview and paraline drawings present mechanical views of an objective reality, linear perspective offers sensory views to the mind's eye of an optical reality. It depicts how objects and space might appear to the eye of a spectator looking in a specific direction from a particular vantage point in space. While our eyes can rove about the surface of a plan or isometric guided by whim or reason, we are invited to read a linear perspective from a fixed position in space.

Linear perspective is valid only for monocular vision. A perspective drawing assumes the spectator sees through a single eye. We almost never view anything in this way. Even with the head in a fixed position, we see through both eyes which are constantly in motion, roving over and around objects and through everchanging environments. Through this constant scanning, we build up experiential data which the mind manipulates and processes to form our perception and understanding of the visual world. Thus, linear perspective can only approximate the complex way the eyes actually function.

Still, linear perspective provides us with a method for correctly placing three-dimensional objects in pictorial space and illustrating the degree to which their forms appear to diminish in size as they recede into the depth of a drawing. The uniqueness of a linear perspective lies in its ability to provide us with an experiential view of space. This distinct advantage, however, also gives rise to the difficulty often connected with perspective drawing. The challenge in mastering linear perspective is resolving the conflict between our knowledge of the thing itself—how we conceive its objective reality—and the appearance of something—how we perceive its optical reality—as seen through a single eye of the spectator.

Perspective projection represents a three-dimensional object by projecting all its points to a picture plane by straight lines converging at a fixed point in space representing a single eye of the spectator. This convergence of sightlines differentiates perspective projection from the other two major projection systems, orthographic projection and oblique projection, in which the projectors remain parallel to each other.

## Perspective Elements

### Station Point (SP)

A fixed point in space representing a single eye of the spectator.

### Sightline

Any of the projectors extending from the station point to various points on an object viewed. The perspective projection of any point on an object is where the sightline to that point intersects the picture plane.

### Central Axis of Vision (CAV)

The sightline determining the direction in which the spectator is assumed to be looking.

### Cone of Vision

A cone described by sightlines radiating outward from the station point and forming a 30° angle with the central axis of vision in linear perspective. The cone of vision serves as a guide in determining what is to be included within the boundaries of a perspective drawing. A 60° cone of vision is assumed to be the normal field of vision within which the principal aspects of the subject should be placed. To minimize distortion of circles and circular shapes, they should fall within a 30° cone of vision. A 90° cone of vision is acceptable for peripheral elements.

We should remember that the cone of vision is three-dimensional even though it is seen as a triangular shape in orthographic plans and elevations. Only a small portion of the immediate foreground falls within the cone of vision. As the cone of vision reaches out to gather in what the spectator sees, it widens its field and the middleground and background become more expansive.

In reality, our field of vision is more like a pyramid than a cone. Most people have a field of view that extends 180° horizontally but only 140° vertically because some of the visual field is blocked by the eyebrows, nose, and cheeks.

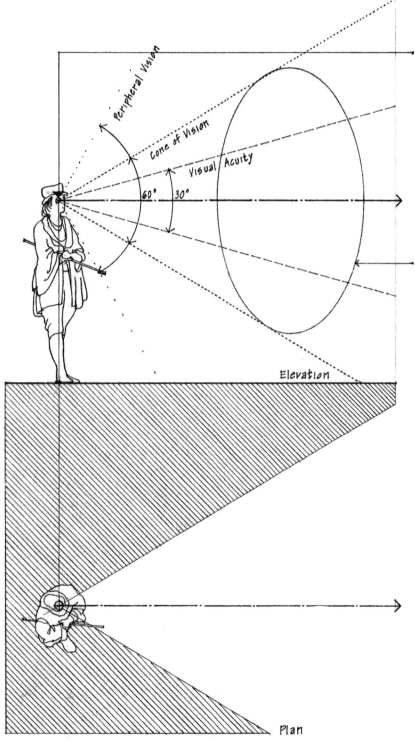

### Picture Plane (PP)

An imaginary transparent plane, coextensive with the drawing surface, on which the image of a three-dimensional object is projected—also called plane of projection. The picture plane slices through the cone of vision and is always perpendicular to the central axis of vision. As long as the central axis of vision is horizontal, the picture plane is vertical. When we shift our line of sight to the left or right, the picture plane moves with it. If we shift our line of sight upward or downward, then the picture plane will be tilted as well.

As we look out through a window, we can draw on the glass surface what we see through it. The glass pane is the physical equivalent of the picture plane. When we draw a perspective, we transfer onto the drawing surface what we see through an imaginary picture plane. The drawing surface becomes the virtual equivalent of the picture plane.

### Center of Vision (CV)

The point on the horizon line at which the central axis of vision intersects the picture plane.

### Horizon Line (HL)

A horizontal line representing the intersection of the picture plane and a horizontal plane passing the station point. The distance from the ground line to the horizon line is equal to the height of the spectator's eye level or station point above the ground plane. For a normal eye-level perspective, the horizon line is at the standing height of the spectator's eye. The horizon line moves down if the spectator sits down in a chair. It moves up if the spectator looks out from a stair landing or a second-story window. It rises still further if the view is from a mountaintop.

Even if not actually seen in a perspective view, the horizon line should always be drawn lightly across the drawing surface to serve as a level line of reference for the entire composition.

### Ground Plane (GP)

A horizontal plane of reference from which heights can be measured in linear perspective. The ground plane is usually, but not always, the surface upon which the spectator stands. It can also be the lake surface on which a boat is sailing, or the ground on which a building rests. It can be the floor plane when drawing a perspective of an interior space, or even the top of a table when sketching a still life.

### Ground Line (GL)

A horizontal line representing the intersection of the ground plane and the picture plane.

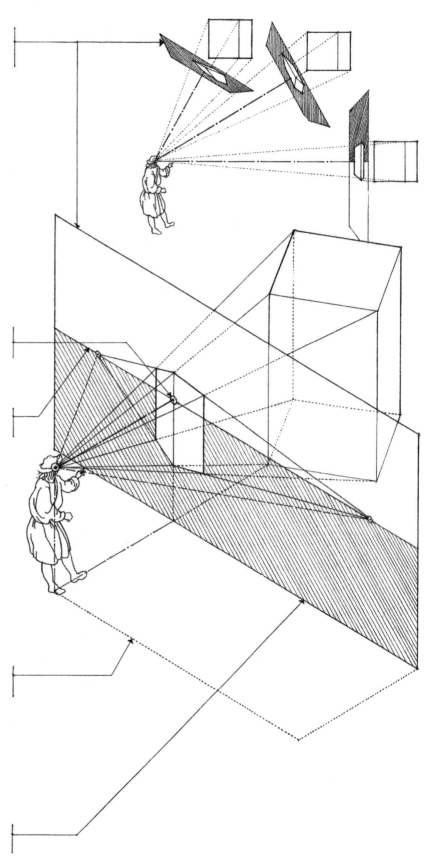

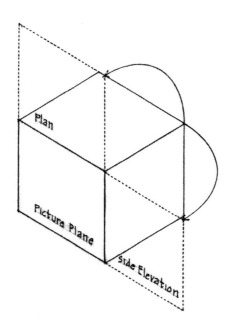

### Direct Projection Method

The direct projection method of perspective construction requires the use of at least two orthographic views: a plan view and a side elevation view. The side elevation is an orthographic projection that is perpendicular to the picture plane, but rotated 90° to be coplanar with the picture plane. The object, picture plane, and station point are shown in both views.

The perspective of any point is where a sightline from the station point to the point in question intersects the picture plane. To find the perspective projection of a point:

1. In the plan view, draw a sightline from the station point to the point in question until it intersects the picture plane.
2. Do the same in the elevation view.
3. Where the sightline in the plan view meets the picture plane, drop a vertical construction line.
4. Where the sightline in the elevation view meets the picture plane, extend a horizontal construction line until it intersects the vertical construction line.
5. This point of intersection is the perspective projection of the point, which lies in the picture plane.

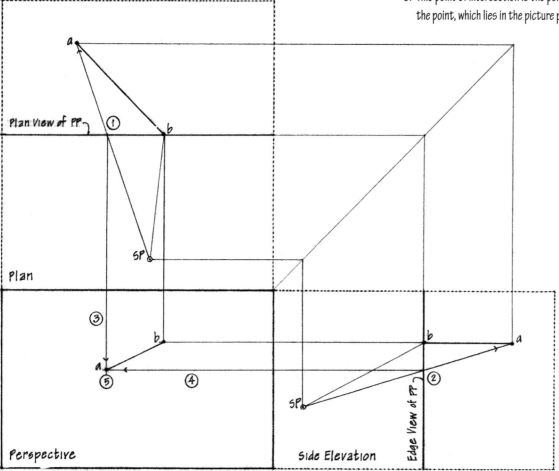

For a point behind the picture plane, draw a sightline from the point in question toward the station point until it meets the picture plane. If the point lies in the picture plane, simply drop the plan position vertically until it meets a horizontal line from the point in the elevation view. If the point is in front of the picture plane, draw a sightline from the station point, through the point, and extend it until it meets the picture plane.

To find the perspective projection of a line, establish the perspective projections of its endpoints and connect the points. If we can establish the perspective projections of points and lines in this way, we can also find the perspective projections of planes or volumes.

In theory, it is not necessary to use vanishing points in the direct projection method. However, the establishment and use of vanishing points greatly simplifies the drawing of a linear perspective and ensures greater accuracy in determining the direction of receding lines.

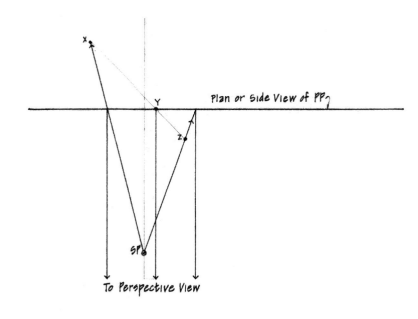

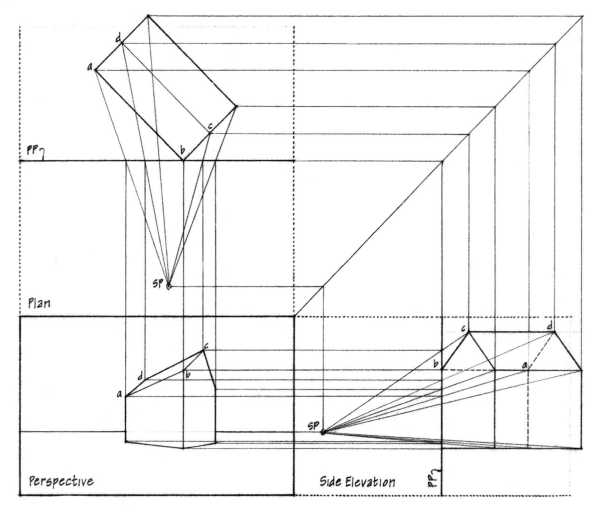

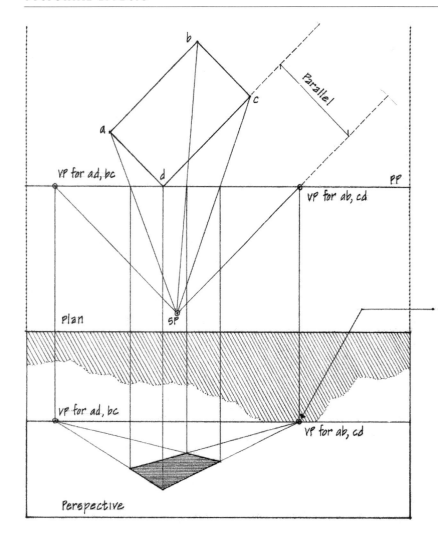

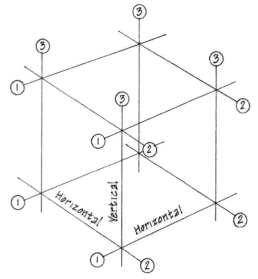

The converging nature of sightlines in linear perspective produces certain pictorial effects. Being familiar with these pictorial effects will help us understand how lines, planes, and volumes should appear in linear perspective and how to correctly place objects in the space of a perspective drawing.

## Convergence

Convergence in linear perspective refers to the apparent movement of parallel lines toward a common vanishing point as they recede. As two parallel lines recede into the distance, the space between them will appear to diminish. If the lines are extended to infinity, they will appear to meet at a point. This point is the vanishing point for that particular pair of lines and all other lines parallel to them.

### Vanishing Point (VP)

A point on the picture plane at which a set of receding parallel lines appears to converge in linear perspective. The vanishing point for any set of parallel lines is the point where a line drawn from the station point parallel to the set intersects the picture plane.

The first rule of convergence is that each set of parallel lines has its own vanishing point. A set of parallel lines consists only of those lines which are parallel to one another. If we look at a cube, for example, we can see that its edges comprise three principal sets of parallel lines, one set of vertical lines parallel to the x-axis, and two sets of horizontal lines, perpendicular to each other and parallel to the y- and z-axes.

In order to draw a perspective, we must know how many sets of parallel lines exist in what we see or envision and where each set will appear to converge. The following guidelines for the convergence of parallel lines is based solely on the relationship between the spectator's central axis of vision and the subject.

## Convergence Principles

We can categorize any line in linear perspective according to its relationship to the picture plane.

### Lines parallel to the picture plane

- If parallel with the picture plane, a set of parallel lines will retain its orientation and not converge to a vanishing point. Each line in the set, however, will diminish in size according to its distance from the spectator. In a similar manner, shapes parallel with the picture plane will retain their shapes but diminish in size according to its distance from the spectator.

### Lines perpendicular to the picture plane

- If perpendicular to the picture plane, a set of parallel lines will appear to converge on the horizon line at the center of vision.

### Lines oblique to picture plane

If oblique to the picture plane, a set of parallel lines will appear to converge toward a common vanishing point as it recedes.

- Horizontal oblique lines: If a horizontal set of parallel lines is oblique to the picture plane, its vanishing point will lie somewhere on the horizon line.
- Inclined oblique lines: If a set of parallel lines rises upward as it recedes, its vanishing point lies above the horizon line. If it slopes downward as it recedes, its vanishing point lies below the horizon line.

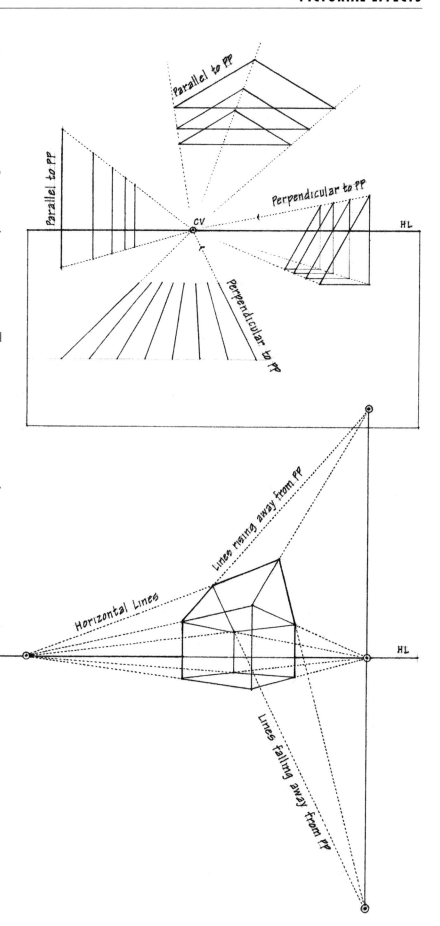

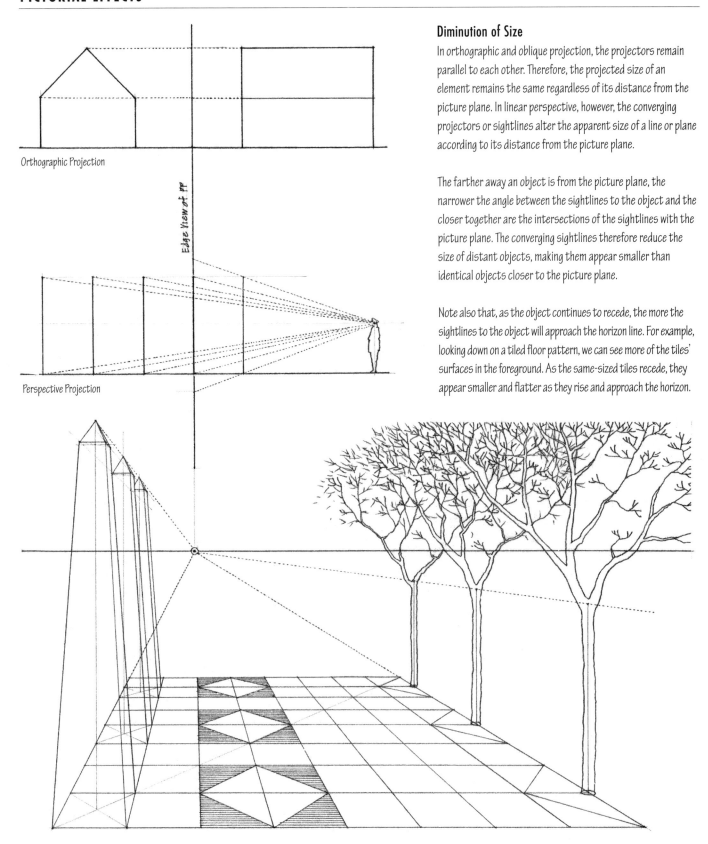

Orthographic Projection

Edge View of PP

Perspective Projection

### Diminution of Size

In orthographic and oblique projection, the projectors remain parallel to each other. Therefore, the projected size of an element remains the same regardless of its distance from the picture plane. In linear perspective, however, the converging projectors or sightlines alter the apparent size of a line or plane according to its distance from the picture plane.

The farther away an object is from the picture plane, the narrower the angle between the sightlines to the object and the closer together are the intersections of the sightlines with the picture plane. The converging sightlines therefore reduce the size of distant objects, making them appear smaller than identical objects closer to the picture plane.

Note also that, as the object continues to recede, the more the sightlines to the object will approach the horizon line. For example, looking down on a tiled floor pattern, we can see more of the tiles' surfaces in the foreground. As the same-sized tiles recede, they appear smaller and flatter as they rise and approach the horizon.

## Foreshortening

Foreshortening refers to the apparent change in form an object undergoes as it rotates away from the picture plane. It is usually seen as a contraction in size or length in the direction of depth so as to create an illusion of distance or extension in space.

Any facet of an object which is not parallel to the picture plane will appear compressed in size or length when projected. In perspective projection, as well as in orthographic and oblique projection, the amount of contraction depends on the angle between the facet of the object and the picture plane. The more a line or plane is rotated away from the picture plane, the less we will see of its length or depth.

In linear perspective, the apparent contraction in depth also depends on the angle between the sightlines to the object and the picture plane. The farther away an object is from the center of vision the greater the angle between the sightlines to the object and the farther apart are the intersections of the sightlines with the picture plane. In other words, as the object moves laterally, parallel to the picture plane, its apparent size will increase. Note that this is the opposite of what occurs as the object recedes away from the spectator. At some point, the size of the object will be exaggerated and its form distorted. We use the cone of vision to limit our view in linear perspective and control this distortion.

While convergence, diminution of size, and foreshortening affect the apparent form of lines and planes, they also influence the compression of spatial relationships in a perspective drawing.

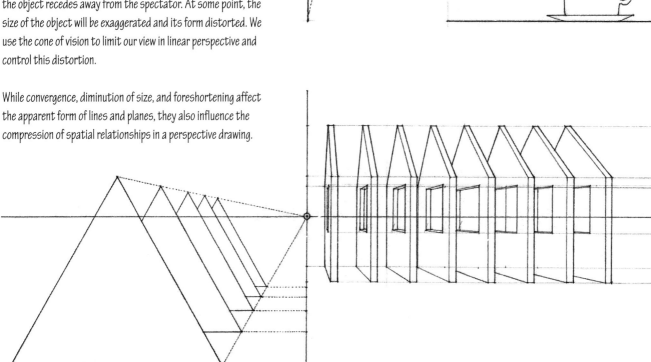

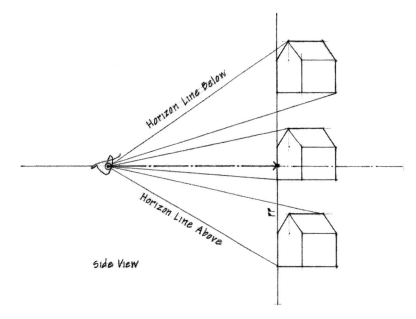

Side View

The spectator's point of view determines the pictorial effect of a perspective drawing. As this viewpoint changes—as the spectator moves up or down, to the left or right, forward or back—the extent and emphasis of what the spectator sees also change. In order to achieve the desired view in perspective, we should understand how to adjust the following variables.

## Height of Station Point

The height of the station point determines whether an object is seen from above, below, or within its own height. Assuming a level central axis of vision, as the station point—the eye of the spectator—moves up or down, the horizon line moves up or down with it. Any horizontal plane at the level of the spectator's eye appears as a line. We see the tops of horizontal surfaces which lie below the spectator's eye level and the undersides of horizontal planes which are above.

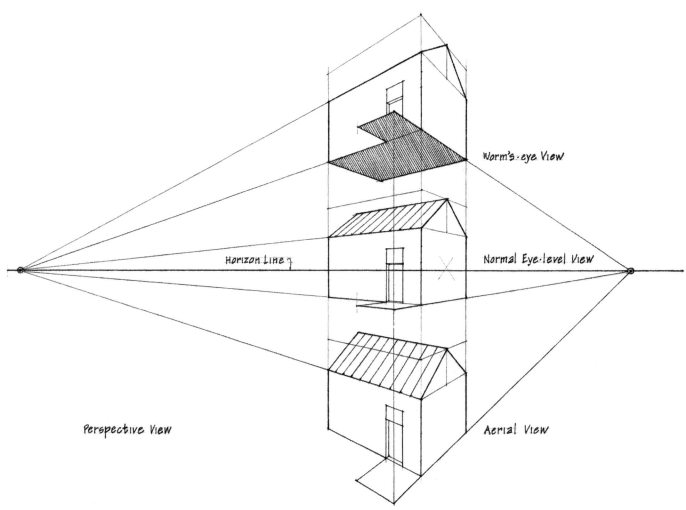

Perspective View

## Distance of Station Point to Object

The distance of the station point to the object influences the rate of foreshortening that occurs in the perspective drawing. As the spectator moves farther away from the object, the vanishing points move farther apart, horizontal lines flatten out, and perspective depth is compressed. As the spectator moves forward, the vanishing points move closer together, horizontal angles become more acute, and perspective depth is exaggerated. In theory, a perspective drawing presents a true picture of an object only when the eye of the viewer is located at the assumed station point of the perspective.

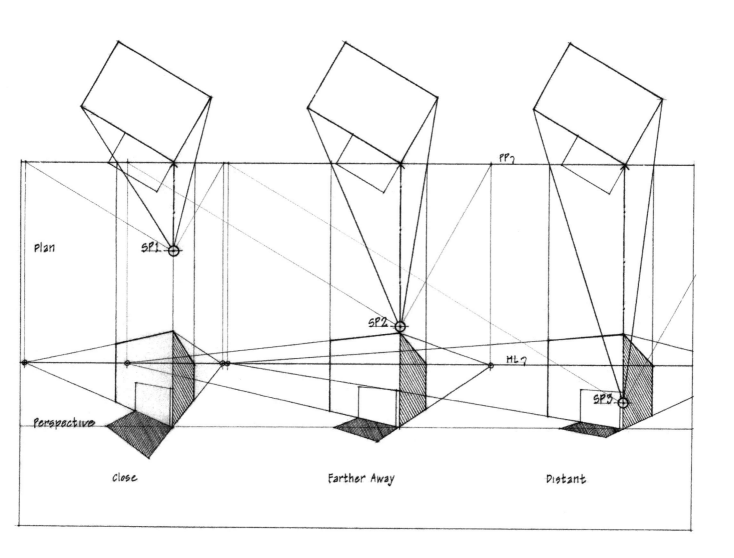

### Angle of View

The orientation of the central axis of vision relative to the object determines which faces of the object are visible and the degree to which they are foreshortened in perspective. The more oblique a plane is to the picture plane, the more it is foreshortened in perspective; the more frontal the plane is, the less it is foreshortened. When a plane becomes parallel to the picture plane, its true shape is revealed.

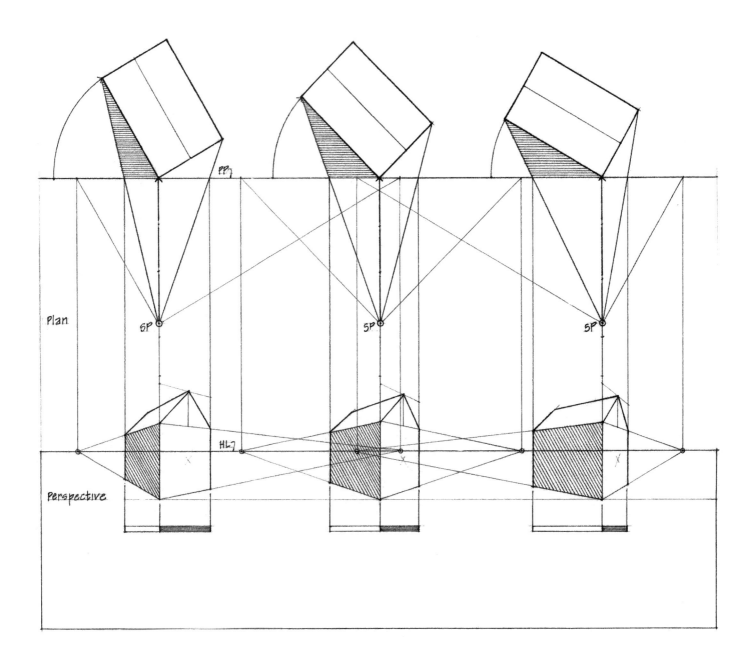

Plan

Perspective

## Location of Picture Plane

The location of the picture plane only affects the size of the perspective image. The closer the picture plane is to the station point, the smaller the perspective image; the farther away the picture plane is, the larger the image. Assuming all other variables remain constant, the perspective images are identical in all respects except size.

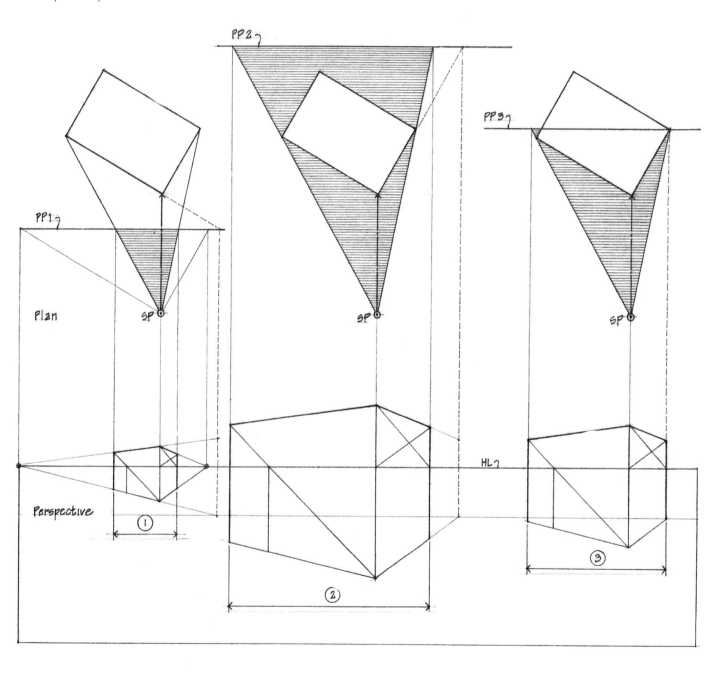

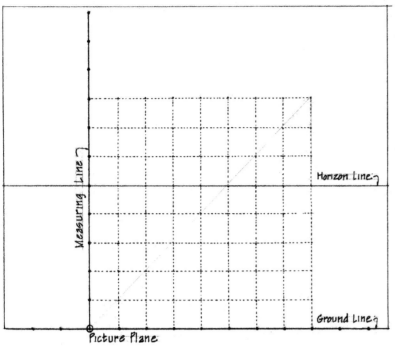

Only lines and planes coincident with the picture plane can be drawn to the same scale. The converging sightlines in linear perspective reduce the size of distant objects, making them appear smaller than identical objects closer to the picture plane. The converging sightlines also increase the apparent size of objects in front of the picture plane. Because of the combined effect of convergence and diminishing size, it is more difficult to make and draw measurements in linear perspective than in other drawing systems. But there are techniques we can use to determine the relative heights, widths, and depth of objects in the pictorial space of a perspective drawing.

## Measuring Height and Width

In linear perspective, any line in the picture plane displays its true direction and true length at the scale of the picture plane. We can therefore use any such line as a measuring line.

### Measuring Line (ML)

Any line that can be used to measure true lengths in a projection drawing. While a measuring line may have any orientation in the picture plane, it typically is vertical or horizontal and used to measure true heights or widths. The groundline is one example of a horizontal measuring line.

Once we establish a height or width, we can transfer the measurement horizontally or vertically, as long as we make the shift parallel to the picture plane. Since parallel lines by definition remain equidistant but appear to converge as they recede in perspective, we can also use a pair of parallel lines to transfer a vertical or horizontal measurement into the depth of a perspective. We can transfer measurements made in this manner vertically or horizontally as long as the shift occurs in a plane parallel to the picture plane.

## Measuring Depth

The measurement of perspective depth is more difficult and requires a certain degree of judgment based on direct observation and experience. The various methods of perspective construction establish depth in different ways. Once we establish an initial depth judgment, however, we can make succeeding depth judgments in proportion to the first.

For example, each time we halve the distance from the ground plane to the horizon line, we double the perspective depth. If we know how far away a point on the ground plane is from the spectator, we can subdivide on a proportional basis the height of the horizon line above the ground plane and establish the position of points further back in the depth of a perspective drawing.

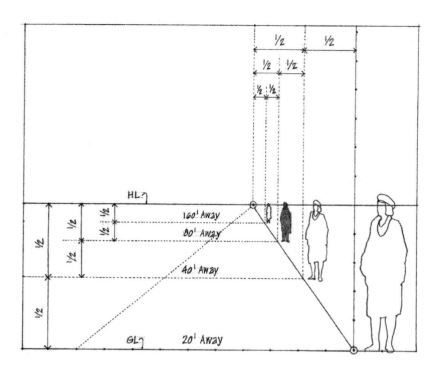

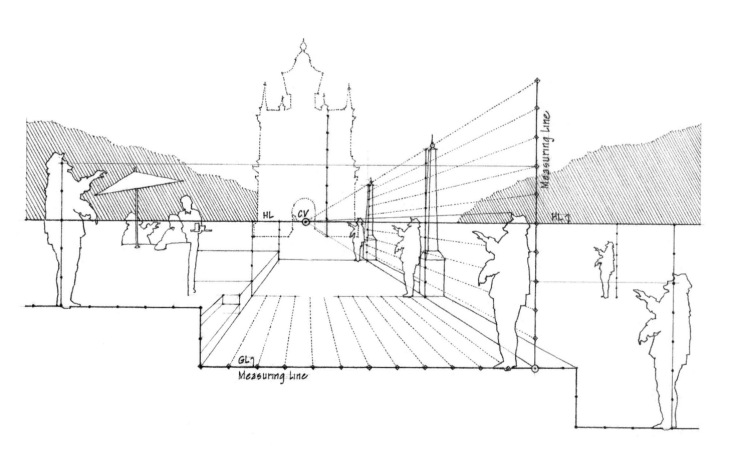

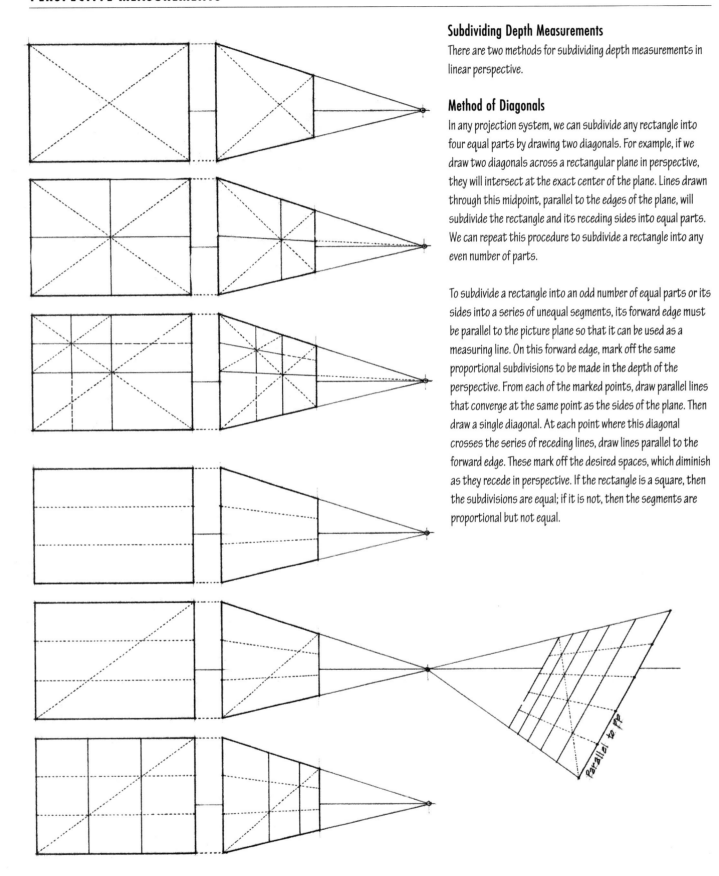

### Subdividing Depth Measurements

There are two methods for subdividing depth measurements in linear perspective.

### Method of Diagonals

In any projection system, we can subdivide any rectangle into four equal parts by drawing two diagonals. For example, if we draw two diagonals across a rectangular plane in perspective, they will intersect at the exact center of the plane. Lines drawn through this midpoint, parallel to the edges of the plane, will subdivide the rectangle and its receding sides into equal parts. We can repeat this procedure to subdivide a rectangle into any even number of parts.

To subdivide a rectangle into an odd number of equal parts or its sides into a series of unequal segments, its forward edge must be parallel to the picture plane so that it can be used as a measuring line. On this forward edge, mark off the same proportional subdivisions to be made in the depth of the perspective. From each of the marked points, draw parallel lines that converge at the same point as the sides of the plane. Then draw a single diagonal. At each point where this diagonal crosses the series of receding lines, draw lines parallel to the forward edge. These mark off the desired spaces, which diminish as they recede in perspective. If the rectangle is a square, then the subdivisions are equal; if it is not, then the segments are proportional but not equal.

Parallel to PP

## Method of Triangles

Since any line parallel to the picture plane can be subdivided proportionately to scale, we can use the line as a measuring line to subdivide any intersecting line into equal or unequal parts. First, define a triangle by connecting the ends of the measuring line and the adjacent line. Then, mark off the desired subdivisions on the measuring line to scale. From each of these points, draw lines parallel to the closing line of the triangle and converge at the same vanishing point. These lines subdivide the adjacent line into the same proportional segments.

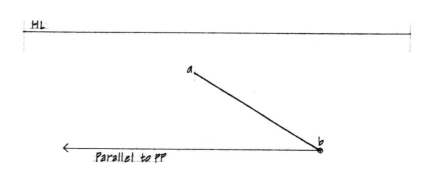

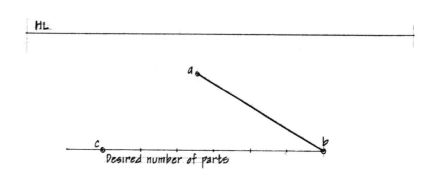

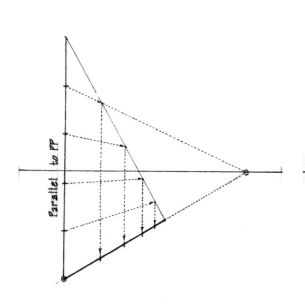

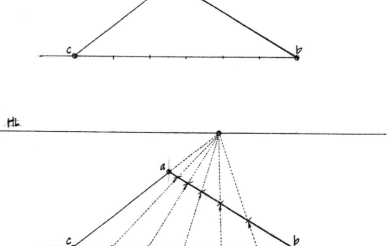

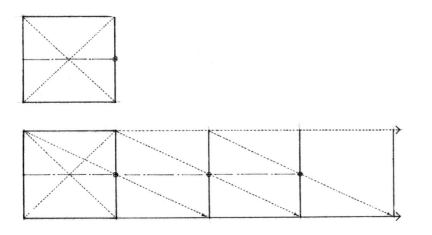

### Extending a Depth Measurement

If the forward edge of a rectangular plane is parallel to the picture plane, we can extend and duplicate its depth in perspective. First establish the midpoint of the rear edge opposite the forward edge of the rectangle. Then extend a diagonal from a forward corner through this midpoint to meet an extended side of the rectangle. From this point draw a line parallel to the forward edge. The distance from the first to the second edge is identical to the distance from the second to the third edge, but the equal spaces are foreshortened in perspective. This procedure can be repeated as often as necessary to produce the desired number of equal spaces in the depth of a perspective drawing.

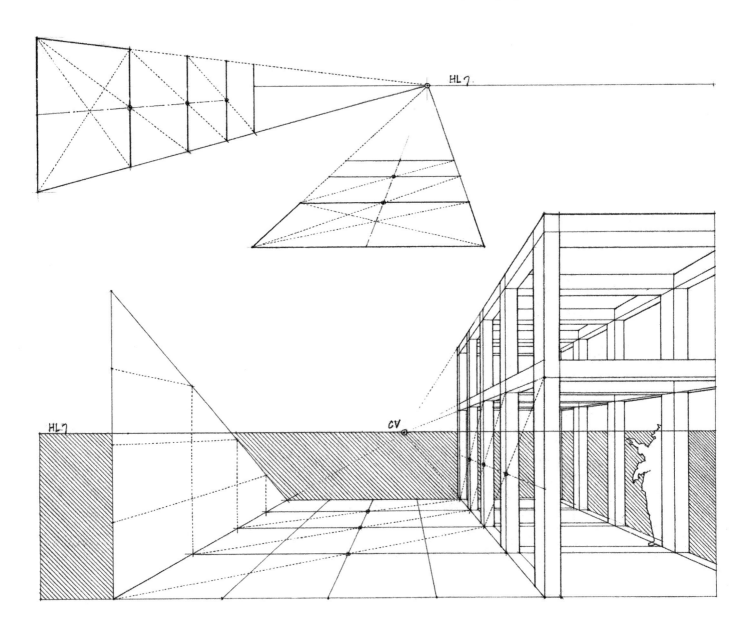

### Exercise 8.1

The perspective view shows four rectangular planes in space. Assume the forward edge of each plane is parallel to the picture plane. Make three copies of the perspective view. On the first copy, subdivide the depth of each of the planes into four equal parts.

### Exercise 8.2

On the second copy, subdivide the depth of each of the planes into five equal parts.

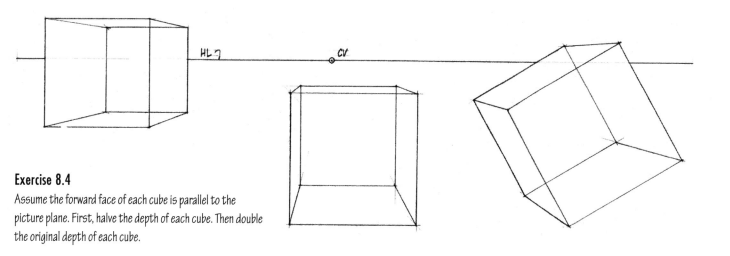

### Exercise 8.3

On the third copy, double the depth of each of the planes.

### Exercise 8.4

Assume the forward face of each cube is parallel to the picture plane. First, halve the depth of each cube. Then double the original depth of each cube.

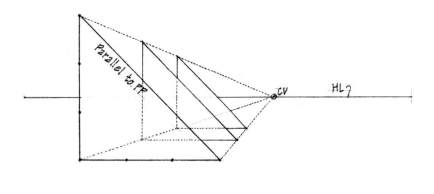

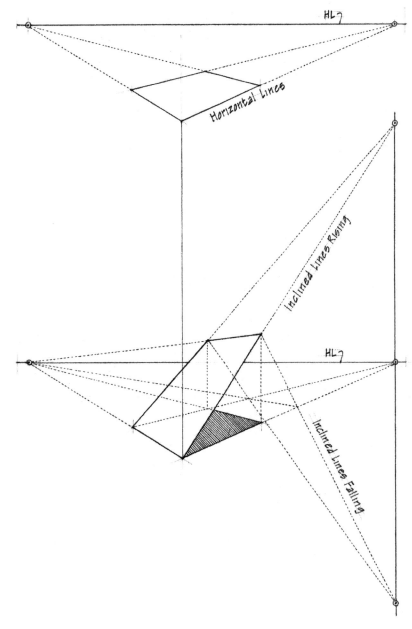

Once we are familiar with how lines parallel to the three principle axes of an object converge in linear perspective, we can use this rectilinear geometry as the basis for drawing perspective views of inclined lines and circles.

## Inclined Lines

Inclined lines parallel to the picture plane retain their orientation but diminish in size according to their distance from the spectator. If perpendicular or oblique to the picture plane, however, an inclined set of lines will appear to a vanishing point above or below the horizon line.

We can draw any inclined line in perspective by first finding the perspective projections of its end points and then connecting them. The easiest way to do this is to visualize the inclined line as being the hypotenuse of a right triangle. If we can draw the sides of the triangle in proper perspective, we can connect the end points to establish the inclined line.

If we must draw a number of inclined parallel lines, as in the case of a sloping roof, a ramp, or a stairway, it is useful to know where the inclined set appears to converge in perspective. An inclined set of parallel lines is not horizontal and therefore will not converge on the horizon line. If the set rises upward as it recedes, its vanishing point will be above the horizon line; if it falls as it recedes, it will be appear to converge below the horizon line.

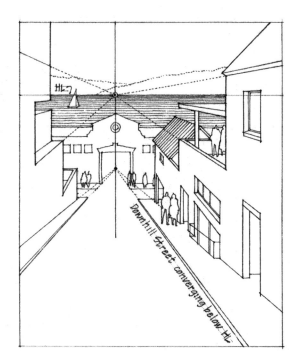

To determine the vanishing point for any inclined set of parallel lines:

- Locate a horizontal line which lies in the same vertical plane as an inclined line in the set.
- Determine the vanishing point for this horizontal line on the horizon line.
- Draw a vertical line through the vanishing point for this horizontal line. This is a vanishing trace for all sets of parallel lines in the vertical plane and all planes parallel to it.
- Extend one inclined line until it intersects this vanishing trace. This intersection is the vanishing point for the inclined line and all other lines parallel to it in the set.

### Vanishing Trace (VT)

A line along which all sets of parallel lines within a plane will appear to converge in linear perspective. The horizon line, for example, is the vanishing trace for all horizontal planes.

The steeper the inclined set of parallel lines, the farther up or down on the vanishing trace will be its vanishing point. If an inclined set of parallel lines rises upward and another set in the same vertical plane falls at the same but opposite angle to the horizontal, the distance of their respective vanishing points above and below the horizon line are equal.

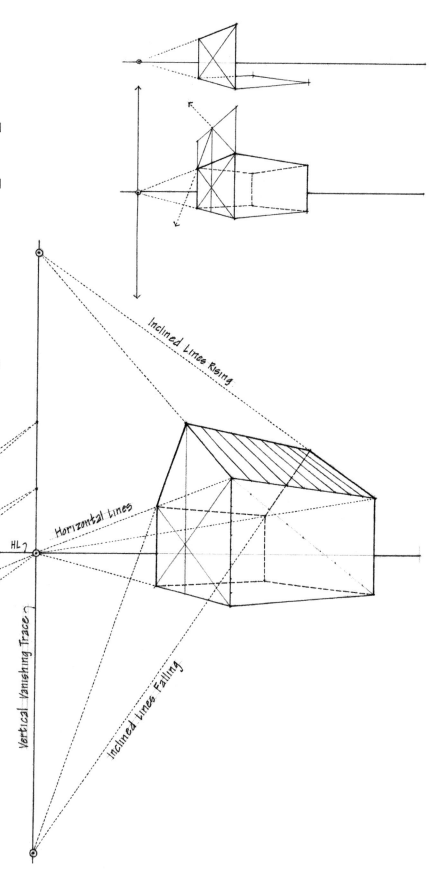

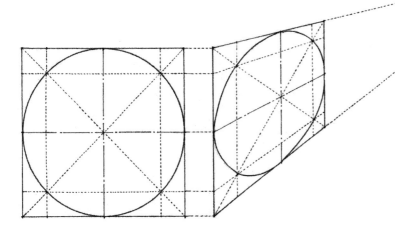

## Circles

The circle is the essential basis for drawing cylindrical objects, arches, and other circular forms. The perspective view of a circle remains a circle when it is parallel to the picture plane. The perspective view of a circle is a straight line when the projectors radiating from the station point are parallel to the plane of the circle. This occurs most frequently when the plane of the circle is horizontal and at the height of the station point, or when the plane of the circle is vertical and aligned with the central axis of vision.

In all other cases, circles appear as elliptical shapes in perspective. To draw a circle in perspective, first draw a perspective view of a square which circumscribes the circle. Construct the diagonals of the square and indicate where the circle crosses the diagonals with additional lines parallel to the sides of the square or tangent to the circumference of the circle. The larger the circle, the more subdivisions are necessary to ensure smoothness of the elliptical shape.

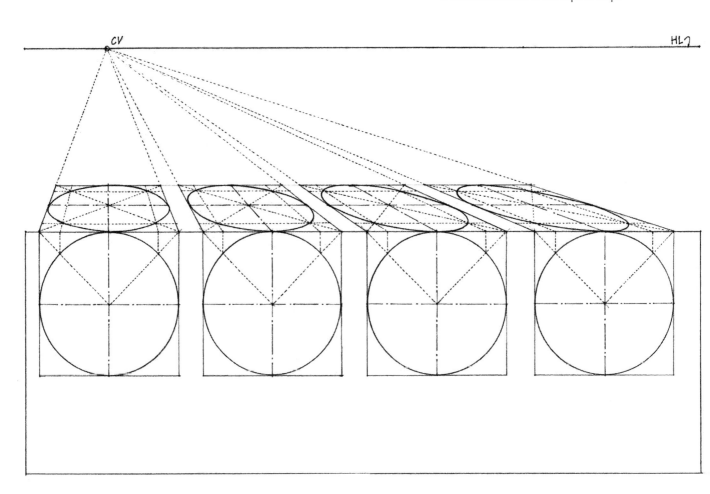

In a plan view of the perspective setup, the sightlines from the station point to tangent points on the circumference of the circle define the widest part of the circle in perspective. This width, which is the major axis of the ellipse representing the circle in perspective, is not coincident with the actual diameter of the circle. Just as the forward half of a square in perspective is greater than the rear half, so is the nearer half of a perspective circle fuller than the far half.

We tend to see things as we believe them to be. So while a circle in perspective appears to be an ellipse, we tend to see it as a circle and thus exaggerate the length of its minor axis. The minor axis should appear to be perpendicular to the plane of the circle. Checking the relationship between the major and minor axes of elliptical shapes helps to ensure accuracy of the foreshortening of circles in perspective.

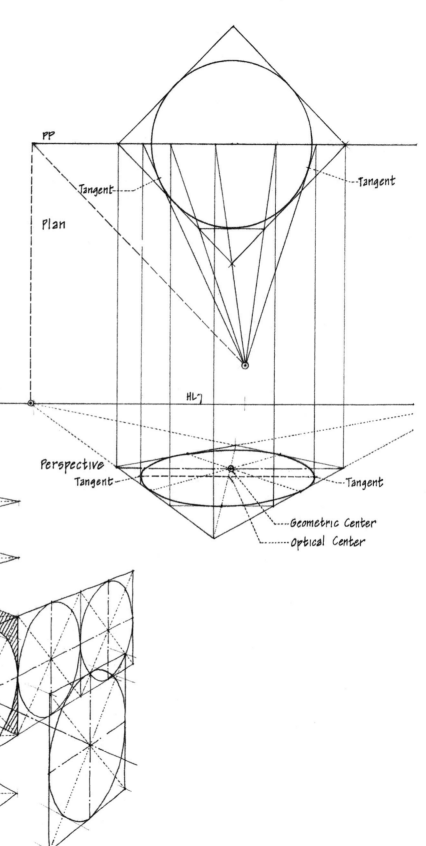

### Exercise 8.5

In the perspective view below, use the principles of perspective geometry to construct the following:

- a ramp rising from point A to point B
- a stairway climbing from point C to point D
- a shed roof ascending from point E to point F
- a cylindrical tower rising from point G to point H.

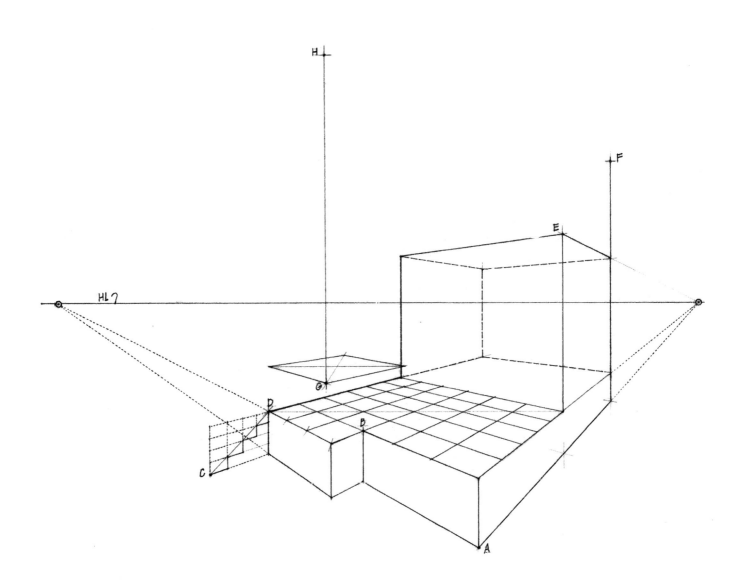

In any rectilinear object, as a cube, each of the three principal sets of parallel lines has its own vanishing point. Based on these three major sets of lines, there are three types of linear perspective: 1-, 2-, and 3-point perspectives. What distinguishes each type is simply the spectator's angle of view relative to the subject. The subject does not change, just our view of it and how the sets of parallel lines will appear to converge in linear perspective.

## One-point Perspective

If we view a cube with our central axis of vision perpendicular to one of its faces, its vertical lines are parallel with the picture plane and remain vertical. The horizontal lines parallel with the picture plane and perpendicular to the central axis of vision also remain horizontal. The lines parallel with the central axis of vision, however, will appear to converge at the center of vision. This is the one point referred to in one-point perspective.

## Two-point Perspective

If we shift our view so that the same cube is viewed obliquely but keep our central axis of vision horizontal, then the vertical lines will remain vertical. The two sets of horizontal lines, however, are now oblique to the picture plane and will appear to converge, one set to the left and the other to the right. These are the two points referred to in two-point perspective.

## Three-point Perspective

If we lift one end of the cube off the ground plane, or if we tilt our central axis of vision to look down or up at the cube, then all three sets of parallel lines will be oblique to the picture plane and appear to converge at three different vanishing points. These are the three points referred to in three-point perspective.

Note that each type of perspective does not imply that there are only one, two, or three vanishing points in a perspective. The actual number of vanishing points will depend on our point of view and how many sets of parallel lines there are in the subject being viewed. For example, if we look at a simple gable-roofed form, we can see that there are potentially five vanishing points since we have one set of vertical lines, two sets of horizontal lines, and two sets of inclined lines.

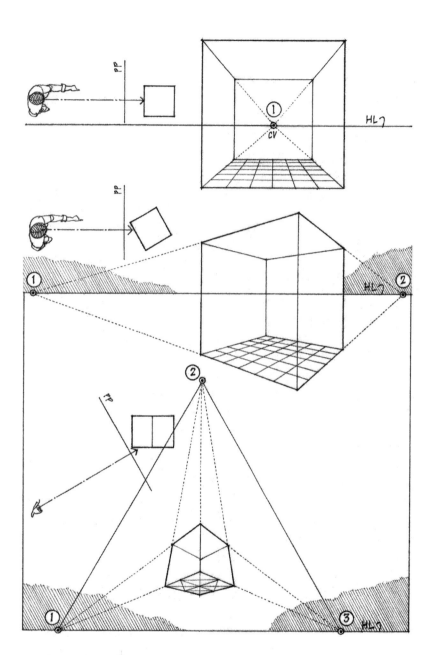

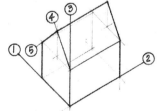

# ONE-POINT PERSPECTIVE

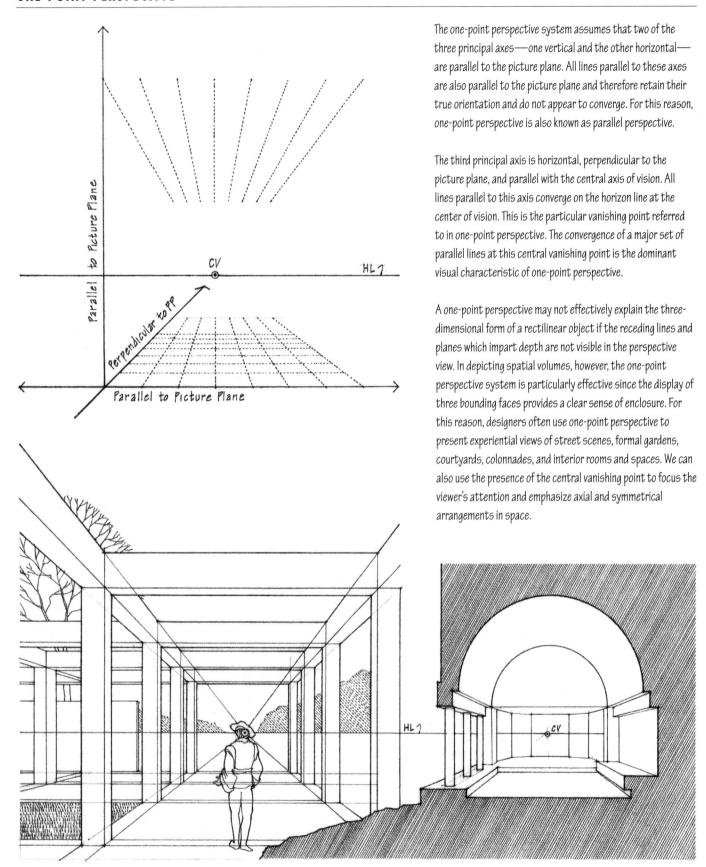

The one-point perspective system assumes that two of the three principal axes—one vertical and the other horizontal—are parallel to the picture plane. All lines parallel to these axes are also parallel to the picture plane and therefore retain their true orientation and do not appear to converge. For this reason, one-point perspective is also known as parallel perspective.

The third principal axis is horizontal, perpendicular to the picture plane, and parallel with the central axis of vision. All lines parallel to this axis converge on the horizon line at the center of vision. This is the particular vanishing point referred to in one-point perspective. The convergence of a major set of parallel lines at this central vanishing point is the dominant visual characteristic of one-point perspective.

A one-point perspective may not effectively explain the three-dimensional form of a rectilinear object if the receding lines and planes which impart depth are not visible in the perspective view. In depicting spatial volumes, however, the one-point perspective system is particularly effective since the display of three bounding faces provides a clear sense of enclosure. For this reason, designers often use one-point perspective to present experiential views of street scenes, formal gardens, courtyards, colonnades, and interior rooms and spaces. We can also use the presence of the central vanishing point to focus the viewer's attention and emphasize axial and symmetrical arrangements in space.

The diagonal point method for constructing a one-point perspective enables us to obtain accurate depth measurements directly within the perspective view without making projections from a plan view. It requires only an elevation or section view, and is therefore especially useful in constructing section perspectives.

The method uses the geometry of a 45° right triangle and the principles of convergence to make depth measurements in perspective. We know that the perpendicular sides of a 45° right triangle are equal in length. Therefore, if we can draw one side of a 45° right triangle to scale, the hypotenuse will mark off an equal length on the perpendicular side.

The technique involves establishing one side of the 45° right triangle in or parallel to the picture plane so that we can use it as a measuring line. Along this side, we measure a length equal to the desired perspective depth. From one endpoint of this length, we draw the perpendicular side that converges at the center of vision. From the other endpoint, we draw the hypotenuse that converges at the vanishing point for lines making a 45° angle with the picture plane. This diagonal marks off a perspective depth along the perpendicular side equal to the scaled length of the parallel side.

## Perspective Setup

We begin with an elevation or section view perpendicular to the spectator's central axis of vision and coincident with the picture plane. The scale of the elevation or section view establishes the size of the perspective drawing.

- Establish the ground line and the horizon line. The ground line is typically the ground line of the elevation or section. The height of the horizon line above the ground line is equal to the height of the eye level of the spectator above the ground plane.
- Establish the spectator's center of vision on the horizon line.

Refer to the discussion of perspective variables to review how varying the distance from the station point to the subject, raising or lowering the horizon line, and locating the picture plane all affect the pictorial nature of a perspective view.

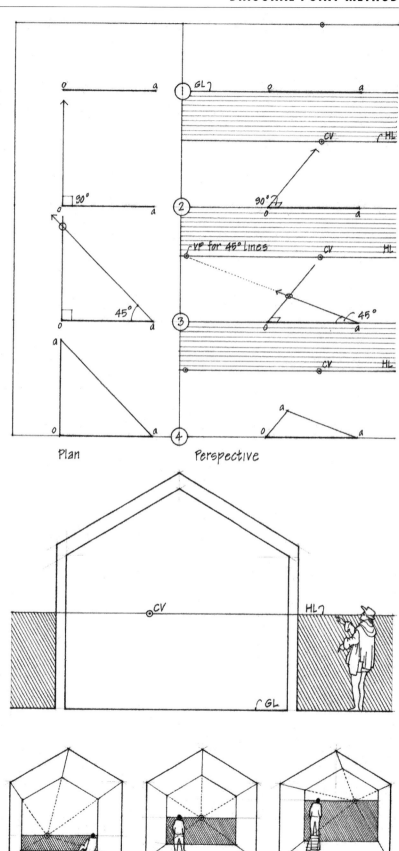

Plan          Perspective

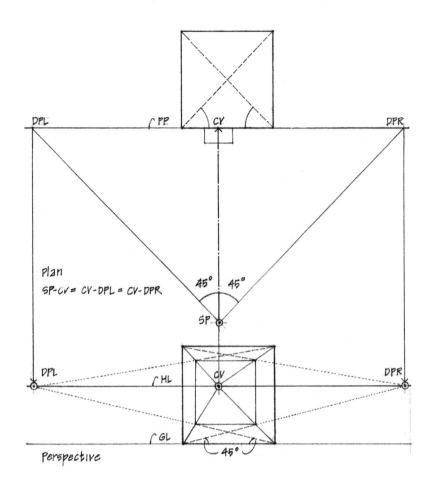

Plan
SP-CV = CV-DPL = CV-DPR

45° 45°

Perspective

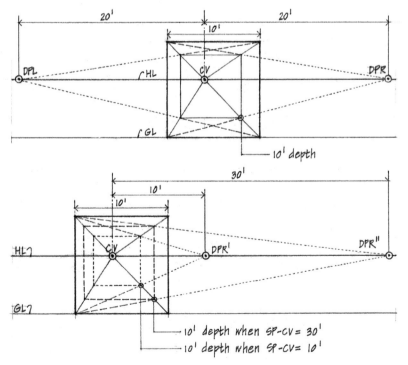

10' depth

10' depth when SP-CV = 30'
10' depth when SP-CV = 10'

## Establishing Diagonal Points

To utilize the diagonal point method, we must locate the vanishing point for a set of parallel lines that make a 45° angle with the picture plane. The vanishing point for any set of parallel lines is that point where a sightline from the station point, drawn parallel to the set, intersects the picture plane. Therefore, if we draw a 45° line from the station point in a plan view of the perspective setup, it will intersect the picture plane at the vanishing point for all 45° diagonals. We call this vanishing point a diagonal point or distance point.

There is one diagonal point for horizontal lines receding to the left at a 45° angle to the picture plane, and another for horizontal lines receding to the right at a 45° angle to the picture plane. Both diagonal points lie on the horizon line, equidistant from the center of vision. From the geometry of the 45° right triangle, we also know that the distance from each diagonal point to the center of vision is equal to the distance from the spectator's station point to the picture plane.

If we understand this geometric relationship, we need not set up a plan view of the perspective setup directly above the perspective view. We can simply locate either or both diagonal points directly in the perspective view, on the horizon line, at a distance from the center of vision equal to the distance of the spectator from the picture plane. For a 60° cone of vision, the distance from the center of vision to either diagonal point should be equal to or greater than the width of the elevation or section view.

For example, if the spectator is standing 20 feet away from the picture plane, the diagonal point on the horizon line will be 20 feet away to the left or right of the center of vision. This distance, measured at the same scale as the picture plane, establishes the vanishing point for all 45° lines receding to the left or right.

If we move the diagonal points toward the center of vision, this is equivalent to the spectator moving closer to the picture plane and seeing more of the receding faces of the space. If we shift the diagonal points farther away from the center of vision, the spectator also moves farther away from the picture plane and the receding faces of the space become more foreshortened.

## Measuring Depth

The basic steps in using a diagonal point to make depth measurements are:

1. Draw lines from the center of vision through each corner of the elevation or section view. These represent the receding horizontal edges of the subject, which are parallel to the central axis of vision and which converge at the center of vision.

2. Establish a horizontal measuring line in the picture plane. This measuring line is usually the ground line, but if the ground line is very close to the horizon line, locate the measuring line below the ground line or well above the horizon line. Doing this results in wider angles of intersection and ensures greater accuracy in triangulating depth measurements.

3. Establish a baseline perpendicular to the picture plane and converging at the center of vision. This baseline, along which we measure perspective depths, is usually the base or top of a major side wall, but it can be any line perpendicular to the picture plane and converging at the center of vision.

4. Along the horizontal measuring line, measure distances at the scale of the picture plane equal to the required perspective depths. Using a left diagonal point, measure to the right of the zero point for depths behind the picture plane and measure to the left of the zero point for points in front of the picture plane.

5. Transfer each of the measurements to the perpendicular baseline with lines that converge at the diagonal point. These diagonals intersect the perpendicular baseline at perspective depths equal to the scaled depths along the measuring line.

6. Once the major perspective depths are determined in the perspective view, we can transfer them horizontally and vertically until they intersect lines and planes receding toward the center of vision.

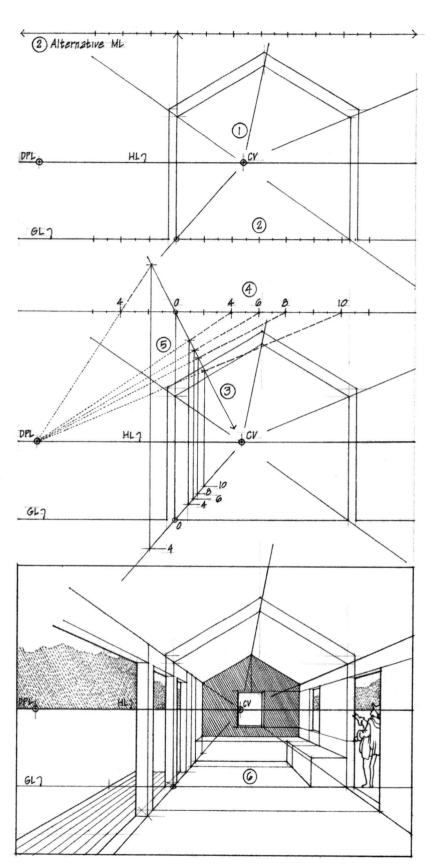

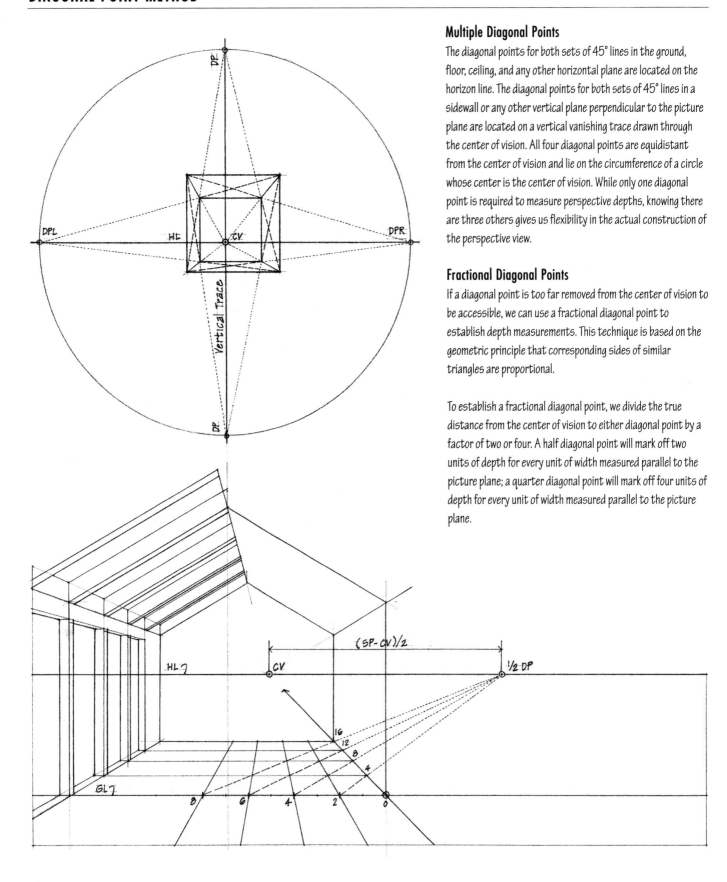

## Multiple Diagonal Points

The diagonal points for both sets of 45° lines in the ground, floor, ceiling, and any other horizontal plane are located on the horizon line. The diagonal points for both sets of 45° lines in a sidewall or any other vertical plane perpendicular to the picture plane are located on a vertical vanishing trace drawn through the center of vision. All four diagonal points are equidistant from the center of vision and lie on the circumference of a circle whose center is the center of vision. While only one diagonal point is required to measure perspective depths, knowing there are three others gives us flexibility in the actual construction of the perspective view.

## Fractional Diagonal Points

If a diagonal point is too far removed from the center of vision to be accessible, we can use a fractional diagonal point to establish depth measurements. This technique is based on the geometric principle that corresponding sides of similar triangles are proportional.

To establish a fractional diagonal point, we divide the true distance from the center of vision to either diagonal point by a factor of two or four. A half diagonal point will mark off two units of depth for every unit of width measured parallel to the picture plane; a quarter diagonal point will mark off four units of depth for every unit of width measured parallel to the picture plane.

## Exercise 8.6

Assume the spectator is standing 15 feet away from the front face of a 10-foot cubic volume and that this face is coincident with the picture plane. Locate the following points in linear perspective:

- A point 6 feet behind the picture plane along line A. Transfer this point vertically to line B.
- A point 4 feet in front of the picture plane along line C.
- A point 3 feet above the ground plane, directly above line D, and 5 feet behind the picture plane.

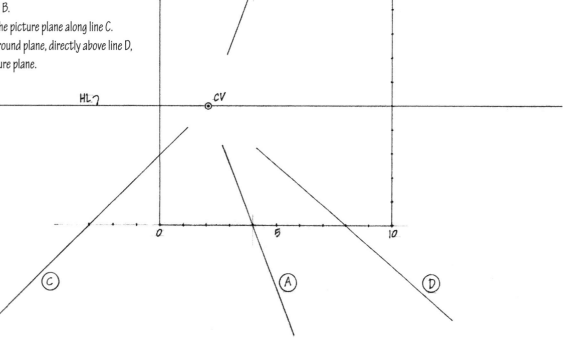

## Exercise 8.7

Assume the spectator is standing 15 feet away from the picture plane and looking toward a wall that is 16 feet wide, 12 feet high, and 30 feet away. Construct a one-point perspective of the space. Within this perspective view, construct:

- A 3' x 7' doorway on the rear wall and one of the side walls, both of which are 8 inches thick.
- A 4' x 4' window with a 3' sill height on the other side wall, 6 feet behind the picture plane. On the same wall, construct an identical window 2 feet in front of the picture plane.
- A 6' x 6' x 1' platform somewhere on the floor.
- A 6' x 6' skylight cut through the 1-foot thick roof structure, directly above the platform.

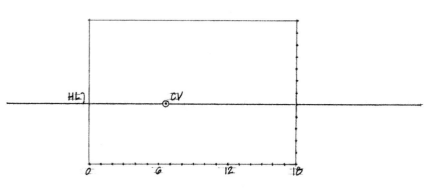

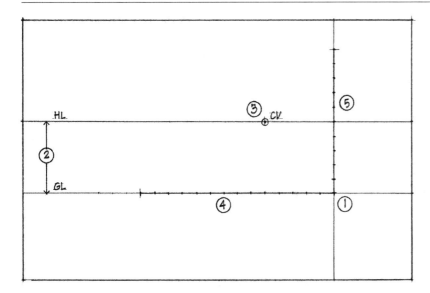

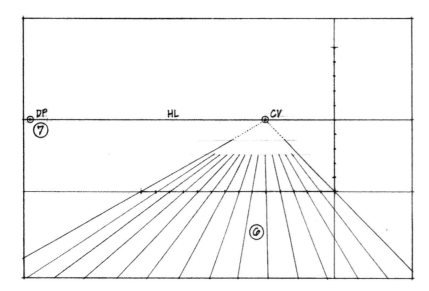

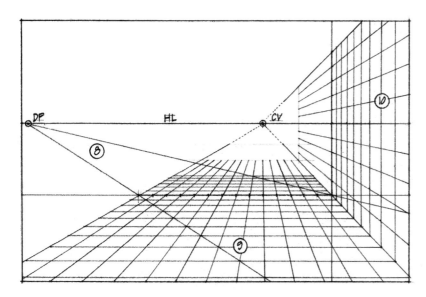

A perspective grid is a perspective view of a three-dimensional coordinate system. The three-dimensional network of uniformly spaced points and lines enables us to correctly establish the form and dimensions of an interior or exterior space as well as regulate the position and size of objects within the space. Several types, varying in scale and point of view, are commercially available. We can also use the following procedure to construct a one-point perspective grid:

1. Decide on a scale for the picture plane, taking into consideration both the dimensions of the space and the desired size of the perspective drawing.
2. At the scale of the picture plane, establish the ground line and the horizon line at the eye level of the spectator.
3. Establish the center of vision close to the middle of the horizon line.
4. Along the ground line, lay out to scale equal increments of measurement. The unit of measurement is typically one foot; we can use smaller or larger increments depending on the scale of the drawing and the amount of detail desired in the perspective view.
5. Do the same along a vertical measuring line drawn through the left or right endpoint of the ground line.
6. Through each of the measured points on the ground line, draw lines on the ground plane from the center of vision forward into the perspective.
7. Establish the diagonal point to the left or right of the center of vision at a distance equal to the distance of the station point to the picture plane. If this is unknown, the distance from the center of vision to the diagonal point should be equal to or greater than the width of the space.
8. From the diagonal point, draw diagonals through both endpoints of the measured ground line.
9. Where these diagonals cross each of the lines converging at the center of vision, draw a horizontal line. The result is a perspective grid of squares on the ground or floor plane.
10. If desired, we can transfer these depth measurements and establish a similar grid along one or both receding sidewalls, as well as on a ceiling or overhead plane.

### Exercise 8.8

Construct a one-point perspective grid on an 8½" x 11" sheet of quality tracing paper or vellum. Assume a scale of ½" = 1'-0" for the picture plane and a horizon line 5 or 6 feet above the ground line. When completed, the perspective grid may be photocopied and enlarged or reduced to any desired scale. By laying tracing paper over the grid, we can utilize the perspective structure to more easily sketch freehand perspective views of both exterior and interior spaces.

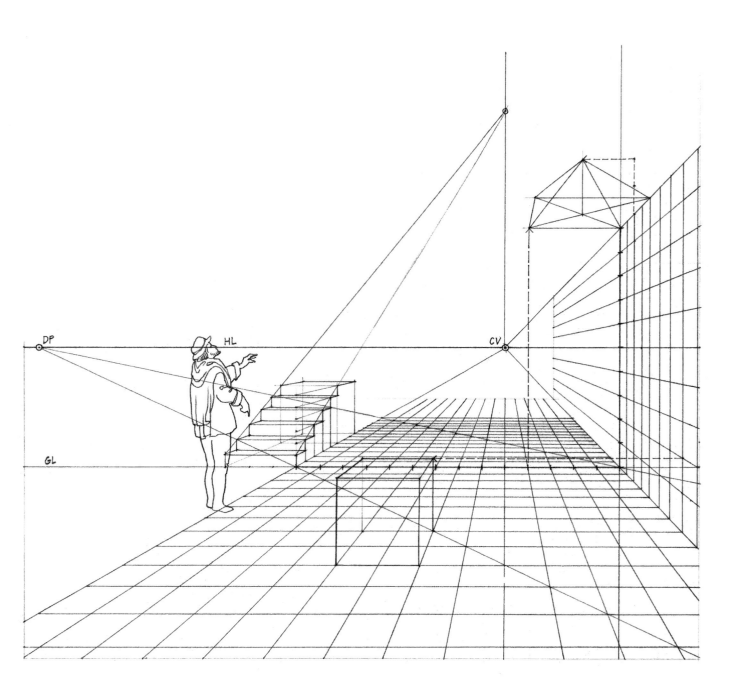

# SECTION PERSPECTIVES

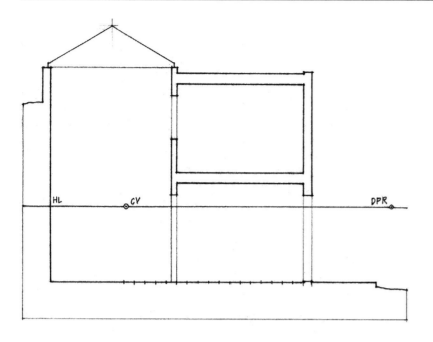

The section perspective combines the scaled attributes of a section drawing and the pictorial depth of a perspective drawing. Therefore, it is able to illustrate both the constructional aspects of a design as well as the quality of the spaces formed by the structure. We begin a section perspective with a building section drawn at a convenient scale. Since the section cut is assumed to be coincident with the picture plane of the perspective, it serves as a ready reference for making vertical and horizontal measurements for the perspective drawing.

- Establish the horizon line and select a center of vision. The height of the horizon line and position of the center of vision affect the emphasis of the resulting view and what we see up, down, and to the left and right.
- On the horizon line, establish the left and right vanishing points for diagonal or 45° lines. As a rule of thumb, the distance from the center of vision to the diagonal points should be at least as great as the width or height of the building section, whichever is larger.
- Use the diagonal point method to construct the one-point perspective.

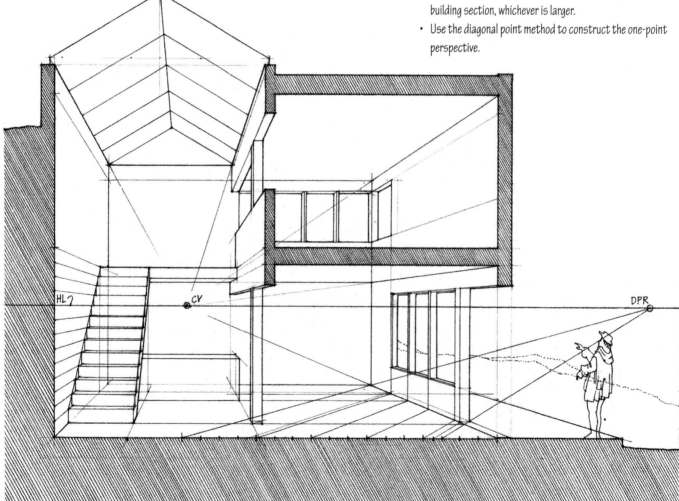

## Exercise 8.9

The schematic building section below is drawn at a scale of ¼" = 1'-0". Given the horizon line, center of vision, and left diagonal point indicated, convert the section into a section perspective.

- Assume the rear wall of the space is 24 feet behind the picture plane which is coincident with the vertical plane of the section cut. Within this space, develop a grid of 3-foot squares on the floor plane.
- Draw three human figures at different depths within the space.
- Shown are three steps rising to a platform. Using these steps as a pattern, develop a stairway along the righthand wall from the platform to a mezzanine which opens out onto the upper level of the site.
- On the lefthand wall, develop a window wall with french doors that open out onto the covered porch. Space the mullions 3 feet on center.
- The roof structure consists of exposed 3 x 10 rafters spaced 3 feet on center. Make an assumption about the orientation of the building and cut a skylight into the roof plane to allow daylight to enter the space.

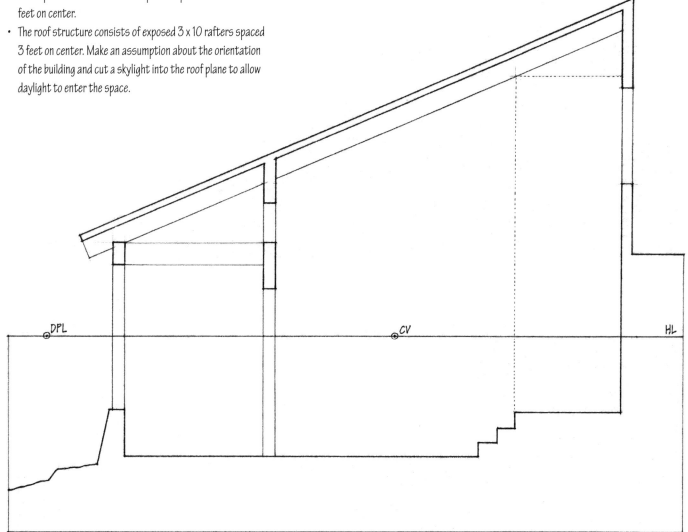

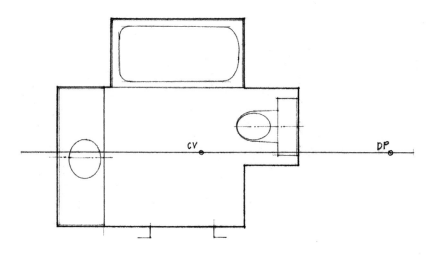

In order to transform a two-dimensional floor plan into a three-dimensional view, we can draw a plan perspective—a one-point perspective view of an interior room or exterior space as seen from above.

We assume the spectator's central axis of vision is vertical and the picture plane is coincident with a horizontal plane passing through the tops of the walls of the space.

- Set the center of vision somewhere in the middle of the floor plan.
- Establish the horizon line through the center of vision and parallel with one of the walls.
- Use the diagonal point method to construct the one-point perspective. The distance from the spectator to the picture plane should be at least as great as the overall width of the plan.

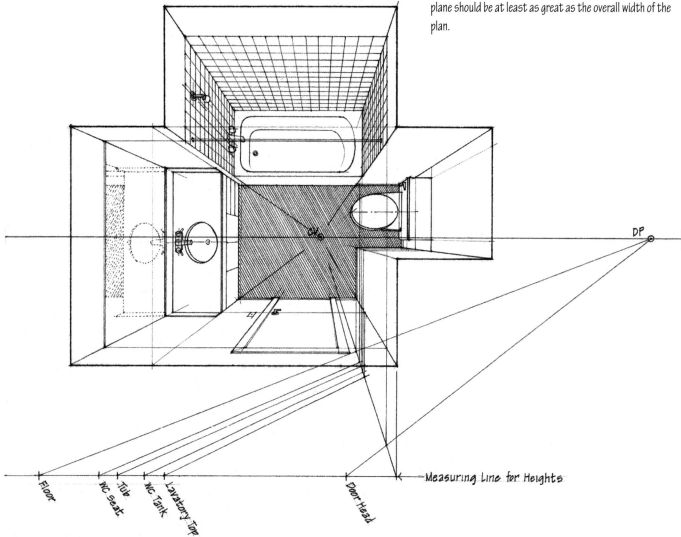

The two-point perspective system assumes that the spectator's central axis of vision is horizontal and the picture plane is vertical. The principal vertical axis is parallel to the picture plane and all lines parallel to it remain vertical and parallel in the perspective drawing. The two principal axes which are horizontal, however, are oblique to the picture plane. All lines parallel to these axes therefore appear to converge to two vanishing points on the horizon line, one set to the left and the other to the right. These are the two points referred to in two-point perspective.

The pictorial effect of a two-point perspective varies with the spectator's angle of view. The orientation of the two horizontal axes to the picture plane determines how much we will see of the two major sets of vertical planes and the degree to which they are foreshortened in perspective. The more oblique a plane is to the picture plane, the more it is foreshortened in perspective; the more frontal the plane is, the less it is foreshortened.

Two-point perspective is probably the most widely used of the three types of linear perspective. Unlike one-point perspectives, two-point perspectives tend to be neither symmetrical nor static. A two-point perspective is particular effective in illustrating the three-dimensional form of objects in space ranging in scale from a chair to the mass of a building.

In depicting a spatial volume, as the interior of a room or an exterior courtyard or street, a two-point perspective is most effective when the angle of view approaches that of a one-point perspective. Any perspective view that displays three bounding faces of a spatial volume provides a clear sense of enclosure. The spectator then becomes an integral part of the space rather than a mere observer looking in from the outside.

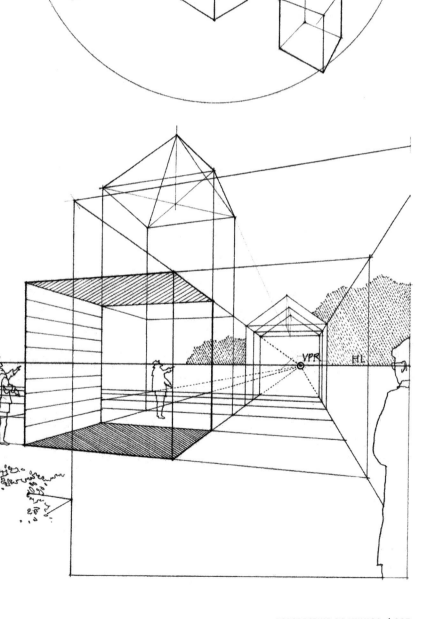

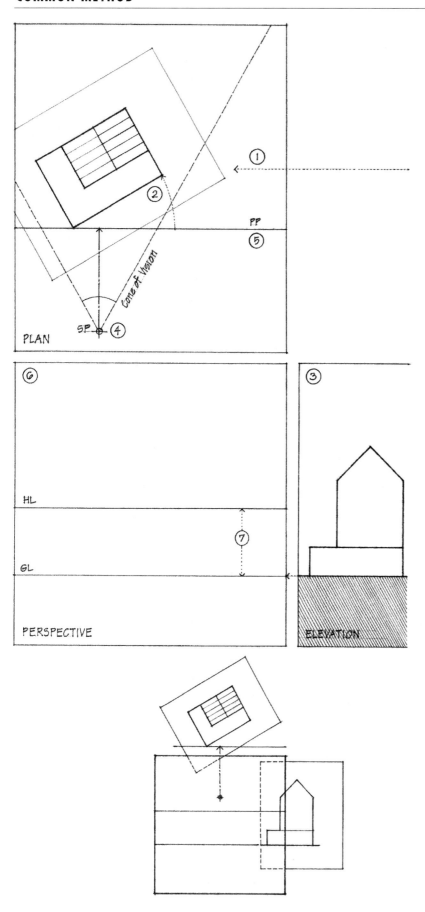

PLAN

PP

Cone of Vision

SP

HL

GL

PERSPECTIVE

ELEVATION

The common method of constructing a two-point perspective is also known as the office method. It requires the use of two orthographic projections: a plan view and an elevation view. The scale of the plan and elevation views establishes the scale of the picture plane in the perspective view.

### Perspective Setup

1. Place the plan view directly above the space where the perspective view is to be constructed.
2. Orient the plan to the desired angle with the picture plane. This angle is typically 30°, 45°, or 60° because of the triangles used in drafting. In theory, however, the exact angle can vary according to how much emphasis we wish to place on each of the major sets of vertical planes.
3. Locate the elevation view off to the side of the area where the perspective view is to be constructed.
4. Establish the station point in the plan view. Check to ensure the major part of the subject falls within a 60° cone of vision and that the central axis of vision focuses on the center of interest. Avoid aligning major vertical planes in the subject with any of the sightlines radiating from the station point.
5. Establish the picture plane in the plan view, perpendicular to the central axis of vision. The picture plane is typically located to pass through a significant vertical edge of the subject so that the edge can be used as a measuring line in the perspective view. Remember that the position of the picture plane affects the size of the perspective image.
6. Tape the sheet of tracing paper on which you will construct the perspective drawing.
7. In the perspective view, establish the ground line and the horizon line. The ground line is typically the ground line of the elevation or section. The height of the horizon line above the ground line is equal to the height of the spectator's eye level above the ground plane.

While the plan, elevation, and perspective views are shown some distance apart for clarity, they can be arranged in a more compact manner to fit a smaller workspace. To do this, move the plan and elevation closer to or under the sheet used for the perspective view, being careful to maintain the proper horizontal and vertical relationships between the three views.

Refer to the discussion of perspective variables to review how varying the distance from the station point to the subject, raising or lowering the horizon line, and locating the picture plane all affect the pictorial nature of a perspective view.

## Vanishing Points

The vanishing point for any set of parallel lines is that point where a sightline from the station point, drawn parallel to the set, intersects the picture plane.

1. Therefore, in the plan view of the perspective setup, draw sightlines from the station point parallel to the plan direction of each major set of vertical planes until they intersect the picture plane. Note that we see vertical planes as lines in the plan view.

2. From these intersections, project vertical construction lines down to meet the horizon line in the perspective view. These points are the vanishing points for horizontal lines in each major set of vertical planes.

3. For rectilinear objects, there are two major sets of vertical planes and therefore two vanishing points on the horizon line for the horizontal lines in these planes. These are the two major vanishing points in two-point perspective.

## Measuring Lines

Any line in the picture plane displays its true length at the scale of the picture plane. Therefore, we can use any such line as a measuring line. While a measuring line may have any orientation in the picture plane, it is usually vertical or horizontal and used to measure true heights and widths.

4. A vertical measuring line occurs wherever a major vertical plane meets or intersects the picture plane.

5. If a major vertical plane lies entirely behind the picture plane, extend it forward to meet the picture plane.

6. Project the position of vertical measuring lines from the plan view down to the perspective view.

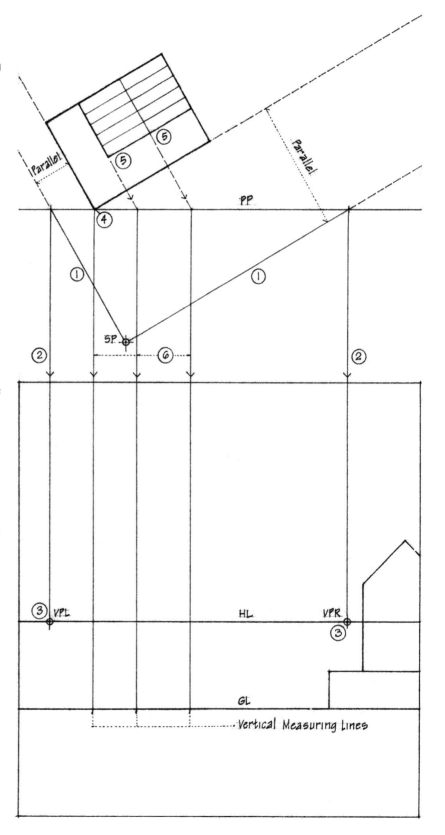

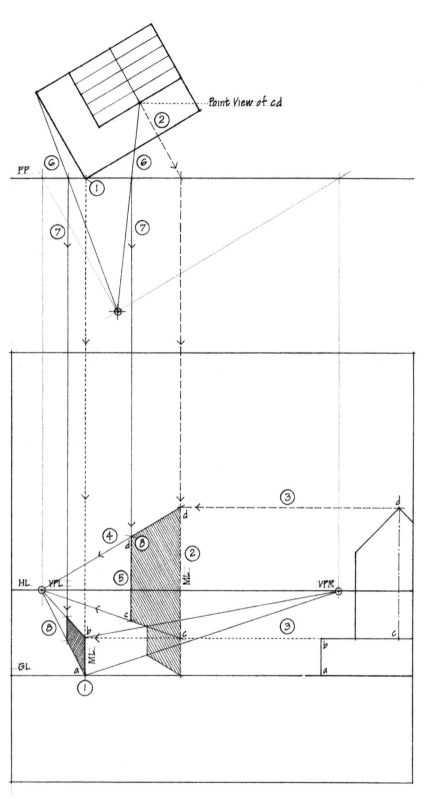

Point View of cd

## Measuring Heights

1. The heights of vertical lines or edges in the picture plane remain true to scale. These lines therefore serve as measuring lines.

2. To determine the perspective height of a vertical line or edge located in front of or behind the picture plane, first establish the measuring line for the vertical plane in which the line occurs.

3. Transfer the true height from the elevation view horizontally to the vertical measuring line in the perspective view.

4. Project the true height forward or back into the perspective along the vertical plane, using a line that converges at the vanishing point for horizontal lines in that plane. As a general rule, transfer the true height on a measuring line into a perspective by following horizontal paths toward either of the two major vanishing points on the horizon line.

5. Since this line and the base of the vertical plane are both horizontal and parallel, the vertical distance between them remains constant as they recede in perspective.

6. To determine the perspective location of the vertical line or edge, draw a sightline from the station point to the point view of the line in plan until it intersects the picture plane. For a vertical line located in front of the picture plane, extend the sightline until it meets the picture plane.

7. From where the sightline intersects the picture plane in plan, drop a vertical construction line to intersect the vertical plane in perspective.

8. The line of intersection represents the perspective height and location of the vertical line or edge.

If we know where the base of a vertical line meets the ground plane in perspective, we can determine its perspective height in two additional ways:

1. From the base of a vertical measuring line, draw a line through the perspective location of the line whose height we wish to determine, and extend it until it meets the horizon line.
2. From this point on the horizon line, draw another line back to the desired height on the vertical measuring line.
3. Since both construction lines converge on the horizon line, they are horizontal and parallel and mark off equal lengths on both the vertical measuring line and the vertical line in the depth of the perspective.

A second method for determining the perspective height of a vertical line involves the height of the horizon line above the ground plane. If this height is known, we can use it as a vertical scale to measure vertical lines anywhere in the depth of a perspective.

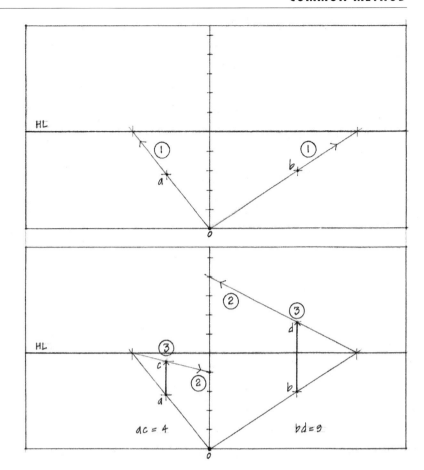

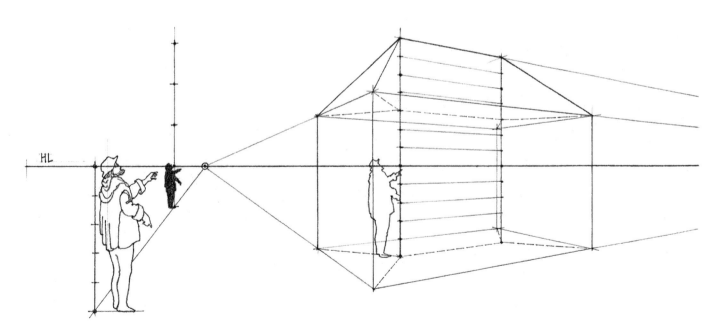

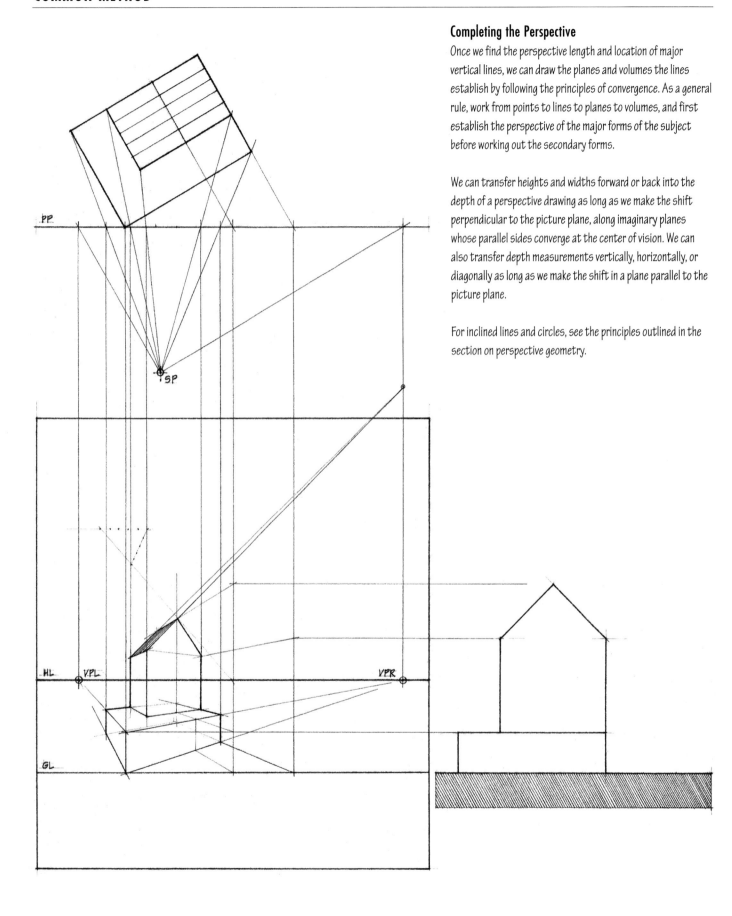

## Completing the Perspective

Once we find the perspective length and location of major vertical lines, we can draw the planes and volumes the lines establish by following the principles of convergence. As a general rule, work from points to lines to planes to volumes, and first establish the perspective of the major forms of the subject before working out the secondary forms.

We can transfer heights and widths forward or back into the depth of a perspective drawing as long as we make the shift perpendicular to the picture plane, along imaginary planes whose parallel sides converge at the center of vision. We can also transfer depth measurements vertically, horizontally, or diagonally as long as we make the shift in a plane parallel to the picture plane.

For inclined lines and circles, see the principles outlined in the section on perspective geometry.

## Exercise 8.10

Construct a two-point perspective of the structure shown in the perspective setup.

## Exercise 8.11

How far back would you have to shift the picture plane in the plan view to double the perspective image?

## Exercise 8.12

Double the height of the horizon line and construct another two-point perspective of the structure.

## Exercise 8.13

Double the distance of the station point from the structure and construct another two-point perspective of the structure.

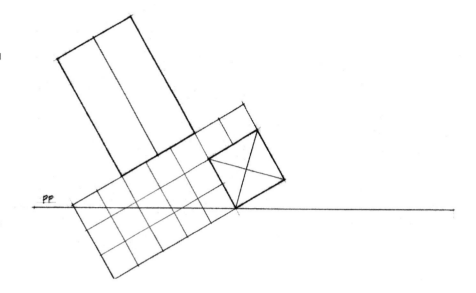

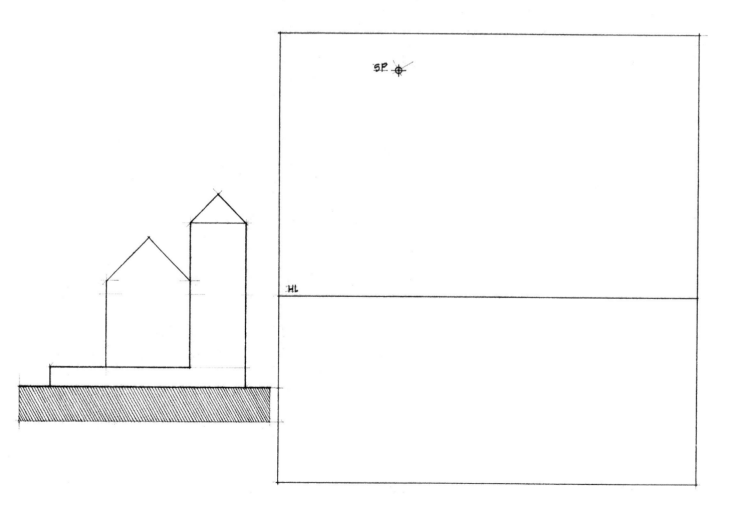

The perspective plan method allows an entire perspective drawing to be laid out from measurements made entirely in the picture plane of the perspective view. It does not require the direct use of an orthographic plan or elevation.

## Plan Diagram

Follow the same procedure as outlined in the common method to construct a plan diagram of the perspective setup. We use this plan diagram to establish the position of the picture plane, station point, vanishing points for major sets of horizontal lines, and locations of vertical measuring lines.

## Measuring Points

We also use the plan diagram to locate measuring points. A measuring point is a vanishing point for a set of parallel lines used to transfer true dimensions along a measuring line in the picture plane to a line in perspective. The diagonal point in one-point perspective is one example of such a measuring point.

In two-point perspective, there are two measuring points for transferring dimensions along a horizontal measuring line in the picture plane to the perspective of a horizontal line in the subject. To determine the location of these measuring points in the plan diagram:

1. With the left vanishing point as the center, swing an arc from the station point to the line of the picture plane. This is the right measuring point.
2. With the right vanishing point as the center, swing an arc from the station point to the line of the picture plane to locate the left measuring point.

Note that chord SP-MPL is parallel to chord AB. MPL is therefore the vanishing point for AB and all other lines parallel to it. We use this set of parallel lines to transfer scale dimensions along the ground line in the picture plane to the perspective of baseline BC in the subject.

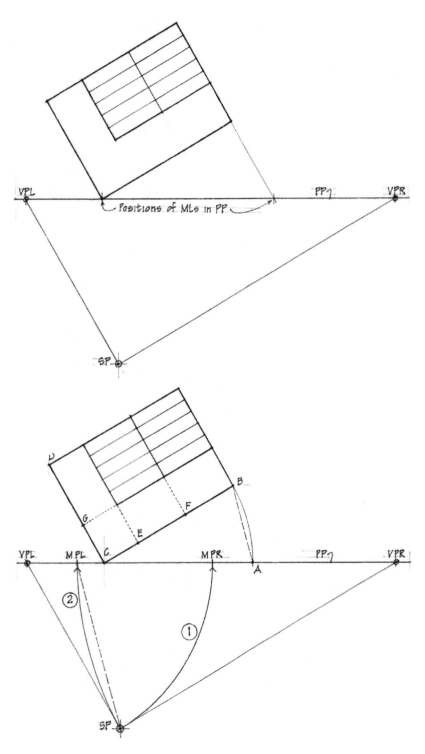

## Perspective Plan

We may construct the perspective plan on the floor or some other horizontal plane of the subject. If this plane is too close to the horizon, however, the perspective plan can become too foreshortened to precisely determine where lines intersect. Being able to discern these intersections is necessary when transferring scaled dimensions along a measuring line in the picture plane to a line in perspective. Because of this, we usually construct the perspective plan at some distance above or below the horizon line in the perspective drawing.

Construct the perspective plan according to the following procedure:

1. Draw the horizon line in the perspective view and lay out the vanishing points, measuring points, and position of measuring lines previously located in the plan diagram. We can establish these points at any scale desired for the size of the perspective drawing; it need not be at the same as the scale of the plan diagram.

2. Establish an auxiliary ground line at any desired distance below or above the horizon line in the perspective drawing.

3. Project the location of a major measuring line down to this ground line. This point serves as a zero point from which we scale plan measurements on the ground line. We lay out the left side measurements of the plan to the left of the zero point. We lay out the right side measurements of the plan to the right of the zero point.

4. From the zero point, draw baselines in perspective that converge to the left and right major vanishing points.

5. Transfer the scale measurements on the ground line to the left baseline in perspective by drawing lines to the right measuring point. Use the left measuring point to transfer measurements to the right baseline. Once we transfer the plan measurements to the left and right baselines, we can complete the perspective plan by following the principles of convergence.

## Fractional Measuring Points

If the scale measurements along the ground line extend beyond the limits of the perspective drawing, we can use a fractional measuring point. To establish a fractional measuring point, we divide the normal distance from the vanishing to the measuring point by a factor of two or four. A half measuring point requires halving the normal units of measurement along the ground line; a quarter measuring point requires using a quarter scale along the ground line.

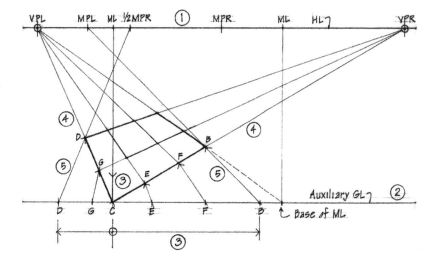

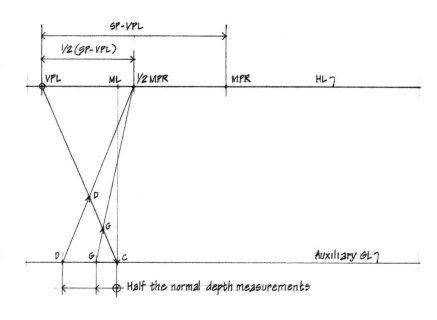

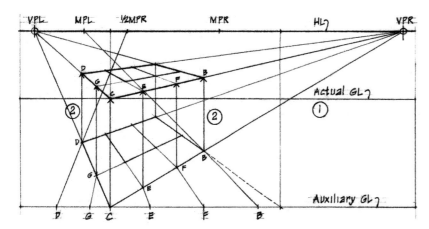

## Perspective View

Once we complete the perspective plan, we begin to construct the perspective view.

1. Establish the actual ground line for the perspective drawing. The distance from the ground line to the horizon line should be equal to the height of the spectator's eye level above the ground plane.
2. Obtain the horizontal spacings of points and vertical lines in the perspective drawing by projecting vertical lines from the perspective plan.
3. Lay out the true heights of elements on vertical measuring lines in the perspective drawing.
4. Transfer these true heights to their correct perspective locations according to the procedure described in the common method of perspective construction. While an elevation view is not required, it can make the construction easier.

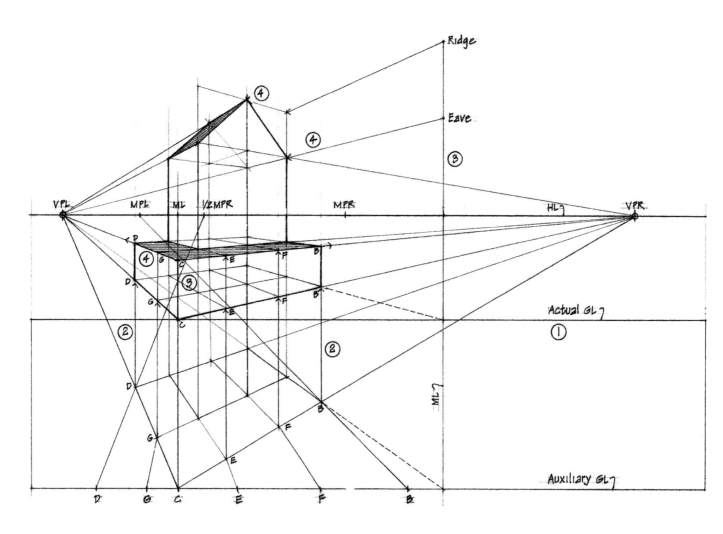

### Exercise 8.14

Use the perspective plan method to construct a two-point perspective of the structure at twice the scale shown in the perspective setup.

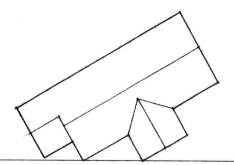

PP

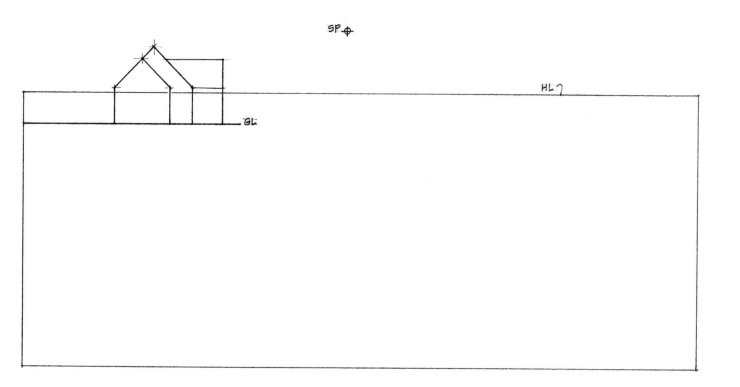

SP

HL

GL

# TWO-POINT PERSPECTIVE GRID

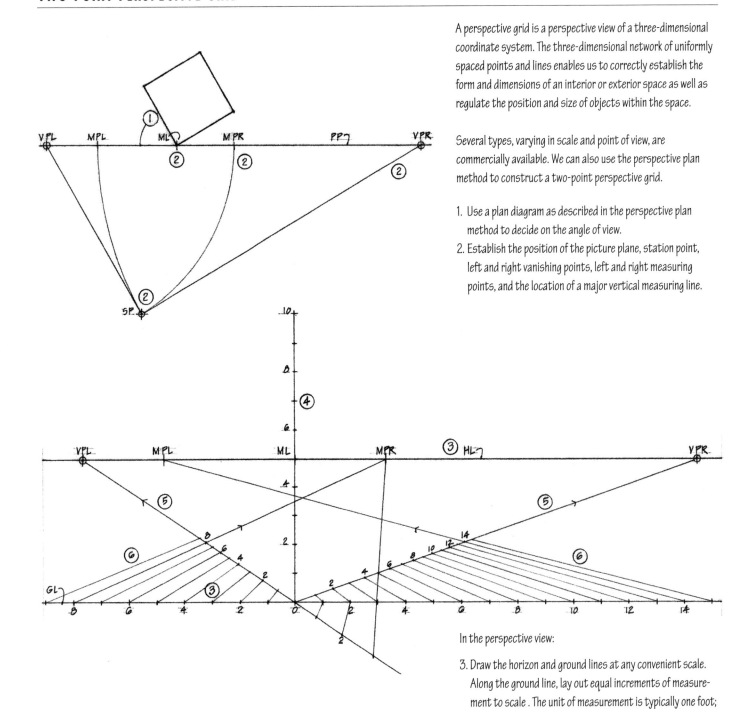

A perspective grid is a perspective view of a three-dimensional coordinate system. The three-dimensional network of uniformly spaced points and lines enables us to correctly establish the form and dimensions of an interior or exterior space as well as regulate the position and size of objects within the space.

Several types, varying in scale and point of view, are commercially available. We can also use the perspective plan method to construct a two-point perspective grid.

1. Use a plan diagram as described in the perspective plan method to decide on the angle of view.
2. Establish the position of the picture plane, station point, left and right vanishing points, left and right measuring points, and the location of a major vertical measuring line.

In the perspective view:

3. Draw the horizon and ground lines at any convenient scale. Along the ground line, lay out equal increments of measurement to scale . The unit of measurement is typically one foot; we can use smaller or larger increments depending on the scale of the drawing and the amount of detail desired in the perspective view.
4. Do the same along a major vertical measuring line.
5. From the left and right vanishing points, draw baselines to where the vertical measuring line meets the ground line.
6. Transfer the units of measurements on the ground line to the left baseline in perspective by drawing lines to the right measuring point. Transfer scale measurements on the ground line to the right baseline by drawing lines to the left measuring point.

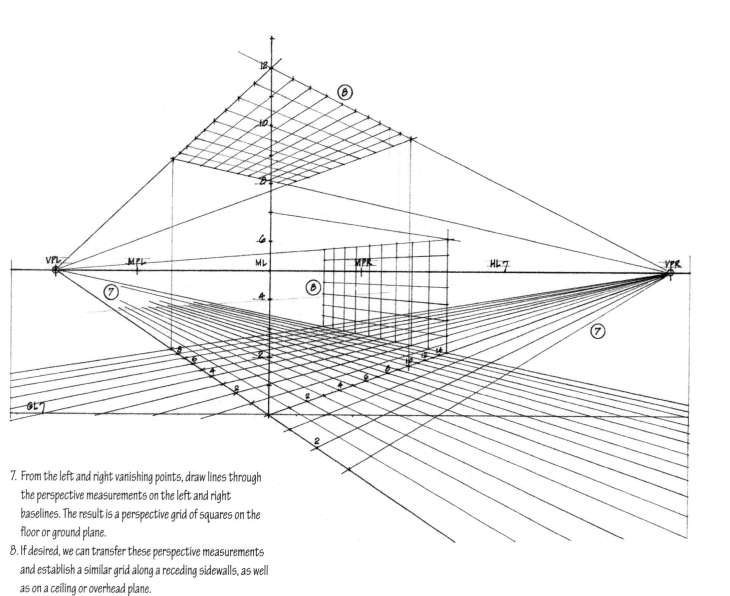

7. From the left and right vanishing points, draw lines through
the perspective measurements on the left and right
baselines. The result is a perspective grid of squares on the
floor or ground plane.

8. If desired, we can transfer these perspective measurements
and establish a similar grid along a receding sidewalls, as well
as on a ceiling or overhead plane.

Over this perspective grid, we can lay tracing paper and freehand or draft a perspective view. It is important to see the perspective grid as a network of points and lines defining transparent planes in space rather than solid, opaque walls enclosing space. The grid of squares not only allows us to plot points in three-dimensional space but also regulates the perspective width, height, and depth of objects and guides the drawing of lines in proper perspective.

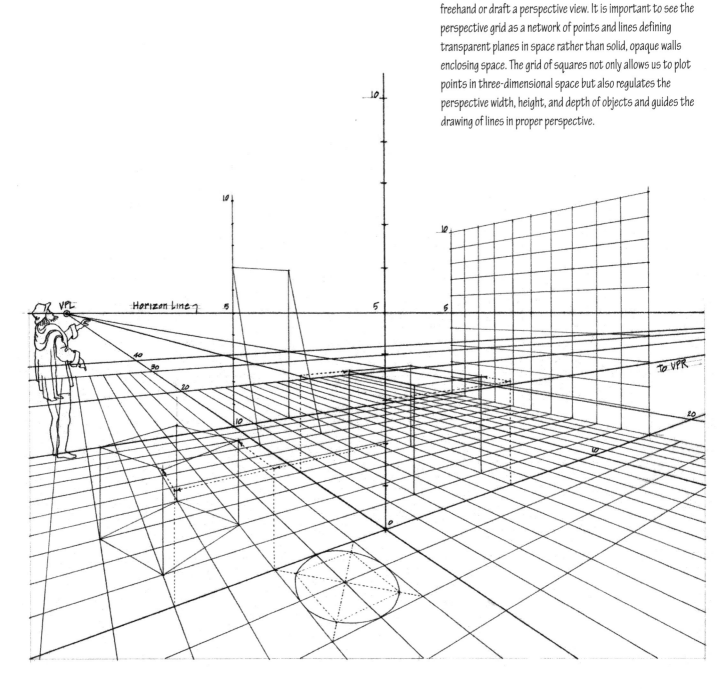

To draw an object within a space, begin by laying out its plan or footprint on the grid of the ground or floor plane. Then elevate each of the corners to their perspective heights using either a vertical grid or the known height of the horizon line above the ground plane. Complete the object by drawing its upper edges, using the principles of convergence and the grid lines to guide their direction. We can use the grid to plot inclined and curved lines as well.

### Exercise 8.15

Construct a two-point perspective grid on a sheet of quality tracing paper or vellum. Assume a scale of $^3/_8" = 1'-0"$ for the picture plane and a horizon line 5 or 6 feet above the ground line. When completed, the perspective grid may be photocopied and enlarged or reduced to any desired scale.

Once constructed, a perspective grid should be saved and reused to draw perspective views of interior and exterior spaces of similar size and scale. Each unit of measurement can represent a foot, four feet, a hundred yards, or even a mile. Rotating and reversing the grid can also vary the point of view. We can therefore use the same grid to draw an interior perspective of a room, an exterior perspective of a courtyard, as well as an aerial view of a city block or neighborhood.

These perspective drawings use the perspective grid developed over the last three pages. In each case, the spectator's height has been selected to portray a specific point of view and the scale of the grid has been altered to correspond to the scale of the subject matter.

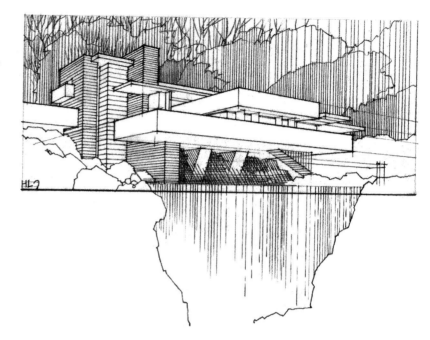

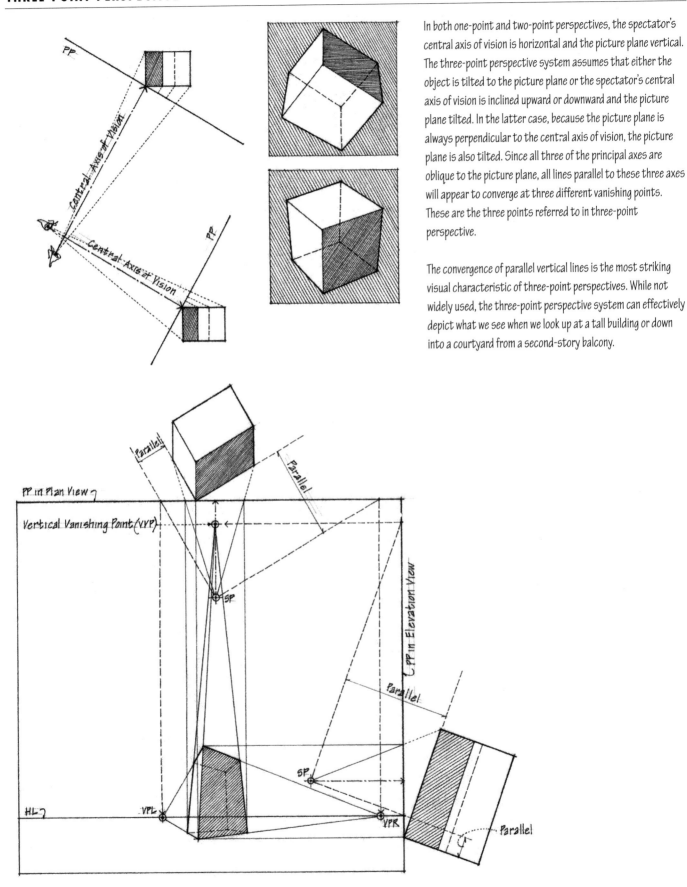

In both one-point and two-point perspectives, the spectator's central axis of vision is horizontal and the picture plane vertical. The three-point perspective system assumes that either the object is tilted to the picture plane or the spectator's central axis of vision is inclined upward or downward and the picture plane tilted. In the latter case, because the picture plane is always perpendicular to the central axis of vision, the picture plane is also tilted. Since all three of the principal axes are oblique to the picture plane, all lines parallel to these three axes will appear to converge at three different vanishing points. These are the three points referred to in three-point perspective.

The convergence of parallel vertical lines is the most striking visual characteristic of three-point perspectives. While not widely used, the three-point perspective system can effectively depict what we see when we look up at a tall building or down into a courtyard from a second-story balcony.

We can use the three points of a triangle as the vanishing points for a cube seen in three-point perspective. One side of the triangle is horizontal and connects the left and right vanishing points for horizontal lines. The third vanishing point for vertical lines is located above or below, depending on our point of view.

Using an equilateral triangle assumes the faces of the cube are at equal angles to the picture plane. Extending the vanishing point for vertical lines away from the horizon alters our point of view and the perspective effect.

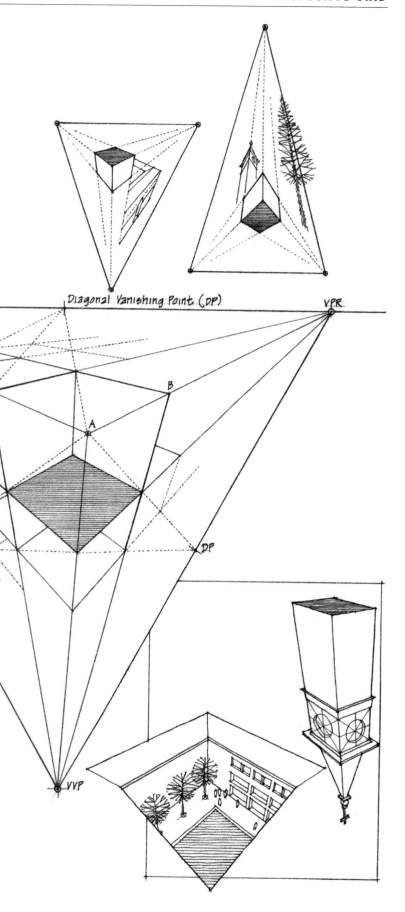

We begin drawing a three-point perspective view of a cube by selecting a point A close to the center of the equilateral triangle. From this point, draw lines to the three vanishing points. Once we establish one edge of the cube, length AB, we can complete it by using diagonals. The vanishing points for these diagonals lie midway between the three major vanishing points.

If we rotate this page 180°, we can see a three-point perspective of the same cube, but in this case, we are looking up at it.

The casting of shades and shadows in linear perspective is similar to their construction in paraline drawings, except that the sloping lines representing the conventional or actual light rays appear to converge when oblique to the picture plane. Light sources behind us illuminate the surfaces we see and cast shadows away from us, while sources in front of us cast shadows towards us and emphasize surfaces that are backlit and in shade. Low light angles lengthen shadows, while high sources shorten them.

To determine the vanishing point for the light rays, construct a triangular shadow plane for a vertical shade line in perspective, having a hypotenuse establishing the direction of the light rays, and a base describing their bearing direction. Because the bearing directions of light rays are described by horizontal lines, their vanishing point must occur somewhere along the horizon line.

Extend the hypotenuse until it intersects a vertical trace through the vanishing point of the bearing direction of the light rays. All other parallel light rays converge at this point. This vanishing point represents the source of the light rays, and is above the horizon when the light source is in front of the observer, and below the horizon when behind the observer.

Since a vertical edge casts a shadow on the ground plane in the direction of the light ray, the shadow converges at the same vanishing point as the bearing direction of the light ray.

Since a horizontal edge is parallel with the ground plane and thus casts a shadow parallel with itself, the shadow cast by that edge converges at the same point as the casting edge itself.

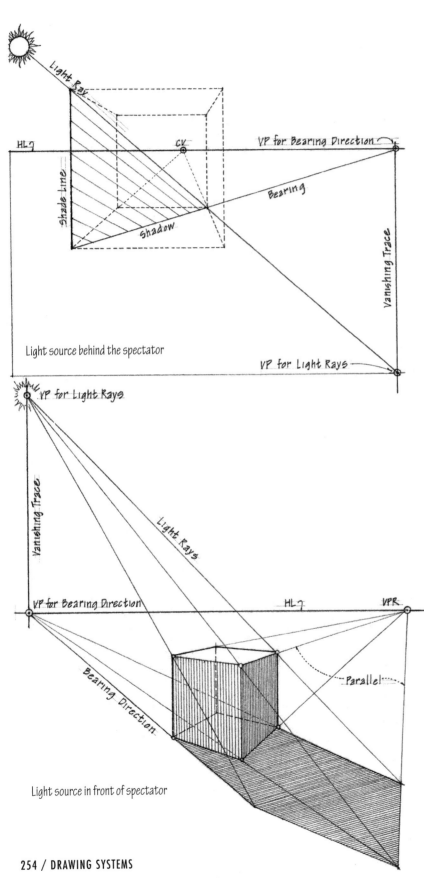

When the light rays originate from either the observer's right or left and are parallel to the picture plane, they remain parallel in perspective and are drawn at their true angular elevation above the ground plane. Their bearing directions remain parallel to each other and the horizon line, and are drawn as horizontal lines.

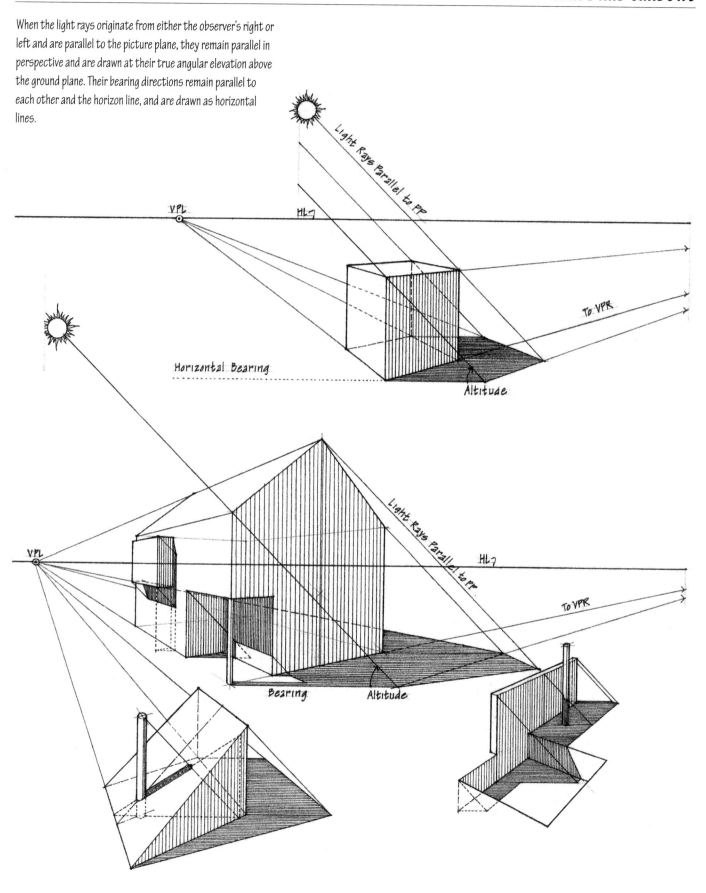

## Exercise 8.16

Given the shadow plane ABC, construct the shade and shadows for the structure in two-point perspective.

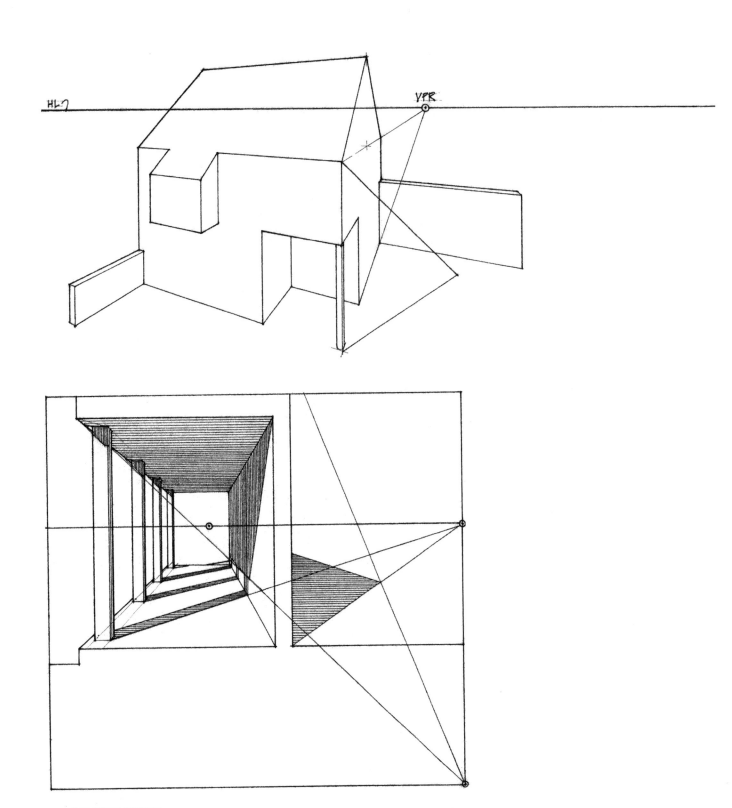

Reflections occur on the horizontal surfaces of bodies of water, the mirrored surfaces of glass, and the polished surfaces of floors. A reflecting surface presents an inverted or mirror copy of the object being reflected. Anything in front of or above a reflecting surface also appears in back of or below the reflecting surface in a direction perpendicular to the surface. Objects appear at the same distance in back of or below the reflecting surface as they are in front of or above the surface.

Any reflecting plane surface parallel to one of the three major sets of parallel lines continues the perspective system of the subject. Therefore, the three major sets of lines in the reflection appear in the same perspective as the lines in the subject, remaining parallel and converging to corresponding vanishing points.

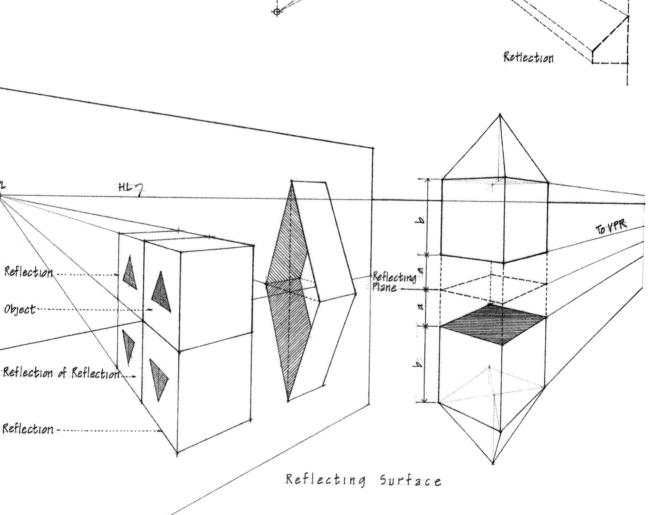

# REFLECTIONS

If sitting directly on the reflecting surface, the reflected image is a direct, inverted copy of the original. Thus, in a perspective view of the reflection, the reflected image follows the same perspective system of lines already established for the original image. If the object being reflected is at some distance from the reflecting surface, then the reflection can reveal normally hidden aspects of the object. First reflect the distance from the object to the reflecting surface, then draw the mirror image of the object. The plane of the reflecting surface should appear to be halfway between the object and its reflected image.

Oblique lines not parallel to the reflecting surface slant at an equal but opposite angle in the reflection.

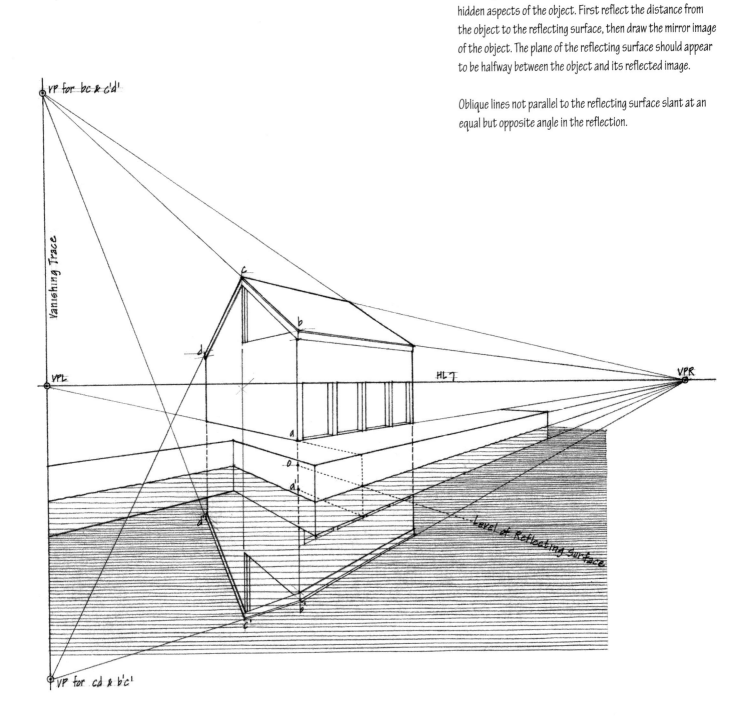

When drawing a perspective of an interior space having a mirrored surface on one or more of its major planes, we extend the perspective system in the manner described above. Sightlines reflect off a mirrored surface at an angle equal to the angle of incidence. Each reflection therefore doubles the apparent dimension of the space in a direction perpendicular to the mirrored surface. A reflection of a reflection will quadruple the apparent size of the space.

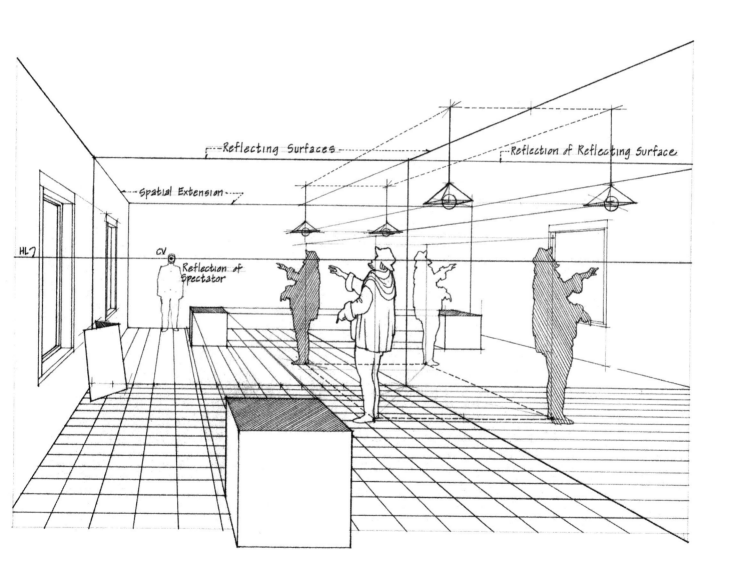

# Drawing from the Imagination

To imagine is to form a mental image of something not present to the senses. Imagination therefore refers to the power of reproducing images stored in memory under the suggestion of associated images—reproductive imagination—or of recombining former experiences in the creation of new images directed at a specific goal or aiding in the solution of problems—creative imagination. We use our creative imagination in design to visualize possibilities, make plans for the future, and speculate on the consequences of our actions. We draw in order to capture and make visible these conceptions that do not yet exist except in the mind's eye.

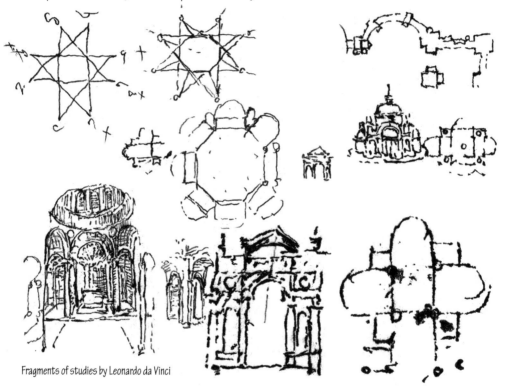

Fragments of studies by Leonardo da Vinci

"Drawing is a means of finding your way about things, and a way of experiencing, more quickly than sculpture allows, certain tryouts and attempts."

—Henry Moore

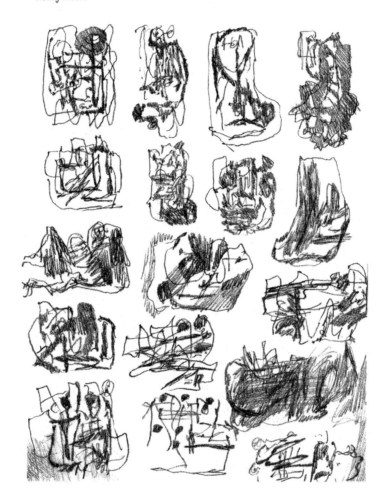

# 9
# Speculative Drawing

To speculate is to engage in thought or reflection. In design, we speculate about the future. As we think about what might be possible in the future, drawing gives material existence to our conceptions so that they can be seen, assessed, and acted upon. The drawing out of these ideas, whether executed quickly or slowly, roughly or carefully, is necessarily speculative in nature. We can never determine beforehand precisely what the final outcome will be. The developing image on paper gradually takes on a life of its own and guides the exploration of a concept as it travels between mind and paper and back again.

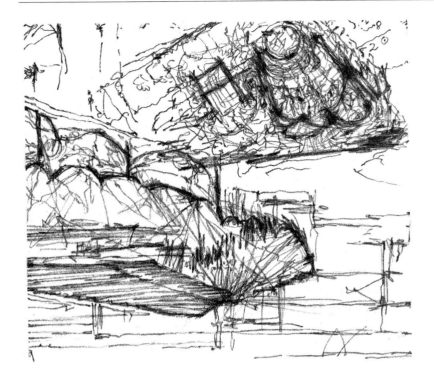

Facsimile of design studies for the Concert and Convention Hall, Helsinki, 1967–71, Alvar Aalto.

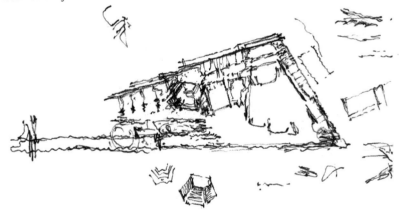

Throughout the design process, we employ a range of drawing techniques and conventions to explore, assess, and refine our ideas. Initially, these drawings may be small diagrammatic sketches intended to stimulate the imagination, test initial thoughts and concepts, and generate a series of alternatives. As a design concept is selected for clarification and development, the drawings we use to represent the idea also become more definitive and refined until the proposal is crystallized and presented for evaluation and implementation.

In the generative and developmental stages of the design process, drawing is distinctly speculative in nature. Thoughts come to mind as we view a drawing in progress, which can alter our perceptions and suggest possibilities not yet conceived. The emerging image on paper allows us to explore avenues that could not be foreseen before the drawing was started, but that generate ideas along the way. Once executed, each drawing depicts a separate reality that can be seen, evaluated, and refined or transformed. Even if eventually discarded, each drawing will have stimulated the mind's eye and set in motion the formation of further conceptions.

Therefore, speculative drawing is different in spirit and purpose from the definitive presentation drawings we use to accurately represent and communicate a fully formed design to others. While the technique and degree of finish of exploratory drawings may vary with the nature of the problem and one's individual way of working, the mode of drawing is always open-ended, informal, and personal. While not intended for public display, these drawings can provide valuable insights into an individual's creative process.

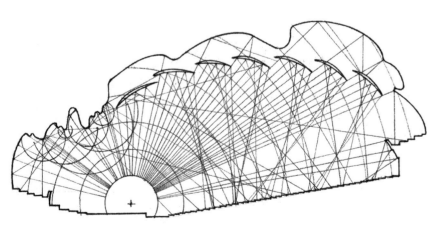

Concert and Convention Hall, Helsinki, 1967–71, Alvar Aalto. Acoustic study of the concert hall.

Speculative drawing is a creative process. The imagination triggers a concept that is seen as a flashing and dimensionless image in the mind's eye. The drawing of that idea, however, does not arrive full-blown and complete. Images rarely exist in the mind fully formed down to the last detail, waiting only to be transferred to a sheet of paper. It develops over time and undergoes a number of transformations as we probe the idea it represents and search for congruence between the image in the mind's eye and the one we are drawing.

If we draw blindly, as if following a recipe, we limit ourselves only to preconceived images and miss opportunities for discovery along the way. While a prior image is necessary to initiate a drawing, it can be a hindrance if we do not see that the evolving image is something we can interact with and modify as we draw. If we can accept this exploratory nature of drawing, we open up the design process to opportunity, inspiration, and invention.

Facsimile of a sketch of the unrealized baldachin for the Cathedral of Mallorca, Antonio Gaudi.

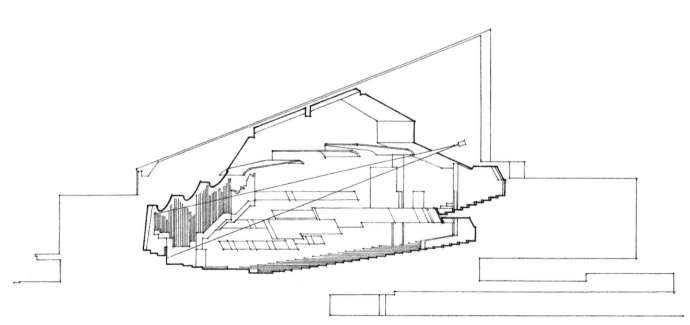

Concert and Convention Hall, Helsinki, 1967–71, Alvar Aalto. Section showing the interior of the concert hall.

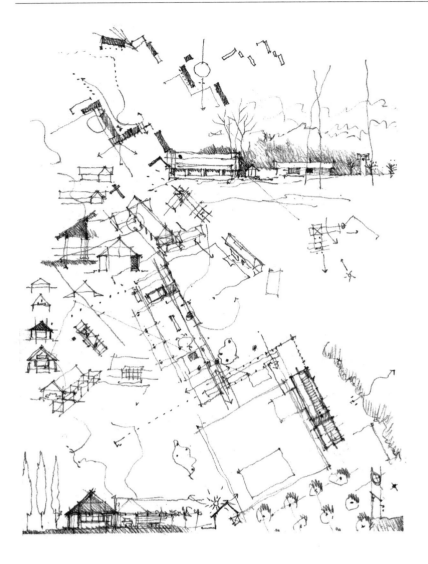

Visual thought is the essential complement to verbal thought in cultivating insights, seeing possibilities, and making discoveries. We also think in visual terms when we draw. Drawing enables the mind to work in graphic form without consciously intending to produce a work of art. Just as thought can be put into words, ideas can take on a visual form to be studied, analyzed, and refined.

In thinking about a design problem, ideas naturally come to mind. Such ideas are often not verbal. The creative process inevitably involves visualizing a potential outcome in the form of images which are not clearly or completely crystallized. It is difficult to hold such ideas in memory long enough to clarify, assess, and develop them. In order to commit an idea to paper quickly enough to keep up with our thoughts, we rely on diagrams and thumbnail sketches. These generative drawings lead the way in formulating possibilities.

The smaller a drawing, the broader the concept it forms. We begin with small sketches since they allow a range of possibilities to be explored. Sometimes a solution will emerge quickly. More often, however, many drawings are required to reveal the best choice or direction to pursue. They encourage us to look at alternative strategies in a fluent and flexible manner and not close on a solution too fast. Being speculative in nature and thus subject to interpretation, they help us avoid the inhibiting nature of a more careful drawing which often leads to premature closure of the design process.

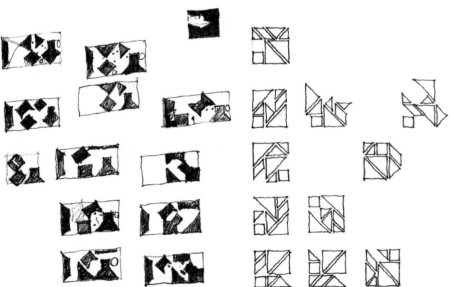

Facsimile of plan compositions for the Fort Wayne Fine Arts Center, Fort Wayne, Indiana, 1961–64, Louis Kahn     Tangram compositions

## Exercise 9.1

Without lifting your pencil from the paper, draw six straight lines that connect all 16 dots. This simple puzzle illustrates both the iterative, trial-and-error nature of problem solving and the need to commit pencil to paper in working through the problem-solving process.

## Exercise 9.2

This cube consists of a 3 x 3 x 3 array of smaller cubes. How many ways can you find to divide the cube into three different shapes, each having an equal volume containing nine of the smaller cubes?

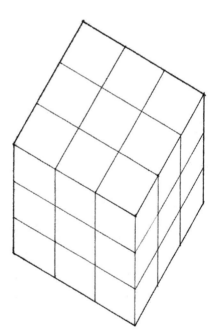

## Exercise 9.3

Circular, triangular, and square shaped holes pierce the solid block. The diameter of the circle, the altitude and base of the triangle, and the sides of the square are equal in dimension. Visualize a single three-dimensional object that will fit exactly and pass completely through each of the apertures. Can you imagine a solution without drawing out the possibilities?

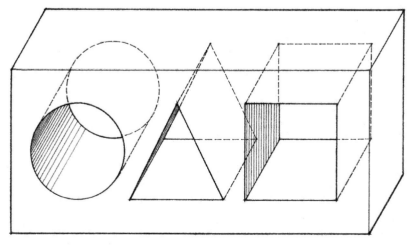

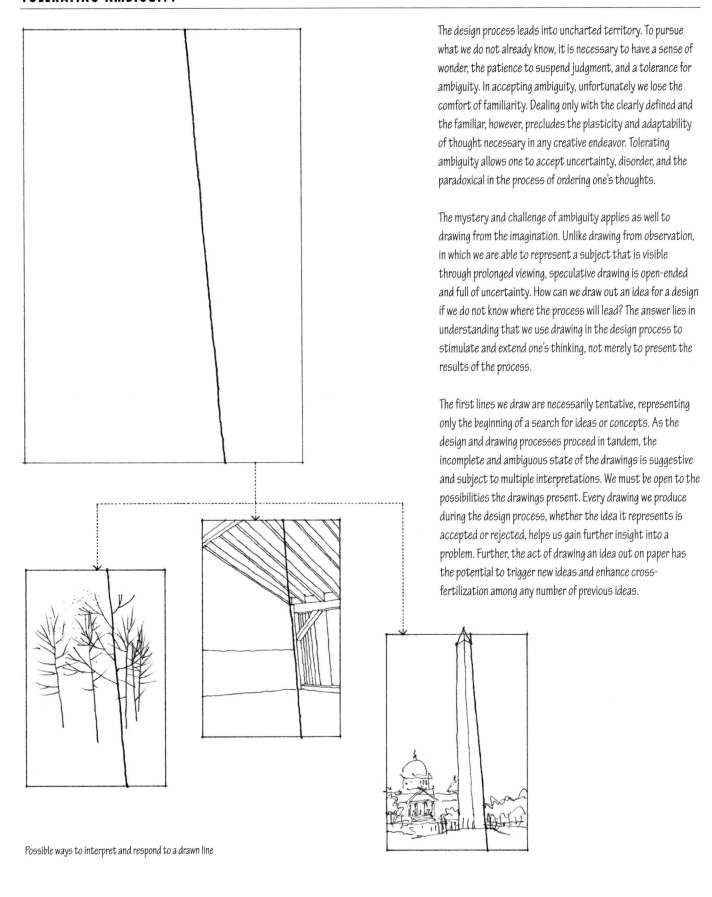

Possible ways to interpret and respond to a drawn line

The design process leads into uncharted territory. To pursue what we do not already know, it is necessary to have a sense of wonder, the patience to suspend judgment, and a tolerance for ambiguity. In accepting ambiguity, unfortunately we lose the comfort of familiarity. Dealing only with the clearly defined and the familiar, however, precludes the plasticity and adaptability of thought necessary in any creative endeavor. Tolerating ambiguity allows one to accept uncertainty, disorder, and the paradoxical in the process of ordering one's thoughts.

The mystery and challenge of ambiguity applies as well to drawing from the imagination. Unlike drawing from observation, in which we are able to represent a subject that is visible through prolonged viewing, speculative drawing is open-ended and full of uncertainty. How can we draw out an idea for a design if we do not know where the process will lead? The answer lies in understanding that we use drawing in the design process to stimulate and extend one's thinking, not merely to present the results of the process.

The first lines we draw are necessarily tentative, representing only the beginning of a search for ideas or concepts. As the design and drawing processes proceed in tandem, the incomplete and ambiguous state of the drawings is suggestive and subject to multiple interpretations. We must be open to the possibilities the drawings present. Every drawing we produce during the design process, whether the idea it represents is accepted or rejected, helps us gain further insight into a problem. Further, the act of drawing an idea out on paper has the potential to trigger new ideas and enhance cross-fertilization among any number of previous ideas.

### Exercise 9.4

The two patterns of lines can serve as the basis for further development of a three-dimensional image. For example, they could suggest how two walls meet a floor. What other ways can you interpret and develop the patterns?

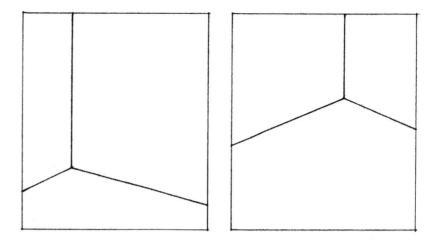

### Exercise 9.5

Draw a wavy line across the middle of a rectangular plane. Then draw parallel lines above and below the wavy line, making them closer to each other at certain points so as to create areas of concentration. As the drawing develops, what does the emerging image suggest or recall to your mind's eye?

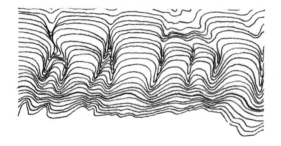

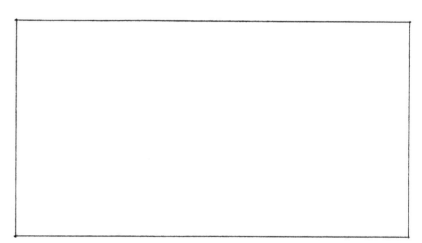

### Exercise 9.6

Imagine what one might see upon looking to the right in the perspective below. First explore a variety of scenarios in the smaller frames and then develop one of them into a perspective view in the larger frame.

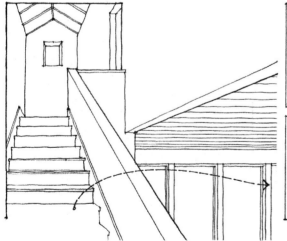

In the search for possibilities and to outline choices, we rely on intuition as a guide. Intuition, however, is based on informed experience. We cannot draw out what is not already within each one of us. Drawing requires understanding of what it is we are drawing. For example, it is difficult to convincingly draw a form whose structure we do not understand. Yet the act of trying to draw it out can lead the way to understanding and guide the intuitive search for ideas.

The first lines we draw are the most difficult. We often fear even beginning until an idea is fully formed in our head. Faced with a blank sheet of paper, what does one draw first? We may start with specific aspects of a particular form or setting, or begin with a more generalized image of a concept or construct. In either case, where we start is not as important as where we end up.

Drawing too carefully in the early stages of the design process can lead to hesitation and disrupt our thinking about the problem. The time and energy spent on the creation of a drawing can inhibit the willingness to explore other possibilities. We should understand that speculative drawing is a trial-and-error process in which the most important step is to set down the first few lines on paper, no matter how tentative they might be. We must trust our intuition if we are to move forward in the drawing process.

"…'How can I design if I do not know what the end result will be like?' is a frequent complaint. 'Why would you need to design if you already knew?' is my response. The need for a prior image is most keenly felt when we do not trust the form as something to work with. There is nothing wrong with having such an image, but it is not a prerequisite and may be a hindrance. When we speak with other people, we need not know what the result of the conversation will be either. We may come out of the conversation with a better sense of the issue; in fact, we may have changed our mind. When we are concerned about 'doing our own thing' and feel we must be on top of the form all the time, we cannot relax and trust the process. Once students find out how one's dialogue with the form will always bear the imprint of one's personality— whether one likes it or not—the complaint is no longer heard."

—John Habraken
*The Control of Complexity. Places/Vol. 4, No. 2*

"One day Alice came to a fork in the road and saw a Cheshire cat in a tree.
'Which road do I take?' she asked.
His response was a question: 'Where do you want to go?'
'I don't know,' Alice answered. 'Then,' said the cat, 'it doesn't matter.'"

—Lewis Carroll
*Alice in Wonderland*

To be fluent in the creative process is to be able to generate a wide range of possibilities and ideas. To be fluent in the drawing process is to be intuitive when placing pen or pencil to paper, responding with ease and grace to our conceptions. We must be able keep up with our thoughts, which can be fleeting.

Writing our thoughts out is an easy, almost effortless task. To develop this same fluency in drawing, we must practice on a regular basis until putting lines down on paper is an automatic reflex, a natural response to what we are seeing or imagining. While speed may come with pushing ourselves to draw faster, speed without discipline is counterproductive. Before drawing can become an intuitive component of our visual thinking, we must first be able to draw slowly, deliberately, and accurately.

A quick mode of drawing is necessary to capture a brief moment in the flow of ideas, which cannot always be directed or controlled. Fluency in drawing therefore requires a freehand technique, with a minimum of tools. Attention paid to the mechanics of drawing with drafting equipment often diverts time and energy from the visual thinking process. We should therefore draw freehand whenever fluency and flexibility are more important in the design process than precision and accuracy.

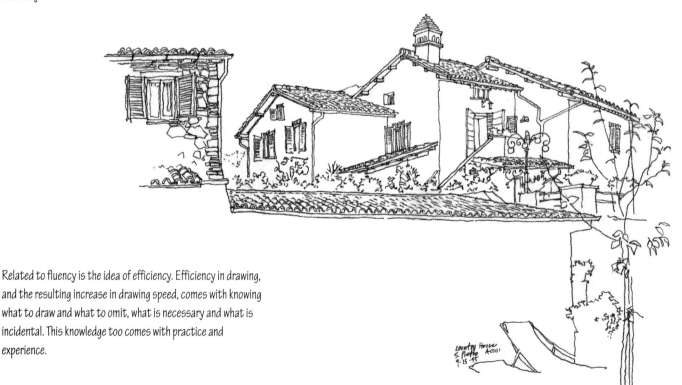

Related to fluency is the idea of efficiency. Efficiency in drawing, and the resulting increase in drawing speed, comes with knowing what to draw and what to omit, what is necessary and what is incidental. This knowledge too comes with practice and experience.

### Exercise 9.7

An effective way to develop fluency and promote drawing on a regular basis is to maintain a sketchbook and to draw in it a half-hour to an hour each day. One possibility is to focus each week on a different architectural element, such as windows, doorways, walls, and rooflines. Another is to focus on specific qualities, such as material textures, shadow patterns, or the ways different materials join or meet each other. The most important thing is to draw subject matter that interests you.

### Exercise 9.8

With just a few quick pencil strokes, try to capture the essence of these images in the adjacent frames.

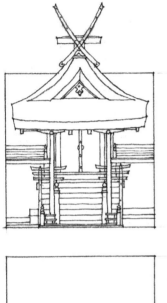

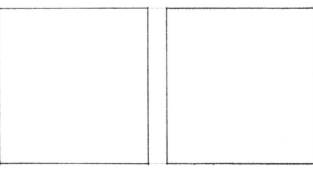

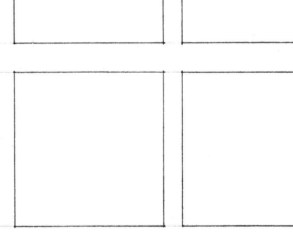

### Exercise 9.9

What simple geometric shapes can you find within these
images? Use a pen or pencil to outline these basic structures.

### Exercise 9.10

Explore how far you can simplify these images and still have
them remain recognizable.

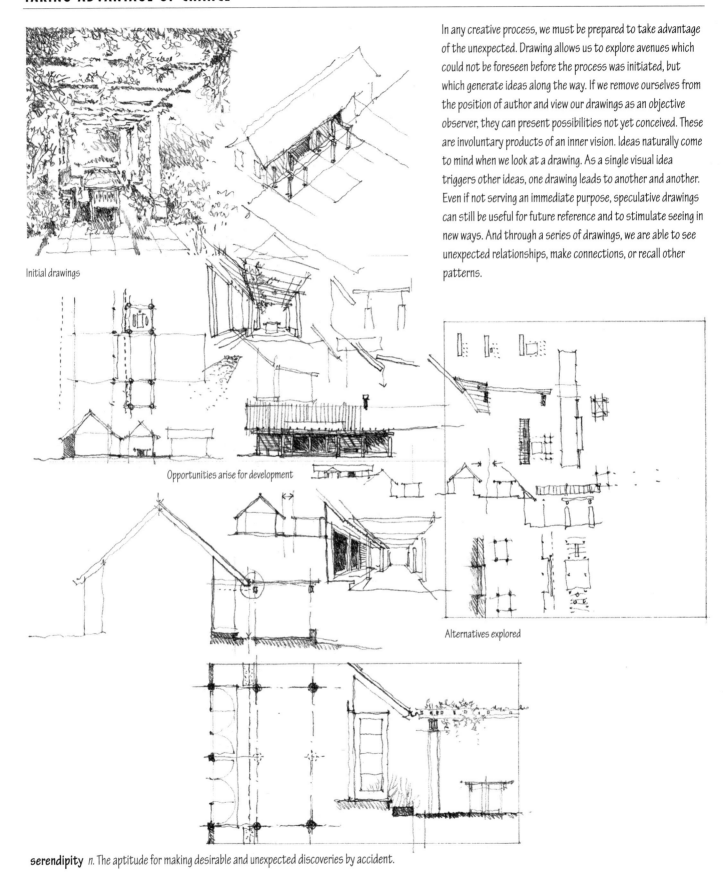

In any creative process, we must be prepared to take advantage of the unexpected. Drawing allows us to explore avenues which could not be foreseen before the process was initiated, but which generate ideas along the way. If we remove ourselves from the position of author and view our drawings as an objective observer, they can present possibilities not yet conceived. These are involuntary products of an inner vision. Ideas naturally come to mind when we look at a drawing. As a single visual idea triggers other ideas, one drawing leads to another and another. Even if not serving an immediate purpose, speculative drawings can still be useful for future reference and to stimulate seeing in new ways. And through a series of drawings, we are able to see unexpected relationships, make connections, or recall other patterns.

Initial drawings

Opportunities arise for development

Alternatives explored

**serendipity** *n.* The aptitude for making desirable and unexpected discoveries by accident.

## Layering

Layering is a graphic mode for both analysis and synthesis. It allow us to quickly and flexibly see patterns and study relationships. Just as we refine our written thoughts by editing and rewriting drafts, we can build up a drawing in layers on a single sheet of paper. We first draw the foundation or structural lines of the image lightly in an exploratory manner. Then, as we make visual judgments on shape, proportion, and composition, we draw over the emerging image in a number of discrete steps. The process may include both sketchy and detailed work as the mind focuses in on some areas for closer inspection while keeping an eye on the whole.

The revision of a drawing can also occur through the physical layering of transparent sheets. Tracing paper allows us to draw over another drawing, retaining certain elements, and refining others. On separate transparent overlays, we can draw patterns of elements, associated forms and groupings, and relevant relationships. Different layers may consist of separate but related processes. We can study certain areas in greater detail and give greater emphasis to certain aspects or features. We can explore alternatives over common ground.

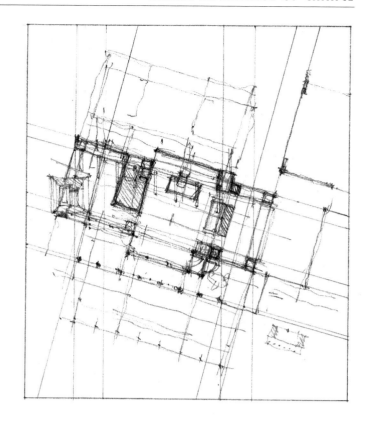

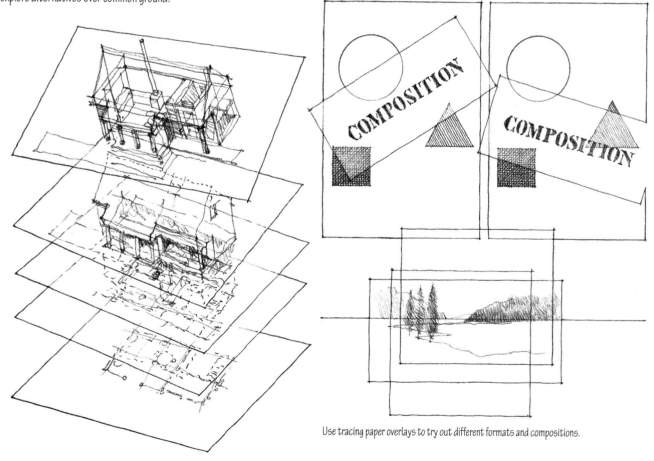

Use tracing paper overlays to try out different formats and compositions.

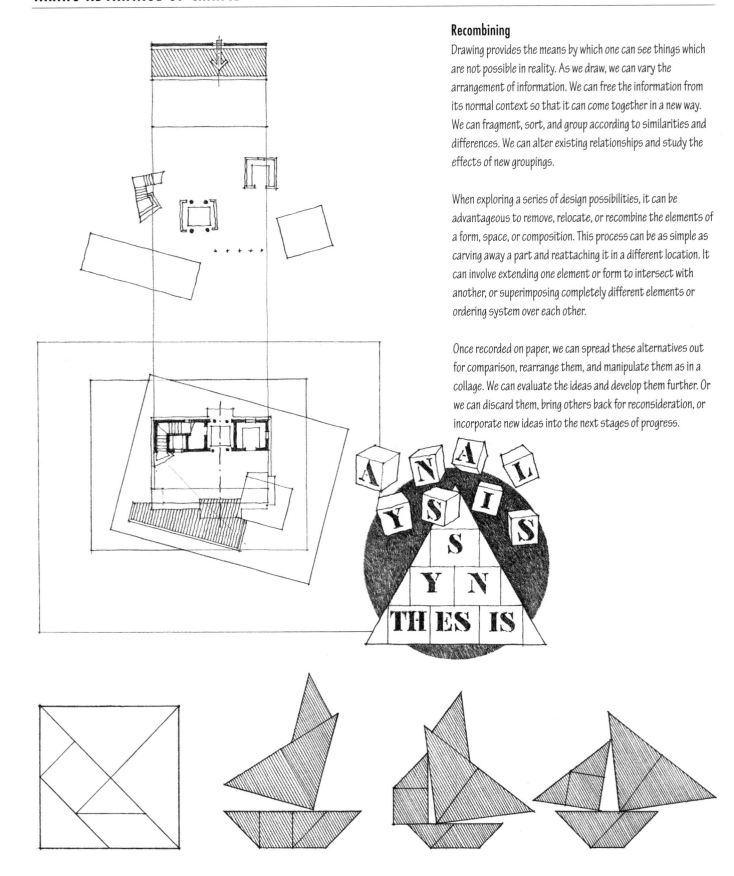

### Recombining

Drawing provides the means by which one can see things which are not possible in reality. As we draw, we can vary the arrangement of information. We can free the information from its normal context so that it can come together in a new way. We can fragment, sort, and group according to similarities and differences. We can alter existing relationships and study the effects of new groupings.

When exploring a series of design possibilities, it can be advantageous to remove, relocate, or recombine the elements of a form, space, or composition. This process can be as simple as carving away a part and reattaching it in a different location. It can involve extending one element or form to intersect with another, or superimposing completely different elements or ordering system over each other.

Once recorded on paper, we can spread these alternatives out for comparison, rearrange them, and manipulate them as in a collage. We can evaluate the ideas and develop them further. Or we can discard them, bring others back for reconsideration, or incorporate new ideas into the next stages of progress.

### Exercise 9.11

Use a series of drawings to illustrate the following operations. First, slice off or carve out a part of the cube. Then remove the piece from the cube. Finally, reattach the piece to the cube in three different ways: touching at a point, adjoining along an edge, and abutting face to face.

### Exercise 9.12

The seven shapes which comprise the Soma cube represent all the ways in which three or four cubes can be arranged other than in straight lines. Use a series of drawings to explore the different ways one could combine these shapes. What is the most compact grouping you can develop? The tallest stable configuration? The interlocking arrangement that encloses the largest volume of space?

### Exercise 9.13

Transfer the plans of the Hardy House and the Jobson House onto separate sheets of tracing paper. Overlay the plans and study the different ways one could reconfigure the plan elements and their relationships. On a third overlay of tracing paper, use drawings to explore how one plan may dominate the composition but incorporate parts of the other, or how an entirely new composition may incorporate parts of both of the original plans. You may repeat this exercise with any other combinations of plans which either contrast sharply or share certain characteristics.

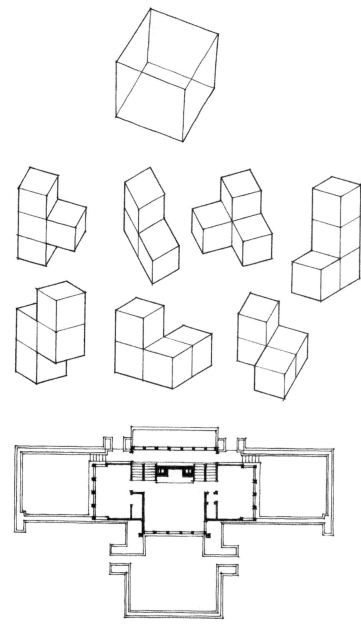

Hardy House, Racine, Wisconsin, 1905, Frank Lloyd Wright

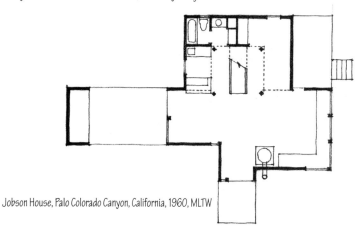

Jobson House, Palo Colorado Canyon, California, 1960, MLTW

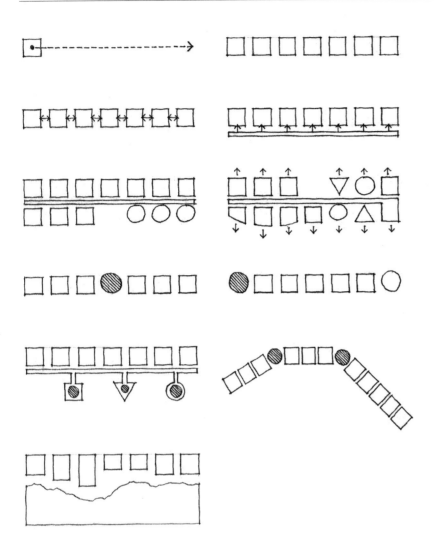

### Transforming

Drawing is only a translation of what we are envisioning. As we commit an image to paper, the mind's eye filters out what is interesting or important. The more important points will tend to rise to the surface, while lesser ones will be discarded in the process. As drawings record our thoughts, they then become independent objects for study, elaboration, and the stimulation of new ideas.

Drawing represents ideas in a tangible form so that they can be clarified, assessed, and acted upon. Every drawing undergoes a number of transformations and evolves as we respond to the emerging image. Once drawn, the graphic images have a physical presence that stands apart from the process of their creation. They serve as catalysts that play back into the mind and provoke further study and development of the ideas in our head.

In the process of exploring an idea and pursuing possibilities as they arise, we develop a series of drawings that we can arrange side by side to compare and evaluate alternatives. We can combine them in new ways; we can transform them into new ideas. The principle of transformation allows a concept to undergo a series of discrete manipulations and permutations in response to certain directives. In order to force a shift in our thinking, we can transform the familiar to the strange and the strange to the familiar.

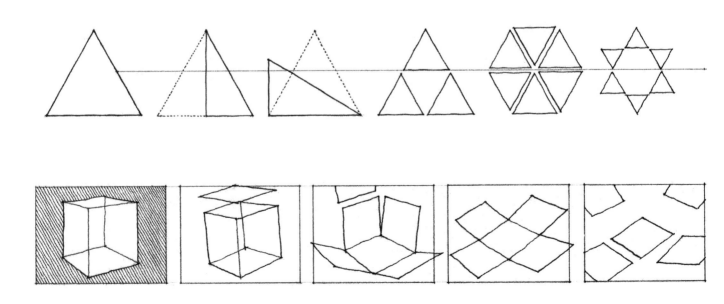

### Exercise 9.14

Through a series of drawings, gradually transform the images on
the left to the ones on the right.

### Exercise 9.15

Create the illusion of depth and movement in a drawing
sequence which relates each pair of images.

### Exercise 9.16

Improvise a sequence of drawings based on the images in the
first frame.

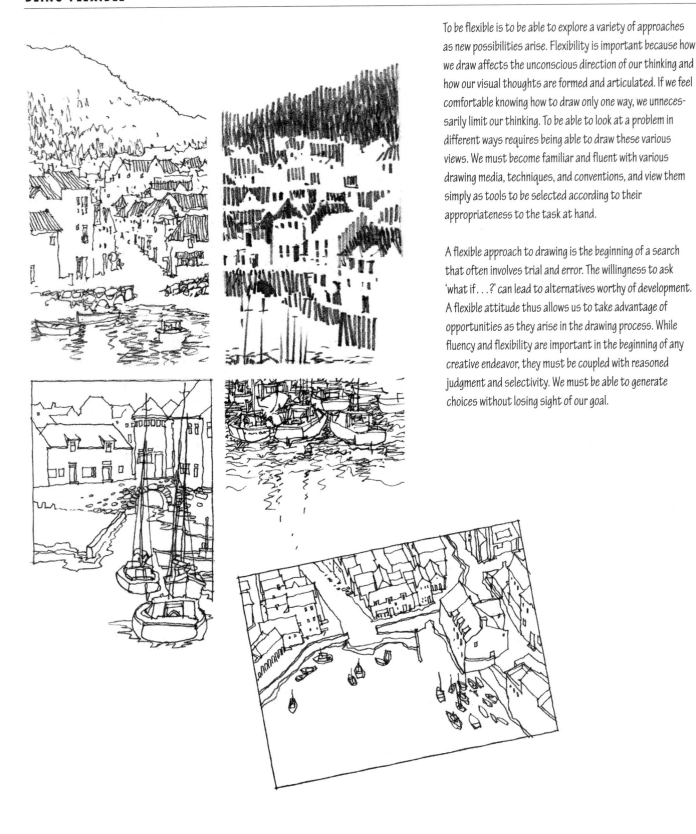

To be flexible is to be able to explore a variety of approaches as new possibilities arise. Flexibility is important because how we draw affects the unconscious direction of our thinking and how our visual thoughts are formed and articulated. If we feel comfortable knowing how to draw only one way, we unnecessarily limit our thinking. To be able to look at a problem in different ways requires being able to draw these various views. We must become familiar and fluent with various drawing media, techniques, and conventions, and view them simply as tools to be selected according to their appropriateness to the task at hand.

A flexible approach to drawing is the beginning of a search that often involves trial and error. The willingness to ask 'what if...?' can lead to alternatives worthy of development. A flexible attitude thus allows us to take advantage of opportunities as they arise in the drawing process. While fluency and flexibility are important in the beginning of any creative endeavor, they must be coupled with reasoned judgment and selectivity. We must be able to generate choices without losing sight of our goal.

### Exercise 9.17

First complete the drawing using a pen and the technique shown. Then redraw the scene using a different medium and technique of your choice. How does changing media affect the resulting image?

After Vincent van Gogh's *Café in Arles*

### Exercise 9.18

On separate sheets of paper, draw the scene described in the following passage from Fyodor Dostoyevsky's *Crime and Punishment* from two different points of view. Use a soft pencil for the first drawing and a pen for the second.

"The old woman paused, as though hesitating; then stepped on one side, and pointing to the door of the room, she said, letting her visitor pass in front of her:

'Step in, my good sir.'

The little room into which the young man walked, with yellow paper on the walls, geraniums and muslin curtains in the windows, was brightly lighted up at that moment by the setting sun.

'So the sun will shine like this then too!' flashed as it were by chance through Raskolnikov's mind, and with a rapid glance he scanned everything in the room, trying as far as possible to notice and remember its arrangement. But there was nothing special in the room. The furniture, all very old and of yellow wood, consisted of a sofa with a huge bent wooden back, an oval table in front of the sofa, a dressing-table with a looking-glass fixed on it between the windows, chairs along the walls and two or three half-penny prints in yellow frames, representing German damsels with birds in their hands—that was all. In the corner a light was burning before a small ikon. Everything was very clean; the floor and the furniture were brightly polished; everything shone."

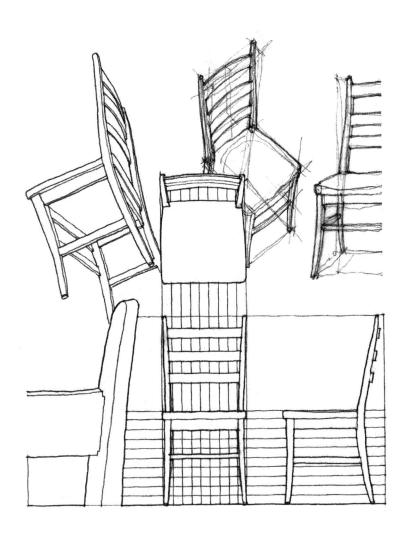

### Shifting Viewpoints

A creative imagination regards old questions from a new angle. Relying on habit and convention can impede the flow of ideas during the design process. If we can see in different ways, we are better able to see hidden opportunities in the unusual, the exceptional, and the paradoxical. To see in new ways requires a keen power of visualization and an understanding of the flexibility drawing offers in presenting new possibilities.

To see with a fresh eye, we can look at a mirror image of what we are drawing. We can turn the drawing upside down or stand back from it to study the visual essence of the image—its basic elements, pattern, and relationships. We can even see it through someone else's eyes. To encourage a shift in view, it is sometimes useful to use a different medium, a different paper, a different technique, or a different drawing system.

Drawing can stimulate our thinking by offering different points of view. Multiview, paraline, and perspective drawing systems comprise a visual language of design communication. We must be able to not only "write" in this language but also to "read" it. This understanding should be thorough enough that we are able to work comfortably back and forth from one drawing system to another. We should be able to transform the flatness of a multiview drawing into a three-dimensional paraline view. Viewing a set of multiview drawings, we should be able to imagine and draw what we would see if we were to stand in a particular position in the plan view.

Vary the point of view.

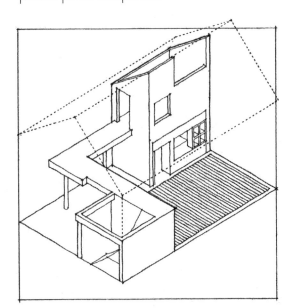

See inside things.

## Rotating

Turning an idea over in our mind enables us to see and study it from different points of view. In a similar fashion, if we can imagine how an object rotates in space, or how it might appear as we move around it, we can explore its many facets from all sides. And if we are able to manipulate a design idea on paper as we turn it over in our mind, we can more fully explore the multiple dimensions of a design idea.

When drawing how something rotates in space, it is much easier to imagine the revolution of a simple geometric element than an entire composition of parts. Therefore, we begin by establishing the ordering device that binds the form or composition together—whether it be an axis, a polygonal shape, or a geometric volume—and analyzing the principles that regulate how the parts are related to the whole.

Then we imagine and draw how the ordering device might appear as it rotates and moves to a new position in space. Once we arrive at this new position, we reestablish the parts in proper relation and orientation to the whole. In building up the image, we utilize regulating lines to form the structure of the object or composition. After checking for accuracy of proportions and relationships, we add thickness, depth, and details to the framework to complete the drawing.

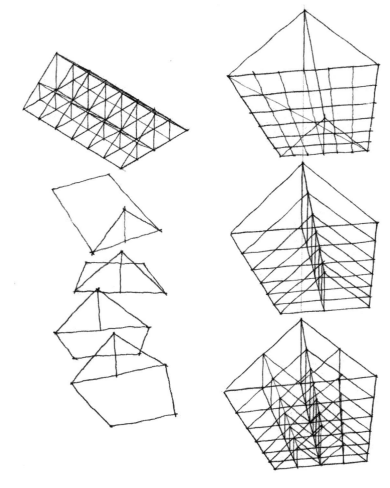

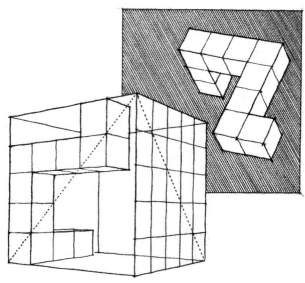

See the whole in the part. . .          and the part in the whole.

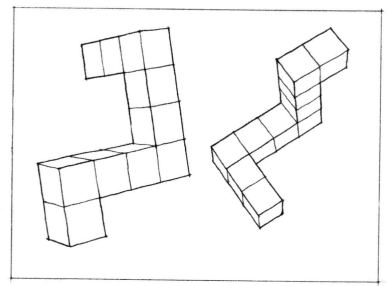

Turn an idea over in the mind.

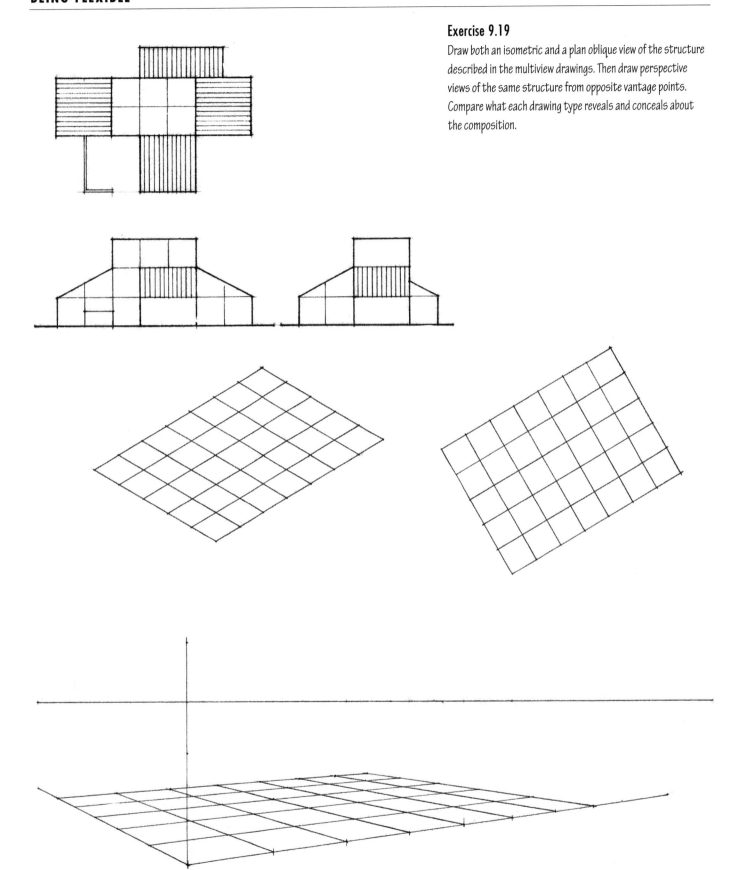

### Exercise 9.19

Draw both an isometric and a plan oblique view of the structure described in the multiview drawings. Then draw perspective views of the same structure from opposite vantage points. Compare what each drawing type reveals and conceals about the composition.

### Exercise 9.20

Imagine the die is moving freely through space. Draw the die at two intermediate positions B and C as it rotates from A to D.

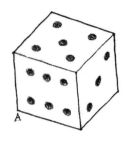

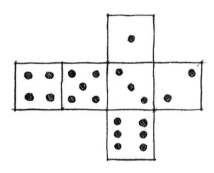

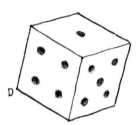

### Exercise 9.21

Imagine the composition is moving freely through space. Draw the composition at two intermediate positions B and C as it rotates from A to D.

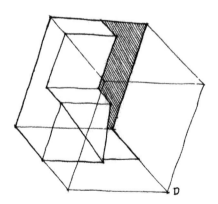

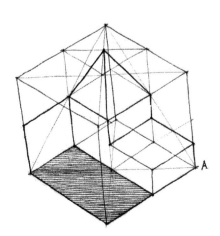

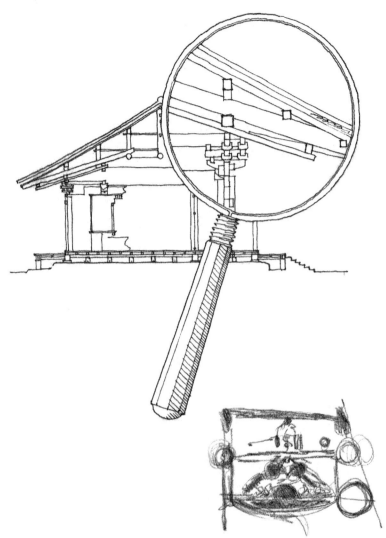

## Changing Scale

In working from the general to the particular, from the broad, overriding issues to the detailed resolution of a problem, we parallel the gradual formulation, refinement, and crystallization of a design. The graphic technique progresses in a corresponding manner from diagrammatic sketches executed in broad strokes to more definitive drawings of concrete ideas and solutions executed with more precise instruments.

We stimulate our design thinking by working at various scales and levels of abstraction. The scale of a drawing establishes which aspects or features we can attend to and likewise those we must ignore. For example, the question of material goes unanswered at a small scale partly because we cannot represent material at that scale. At a larger scale, however, this question would arise. Unless the material question is resolved, such a drawing would seem too large for its content. Changing the scale of the drawings we use during the design process allows us to distill an idea down to essentials as well as expand the idea to incorporate issues of material and detail.

The interdependence of design issues and scale is a question not only of perception but also of craft. Our choice of a drawing medium depends on the scale of a drawing and determines the degree of representation or abstraction we are able to illustrate. For example, drawing with a fine-tipped pen would encourage us to draw small and enable us to attend to detail. Drawing with a broad-tipped marker, on the other hand, would allow us to cover more ground as well as study the broader issues of pattern and organization.

Capital Complex of Bangladesh, Dacca, Bangladesh, 1962, Louis Kahn.
An early plan sketch, section through the stair gallery, and a detail of the composite wall construction.

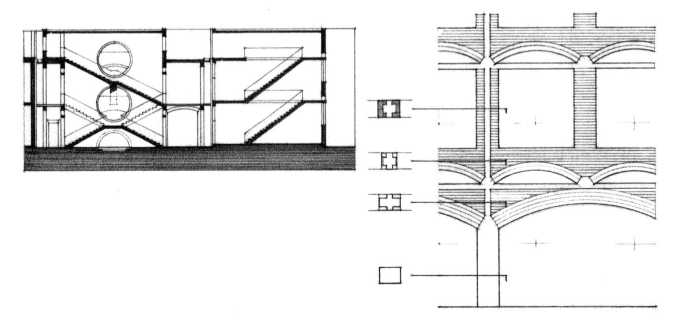

## Exercise 9.22

Reduce the scale of the column capital in each succeeding frame by a half. How much detail can you eliminate in each drawing without sacrificing the identity of the capital?

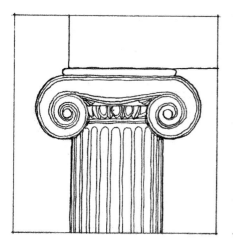

## Exercise 9.23

Find and select a building element, such as a window, doorway, ornamental frieze. Draw the element from a distance of 30 feet, then 15 feet, and finally 5 feet. In each successive view, increase both the scale and the amount of detail.

## Exercise 9.24

Repeat the above exercise with another building element. This time, reverse the procedure by first drawing the element from 5 feet away, then 15 feet, and finally 30 feet. In each successive view, decrease both the scale and the amount of detail.

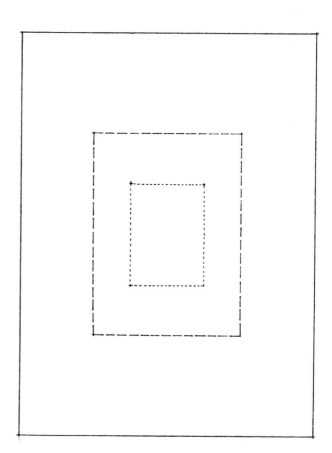

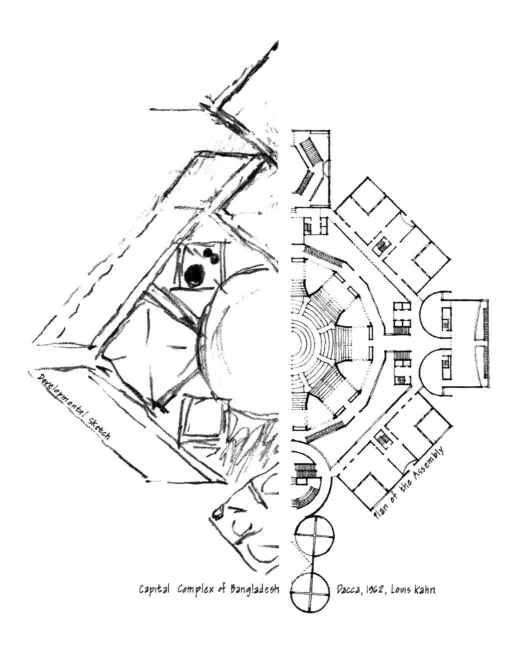

Developmental Sketch

Plan of the Assembly

Capital Complex of Bangladesh    Dacca, 1962, Louis Kahn

# 10
# Diagraming

No drawing is ever the thing it endeavors to represent. All drawings are to some degree abstractions of a perceived reality or an imaginary conception. In design drawing, we operate at varying levels of abstraction. At one end of the spectrum lies the presentation drawing, which attempts to simulate as closely as possible the future reality of a design proposal. At the other end is the diagram, which has the ability to describe something without representing it in a pictorial way.

A diagram is any drawing that explains or clarifies the parts, arrangement, or operation of something. The hallmark of a diagram is its ability to simplify a complex notion into essential elements and relationships by a process of elimination and reduction. Professionals in many different fields use diagrams to expedite their thinking. Mathematicians, physicists, and even musicians and dancers use their own abstract languages of symbols and notations to deal with the complexities of their endeavors. Designers, too, use diagrams to stimulate and clarify their visual thinking.

While every design process must eventually converge on a solution to a problem, the beginning phases should be characterized by divergent thinking about possibilities. Design involves making choices; without alternatives, there is no choice to be made. By focusing on the general rather than the particular, diagrams discourage closing on a solution too quickly and encourage the exploration of possible alternatives. The activity of diagraming, therefore, provides a convenient way to think about how to proceed in generating a series of viable alternatives to a given design problem. Their abstract nature enables us to analyze and understand the essential nature of program elements, to consider their possible relationships, and to seek ways in which these parts can be organized to make a unified whole.

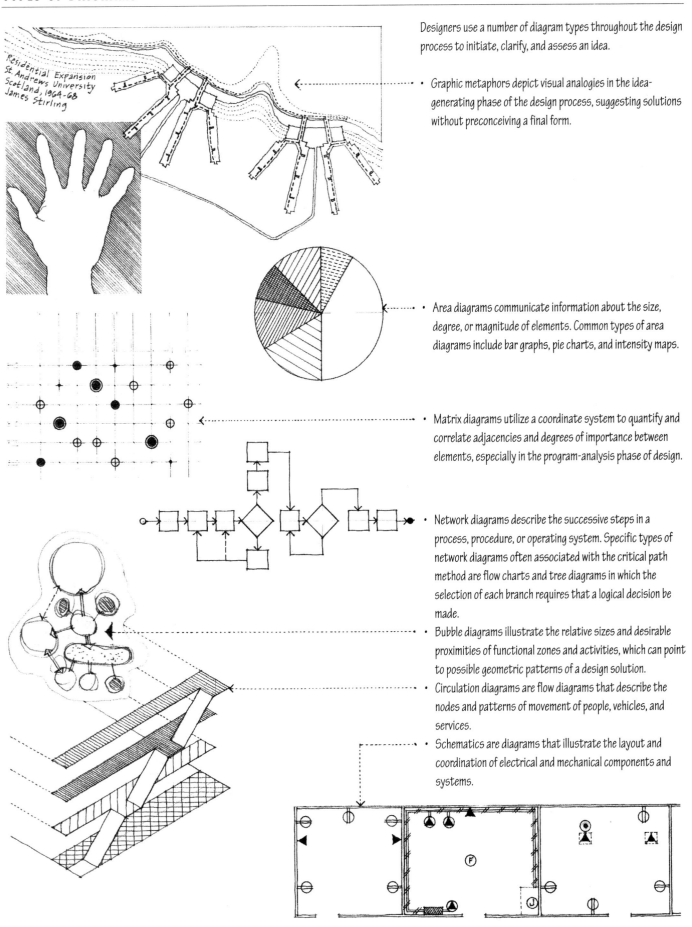

Residential Expansion
St. Andrews University
Scotland, 1964-68
James Stirling

Designers use a number of diagram types throughout the design process to initiate, clarify, and assess an idea.

- Graphic metaphors depict visual analogies in the idea-generating phase of the design process, suggesting solutions without preconceiving a final form.

- Area diagrams communicate information about the size, degree, or magnitude of elements. Common types of area diagrams include bar graphs, pie charts, and intensity maps.

- Matrix diagrams utilize a coordinate system to quantify and correlate adjacencies and degrees of importance between elements, especially in the program-analysis phase of design.

- Network diagrams describe the successive steps in a process, procedure, or operating system. Specific types of network diagrams often associated with the critical path method are flow charts and tree diagrams in which the selection of each branch requires that a logical decision be made.

- Bubble diagrams illustrate the relative sizes and desirable proximities of functional zones and activities, which can point to possible geometric patterns of a design solution.

- Circulation diagrams are flow diagrams that describe the nodes and patterns of movement of people, vehicles, and services.

- Schematics are diagrams that illustrate the layout and coordination of electrical and mechanical components and systems.

Analytical diagrams examine and explain the arrangement and relations of the parts of a whole. We use a variety of analytical diagrams in design. Site analyses explore how the siting and orientation of a design respond to environmental and contextual forces. Program analyses investigate how a design organization addresses programmatic requirements. Formal analyses examine the correspondence between structural pattern, spatial volumes, and elements of enclosure.

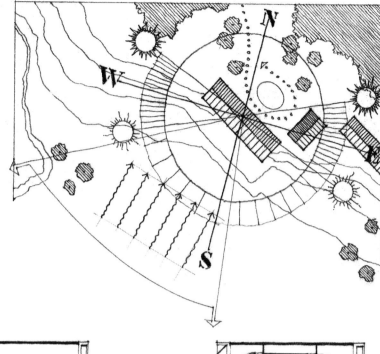

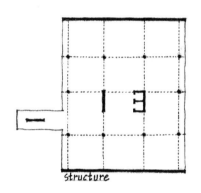
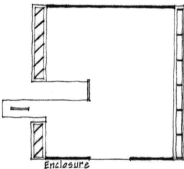
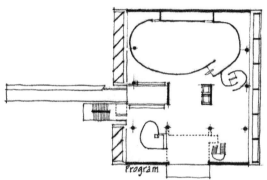

Millowners' Association, Ahmedabad, India, 1954, Le Corbusier

We can use any of the drawing systems to define the viewpoint of a diagram. When a diagram isolates a single issue or set of relationships for study, a two-dimensional format is usually sufficient. However, when we begin to explore the complex spatial and relational attributes of a design, a three-dimensional drawing system becomes necessary. Particularly effective vehicles for studying the volumetric massing and spatial dimensions of a design are cutaway, expanded, and phantom views.

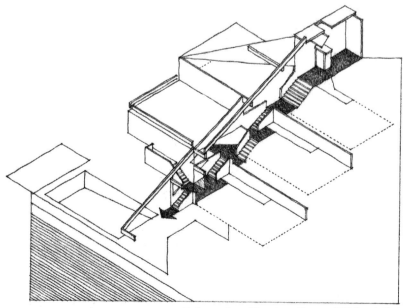

Bookstaver House, Westminster, Vermont, 1972, Peter L. Gluck

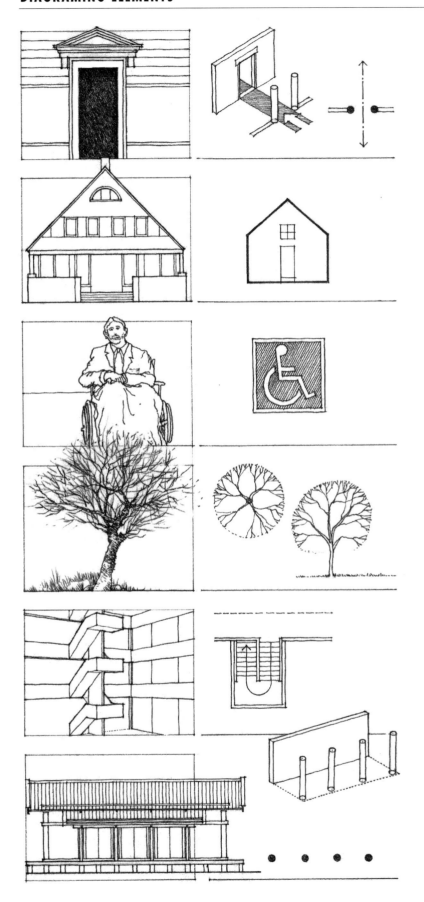

The efficiency of using diagrams to study, analyze, and make design decisions results from their use of signs and symbols. These abstract figures represent more complex entities, actions, or ideas in a form more suitable for editing, manipulation, and transformation than representational images. Their use allows us to respond to the swift and speculative nature of thought during the design process.

## Symbol

A symbol is a graphic figure that stands for something else by association, resemblance, or convention, deriving its meaning chiefly from the structure in which it occurs. Representational symbols are simplified pictures of what they represent. To be useful and meaningful to a broad audience, they must be generalized and embody the structural features of what they refer to. Highly abstract shapes, on the other hand, can be very broad in application, but usually need a context or caption to explain their meaning. When symbols become more abstract and lose any visual connection to what they refer, they become signs.

## Sign

A sign is a graphic symbol, figure, or mark having a conventional meaning and used as an abbreviation for the word, phrase, or operation it represents. Signs do not reflect any of the visual characteristics of its referent. They can be understood only by convention or common agreement.

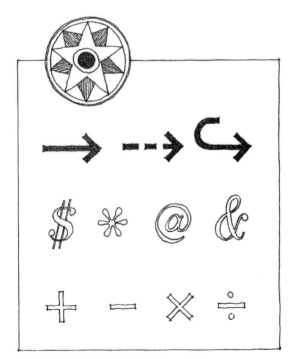

Symbols and signs are not as suitable as words in expressing subtle degrees of difference or slight nuances of meaning, but nevertheless they efficiently communicate the identity of elements and the nature of actions or processes. Such visual abstractions can often communicate more swiftly than is possible through words alone. Even so, we often use explanatory text clarify the symbols of a diagram, even if only in the abbreviated form of a key or legend.

We can modify the graphic display and meaning of symbols and signs by altering the following characteristics:

- The relative size of each symbol or sign can describe quantifiable aspects of each element as well as establish a hierarchical ranking among the elements.
- A grid or other geometric ordering device can regulate the positioning and layout of entities or subjects within the field of the diagram.
- Relative proximities indicate the intensity of relationship among entities. Elements in close proximity to each other reveal a stronger relationship than more distant ones.
- Similarities and contrasts of shape, size, or tonal value establish categories among selected objects or ideas. Reducing the number of elements and variables helps maintain an appropriate and manageable level of abstraction.

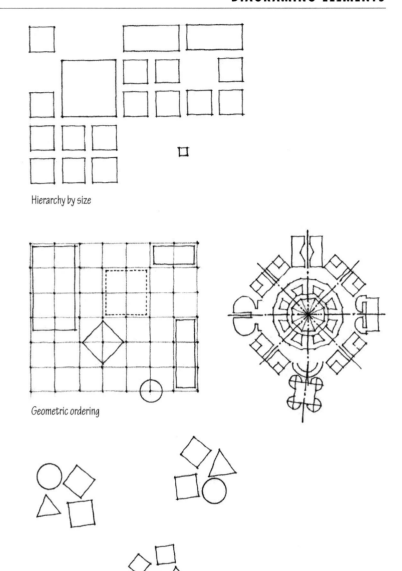

Hierarchy by size

Geometric ordering

Organizing by proximity

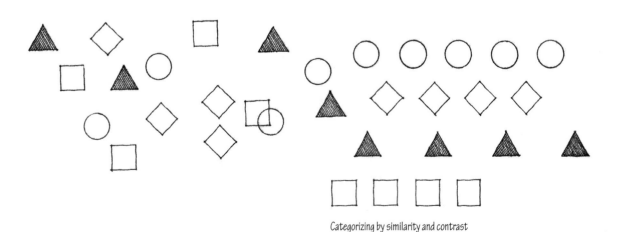

Categorizing by similarity and contrast

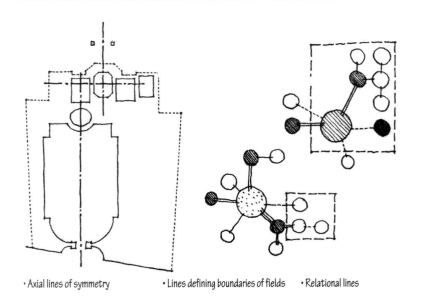

· Axial lines of symmetry          · Lines defining boundaries of fields          · Relational lines

In order to make the relationships among the elements of a diagram more visible, we use the grouping principles of proximity, continuity, and similarity. To further clarify and emphasize specific types of linkages or the nature of interactions among the entities, we can employ a variety of lines and arrows. And by varying the width, length, continuity, and tonal value of these linking elements, we can also describe varying degrees, levels, and intensities of connection.

## Lines

We use the organizing power of lines in diagraming to define the boundaries of fields, denote the interdependencies of elements, and structure formal and spatial relationships. In clarifying the organizational and relational aspects of a diagram, lines make both abstract and pictorial concepts visible and understandable.

## Arrows

Arrows are a special type of connecting line. The wedge-shaped ends can signify one- or two-way movement from one element to another, indicate the direction of a force or action, or denote the phase of a process. For clarity, we use different types of arrows to distinguish between the types of relationships as well as varying degrees of intensity or importance.

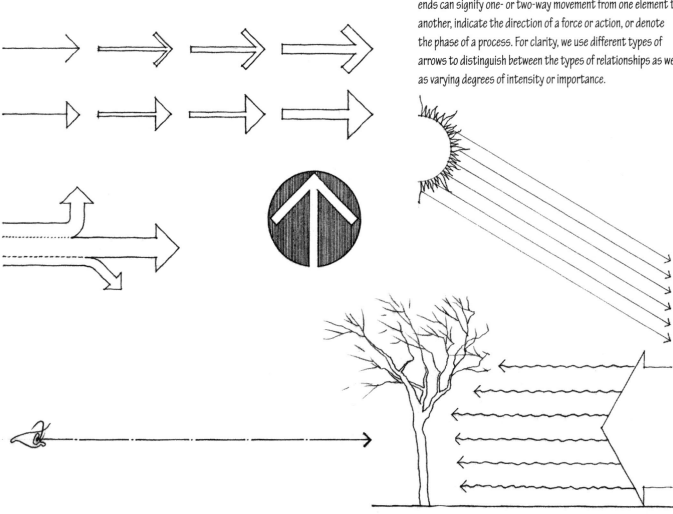

### Exercise 10.1

Diagram the spatial composition of the building designs below.

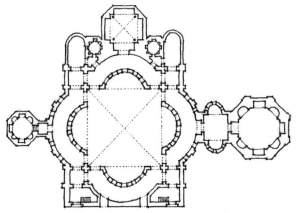

San Lorenzo Maggiore, Milan, Italy, c. A.D. 480

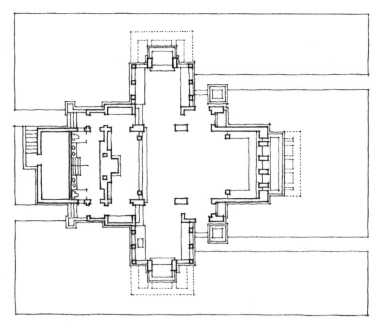

Coonley Playhouse, Riverside, Illinois, 1912, Frank Lloyd Wright

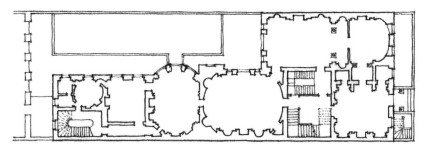

Lord Derby's House, London, 1777, Robert Adam

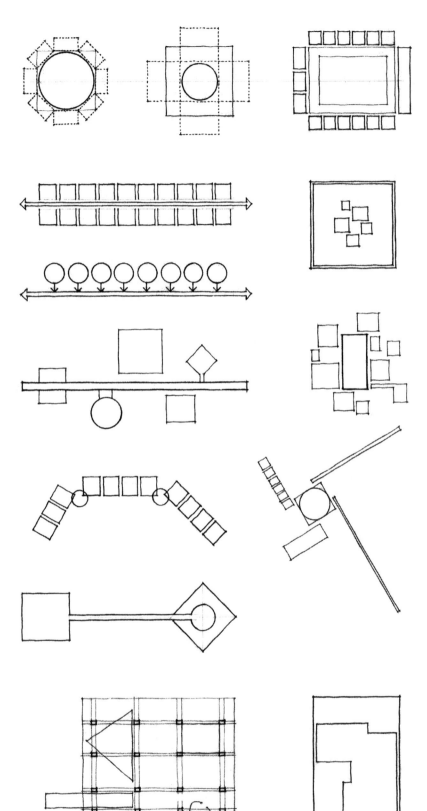

We use diagrams in the initial stages of the design process to to study existing conditions and to generate, explore, and clarify concepts. We also use diagrams in the presentation phase of the design process to explain the conceptual basis for a design proposal.

## Parti

A concept is a mental idea or image capable of generating and guiding the development of a design. We use the term parti when referring to the concept or primary organizing idea for an architectural design. Drawing a concept or parti out in diagrammatic form enables a designer to quickly and efficiently investigate the overall nature and organization of a scheme. Instead of concentrating on how a design might appear, the concept diagram focuses on the key structural and relational features of an idea.

A suitable concept should of course be appropriate and relevant to the nature of the design problem. In addition, both a design concept and its graphic portrayal in a diagram should have the following characteristics.

A concept diagram should be:

- Inclusive: capable of addressing the multiple issues of a design problem
- Visually descriptive: powerful enough to guide the development of a design
- Adaptable: flexible enough to accept change
- Sustainable: able to endure manipulations and transformations during the design process without a loss of identity

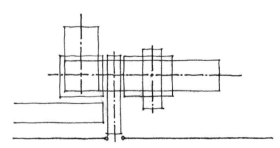

## Exercise 10.2

On the previous page are a number of examples of parti diagrams. For each building plan illustrated below, select the diagram that most closely corresponds to the organizational idea of the scheme. Modify the selected diagram to develop the parti for each of the plans.

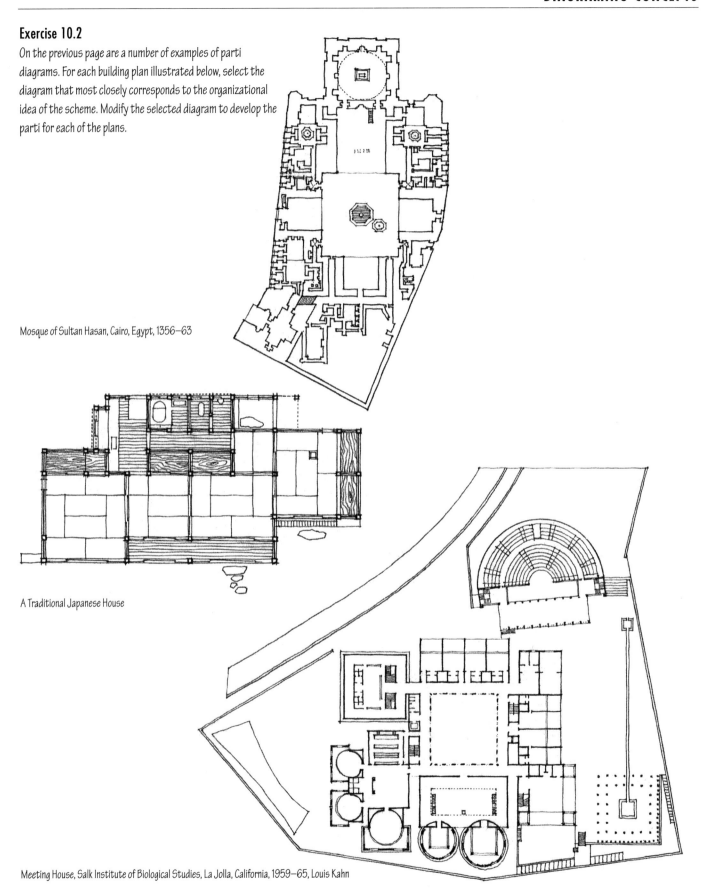

Mosque of Sultan Hasan, Cairo, Egypt, 1356–63

A Traditional Japanese House

Meeting House, Salk Institute of Biological Studies, La Jolla, California, 1959–65, Louis Kahn

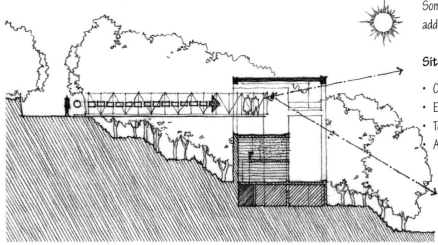

Some of the issues which concept diagrams can effectively address include:

### Site:

- Contextual constraints and opportunities
- Environmental forces of sun, wind, and precipitation
- Topography, landscape, and water features
- Approach, access, and paths through a site

Residence at Riva San Vitale, on the shore of Lugano Lake, Switzerland, 1971–73, Mario Botta

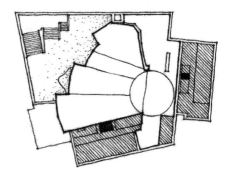
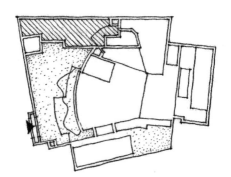
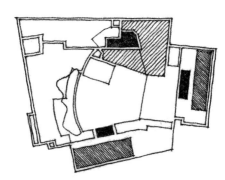

Theater in Seinäjoki, Finland, 1968–69, Alvar Aalto

### Program:

- Spatial dimensions required for activities
- Functional proximities and adjacencies
- Relationship between served and service spaces
- Zoning of public and private functions

### Circulation:

- Pedestrian, vehicular, and service
- Approach, entry, nodes, and paths of movement
- Horizontal and vertical

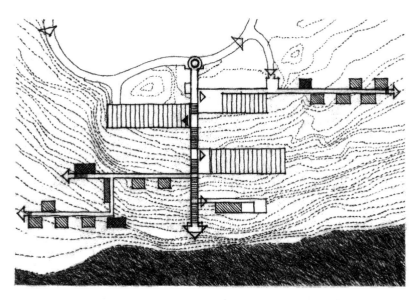

Haystack Mountain School of Arts and Crafts, Deer Isle, Maine, 1960, Edward Larabee Barnes

**Formal issues:**

- Figure-ground and solid-void relationships
- Ordering principles, such as symmetry and rhythm
- Structural elements and pattern
- Elements and configuration of enclosure
- Spatial qualities, such as shelter and outlook
- Hierarchical organization of spaces
- Formal massing and geometry
- Proportion and scale

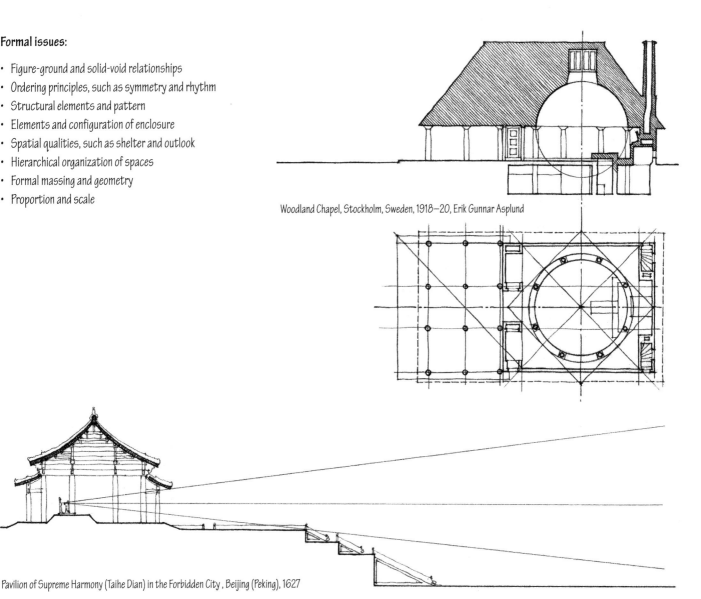

Woodland Chapel, Stockholm, Sweden, 1918–20, Erik Gunnar Asplund

Pavilion of Supreme Harmony (Taihe Dian) in the Forbidden City , Beijing (Peking), 1627

**Systems:**

- Layout and integration of structural, lighting, and environmental control systems

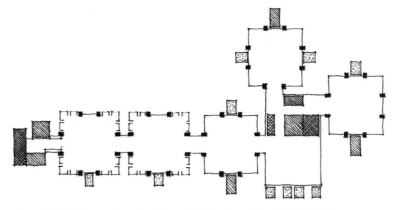

Richards Medical Research Laboratory, University of Pennsylvania, Philadelphia, 1957–61, Louis Kahn

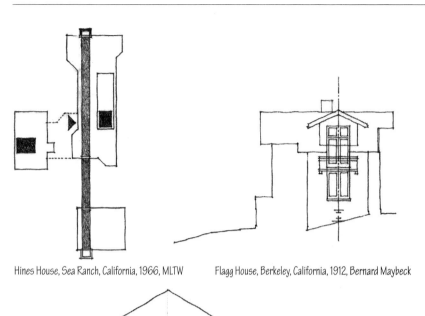

Hines House, Sea Ranch, California, 1966, MLTW

Flagg House, Berkeley, California, 1912, Bernard Maybeck

In generating, developing, and utilizing concept diagrams, certain principles can help stimulate our thinking.

- Keep concept diagrams concise. Drawing small condenses the information to a manageable level.
- Delete extraneous information as needed to focus on a particular issue and enhance the overall clarity of the diagram.
- Overlay or juxtapose a series of diagrams to see how certain variables affect the nature of a design, or how the various parts and systems of a design fit together to form a whole.
- Reverse, rotate, overlap, or distort an element or linkage in order to provide new ways of viewing the diagram and to discover new relationships.
- Utilize the modifying factors of size, proximity, and similarity to reorganize and prioritize the elements as you search for order.
- Add relevant information when necessary to take advantage of newly discovered relationships.

In all cases, the visual clarity and organization of the diagram should please the eye as well as impart information to the viewer.

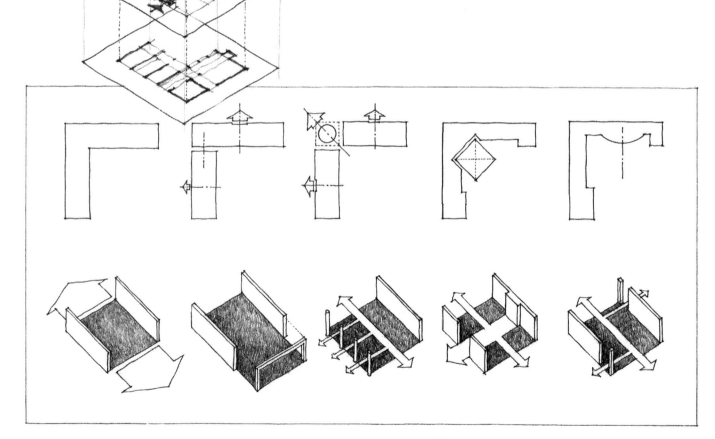

## Exercise 10.3

Analyze the plan and cross section of the Library of Mount Angel Benedictine College. Develop diagrams which convey the following information:

- Structural pattern
- System of enclosure
- Spatial organization
- Functional zoning
- Pattern of circulation

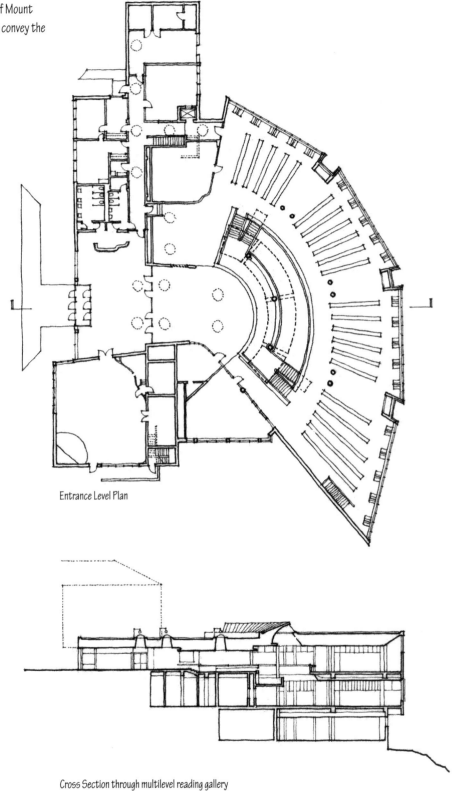

Entrance Level Plan

Cross Section through multilevel reading gallery

Library of Mount Angel Benedictine College, Mount Angel, Oregon, 1965–70, Alvar Aalto

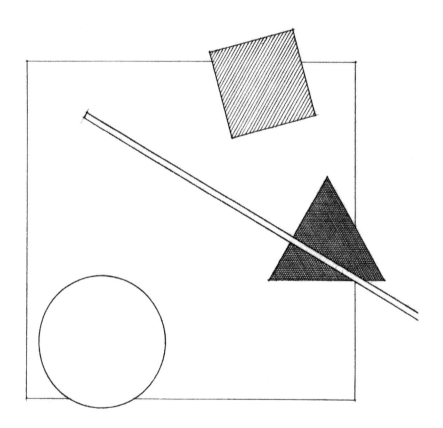

# 11
# Drawing Composition

Drawing is a system of design. Neither the appropriate choice of viewpoint nor beauty of technique is sufficient without a concern for composition. In composing a drawing, we manipulate the fundamental graphic elements of line, shape, and tone into coherent figure-ground patterns which convey visual information. Through the organization and relationship of these elements, we define both the content and the context of a drawing. Planning this composition is therefore critical to the message it communicates.

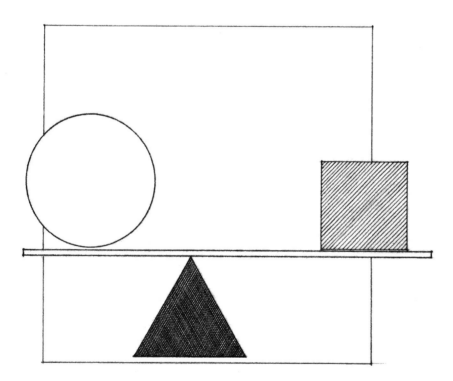

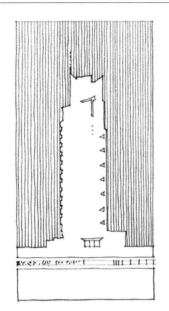

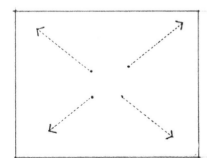

The first step in composing a drawing is to determine the shape, size, and proportions of its field relative to the dimensions of the drawing sheet or board. This field should be large enough to incorporate a portion of the design context as well as space for the drawing title, graphic scale, and associated symbols.

The field of a drawing may be square, rectangular, circular, elliptical, or irregular. Rectangular fields are the most common and may be oriented either vertically or horizontally. Regardless of the shape of a drawing's field, certain fundamental principles apply to the organization of elements within it.

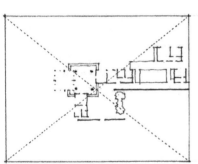

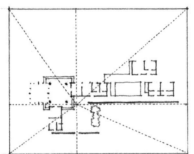

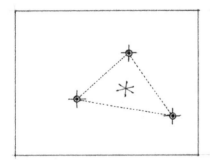

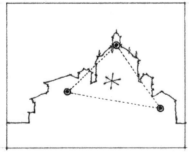

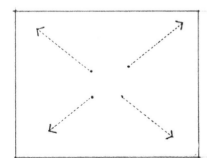

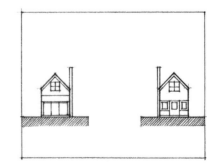

- To create visual interest and movement, place the focal point of a drawing off-center but not too close to the edges of a field. Placing the focal point in the exact center of the field can lead the eye past important points in the drawing.
- When multiple centers of interest lead the eye through and around the field of a drawing, there is a balance point or center of gravity which should be located near the center of the drawing field.
- The eye follows lines of force established by centers of interest. Avoid diagonal lines that lead the eye to the corners of a drawing field. Establish instead concentric lines of force which keep the eye within the field of a drawing.
- Avoid placing two centers of attention close to opposite edges of a field, thereby creating a center space devoid of interest.

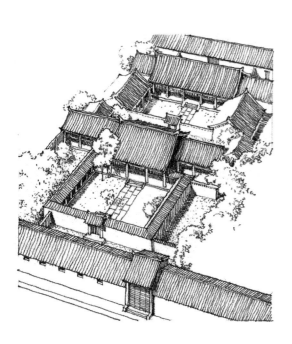

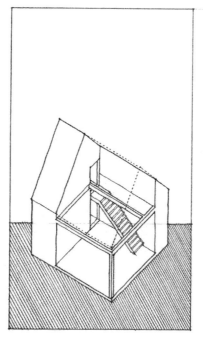

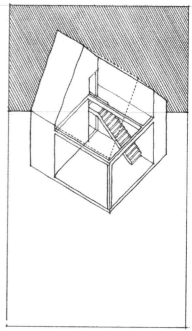

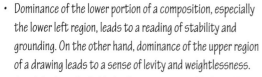

- Dominance of the lower portion of a composition, especially the lower left region, leads to a reading of stability and grounding. On the other hand, dominance of the upper region of a drawing leads to a sense of levity and weightlessness.
- Avoid dividing the field of a drawing into equal halves. The resulting symmetrical division can lead to bland and uninteresting compositions.
- We read from left to right and therefore tend to expect information to begin on the left-hand side of a page. Placing information or a focal point on the right-hand side of a field creates tension, which may require redirecting the eye back into the field of the drawing.
- Allowing certain graphic elements to break through the boundaries of a field can enhance the dynamic quality and emphasize the pictorial depth of a drawing.

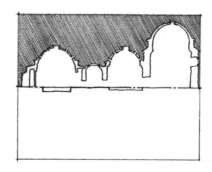

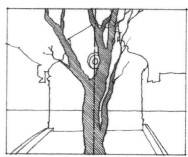

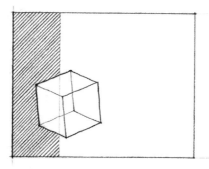

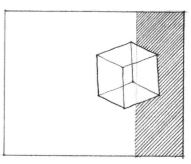

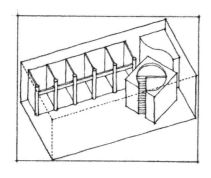

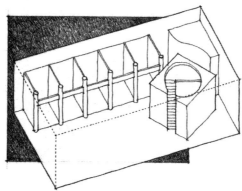

Design drawings are reduced versions of full-size objects or constructions. In selecting an appropriate scale for a drawing, there are several factors to consider.

First, there is an obvious relationship between the scale of a drawing and the size of the drawing surface. The larger a design, the smaller its representation on the sheet or board; the smaller the design, the larger its scale can be. Also influencing drawing scale is the manner in which drawings are laid out in a presentation. For example, when plans, sections, and elevations comprise a set of cross-referenced information, their scale must enable the entire set to fit on a single sheet or board.

Second, the scale of a drawing regulates the perceived distance between the mind's eye of the viewer and the representation of a design. Close-up views provide a detailed look at the features of the subject. Small-scale drawings increase this perceptual distance but enable the entirety of an idea to be grasped quickly. At the same time, these distant views minimize the amount of detail that can be depicted.

Large-scale drawings, on the other hand, are close-up views which allow a greater degree of detail and complexity to be revealed, as well as a greater range of tonal values to be rendered. As the scale of a drawing increases, the amount of detail required for legibility and credibility also becomes greater. Not including enough detail at larger scales can make a drawing look sparse and diagrammatic.

Finally, the scale of a drawing influences the type of drawing tool and technique we use. Fine-tipped instruments, such as pens and thin-lead pencils, encourage drawing at a small scale and enable us to focus on fineness of detail. Broad-tipped tools, such as color markers and charcoal, promote large-scale drawing and discourage the study of small-scale features.

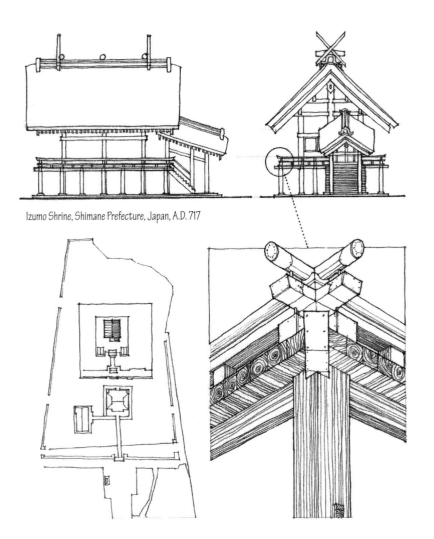

Izumo Shrine, Shimane Prefecture, Japan, A.D. 717

The size of a graphic image relative to the size of its field determines how we read the figure.

### Vignette

Situating the drawing in a large field emphasizes its individuality. The space between a drawing and the edge of a sheet typically should be similar to or larger than the dimensions of the drawing.

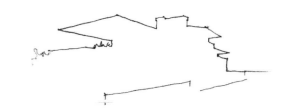

### Interacting

If we enlarge the drawing or reduce the size of its field, its figure begins to interact visually with its background. The field begins to have a recognizable shape or figural quality of its own.

### Ambiguous

Enlarging the drawing or reducing its field still further establishes an ambiguous figure-ground relationship in which the field elements can also be seen as figures.

When a paraline drawing, perspective drawing, or other graphic image does not have a rectangular shape, it tends to float in its field. We can stabilize the image with either a title block or a horizontal band of color or value.

When framing a drawing, avoid using a double or triple mat. Doing so can create the impression of a figure on a background that itself has a background. Therefore, attention would be diverted from the figure where it belongs to the frame around it.

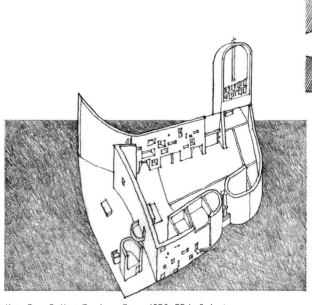

Notre Dame Du Haut, Ronchamp, France, 1950–55, Le Corbusier

Drawing composition concerns the relationships among the parts of a graphic image rather than the rendering of any particular part. We can apply certain principles of visual design to regulate the organization of a drawing composition in order to promote a sense of order and unity.

## Unity and variety

The following ordering principles, in promoting unity, do not exclude the pursuit of variety and visual interest. Rather, the means for achieving order are intended to include in their patterns the presence of dissimilar elements and characteristics.

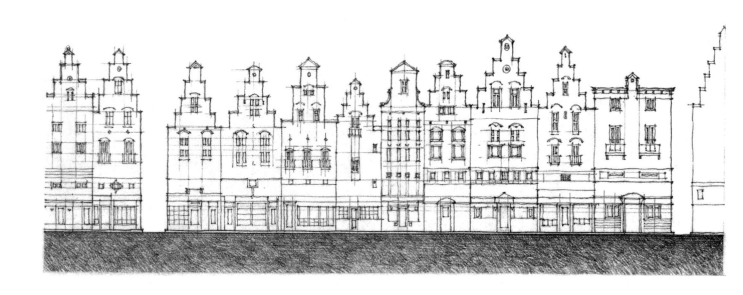

In scanning an image, the eye is attracted to certain graphic elements. The eye seeks out areas of:

· exceptional size or proportion
· contrasting or unusual shape
· sharp tonal contrast
· finely resolved or elaborate detail

We can also stress the importance of an element by isolating it within the drawing composition. We use these points or areas of interest to define the focus of a drawing. In each case, a discernible contrast must be established between the dominant element and the subordinate aspects of the composition. Without contrast, nothing can dominate.

There may exist not one but several focal points in a drawing. One may dominate while others serve as accents. We must be careful that multiple centers of interest do not cause confusion. When everything is emphasized, nothing dominates.

Moore House, Orinda, California, 1961, Charles Moore

# BALANCE

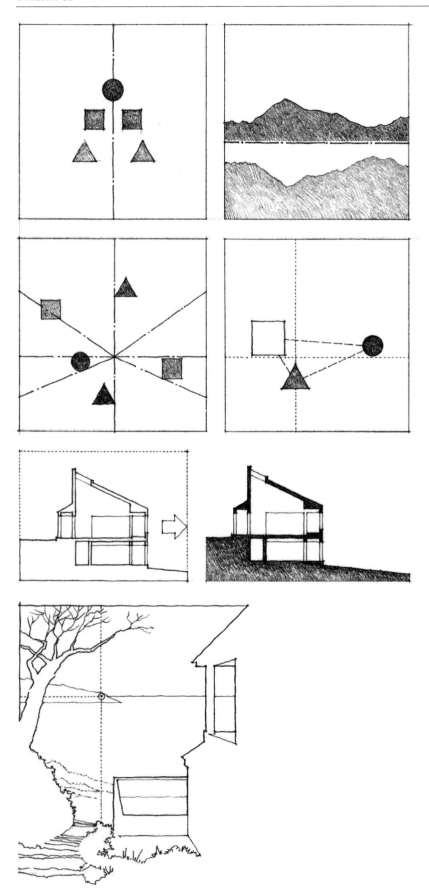

In any drawing, there will naturally be a mix of shapes and tonal values. How we organize these elements should result in a visual sense of balance. Balance refers to the pleasing or harmonious arrangement or proportion of parts or elements in a design or composition. The principle of balance involves reaching equilibrium among visual forces of weight, compression, and tension in a drawing.

There are two principal types of balance: symmetrical and asymmetrical. Symmetry refers to the exact correspondence in size, shape, and arrangement of parts on opposite sides of a dividing line or axis. Bilateral or axial symmetry results from the arrangement of similar parts on opposite sides of a median axis. This type of symmetry leads the eye to the mediating axis in a quiet manner.

Radial symmetry results from the arrangement of similar radiating parts about a center point or central axis. This type of symmetry stresses the centerpoint or middleground of a composition.

We recognize asymmetry by the lack of correspondence in the size, shape, or tonal value of elements in a composition. In order to achieve visual or optical balance, an asymmetrical composition must take into account the visual weight or force of each of its elements and employ the principle of leverage in their arrangement. Elements that are visually forceful and attract our attention must be counterbalanced by less forceful elements which are larger or placed farther away from the center of gravity of the composition.

## Exercise 11.1

Explore ways to compose this fragment of a Spanish town within a larger drawing field. How could you compose the view to emphasize the town's position atop a hill? How could you alter the composition to stress instead its relationship to a distant mountain range?

## Exercise 11.2

Explore ways to compose this view of the Sydney Opera House designed by Jørn Utzon in 1956, within a larger square or rectangular field. How could you place the structure to emphasize its soaring roof forms as well as their relationship to the harbor on which they front?

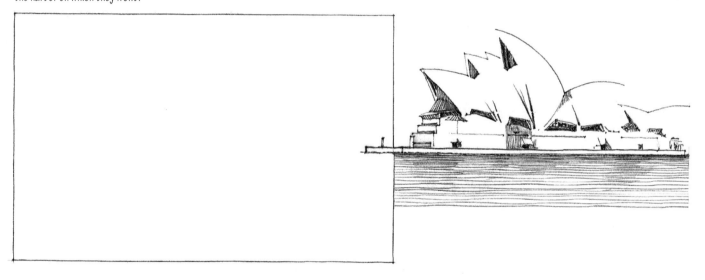

## Exercise 11.3

Shown is a plan diagram of the Capitol Complex at Islamabad, Pakistan, designed by Louis Kahn in 1965. Explore how you could achieve a balanced composition within a rectangular field. How could you maintain the same balance within a square field? How would rotating the plan 90° affect the compositional possibilities?

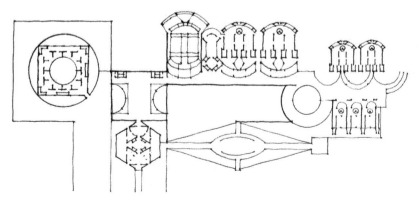

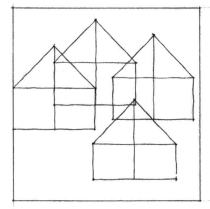

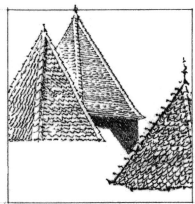

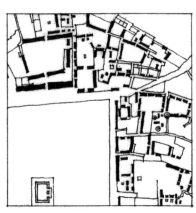

Harmony refers to consonance or to the pleasing agreement of the parts in a design or composition. While balance achieves unity through the careful arrangement of both similar and dissimilar elements, the principle of harmony involves the careful selection of elements which share a common trait or characteristic:

- common size
- common shape
- common tonal value or color
- similar orientation
- similar detail characteristics

Perhaps the most natural way to produce harmony in a drawing is the use of a common medium and technique throughout the composition. Employing the principle of harmony too rigorously can result in a unified but uninteresting composition. Drawings need diversity as an antidote to monotony. But variety, when carried to an extreme for the sake of interest, can result in visual chaos and a fragmented message. It is the careful and artistic tension between order and disorder—between unity and variety—that enlivens harmony. Stability and unity emerge from stimulating the action of contrasts as well as the union of similarities.

Since we design and evaluate architecture in relation to its environment, it is important to incorporate the context in the drawing of a design proposal. In each of the major drawing systems, we do this by extending the ground line and plane to include adjacent structures and site features. In addition to the physical context, we should indicate the scale and intended use of spaces by including human figures and furnishings. We can also attempt to describe the ambience of a place by depicting the quality of light, the colors and textures of materials, the scale and proportion of the space, or the cumulative effect of details.

These elements are simply parts of a greater whole, and the amount of interest and attention we give them should be proportional to their importance in the overall composition. Therefore, the following guidelines apply to the drawing of contextual devices:

- Use only those contextual devices necessary to communicate context, scale, and use.
- Draw contextual devices simply and with an appropriate level of detail.
- Never obscure important structural or space-defining elements and their relationships.
- Consider the shape, size, and tonal value of contextual devices as important elements in the composition of a drawing.

Approach to Notre Dame Du Haut, Ronchamp, France, 1950–55, Le Corbusier

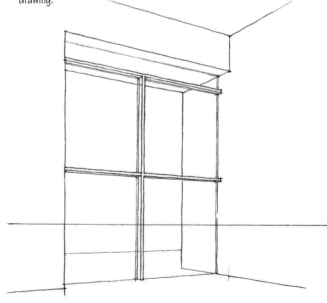

Interior of Barrágan House and Atelier, Tacubaya, Mexico City, 1947, Luis Barrágan

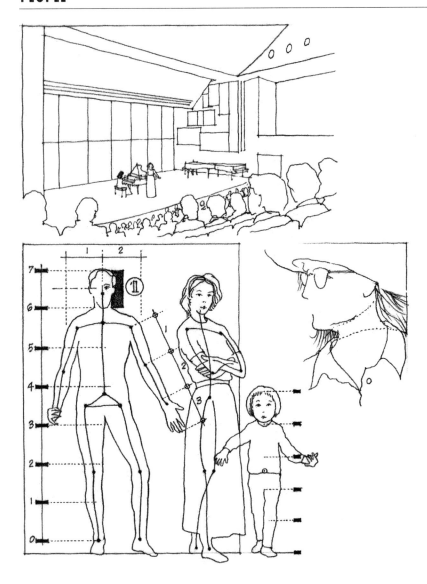

The viewer of a drawing relates to the human figures within it, becomes one of them, and thus is drawn into the scene. Therefore, in the drawing of architectural and urban spaces, we include people to:

- indicate the scale of a space
- express spatial depth and changes of level
- animate a space with signs of life and habitation

## Scale

The figures we use to populate a drawing should be in scale with the environment. Therefore, we need to draw human figures in proper size and proportion. We can divide the standing human figure into seven or eight equal parts, with the head being $\frac{1}{7}$ or $\frac{1}{8}$ of the total body height.

- Establish the height of each figure and the proportions of the parts, the most critical being the size of the head.
- The jaw line leads to where the head joins the spine.
- The back of the neck is usually higher than the jaw.
- The shoulder slopes from the nape of the neck down to the arms.
- The height of the nose and the ears are equivalent.
- Use glasses to suggest eyes.
- Stop short of drawing eyes and mouth; imply their presence by subtly shading their undersides.
- At the scale of most architectural drawings, the drawing of fingers is not necessary and is almost always distracting.
- Hands extend down to almost touch the knees.

- Give the figures a sense of volume, especially in paraline and perspective views.
- Avoid drawing outlined frontal views of people which appear like flat, cardboard cutouts.
- Clothe the figure appropriately, avoiding unnecessary details that might distract from the focus of the drawing.

- Establish attitude and gesture, paying particular attention to the contour of the spine and support points for the body.
- Use the relative proportions of body parts as a guide when drawing different postures and gestures.
- Show people gesturing with their arms and hands.
- Use the chin and nose to direct attention.

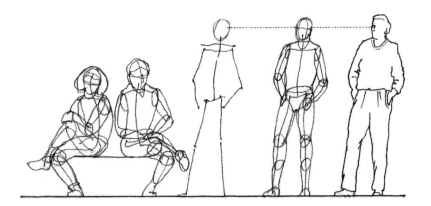

In orthographic multiview drawings, we can simply scale the five- or six-foot height. Remember that in orthographic projection, the height and width of elements remain constant regardless of their depth within the projected view. We can also scale the height of human figures in paraline views. Since the view is downward, the figures should have some degree of roundness to indicate their volume.

In perspective drawings, the placement of human figures can indicate not only spatial depth but also changes in level. It is generally easiest to begin by locating where each person is standing. Then extend this spot vertically and place the eyes of the head of each figure on the horizon line. Once the height of a figure is established, we can use the principles of linear perspective to shift the figure right or left, up or down, or into the depth of the perspective. Figures above or below the level of the spectator should first be sized as if on the same level, and then shifted up or down as required. When drawing people in a sitting position, it is usually best to draw first a person standing alongside the chair. Then use the established proportions to draw the same person sitting down.

## Disposition

The human figures we use to indicate scale and use also become important elements in a composition and should not conceal or distract from the focus and essential features of a drawing. Utilize both groups and solitary figures and the principle of overlap to convey depth.

## Activity

We indicate activity in a drawing by the number, disposition, posture, and dress of human figures. The figures should convey the nature of the activity and be appropriate to the place and setting. The manner in which we draw them should answer the fundamental question: What activity should go on in this room or space?

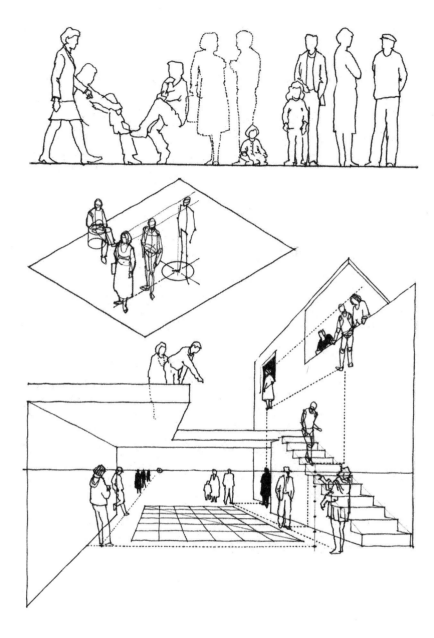

### Exercise 11.4

Bring a pen, pencils, and a sketchbook to a public place where people gather. Practice drawing the people you see. Draw people standing as well as sitting; sketch small, distant figures as well as closer ones. Begin by working out the structure, proportions, and gesture of each individual, then build up a sense of volume, and finally add necessary details. Start slowly in the first session. In each succeeding session, gradually shorten the time you take to draw each figure and reduce the amount of detail accordingly.

### Exercise 11.5

In this linear perspective, use analytical lines and the principles of convergence to transfer the human figure to locations A, B, C, and D.

In addition to people, there are other elements which we can use to suggest the context of a drawing. These typically include topography and entourage—the landscaping and other environmental features shown in the rendering of a building.

In addition to indicating scale, trees and other landscape features portray the geography and character of a site, whether hilly or flat, wooded or barren, urban or rural. This entourage should never compete with but rather act as a foil for the design that is being illustrated.

Drawing trees and shrubs follows in a similar manner to how we construct a scene. We begin with the branch structure, following the pattern of growth from the ground upward. To this framework, we can add the overall shape and massing of the foliage, paying close attention to texture, tonal value, and degree of opacity and transparency. Be economical. The amount of detail rendered should be consistent with the scale and style of the drawing.

Trees and other plant materials are important means of providing tonal values and textures in a drawing. How we portray these natural elements is therefore a consideration in planning the tonal range and pattern of a composition.

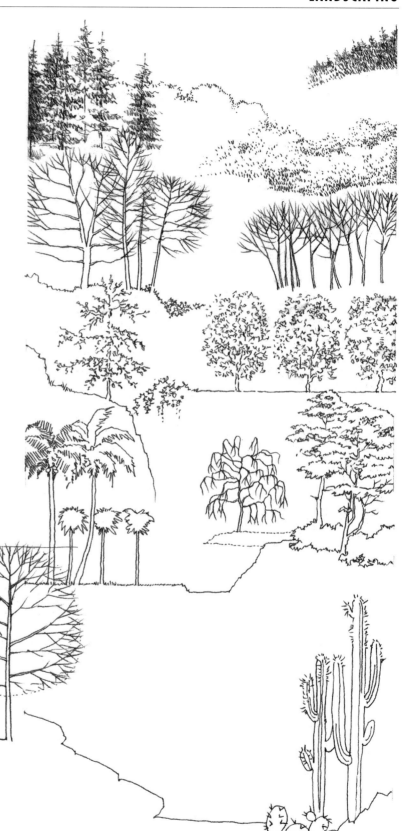

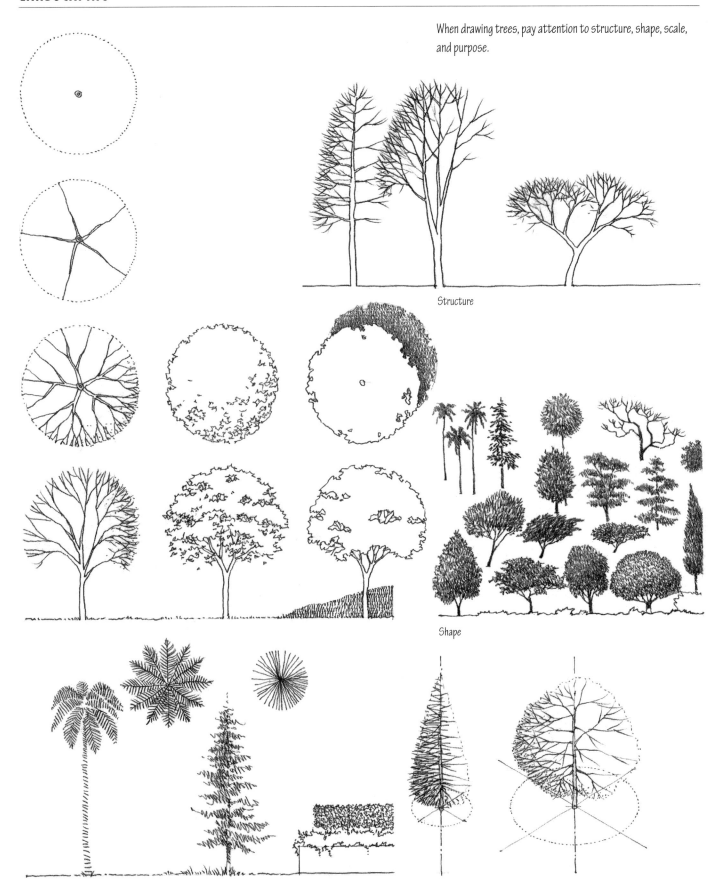

When drawing trees, pay attention to structure, shape, scale, and purpose.

Structure

Shape

## Exercise 11.6

Bring a pen, pencils, and a sketchbook to a public park. Practice drawing a variety of trees and other plant life you see. Draw small, distant trees as well as closer ones. Begin by blocking out the branch structure of the subject. Over this framework, build up the shape, texture, mass, and tonal value of the foliage.

## Exercise 11.7

Draw a series of timed sketches of a deciduous tree from direct observation. Begin with a 5-minute drawing, then do a 3-minute sketch, and end with a 1-minute sketch. Build up each drawing from structure to shape and tonal value. Repeat this exercise for a conifer.

## Exercise 11.8

Draw a series of sketches of a deciduous tree from direct observation. Begin by drawing the subject from a distance of 25 feet. Move to a distance of 50 feet and draw the same tree again. Draw the tree one more time from a distance of 100 feet. Each time you move farther away, pay attention to how the foliage shifts from texture gradient to a shape of tonal value. Repeat this exercise for a conifer.

The type and arrangement of furnishings are important indicators of use and activity in a space. Their placement reminds us that there should be places on which to sit, lean, rest our elbow or foot, or to simply touch.

Drawing furniture in conjunction with people helps establish their scale and maintain the proper proportion of their parts. Except when furniture is the subject of a design, use real, well-designed examples, and proceed from their geometric basis. Once the structural framework for the form is established, we can add indications of material, thickness, and details.

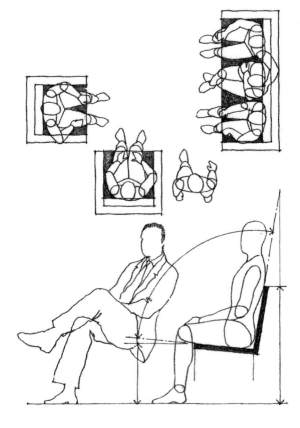

Traditional Wing Chair

Louis XVI Armchair

Bar Harbor Wicker

Shaker Ladderback

Thonet Bentwood

Wassily Chair - Marcel Breuer

We include a variety of vehicles—cars, trucks, buses, and even bicycles—to indicate roadways and parking areas in exterior scenes. Be realistic with their placement and scale.

Drawing vehicles in conjunction with people helps establish their scale. Use real examples whenever possible, and as in the drawing of furniture, proceed from their geometric basis. If we overdraw these elements and include too much detail, they can easily become unintended distractions from the focus of a drawing.

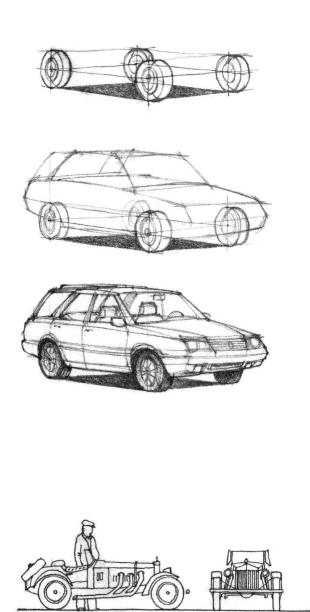

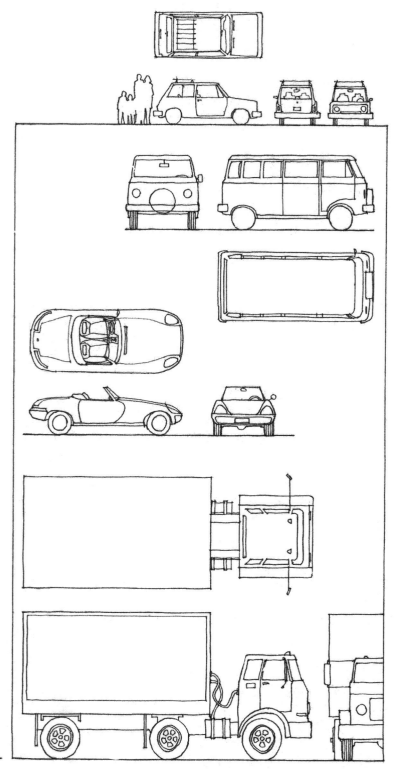

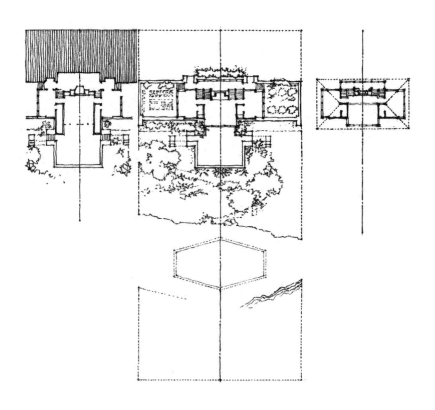

# 12
# Presentation Drawing

Presentation drawings are those we typically think of when the term *design drawing* is used. These drawings describe a design proposal in a graphic manner intended to persuade an audience of its value. The audience may be a client, a committee, or merely someone browsing for an idea. Whether produced to assist the client's imagination or to obtain a commission, either privately or through a competition, presentation drawings should communicate as clearly and accurately as possible the three-dimensional qualities of a design. Although the drawings that comprise a presentation may be excellent two-dimensional graphics worthy of an exhibition, they are merely tools for communicating a design idea, never ends in themselves.

Hardy House, Racine, Wisconsin, 1905, Frank Lloyd Wright

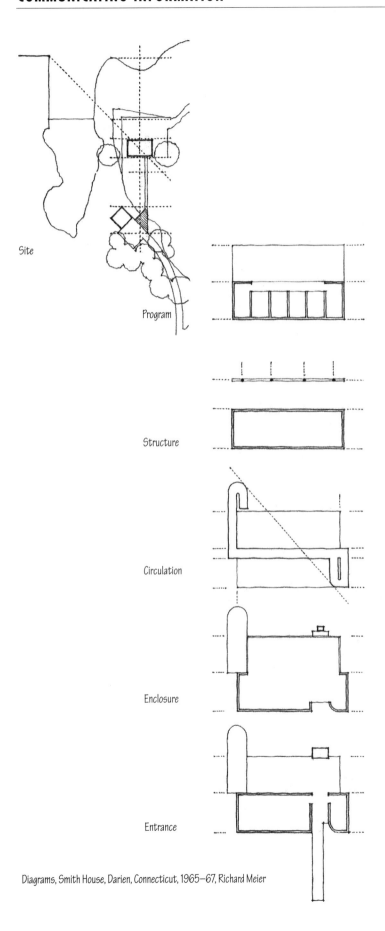

Site

Program

Structure

Circulation

Enclosure

Entrance

Diagrams, Smith House, Darien, Connecticut, 1965–67, Richard Meier

Unless presentation drawings are comprehensible and persuasive—their conventions understood and their substance meaningful—a presentation will be weak and ineffective. An effective presentation, however, also possesses collective characteristics that can enhance the readability of the individual drawings themselves.

### Point of View

Be clear about design intent. A presentation should communicate the central idea or concept of a design scheme. Graphic diagrams and text are effective means of articulating and clarifying the essential aspects of a design scheme, especially when they are visually related to the more common types of design drawings.

### Efficiency

Be economical. An effective presentation employs economy of means, utilizing only what is necessary to communicate an idea. If any of the graphic elements of a presentation become overly expressive and ends in themselves, the intent and purpose of the presentation are obscured.

### Clarity

Be articulate. At a minimum, presentation drawings should explain a design clearly and in enough detail so that persons unfamiliar with it will be able to understand the design proposal. Eliminate unintended distractions such as those caused by ambiguous figure-ground relationships or inappropriate groupings of drawings. Too often, we are blind to these glitches since we know what we want to communicate and therefore cannot read our own work in an objective manner.

### Accuracy

Avoid distorting or presenting incorrect information. Presentation drawings should accurately simulate a possible reality and the consequences of future actions so that the decisions made based on the information presented are sound and reasonable.

## Unity

Be organized. In an effective presentation, no one segment is inconsistent with or detracts from the whole. Unity, not to be confused with uniformity, depends on:

- a logical and comprehensive arrangement of integrated graphic and verbal information;
- a synthesis of format, scale, medium, and technique appropriate to the design as well as to the place and audience for which the presentation is intended.

## Continuity

Each segment of a presentation should relate to what precedes it and what follows, reinforcing all the other segments of the presentation.

The principles of unity and continuity are mutually self-supporting; one cannot be achieved with the other. The factors that produce one invariably reinforce the other. At the same time, however, we can bring into focus the central idea of a design through the placement and pacing of the major and supporting graphic and verbal element that comprise the presentation.

Anti-Villa, Napa Valley, California, 1977–78, Batey & Mack

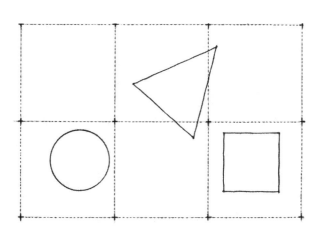

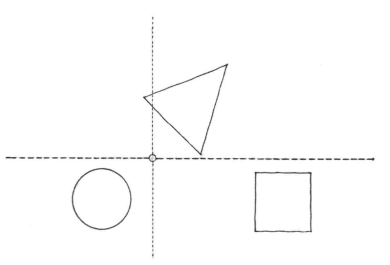

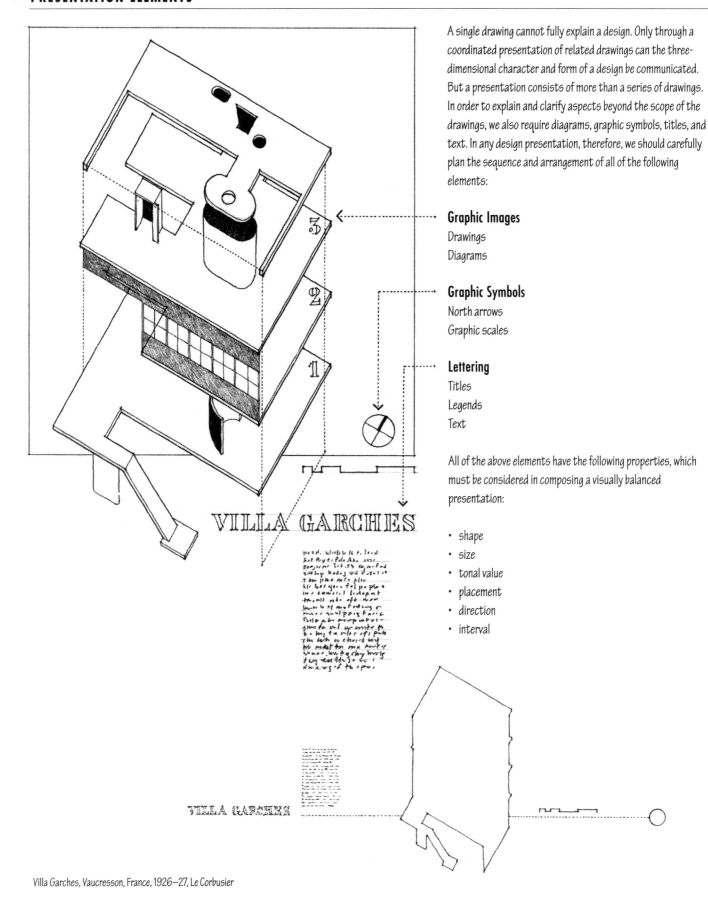

A single drawing cannot fully explain a design. Only through a coordinated presentation of related drawings can the three-dimensional character and form of a design be communicated. But a presentation consists of more than a series of drawings. In order to explain and clarify aspects beyond the scope of the drawings, we also require diagrams, graphic symbols, titles, and text. In any design presentation, therefore, we should carefully plan the sequence and arrangement of all of the following elements:

**Graphic Images**
Drawings
Diagrams

**Graphic Symbols**
North arrows
Graphic scales

**Lettering**
Titles
Legends
Text

All of the above elements have the following properties, which must be considered in composing a visually balanced presentation:

- shape
- size
- tonal value
- placement
- direction
- interval

VILLA GARCHES

*Villa Garches, Vaucresson, France, 1926–27, Le Corbusier*

We generally read design presentations from left to right and from top to bottom. Slide and computerized presentations, however, involve a sequence in time. In either case, the subject matter presented should progress in sequence from small-scale to large-scale, and from the general or contextual view to the specific.

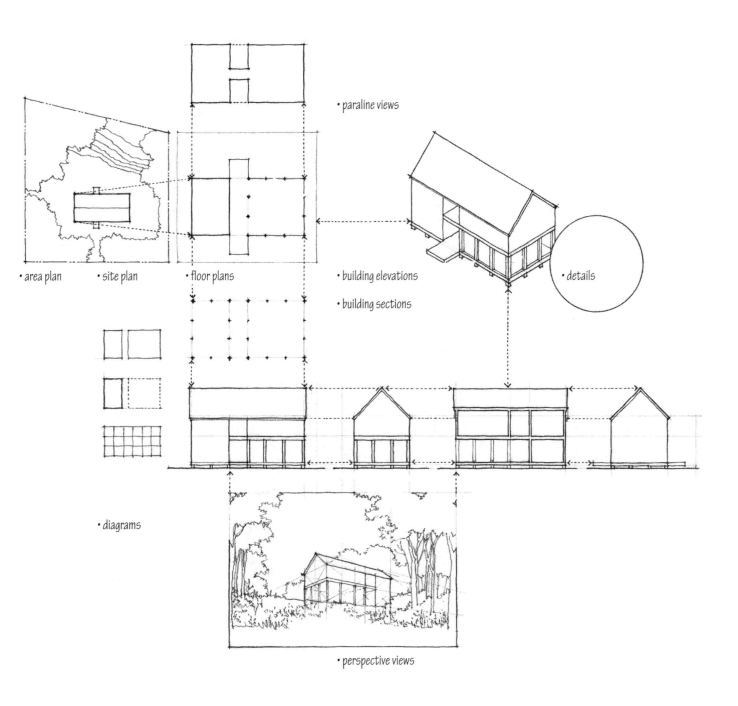

• paraline views

• area plan          • site plan          • floor plans

• building elevations

• building sections

• details

• diagrams

• perspective views

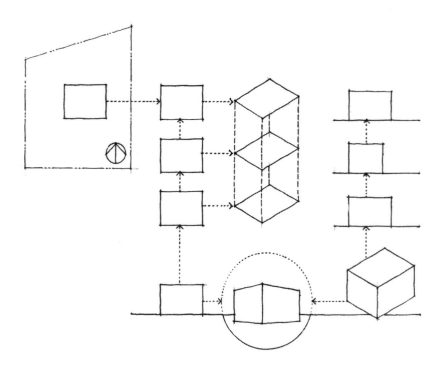

### Drawing Relationships

The sequence and alignment of the drawings should reinforce their projected relationships.

- Orient all plans in a similar manner. Whenever possible, orient plan drawings with north up or upward on the sheet.
- Relate floor plans of multistory buildings either vertically or horizontally, preferably along their longer dimensions.
- Arrange building elevations either vertically or horizontally, correlating them whenever possible to the floor plans.
- Likewise, organize building sections either vertically or horizontally and relate them whenever possible to the floor plans or building elevations.
- Lay out a related series of paraline drawings vertically or horizontally. When each drawing successively builds on the preceding one, work from the bottom up or proceed from left to right.
- Relate paraline and perspective drawings as directly as possible to the plan drawing that best shows their context.
- Include people and furniture to show the scale and use of spaces in all drawings.

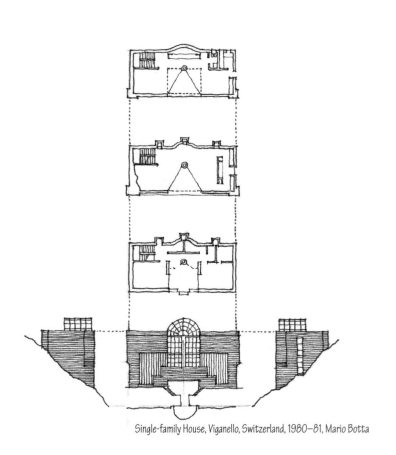

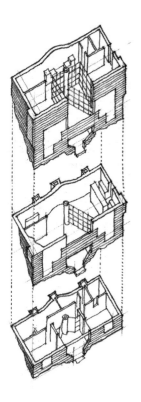

Single-family House, Viganello, Switzerland, 1980–81, Mario Botta

## Exercise 12.1

Develop two different presentation layouts for the site plan, floor plans, and paraline drawing, one based on a horizontal format and another based on a vertical format.

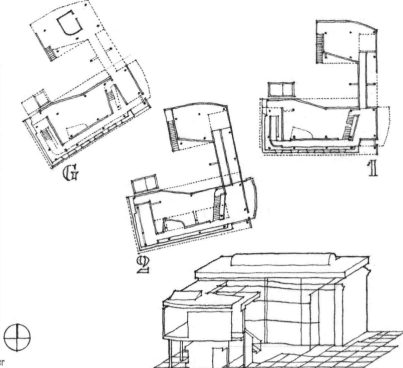

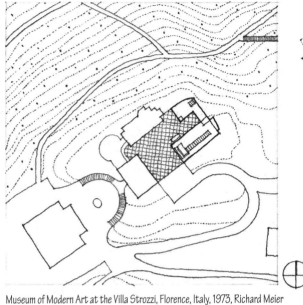

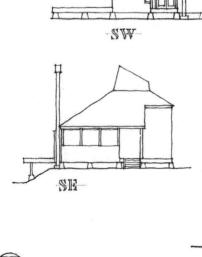

Museum of Modern Art at the Villa Strozzi, Florence, Italy, 1973, Richard Meier

## Exercise 12.2

Develop two different presentation layouts for the plan, section, and elevation drawings, one based on a horizontal format and another based on a vertical format.

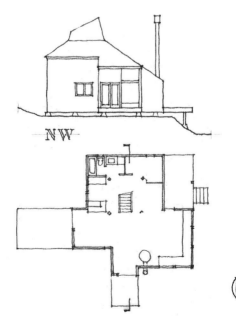

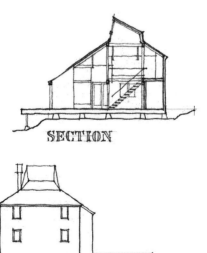

Jobson House, Palo Colorado Canyon, California, 1961, Charles Moore

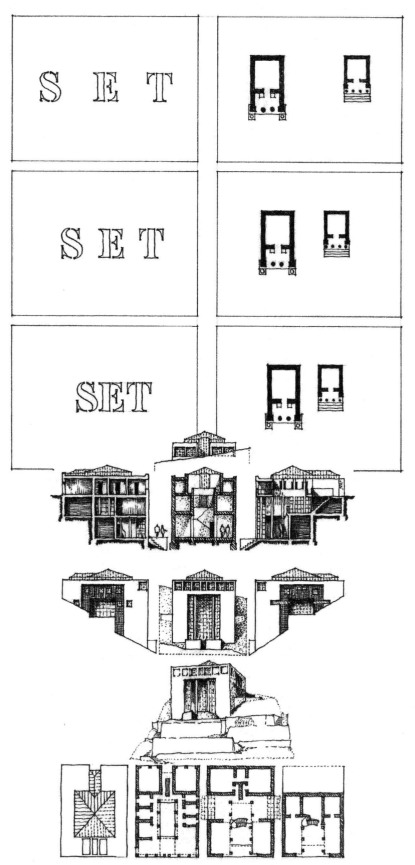

We usually present design drawings as a related set or group of figures. Typical examples include a series of floor plans for a multistory building or a sequence of building elevations. The spacing and alignment of these individual drawings, as well as similarity of shape and treatment, are the key factors in determining whether we read these drawings as a set of related information or as individual figures.

- Use white space and alignment to reinforce the organization of the graphic and verbal information of a presentation. Do not fill up white space unless absolutely necessary.
- If we want two drawings to be read as individual figures, the space between them should be equal to the space between each drawing and the nearest edge of the field.
- Moving the two drawings closer together causes them to be read as a related group.
- If we move the drawings closer still, they will appear to be a single view rather than two related but individual views.

- Properly related drawings which form a visual set can themselves define an edge of a field for another drawing or set of figures.
- Lines can serve to separate as well as to unify, to emphasize, and to outline. Avoid using lines, however, when spacing or alignment can achieve the same purpose.
- Boxes can establish a field within a larger field or within the boundaries of the sheet or board. Be aware, however, that using too many frames can establish confusing figure-ground relationships.

Project for Weidemann House, Stuttgart, Germany, 1975, Rob Krier

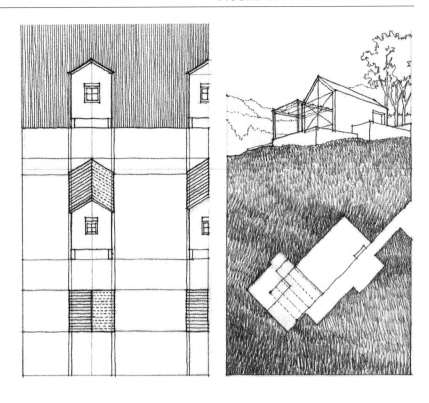

- We can use a tonal value to define a field within a larger field. A darker background for an elevation drawing, for example, can merge with a section drawing. The foreground for a perspective can become the field for a plan view of the building.

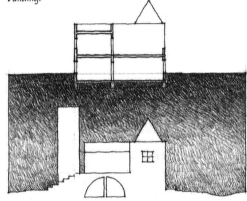

### Exercise 12.3

Develop two different strategies for laying out the plan, elevation, and section shapes in order to form three distinct but related visual sets of information: a plan set, an elevation set, and a section set. How could a field of tonal value be used to create or reinforce one or more of the visual sets?

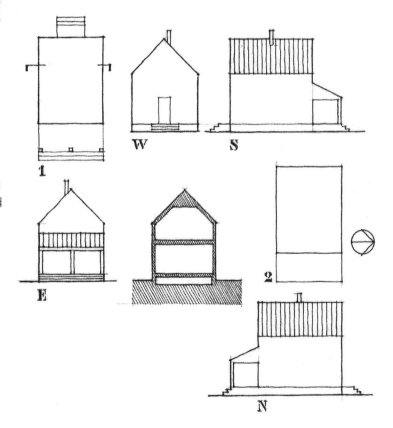

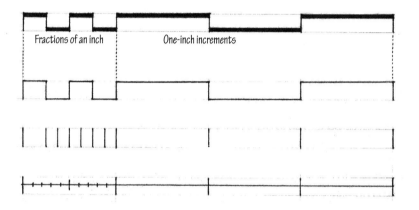

Fractions of an inch One-inch increments

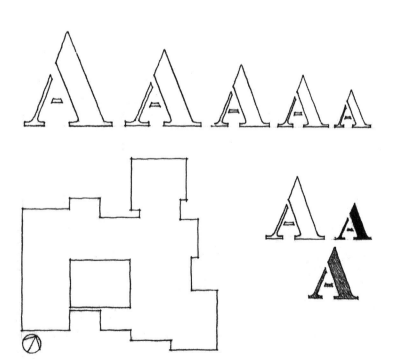

GROUND FLOOR PLAN

### Graphic Symbols

Graphic symbols help the viewer identify the various aspects and features of a drawing or presentation. Two principal types are the north arrow and graphic scale.

- North arrows indicate the major compass points on architectural plans so that the viewer is able to grasp the orientation of a building and its site.

- Graphic scales are graduated lines or bars representing proportionate size. These scales are especially useful because they remain proportional when a drawing is enlarged or reduced.

Graphic symbols rely on conventions to convey information. To be easily recognizable and readable, keep them simple and clean—free of extraneous detail and stylistic flourishes. In enhancing the clarity and readability of a presentation, these devices also become important elements in the overall composition of a drawing or presentation.

The impact of graphic symbols and lettering depends on their size, visual weight, and placement.

### Size

The size of a graphic symbol or lettering should be in proportion to the scale of the drawing and readable from the anticipated viewing distance.

### Visual Weight

The size and tonal value determines the visual weight of graphic symbols and lettering. If a large symbol or typeface is required for readability but a low value is mandatory for a balanced composition, then use an outline symbol or letter style.

### Placement

Place graphic symbols, titles, and text as close to the drawing to which they refer. Whenever possible, use spacing and alignment instead of boxes or frames to form visual sets of information.

## Lettering

The most important characteristics of lettering are legibility, and consistency. The character of the typeface we use should be appropriate to the design being presented and not detract from the drawings themselves. A wealth of well-designed typefaces is available in the form of pressure-sensitive, dry transfer sheets as well as in computerized typography. Therefore, we should spend time on the appropriate selection and use of fonts rather than trying to design new ones.

# TYpO GRa PHY

• We space letters by optically equalizing the areas between the letterforms rather than by mechanically measuring the distance between the extremities of each letter.

Correct spacing of equal areas      Incorrect spacing of letterforms

• Lowercase lettering is appropriate if executed consistently throughout a presentation. It is generally easier to read than text consisting of all capitals because the differences among lowercase characters are more distinct and recognizable.

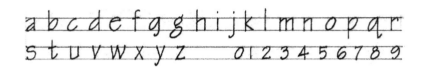

• Serifs are the fine lines used to finish off the main strokes of a letter form. They enhance the recognition and readability of letterforms. Avoid mixing serif and sans serif typefaces.

SERIFS Serifs

• The use of guidelines to control the height and line spacing of hand lettering is essential. The maximum size for a hand lettering is $3/16$ of an inch. Beyond this size, the strokes require a width beyond what a pen or pencil is capable of producing.

ABCDEFGHIJKLMNOPQRSTUV
WXYZ     1234567890

• Determine the range of lettering sizes by judging the distance from which the audience will view the presentation. Keep in mind that we may read different portions of a presentation—project overviews, diagrams, details, text, etc.—at different distances.

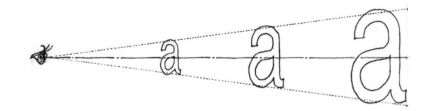

ABCDEFGHIJKLMNOPQRSTUVWXYZ 1234567890 abcdefghijklmnopqrstuvwxyz

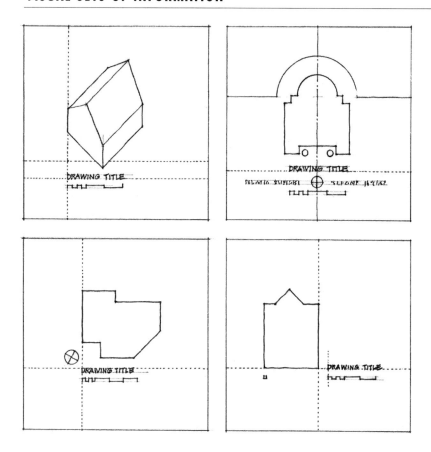

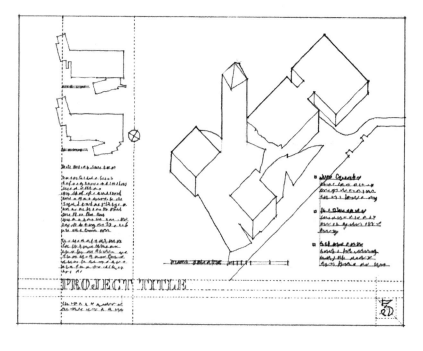

Lettering in an design presentation should be carefully integrated into the composition of drawings on each sheet or board.

## Drawing Titles

Relate titles and graphic symbols which identify and explain the contents of a specific drawing to that drawing. By convention, we always place titles directly below a drawing. In this position, titles can help stabilize drawing fields, especially irregularly shaped ones. Use symmetrical layouts with symmetrical drawings and designs. In all other cases, it is usually easier to justify—align vertically—a drawing title with either the drawing itself or its field.

## Text

Organize text into visual sets of information and relate these sets directly to the portion of the drawing to which they refer. The line spacing of text should be from one to one-and-a-half of the letter height used. The space between blocks of text should be equal to or greater than the height of two lines of text.

## Project Title

The project title and associated information should relate to the overall sheet or board, not to any single drawing within the field of the panel.

A set of related drawings may by laid out in a vertical, horizontal, or grid format. In planning the layout for a presentation, we first identify the essential relationships we want to achieve. Then we use a storyboard or small-scale mock-up of the presentation to explore alternative drawing arrangements, alignments, and spacing prior to beginning the final presentation drawings.

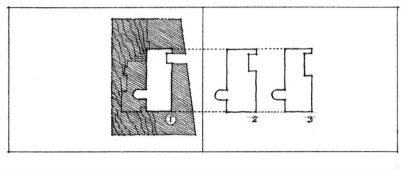

- Remember to explore potential relationships between the sheets or panels.
- Maintain horizontal continuity across sheets with a ground line or by the alignment of drawing titles.
- Do not include dimensions or employ borders and title blocks; these are conventions for construction or working drawings.

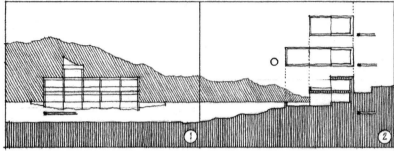

When a presentation consists of more than one sheet, board, or panel, identify each panel by a number. This information should be in the same relative position on each panel. If the panels of a presentation are to be displayed in a specific manner, we can use more graphic means to identify the relative position of each panel in the display.

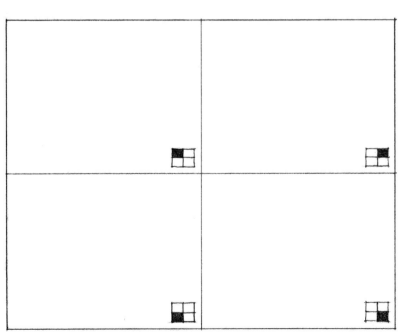

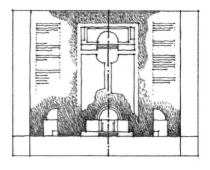

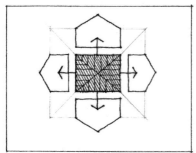

A symmetrical layout works best in presenting symmetrical designs.

Centralized formats are suitable when presenting a plan surrounded by elevation views, an expanded paraline drawing, or a key drawing surround by detailed portions drawn at a larger scale.

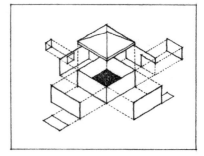

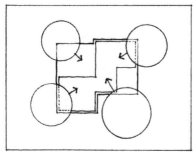

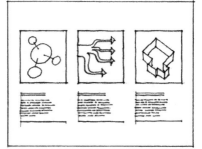

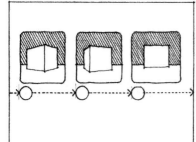

If a series of related drawings are treated in different ways or are of different types, we can unify them by framing or boxing them in a uniform manner.

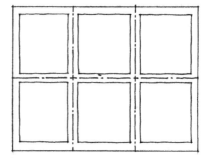

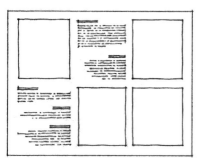

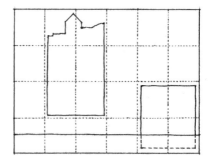

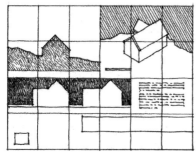

A grid provides the greatest flexibility for laying out a series of drawing and informational text on a panel or series of boards. The underlying sense of order created by the grid allows a great variety of information to be presented in a uniform manner.

- The grid may be square or rectangular.
- We can display drawings, diagrams, and text in individual boxed or frames.
- We can display drawings horizontally with text below each drawing to form related columns.
- An important drawing may take up more than one box or frame.
- Graphics and text may be integrated in an organic manner.

## Exercise 12.4

Handletter the following quotation using one-eighth-inch high letters and text lines spaced one-quarter of an inch apart.

*"From the age of six I had a mania for drawing forms of things. By the time I was fifty I had published an infinity of drawings, but all I have produced before the age of seventy is not worth taking into account. At seventy-five I learned a little about the structure of nature—of animals, plants, and bees, birds, fishes and insects. In consequence when I am eighty I shall have made a little more progress. At ninety I shall certainly have reached a marvelous stage, and when I am a hundred and ten, everything I do—be it but a line or a dot—will be alive."*

—*The Manga*, Hokusai (1760–1849)

## Exercise 12.5

Design a page layout using your handlettered copy and the image of the *Mad Poet*.

In order to use drawing as a tool for visualizing, exploring, and communicating design ideas, we must understand the pictorial language of drawing. The CD-ROM that accompanies this book facilitates further exploration into the relationship between a three-dimensional subject and its two-dimensional representation in a drawing. With the benefit of three-dimensional animations, Quicktime video clips, and explanatory audio, the lesson units on this CD-ROM elucidate the principal projection systems and drawing techniques in a way that is not possible on the printed page. In many ways, this CD-ROM represents an experiment in communicating design drawing concepts and techniques in an entirely new medium, and thus I welcome you to share your feedback with the publisher. The use of multimedia technology in the teaching of design drawing is still in an early stage; however, if this CD-ROM proves as helpful as I hope it will be, there may well be revised editions, as well as innovations in the way architectural drawing is taught in years to come.

Windows®

Processor - 486DX 66 MHz (Pentium recommended) RAM - 16 MB
Hard disk space available - 10 MB
Graphics card and monitor - 640 x 480 SVGA display/256 ColorSound Blaser compatible sound card and external speakers
Windows® 3.1 or Windows '95®
4X CD-ROM Drive

Macintosh®

Processor - 68040 25 MHz or PowerMac 601 (Quadra 650 or/PowerMac 6100 or better)
RAM 16 MB
Hard disk space available - 10 MB
Monitor - 256 colors (640x480)
Standard internal Mac sound (external speakers optional) Operating System: System 7 or later
4X CD-ROM drive